STUDIES IN AMERICAN INDIAN LITERATURE

Critical Essays and Course Designs

Edited by Paula Gunn Allen

The Modern Language Association of America

Paula Gunn Allen, "The Sacred Hoop: A Contemporary Perspective," is reprinted in revised form from *Literature of the American Indians*, edited by Abraham Chapman. Gretchen Bataille, "Transformation of Tradition: Autobiographical Works by American Indian Women," in an expanded form, appears in *Native American Women in a Changing World*, by Gretchen Bataille and Kathleen M. Sands (University of Nebraska Press). Kenneth M. Roemer, "Bear and Elk: The Nature(s) of Contemporary American Indian Poetry," is reprinted in revised form from *The Journal of Ethnic Studies*, 5, No. 2, by permission of the editor. Patricia Clark Smith, "Coyote Ortiz: *Canis latrans latrans* in the Poetry of Simon Ortiz," is reprinted in revised form from *Minority Voices: An Interdisciplinary Journal of Literature and the Arts*, 3, No. 2.

The cover illustration in the paperback edition is by James Trujillo.

Library of Congress Cataloging in Publication Data
Main entry under title:

Studies in American Indian literature.

Bibliography: p.
Includes index.
1. American literature—Indian authors—Study and teaching. 2. American literature—Indian authors—History and criticism. 3. Indian literature—Study and teaching. 4. Indian literature—History and criticism. 5. Indians in literature.
I. Allen, Paula Gunn. II. Title.
PS153.I52S8 1983 810'.9'897 82-12516
ISBN 0-87352-354-7
ISBN 0-87352-355-5 (pbk.)

Published by The Modern Language Association of America
62 Fifth Avenue, New York, New York 10011

Contents

Introduction

Paula Gunn Allen

The nature of literature emerges most clearly under the referential aspect. The center of literary art is obviously to be found in the traditional genres of the lyric, the epic, the drama. In all of them, the reference is to a world of fiction, of imagination. The statements in a novel, in a poem, or in a drama are not literally true; they are not logical propositions. There is a central and important difference between a statement, even in a historical novel by Balzac which seems to convey "information" about actual happenings, and the same information appearing in a book of history or sociology.

René Wellek and Austin Warren
Theory of Literature

> IT'S WITH TERROR, SOMETIMES
> THAT I HEAR THEM CALLING ME
> BUT IT'S THE LIGHT SKIP OF A COUGAR
> DETACHING ME FROM THE GROUND
> TO LEAVE ME ALONE
> WITH MY CRAZY POWER
> TILL I REACH THE SUN MAKERS
> AND FIND MYSELF AGAIN
> IN A NEW PLACE.
> Serain Stump
> *There Is My People Sleeping*

One major commitment of the Modern Language Association of America in recent years has been the support of ethnic and racial minority literary studies in the university. Through its Commission on the Languages and Literatures of America, MLA has sponsored summer seminars on the study of minority languages and literatures and analogous programs designed to develop critical understanding of minority literatures and to serve the academic and ethnic literary communities simultaneously.

As part of its new direction in this effort, MLA and its commission are developing publications through the summer seminars on minority literatures. This is the second volume published under this program. *Studies in American Indian Literature: Critical Essays and Course Designs* begins to make available needed critical and pedagogical approaches. This volume features critical studies in American Indian literature that explain and/or use basic themes, motifs, structures, and symbols found in traditional and modern American Indian literature. In conjunction with the essays, the book provides basic course designs that instructors can implement singly or sequentially, as funding and policy allow. We believe that placing pertinent essays with those courses they most relate to will enable the reader more readily to perceive the critical foundations that underlie the suggested courses.

The suggested curriculum is wide-ranging. It includes the basic introductory and survey courses usually found at the university level in this area. Additionally, it goes beyond these with courses that allow specialized study. This broadening of the field of American Indian literature is necessary if students are to gain something approaching a realistic understanding of literatures that represent several hundred different tribes and cover several thousand years.

The book includes the following general categories: introductory and survey courses, regional studies in the oral tradition, transitional literature, feminist and interdisciplinary approaches to the study of these literatures, modern and contemporary American Indian literature, and Indian themes and perspectives in American literature. The courses incorporate many useful approaches to the study and teaching of American Indian literature, though they by no means exhaust the possibilities available for study and teaching in this rich area. The course designs will serve as guides; innovative instructors or researchers will make use of the resources unique to their region of the country and the local tribes and local contemporary Indian authors who live nearby.

The volume has several basic purposes:

1. To integrate American Indian literary traditions into the study of American literature at every level. We believe that American literature has drawn heavily on American Indian literature and philosophies. Two essays in this volume examine that contention at length.
2. To provide tools to broaden the scope, insights, and approaches of criticism. The writing of literary criticism is a dynamic process; the study of literatures that differ in aesthetics, structure, and style can offer new insights into the aesthetic and expressive dimensions of human experience, and these insights can expand our understanding of the varied modes of

human consciousness and the alternatives for living that these differences imply.

3. To enrich university curricula by increasing the number of courses offered and by expanding the content of existing courses to include American Indian materials.

4. To acquaint scholars with the multitude of possibilities for further research presented by American Indian literature. Much necessary research remains to be done in this area.

5. To provide Indian and non-Indian Americans with an understanding, based on sound academic and disciplinary scholarship, of the depth and variety of literary experience to which we are all heir.

This volume grew out of the lectures and workshops of the 1977 Modern Language Association–National Endowment for the Humanities Summer Seminar on American Indian Literature, and out of a series of later exchanges among participants and staff of that seminar, along with their students and colleagues. The tasks of this volume are to address critical problems that arise in the study of American Indian literature, traditional or modern, and to design courses related to that study.

Wellek and Warren's comforting division of human experience into fact or fancy and of literary study into the obvious traditional genres is not a division that one can safely apply to the study of American Indian literature, traditional or modern. For within the tribal world of the contemporary or traditional American Indian, many statements that stem from the "imagination" are taken to be literally true, even though they are not based on sociological or historical "facts." Momaday, for example, says that "An Indian is an idea which a given man [and I might add, woman] has of himself" and goes on in that essay to discuss exactly what *imagination* means to an Indian. Having nearly completed his manuscript for *The Way to Rainy Mountain*, Momaday sat contemplating the last page. He writes of that moment: "Then it was that that ancient, one-eyed woman Ko-sahn stepped out of the language and stood before me on the page. I was amazed."

In his amazement, and because of his acquaintance with the world also inhabited by René Wellek and Austin Warren, he protests her presence:

> "But all of this, this imagining," I protested, "this has taken place—is taking place in my mind. You are not actually here, not in this room. . . . "
> . . . You imagine that I am here in this room, do you not? [she answers]
> . . . You see, I have existence, whole being, in your imagination. It is but one kind of being, to be sure, but it is perhaps the best of all kinds. If I am not here in this room, grandson, then surely neither are you.[1]

Ideas of beauty—intellectual harmony, structural balance, thematic or symbolic unity—differ in various American Indian and European-American cultures, though, of course, both larger groups embrace responses and judgments that might properly be termed aesthetic. "Aesthetics," in a tribal context, takes on a meaning that necessarily includes utility or integration into daily pursuits. But if the aesthetic dimension is one aspect of literary significance, we must find a suitable way of critically evaluating that dimension in the literature of American Indians.

Significance, like beauty, is usually related to expectations, to emotional and intellectual patterns, and to deep values, all of which one learns within a cultural framework. Symbolic referents are not all that transferable from one society to another, nor do cognitive and imaginative processes seem much more so. But perhaps it is possible to agree on a definition, or definitions, of the word "significance" that will satisfy the critical judgments of both cultural groups and that will also apply to their literatures.

Significance is, of course, necessarily connected to specificity, or particularity, which is thought to be a distinguishing characteristic of good literature. Particularity triggers imaginative involvement and allows a reader to experience a literary work and thus appreciate, understand, and perhaps grow toward a new level of consciousness. Particulars of a definite sort are not necessary; what is particular to one set of people might be general to another.

Nor is the matter simply one of particulars or details, for the sequence in which these details occur, their juxtaposition to one another, and their relation to the total context are primary sources of meaning for writer (singer) and audience (participant) alike. Associations that are highly significant in one culture may be meaningless in another. The critic, therefore, not only must clarify symbols and allusions but also must define or describe whole perceptual-interpretative systems.

Simply put, the teachers and critics of American Indian literature must place the document within a context that allows readers and students to understand it in terms that do not distort it. They must use historical and traditional information in preparing students and readers to work with the materials under consideration. If they are teaching N. Scott Momaday, for example, they must introduce materials from Kiowa oral tradition, history, and contemporary life, along with information about contemporary literary standards and modes. *House Made of Dawn* is a complex novel that relies on Navajo, Pueblo, and Kiowa traditions, histories, and present situations, both on the reservation and in urban enclaves. Its structure derives from contemporary literary modes and from the oral tradition. To do the book justice, the teacher/critic must be aware of the multiple factors that combine to make it a singularly Indian book that is accessible to literate non-Indian readers.

Leslie Marmon Silko's *Ceremony* requires the same attention to Laguna traditions, history, and present conditions. Without such attention one could make a serious error such as that made by a critic who asserts that

Ts'its'tsi'nako (Thought Woman—God) is a persona of Silko. The critic seems unaware that most of the "poems" in the novel are not poems in the European sense. The poem he refers to as "a central body or story with its own thematic variations" is actually a story from the Laguna oral tradition. As a result, the layout of the poem is the only choice Silko made and the only aspect on which she had any effect. Ignorance of Laguna lore leads the critic to say:

> Silko has thus projected two voices of herself in the novel: we know she is the author of the wider narrative called *Ceremony*, yet she has secreted a second persona of herself into the poems. . . . The emphasis is upon the imagination— the poet's gift to the world.[2]

While such a distortion represents an honest attempt to deal with the novel respectfully, it results in a misperception of what the author is up to, creates a misunderstanding of the story itself, and dislocates the writer and the book. By using only the techniques of explication, without seeking to understand the context from which the materials derive, the critic has removed the book and its author from the living web of the people and tradition from which they both arose. This removal allows the critic to feel sympathetic toward Indians and to defend them somewhat militantly against the evils of a greedy white world (as he sees it), but it denies the Laguna people their real humanity and the dignity that people in difficult circumstances most need.

Thus, the course designs, critical papers, and bibliography included in this volume were designed to demonstrate appropriate methods of approaching the study of American Indian literature. Professors who intend to embark on the teaching of courses using American Indian materials—traditional or modern—must study carefully the traditions, history, and present-day settings of the tribe from which the document comes or to which it refers. The faculty and participants at the Flagstaff seminar agreed that context and continuity are two of the most important areas to be taken into account in the study and teaching of American Indian literature. To this end, seminar leaders devoted lectures to historical and ethnographic accounts of American Indians and to the world views that characterize them and distinguish them from non-Indian Americans.

In terms of "pure" criticism, few definable sets of criteria are available to critics of American Indian literature, beyond the rather broad categories mentioned: significance and context, aesthetic quality and the interrelationship of structure, content, and the oral tradition. Universality of meaning may necessarily be required of all works of literature, but it may be that such universality must be got at from a very particular point of view. If this is so, the critic in American Indian literature becomes important—not as a scholarly adjunct to the creating and re-creating that are always the component parts of the synergy between teller and listener, but as a mediator who allows teller and listener to share a particular understanding even though they come from widely divergent traditions.

Critics and teachers must avoid the danger of taking a paternalistic attitude toward the materials and the people they reflect. Many scholars find it difficult, given the history of Indian-white relations, to maintain a balanced posture toward Indians. The present political and social climate encourages an overly romantic response to Indians, their values, and their traditions, and teachers or critics must not allow natural sympathies or political biases to color their presentation of the materials.

There are several reasons for this caution. First, instructors should present these literatures as they were intended to appear to the primary audiences, so that the student or reader can enter into the universe in which the material belongs. Second, exercises in literary colonialism are dangerous to the Indian people, for they can lead to intellectual confusion, self-hatred, or rejection of the education such study is designed to further. And third, interpreting Indian cultures and artifacts as examples of unalloyed primitivism or nobility can lead to feelings of contempt for American Indians, feelings that can often result in political action against them. When Americans cannot view American Indians as people with histories, cultures, customs, and understandings worthy of study and dispassionate observation, they ignore the real plight of too many Indian people who must go without jobs, food, decent housing, or, far too often, the simple human right to survive. Far too many Indians are treated contemptuously, unemployed, sterilized without their knowledge, and murdered in today's United States, and their mistreatment goes unremarked and uninvestigated far too often. These abuses are frequently the subject of the works of contemporary American Indian writers.

Those who would study and teach American Indian literature consider these issues in the context of competent criticism of any literature. What American Indian literature is and how it functions are the central concerns of this volume. The essays and curriculum outlines illuminate a variety of subjects. This vast field offers challenging and consuming work to all who are psychologically and professionally able to devote the necessary time and thought to its study. Those who make this commitment will find themselves greatly enriched by their pursuit.

The materials in this volume were designed to create a coherent basic framework for such a pursuit, in the hope that serious, responsible critical studies will result.

Five scholars in the field of American Indian studies composed the staff of the seminar: Dexter Fisher of the Modern Language Association; Terry Wilson (Potawatomi), director of American Indian studies, University of California, Berkeley (history); John M. Rouillard (Santee Sioux), director of American Indian studies, San Diego State University, San Diego (musicology);

Larry Evers, University of Arizona, Tucson (literature, ethnography, and communications); and Paula Gunn Allen (Laguna Sioux), poet and critic, former director of American Indian studies, San Francisco State University. Under the guidance of this staff, participants from all over the United States and Canada gathered to develop critical and pedagogical approaches to American Indian literature that would place it firmly within departments of literature and expand its use beyond studies in folklore, where it remained too long.

Because this seminar was the first of its kind, certain basic issues were discussed concerning viable approaches to criticism and curriculum design. The multidisciplinary nature of both the staff and the participants reflected the staff's desire to present American Indian literature in the total context from which it derives. As traditional literatures are generally sung or chanted, a musicologist was necessary. Since literature studied in the absence of historical information is often incomprehensible, a historian was necessary. And because the study of both traditional and contemporary American Indian literature rests squarely on the whole oral tradition, which includes nonliterary materials, an ethnographer was required. Further, as the study and teaching of American Indian literature are necessarily bicultural operations, an equal number of Indians and non-Indians participated.

The essays in this volume reflect diverse approaches to the study of American Indian literature. Evers originally delivered his "Cycles of Appreciation" at the seminar. Participants and other scholars wrote the other essays after the seminar, but all represent the kinds of concerns and approaches that the staff and participants, during the two weeks in Flagstaff, collectively agreed on as accurate, undistorted, and critically viable. Seminar participants wrote the curriculum designs during the seminar (with the exception of the nineteenth-century design by LaVonne Ruoff), and their contributions are gratefully acknowledged. They are Olga Arenivar, Joseph M. Backus, Helen Bannan, Gretchen Bataille, Barney Bush, Michael Castro, Bud Cochran, Elizabeth Cook-Lynn, Patricia D'Andrea, Sandra Davis, Lester Faigley, Joy Harjo, Helen Harris, Elaine Jahner, Victor Masayesva, Raoul McKay, Delilah Orr, Charles E. Roberts, Kenneth Roemer, LaVonne Ruoff, James Ruppert, Priscella A. Russo, Kathleen Sands, Michael Taylor, and Andrew Wiget. Thanks also go to guest scholars and artists. Without them, much of this work, and the participants' understanding of it, could not have come about: Mike Kabotie and the Artists Hopid, Harold Littlebird, Kenneth Lincoln, and Leslie Marmon Silko. The tribes represented at the seminar included Navajo, Laguna, Hopi, Cherokee, Sioux, Creek, Chocktaw, Shawnee, and Cayuga, representing the northeastern, midwestern, southwestern, and southeastern parts of the country.

Appreciation also goes to Northern Arizona State University at Flagstaff for opening its doors to the seminar, and, for making possible both the seminar and the publication of this volume, we are grateful to the Modern Language Association and the National Endowment for the Humanities.

Notes

1   Momaday, "The Man Made of Words," pp. 97, 98, 99.

2   Larson, *American Indian Fiction*, pp. 158, 159. This "second persona" exists only if it is identified as Silko's tribal self.

3   In the five years since the seminar, much fine critical work has been published. Of this work the following should be mentioned as they will be particularly useful to scholars and instructors using the course outlines in this volume: Kenneth Lincoln's forthcoming comprehensive study of contemporary literature, *Native American Renaissance,* and Allen and Smith's overview of American Indian literature since 1968, "Chee Dostoyevsky Rides the Reservation: American Indian Literature since Momaday"; Lincoln's article, "The Now Day Indi'n," and Jahner's *American Indians Today,* a collection of essays on arts, literature, and thought should be especially interesting to those studying and teaching modern American Indian authors.

For recent publications in oral literature, two volumes should prove useful: Brian Swann's *Smoothing the Ground,* a collection of articles by Jahner, Lincoln, Jarold Ramsey, Barre Toelken, Karl Kroeber, and others; and Swann's *Song of the Sky,* traditional songs reworked from Densmore, Curtis, and other early collectors. For new materials from the Lakota oral tradition, see Jahner and De Mallie's *Lakota Belief and Ritual,* De Mallie's *Lakota Society,* and Jahner's *Lakota Myth.*

Oral Literature

The Sacred Hoop: A Contemporary Perspective

Paula Gunn Allen

Literature is one facet of a culture. The significance of a literature can be best understood in terms of the culture from which it springs, and the purpose of literature is clear only when the reader understands and accepts the assumptions on which the literature is based. A person who was raised in a given culture has no problem seeing the relevance, the level of complexity, or the symbolic significance of that culture's literature. We are all from early childhood familiar with the assumptions that underlie our own culture and its literature and art. Intelligent analysis becomes a matter of identifying smaller assumptions peculiar to the locale, idiom, and psyche of the writer.

The study of non-Western literature poses a problem for Western readers who naturally tend to see alien literature in terms that are familiar to them, however irrelevant those terms may be to the literature under consideration. Because of this, students of traditional American Indian literatures have applied the terms "primitive," "savage," "childlike," and "pagan" to these literatures. Perceiving only the most superficial aspects of American Indian literary traditions, Western scholars have labeled the whole body of these literatures "folklore," even though the term specifically applies only to those parts of the literatures that are the province of the general populace.

The great mythic[1] and ceremonial cycles of the American Indian peoples are neither primitive, in any meaningful sense of the word, nor necessarily the province of the folk; much of the literature, in fact, is known only to educated, specialized persons who are privy to the philosophical, mystical, and literary wealth of their own tribe.

Much of the literature that was in the keeping of such persons, engraved perfectly and completely in their memories, was not known to most other men and women. Because of this, much literature has been lost as the last initiates of particular tribes and societies within the tribes died, leaving no successors.

Most important, traditional American Indian literature is not similar to Western literature, because the basic assumptions about the universe and, therefore, the basic reality experienced by tribal peoples and by Western peoples are not the same, even at the level of folklore. This difference has confused non-Indian students for centuries. They have been unable or unwilling to accept this difference and to develop critical procedures to illuminate the materials without trivializing or otherwise invalidating them.

For example, American Indian and Western literary traditions differ greatly in the assumed purposes they serve. The purpose of traditional American Indian literature is never simply pure self-expression. The "private soul at any public wall" is a concept alien to American Indian thought. The tribes do not celebrate the individual's ability to feel emotion, for they assume that all people are able to do so. One's emotions are one's own; to suggest that others should imitate them is to impose on the personal integrity of others. The tribes seek—through song, ceremony, legend, sacred stories (myths), and tales—to embody, articulate, and share reality, to bring the isolated private self into harmony and balance with this reality, to verbalize the sense of the majesty and reverent mystery of all things, and to actualize, in language, those truths that give to humanity its greatest significance and dignity. To a large extent, ceremonial literature serves to redirect private emotion and integrate the energy generated by emotion within a cosmic framework. The artistry of the tribes is married to the essence of language itself, for through language one can share one's singular being with that of the community and know within oneself the communal knowledge of the tribe. In this art, the greater self and all-that-is are blended into a balanced whole, and in this way the concept of being that is the fundamental and sacred spring of life is given voice and being for all. American Indian people do not content themselves with simple preachments of this truth, but through the sacred power of utterance they seek to shape and mold, to direct and determine, the forces that surround and govern human life and the related lives of all things.

An old Keres song says:

> I add my breath to your breath
> That our days may be long on the Earth
> That the days of our people may be long
> That we may be one person
> That we may finish our roads together
> May my father bless you with life
> May our Life Paths be fulfilled.

In this way one learns how to view oneself and one's tradition so as to approach both rightly. Breath is life, and the intermingling of breaths is the purpose of good living. This is in essence the great principle on which all productive living must rest, for relationships among all the beings of the universe must be fulfilled; in this way each individual life may also be fulfilled.

This idea is apparent in the Plains tribes' idea of a medicine wheel[2] or sacred hoop.[3] The concept is one of singular unity that is dynamic and encompassing, including, as it does, all that is contained in its most essential aspect, that of life. In his introduction to Geronimo's autobiography, Frederick Turner III incorrectly characterizes the American Indian cultures as static.[4] Stasis, however, is not characteristic of the American Indians' view of things. As any American Indian knows, all of life is living—that is, dynamic and aware, partaking as it does in the life of the All-Spirit and contributing as it does to the continuing life of that same Great Mystery. The tribal systems are static in that all movement is related to all other movement—that is, harmonious and balanced or unified; they are not static in the sense that they do not allow or accept change. Even a cursory examination of tribal systems will show that all have undergone massive changes while retaining those characteristics of outlook and experience that are the bedrock of tribal life.[5] So the primary assumptions tribespeople make can be seen as static only in that these people acknowledge the essential harmony of all things and see all things as being of equal value in the scheme of things, denying the opposition, dualism, and isolation (separateness) that characterize non-Indian thought. Christians believe that God is separate from humanity and does as he wishes without the creative assistance of any of his creatures, while the non-Christian tribal person assumes a place in creation that is dynamic, creative, and responsive. Further, tribal people allow all animals, vegetables, and minerals (the entire biota, in short) the same or even greater privileges. The Indian participates in destiny on all levels, including that of creation. Thus this passage from a Cheyenne tale in which Maheo, the All-Spirit, creates out of the void four things—the water, the light, the sky-air, and the peoples of the water:

> "How beautiful their wings are in the light," Maheo said to his Power, as the birds wheeled and turned, and became living patterns against the sky.
> The loon was the first to drop back to the surface of the lake. "Maheo," he said, looking around, for he knew that Maheo was all about him, "You have made us sky and light to fly in, and you have made us water to swim in. It sounds ungrateful to want something else, yet still we do. When we are tired of swimming and tired of flying, we should like a dry solid place where we could walk and rest. Give us a place to build our nests, please, Maheo."
> "So be it," answered Maheo, "but to make such a place I must have your help, all of you. By myself, I have made four things. . . . Now I must have help if I am to create more, for my Power will only let me make four things by myself."[6]

In this passage we see that even the All-Spirit, whose "being was a Universe,"[7] has limited power as well as a sense of proportion and respect for the powers of the creatures. Contrast this spirit with the Judeo-Christian God, who makes everything and tells everything how it may and may not function if it is to gain his respect and blessing and whose commandments make no allowance for change or circumstance. The American Indian universe is based on dynamic self-esteem, while the Christian universe is based primarily on a sense of separation and loss. For the American Indian, the ability of all creatures to share in the process of ongoing creation makes all things sacred.

In Paradise, God created a perfect environment for his creatures. He arranged it to their benefit, asking only that they forbear from eating the fruit of one particular tree. In essence, they were left with only one means of exercising their creative capacities and their ability to make their own decisions and choices. Essentially, they were thus prevented from exercising their intelligence while remaining loyal to the creator. To act in a way that was congruent with their natural curiosity and love of exploration and discovery, they were forced to disobey God and thus be exiled from the perfect place he had made for them. They were severely punished for exercising what we might call liberty—Eve more than Adam, for hers was the greater sin (or so the story goes):

> And the LORD God commanded the man, saying, Of every tree of the garden thou mayest freely eat:
> But of the tree of the knowledge of good and evil, thou shalt not eat: for in the day that thou eatest thereof thou shalt surely die. (Genesis ii. 16–17)

The Cheyennes' creator is somewhat wiser. He gives his creatures needs so that they can exert their intelligence and knowledge to satisfy these needs by working together to solve a common problem or attain a common goal. Together Maheo, the creator, and the water-beings create the earth, and with the aid of these beings, Maheo creates first man and first woman and the creatures and environment they will need to live good and satisfying lives. These creation stories demonstrate the basic ordering principles of two different cultures. The Judeo-Christian view is hierarchical. God commands first; within the limits of those commands, man rules; woman is subject to man, as are all the creatures, for God has brought them to Adam for him to name (Genesis ii. 18–24; iii. 16). In this scheme, the one who is higher has the power to impose penalties or even to deny life to those who are lower:

> And the LORD God said, Behold, the man is become as one of us, to know good and evil; and now, lest he put forth his hand, and take also of the tree of life, and eat, and live for ever;
> Therefore, the LORD God sent him forth from the garden of Eden to till the ground from whence he was taken. (Genesis iii. 22–23)

The sin Adam and Eve committed in the Garden of Eden was that of attempting to become knowledgeable. Their attempt opened the further possibility that, with knowledge, they might become immortal. This, apparently, was not acceptable, not because knowledge and immortality were sinful, but because the possession of them by human beings would reorder the hierarchical principles on which the Judeo-Christian universe is posited. Those reared in a Christian society are inclined to perceive social relationships—and literary works—in this context; they order events and phenomena in hierarchical and dualistic terms. Those reared in traditional American Indian societies are inclined to relate events and experiences to one another. They do not organize perceptions or external events in terms of dualities or priorities. This egalitarianism is reflected in the structure of American Indian literature, which does not rely on conflict, crisis, and resolution for organization, nor does its merit depend on the parentage, education, or connections of the author. Rather, its significance is determined by its relation to creative empowerment, its reflection of tribal understandings, and its relation to the unitary nature of reality.

The way the loon prays in the Cheyenne creation story is indicative of that difference. The loon looks around him as he addresses Maheo, "for he knew that Maheo was all about him," just as earlier in the story the snowgoose addressed Maheo in these words: "I do not know where you are, but I know you must be everywhere."[8]

Another difference between these two ways of perceiving reality lies in the tendency of the American Indian to view space as spherical and time as cyclical, whereas the non-Indian tends to view space as linear and time as sequential. The circular concept requires all "points" that make up the sphere of being to have a significant identity and function, while the linear model assumes that some "points" are more significant than others. In the one, significance is a necessary factor of being in itself, whereas in the other, significance is a function of placement on an absolute scale that is fixed in time and space. In essence, what we have is a direct contradiction of Turner's notion about the American Indian universe versus that of the West: the Indian universe moves and breathes continuously, and the Western universe is fixed and static. The Christian attitude toward salvation reflects this basic stance: one can be "saved" only if one believes in a Savior who appeared once and will not come again until "the end of time." The idea "once a saint always a saint" is another expression of the same underlying perception and experience.

The notion that nature is somewhere over there while humanity is over here, or that a great hierarchical ladder of being exists on which ground and trees occupy a very low rung, animals a slightly higher one, and man (never woman)—especially "civilized" man—a very high one indeed is antithetical to tribal thought. The American Indian sees all creatures as relatives (and in tribal systems relationship is central), as offspring of the Great Mystery, as cocreators, as children of our mother, and as necessary parts of an ordered, balanced, and living whole. This concept applies to what non-Indian Americans think of as the supernatural, and it applies as well to the more tangible (phenomenal) aspects of the universe. American Indian thought makes no such dualistic division, nor does it draw a hard and fast line between what is material and what is spiritual, for it regards the two as different expressions of the same reality, as though life has twin manifestations that are mutually interchangeable and, in many instances, virtually identical aspects of a reality that is essentially more spirit than matter or, more correctly, that manifests its spirit in a tangible way. The closest analogy in Western thought is the Einsteinian understanding of matter as a special state or condition of energy. Yet even this concept falls short of the American Indian understanding, for Einsteinian energy is believed to be unintelligent, while energy, according to the Indian view, is intelligence manifested in yet another way.

Many non-Indians believe that human beings possess the only intelligence in phenomenal existence (often in any form of existence). The more abstractionist and less intellectually vain Indian sees human intelligence as rising out of the very nature of being, which is, of necessity, intelligent in and of itself, as an attribute of being. Again, this idea probably stems from the Indian concept of a circular, dynamic universe in which all things are related and are of one family. It follows that those attributes possessed by human beings are natural attributes of *all* being. The Indian does not regard awareness of being as an abnormality peculiar to one species, but, because of a sense of relatedness to (instead of isolation from) what exists, the Indian assumes that this awareness is a natural by-product of existence itself.

In English, one can divide the universe into two parts: the natural and the supernatural. Humanity has no real part in either, being neither animal nor spirit—that is, the supernatural is discussed as though it were apart from people, and the natural as though people were apart from it. This necessarily forces English-speaking people into a position of alienation from the world they live in. This isolation is entirely foreign to American Indian thought. At base, every story, every song, every ceremony tells the Indian that each creature is part of a living whole and that all parts of that whole are related to one another by virtue of their participation in the whole of being.

In American Indian thought, God is known as the All-Spirit, and other beings are also spirit—more spirit than body, more spirit than intellect, more spirit than mind. The natural state of existence is whole. Thus healing chants and ceremonies emphasize restoration of wholeness, for disease is a condition of division and separation from the harmony of the whole. Beauty is wholeness. Health is wholeness. Goodness is wholeness. The Hopi refer to a witch—a person who uses the powers of the universe in a perverse or inharmonious way—as a two-hearts, one who is not whole but split in two at the center of being. The circle of being is not physical, but it is dynamic and alive. It is what lives and moves and knows, and all the life forms we recognize—animals, plants, rocks, winds—partake of this greater life. Acknowledgment of this allows healing chants such as this from the Night Chant to heal (make the person whole again):

> Happily I recover.
> Happily my interior becomes cool.
> Happily I go forth.
> My interior feeling cool, may I walk.
> No longer sore, may I walk.
> As it used to be long ago, may I walk.
> Happily, with abundant dark clouds, may I walk.
> Happily, with abundant showers, may I walk.
> Happily, with abundant plants, may I walk.
> Happily, on a trail of pollen, may I walk.
> Happily, may I walk.[9]

Because of the basic assumption of the wholeness or unity of the universe, our natural and necessary relationship to all life is evident; all phenomena we witness within or "outside" ourselves are, like us, intelligent manifestations of the intelligent universe from which they arise, as do all things of earth and the cosmos beyond. Thunder and rain are specialized aspects of this universe, as is the human race. Consequently the unity of the whole is preserved and reflected in language, literature, and thought, and arbitrary divisions of the universe into "divine" and "worldly" or "natural" and "unnatural" beings do not occur.

Literature takes on more meaning when considered in terms of some relevant whole (like life itself), so let us consider some relationships between specific American Indian literary forms and the symbols usually found in them. The two forms basic to American Indian literature are the ceremony and the myth. The ceremony is the ritual enactment of a specialized perception of a cosmic relationship, while the myth is a prose record of that relationship. Thus, the *wiwanyag wachipi* (sun dance) is the ritual enactment of the relationship the Plains people see between consecration of the human spirit to Wakan Tanka as manifested as Sun, or Light, and Life-Bestower. Through purification, participation, sacrifice, and supplication, the participants act as instruments or transmitters of increased power and wholeness, which bestows health and prosperity, from Wakan Tanka.

The formal structure of a ceremony is as holistic as the universe it purports to reflect and respond to, for the ceremony contains other forms such as incantation, song (dance), and prayer, and it is itself the central mode of literary expression from which all allied songs and stories derive. The Lakota view all the ceremonies as related to one another in various explicit and implicit ways, as though each were one face of a multifaceted prism. This interlocking of the basic forms has led to much confusion among non-Indian collectors and commentators, and this complexity makes all simplistic treatments of American Indian literature more confusing than helpful. Indeed, the non-Indian tendency to separate things from one another—be they literary forms, species, or persons—causes a great deal of unnecessary difficulty and misinterpretation of American Indian life and culture. It is reasonable, from an Indian point of view, that all literary forms should be interrelated, given the basic idea of the unity and relatedness of all the phenomena of life. Separation of parts into this or that category is not agreeable to American Indians, and the attempt to separate essentially unified phenomena results in distortion.

For example, to say that a ceremony contains songs and prayers is misleading, for prayers are one form of address and songs are another. It is more appropriate to say that songs, prayers, dances, drums, ritual movements, and dramatic address are compositional elements of a ceremony. It is equally misleading to single out the *wiwanyag wachipi* and treat it as an isolated ceremony, for it must of necessity include the *inipi* (rite of purification) and did at one time contain the *hanblecyeyapi* (vision quest), which was how the Lakota learned about it in the first place.[10] Actually, it might best be seen as a communal vision quest.

The purpose of a ceremony is to integrate: to fuse the individual with his or her fellows, the community of people with that of the other kingdoms, and this larger communal group with the worlds beyond this one. A raising or expansion of individual consciousness naturally accompanies this process. The person sheds the isolated, individual personality and is restored to conscious harmony with the universe. In addition to this general purpose, each ceremony has its own specific purpose. This purpose usually varies from tribe to tribe and may be culture-specific. For example, the rain dances of the Southwest are peculiar to certain groups, such as the Pueblos, and are not found among some other tribes, while war ceremonies, which make up a large part of certain Plains tribes' ceremonial life, are unknown among many tribes in California.[11] But all ceremonies, whether for war or healing, create and support the sense of community that is the bedrock of tribal life. This community is not made up only of members of the tribe but necessarily includes all beings that inhabit the tribe's universe.

Within this context the dynamic characteristics of American Indian literature can best be understood. The structures that embody expressed and implied relationships between human and nonhuman beings, as well as the symbols that signify and articulate them, are designed to integrate the various orders of consciousness. Entities other than the human participants are present at ceremonial enactments, and the ceremony is composed for their participation as well as for that of the human beings who are there. Some tribes understand that the human participants include members of the tribe who are not physically present and that the community as a community, not simply the separate persons in attendance, enact the ceremony.

Thus devices such as repetition and lengthy passages of meaningless syllables take on significance within the context of the dance. Repetition has an entrancing effect. Its regular recurrence creates a state of consciousness best described as "oceanic," but without the hypersentimental side effects implied by that term. It is hypnotic, and a hypnotic state of consciousness is the aim of the ceremony. The participant's attention must become diffused. The distractions of ordinary life must be put to rest and emotions redirected and integrated into a ceremonial context, so that the greater awareness can come into full consciousness and functioning. In this way the person becomes literally one with the universe, for he or she loses consciousness of mere individuality and shares the consciousness that characterizes most orders of being.

In some sense repetition operates like the chorus in Western dramā, serving to reinforce the theme and to focus the participants' attention on central concerns, while intensifying their involvement with the enactment. One suits one's words and movements (if one is a dancer) to the repetitive pattern. Soon breath, heartbeat, thought, emotion, and word are one. The repetition serves to integrate or fuse, allowing thought and word to coalesce into one rhythmic whole, which is not as jarring to the ear as rhyme.

Margot Astrov suggests that this characteristic device stems from two sources, one psychic and one magical:

> . . . this drive that forces man to express himself in rhythmic patterns has its ultimate source in psychic needs, for example the need of spiritual ingestion and proper organization of all the multiform perceptions and impressions rushing forever upon the individual from without and within. . . . Furthermore, repetition, verbal and otherwise, means accumulation of power.[12]

She finds evidence that the first, the need to organize perception, predominates in the ceremonies of some tribes, such as the Apaches, and that the second, a "magically creative quality," is more characteristic of others, such as the Navajo. In other words, some tribes appear to stress form while others stress content, but either way the tribe will make its selection in terms of which emphasis is best likely to bring about fusion with the cosmic whole in their group and environment. This fusion depends on the emphasis that is most congenial to the aesthetic and psychic sense of the tribe.

One should remember, when considering rhythmic aspects of American Indian poetic forms, that all ceremony is chanted, drummed, and danced. American Indians often refer to a piece of music as a dance instead of a song, because song without dance is very rare, as is song without the use of a drum or other percussion instrument. One must also note that the drum does not "accompany" the song, for that implies separation between instrument and voice where no separation is recognized. Words, structure, music, movement, and drum combine to form an integral whole, and accompaniment per se is foreign to the ceremony, though it is common in Western music. The ceremony may be enacted before people who are neither singing nor dancing, but their participation is nevertheless assumed. For participation is a matter of attention and attunement, not of activity.

Repetition is of two kinds, incremental and simple. In the first, variations will occur. A stanza may be repeated in its entirety four times—once for each of the directions—or six times—once for each lateral direction with above and below added—or seven times—once for each direction plus the center "where we stand." Alternatively, the repetition may be of a phrase only, as in the *Yei be chi*, or of a phrase repeated four times with one word—the ceremonial name for each of four mountains, say, or the names of significant colors, animals, or powers—inserted in the appropriate place at each repetition, as in this Navajo Mountain Chant:

> Seated at home behold me,
> Seated amid the rainbow;
> Seated at home behold me,
> Lo, here, the Holy Place!
> > Yea, seated at home behold me.
> At Sisnajinni, and beyond it,
> > Yea, seated at home behold me;
> The Chief of Mountains, and beyond it,
> > Yea, seated at home behold me;
> In Life Unending, and beyond it,
> > Yea, seated at home behold me;
> In Joy Unchanging, and beyond it,
> > Yea, seated at home behold me.
>
> Seated at home behold me,
> Seated amid the rainbow;
> Seated at home behold me,
> Lo, here, the Holy Place!
> > Yea, seated at home behold me.
> At Tsodschl, and beyond it,
> > Yea, seated at home behold me;
> The Chief of Mountains, and beyond it,
> > Yea, seated at home behold me;
> In Life Unending, and beyond it,
> > Yea, seated at home behold me;
> In Joy Unchanging, and beyond it,
> > Yea, seated at home behold me.
>
> Seated at home behold me,
> Seated amid the rainbow;
> Seated at home behold me,
> Lo, here, the Holy Place!
> > Yea, seated at home behold me.

At Doko-oslid, and beyond it,
>   Yea, seated at home behold me;
The Chief of Mountains, and beyond it,
>   Yea, seated at home behold me;
In Life Unending, and beyond it,
>   Yea, seated at home behold me;
In Joy Unchanging, and beyond it,
>   Yea, seated at home behold me.

Seated at home behold me,
Seated amid the rainbow;
Seated at home behold me,
Lo, here, the Holy Place!
>   Yea, seated at home behold me.
At Depenitsa, and beyond it,
>   Yea, seated at home behold me;
The Chief of Mountains, and beyond it,
>   Yea, seated at home behold me;
In Life Unending, and beyond it,
>   Yea, seated at home behold me;
In Joy Unchanging, and beyond it,
>   Yea, seated at home behold me.[13]

Some critics have said that this device results from the oral nature of American Indian literature, that repetition ensures attention and makes the works easy to remember. If this is a factor at all, however, it is a peripheral one, for nonliterate people have more finely developed memories than do literate people. The child learns early to remember complicated instructions, long stories—often verbatim—multitudes of details about plants, animals, kinship and other social relationships, privileges, and responsibilities, all "by heart." For a person who can't run to a bookshelf or a notebook to look up either vital or trivial information, reliance on memory becomes very important in everyday life. This highly developed everyday memory is not likely to fail on ceremonial occasions, so the use of repetition for ease of memorization is not important.

Astrov, in her discussion of the "psychic" basis of the device, touches on another reason folklorists give for the widespread use of repetition in oral ceremonial literature:

> A child repeats a statement over and over for two reasons. First, in order to make himself familiar with something that appears to him to be threateningly unknown and thus to organize it into his system of familiar phenomena; and, second, to get something he wants badly.[14]

Astrov implies that repetition is childish on two counts: that it (rather than rational thought) familiarizes and defuses threat and that the person, irrationally, believes that oral repetition of a desire will ensure its gratification. Let us ignore the obvious fact that shamans, dancers, and other adult participants in the ceremony are not children, and concentrate on actual ceremonies to see whether they contain factors that are or might appear "threatening" to the tribe or whether they simply repeat wishes over and over. Nothing in the passages quoted so far could be construed as threatening, unless beauty, harmony, health, strength, rain, breath, life unending, or sacred mountains can be so seen. Nor are any threatening unknowns mentioned in the songs and chants Astrov includes in her collection; there are threats implicit in death or great powers, but while these constitute unknowns to many civilized people, they are familiar to the tribes. And, by Astrov's own admission, the works approach death or severe illness in positive ways, as in this death song:

> From the middle
> Of the great water
> I am called by the spirits.[15]

"Light as the last breath of the dying," she comments, "these words flutter out and seem to mingle with the soft fumes and mists that rise from the river in the morning"—hardly a threatening description. She continues:

> It is as though the song, with the lightness of a bird's feather, will carry the departing soul up to where the stars are glittering and yonder where the rainbow touches the dome of the sky.[16]

Nowhere in her discussion of Indian songs does Astrov indicate that the singers feel threatened by the chants. Instead, she points out that they express serenity and even joy in the face of what might seem frightening to a child. Nor do there appear any passages, in her extensive collection, that are the equivalent of "Lord, Won't You Buy Me a Color TV," and the absence of such material weakens the childhood-magic theory of repetition. In fact, the usual American Indian perception of humanity (collectively, not individually) as cocreator discourages the people from perceiving the deity as a sort of cosmic bellhop who alone is responsible for their personal well-being. This perception simultaneously discourages people from setting themselves up as potentates, tyrants, dictators, or leaders of any other kind.

The failure of folklorists to comprehend the true metaphysical and psychic nature of structural devices such as ceremonial repetition is a result of the projection of one set of cultural assumptions onto another culture's customs and literatures. People of the Western cultures, particularly those in professions noted for their "objectivity" and intellectual commitment to Freudian tenets, are likely not to interpret psychic components of ceremonial literature in its extramundane sense but rather in its more familiar psychological sense. The twin assumptions that repetition serves to quiet childish psychological needs and to assure participants in a ceremony that they are exerting control over external phenomena—getting something they want badly—are projections. The participants do indeed believe that they can exert control over natural phenomena, but not because they have childishly repeated some syllables. Rather, they assume that all reality is internal in some sense, that the dichotomy of the isolate individual versus the "out there" only appears to exist, and that ceremonial observance can help them transcend this delusion and achieve union with the All-Spirit. From a position of unity within this larger Self, the ceremony can bring about certain results, such as healing one who is ill, ensuring that natural events move in their accustomed way, or bringing prosperity to the tribe.

The Westerner's bias against nonordinary states of consciousness is as unthinking as the Indian's belief in them is said to be. The Westerner's bias is the result of an intellectual climate that has been carefully fostered in the West for centuries, that has reached its culmination in Freudian and Darwinian theories, and that only now is beginning to yield to the masses of data that contradict it. This cultural bias has had many unfortunate side effects, only one of which is the deep misunderstanding of tribal literatures that has for so long marked the learned and popular periodicals that deal with tribal culture.

In his four-volume treatise on nonordinary reality, Carlos Castañeda has described what living in the universe as a shaman is like. Unfortunately, he does not indicate that this experience is rather more common to ordinary than to extraordinary people, that the state of consciousness created through ceremony and ritual and detailed in mythic cycles is exactly that of the "man of knowledge," or sage. He makes the whole thing sound exotic, strange, beyond the reach of most persons; yet the great body of American Indian literature suggests quite a different conclusion. This literature can best be approached as a psychic journey. Only in the context of the consciousness of the universe can it be understood.

American Indian thought is essentially mystical and psychic in nature. Its distinguishing characteristic is a kind of magicalness—not the childish sort described by Astrov, but rather an enduring sense of the fluidity and malleability, or creative flux, of things. This is a reasonable attitude in its own context, derived quite logically from the central assumptions that characterize tribal thought. The tribal person perceives things, not as inert, but as viable and alive, and he or she knows that living things are subject to processes of growth and change as a necessary component of their aliveness. Since all that exists is alive and since all that is alive must grow and change, all existence can be manipulated under certain conditions and according to certain laws. These conditions and laws, called "ritual" or "magic" in the West, are known to American Indians variously. The Sioux refer to them as "walking in a sacred manner," the Navajo as "standing in the center of the world," and the Pomo as "having a tradition." There are as many ways of referring to this phenomenon as there are tribes.

The symbolism in American Indian ceremonial literature, then, is not symbolic in the usual sense; that is, the four mountains in the Mountain Chant do not stand for something else. They are those exact mountains perceived psychically, as it were, or mystically. The color red, as used by the Lakota, doesn't stand for sacred or earth, but is the quality of a being, the color of it, when perceived "in a sacred manner" or from the point of view of the earth itself. That is, red is a psychic quality, not a material one, though it has a material dimension, of course. But its material aspect is not its essential one: or as the great metaphysician Madame Blavatsky put it, the physical is not a principle, or, as Lame Deer the Lakota shaman suggests, the physical aspect of existence is only representative of what is real:

> The meat stands for the four-legged creatures, our animal brothers, who gave of themselves so that we should live. The stream [from the stewpot] is living breath. It was water; now it goes up to the sky, becomes a cloud again. . . .
>   We Sioux spend a lot of time thinking about everyday things, which in our mind are mixed up with the spiritual. We see in the world around us many symbols that teach us the meaning of life. We have a saying that the white man sees so little, he must see with only one eye. We see a lot that you no longer notice. You could notice if you wanted too, but you are usually too busy. We Indians live in a world of symbols and images where the spiritual and the commonplace are one. To you symbols are just words, spoken or written in a book. To us they are part of nature, part of ourselves, even little insects like ants and grasshoppers. We try to understand them not with the head but with the heart, and we need no more than a hint to give us the meaning.[17]

Not only are the "symbols" statements of perceived reality rather than metaphorical or poetic statements but the formulations that are characterized by brevity and repetition are also expressions of that perception. One sees life as part of oneself; a hint as to which particular part is all that is needed to convey meaning. This accounts for the "purity" and "simplicity" that apparently characterize traditional American Indian literatures. The works are simple in that they concern themselves with what is known and familiar, not in that they are childlike or unsophisticated.

In a sense, the American Indian perceives all that exists as symbolic. This outlook has given currency to the concept of the Indian as one who is close to the earth, but the closeness is actual, not a quaint result of savagism or childlike naiveté. An Indian, at the deepest level of being, assumes that the earth is alive in the same sense that human beings are alive. This aliveness is seen in nonphysical terms, in terms that are perhaps familiar to the mystic or the psychic, and this view gives rise to a metaphysical sense of reality that is an ineradicable part of Indian awareness. In brief, we can say that the sun or the earth or a tree is a symbol of an extraordinary truth.

This attitude is not anthropomorphic. No Indian would regard personal perception as the basic, or only, unit of universal consciousness. Indians believe that the basic unit of consciousness is the All-Spirit, the living fact of intelligence from which all other perceptions arise and derive their power:

> I live, but I will not live forever.
> Mysterious moon, you only remain,
> Powerful sun, you alone remain,
> Wonderful earth, you remain forever.
> All of us soldiers must die.[18]

This attitude is not superstitious, though it can degenerate into superstition when the culture disintegrates. It is based very solidly on experience, and most members of the tribe share that experience to some degree. The experience is verified by hundreds and thousands of years of experience and is a result of actual perception—sight, taste, hearing, smell—as well as more indirect social and natural phenomena. In the West, if a person points to a building and says, "There is a building," and if other people looking in the direction indicated agree, and if that building can be entered, walked through, touched, then the building is said to be really there.

In the same way, traditional American Indians encounter and verify metaphysical reality. No one's experience is idiosyncratic. The singer who tells of journeying to the west and climbing under the sky speaks of a journey that many have taken in the past and will take in the future. Every traveler will describe the same sights and sounds and will enter and return in like fashion.

Generations of Western observers have noticed this peculiarity of psychic travel, and many attempt to explain it in psychoanalytic terms, referring to Jung's "collective unconscious," for example, or to Freud's notion of the projection of repressed conflict. Nevertheless, the evidence, however one interprets it, suggests that the psychic life of all humanity is the same. Western sophisticates presume that the experiences—sights, sounds, and beings encountered on psychic journeys—are imaginary and hallucinatory; they are equally inclined to presume that thoughts are idiosyncratic events of no real consequence. Nowhere in the literature on ceremonialism have I encountered a Western writer willing to suggest that the "spiritual and the commonplace are one."[19] Many argue that these "hallucinations" are good, others that they are the product of a diseased mind,[20] but none suggests that one may *actually* be "seated amid the rainbow."

Symbols in American Indian systems are not symbolic in the usual sense of the word. The words articulate reality—not "psychological" or imagined reality, not emotive reality captured metaphorically in an attempt to fuse thought and feeling, but that reality where thought and feeling are one, where objective and subjective are one, where speaker and listener are one, where sound and sense are one.

terms of another culture, whether it be that of Maya or of England, because those other cultures have different imperatives and have grown on different soil, under a different sky within the nexus of different spirits, and within a different traditional context. "Owl" in one situation will have a very different significance from "owl" in another, and a given color—white or blue—will vary from place to place and from ceremony to ceremony in its significance, intensity, and power. In other words, the rules that govern traditional American Indian literatures are very different from those that govern Western literature, though the enormity of the difference is, I think, a fairly recent development. Literature must, of necessity, express and articulate the deepest perceptions, relationships, and attitudes of a culture, whether it does so deliberately or accidentally. Tribal literature does this with a luminosity and clarity that is largely free of pretension, stylized "elegance," or show. Experiences that are held to be the most meaningful—from those that completely transcend ordinary experience to those that are commonplace—are celebrated in the songs and ceremonial cycles of the people.

The more commonplace experiences are celebrated in popular tales and songs, which may be humorous, soothing, pedagogical, or entertaining. In this category are lullabies, corn-grinding and ditch-digging songs, jokes, *pourquoi* tales, "little" stories, and stories with contemporary settings. Included here, too, are those delightful dances called '49s.[23] All but the '49s appear in collections of Indian lore, sometimes masquerading as true myths or simple songs. This masquerade, of course, does little to clear up misunderstandings regarding American Indian literature, for frequently those "myths" that seem childlike are forms developed for children and bear only a slight resemblance to the true mythic chants from which they derive.

Between the trivial, popular forms and the ceremonial works are songs and stories such as the various games; incantations and other simple forms of magic; prose cycles such as the Trickster tales recorded by Paul Radin; some journey and food-related songs and legends.

Individual songs may be difficult to classify, though the level of symbolism they contain and the amount of prescribed ritual and associated ceremony, the number and special qualifications of the celebrants, and the physical setting and costume used can help distinguish one kind from another. In order to classify any given song, though, one needs more than a nodding acquaintance with the locality and the tribe whose song or story is under consideration.

Another important factor to consider in classification of a song is the relative secrecy of parts or all of the ceremony, especially when tourists, cameras, or tape recorders are present. The amount of secrecy will vary to some extent from tribe to tribe, some being more open than others, but some secrecy is nearly always the rule.

Another such indicator, particularly valuable for classroom work, is the source of the song or story. Only very erudite tomes are likely to have much that is really sacred, and even those have usually been altered in some way. Popular books are likely to carry mainly popular literature, with a few selections from the next more powerful category. It would be well to mention, in this connection, that the use of really sacred materials by ordinary mortals and publishers is generally forbidden. Also, these works do not make good classroom materials for a variety of reasons: they are arcane; they are usually taboo; they tend to confuse non-Indian students; they may cause resentment among Indian students; and they create questions and digressions that are usually beyond the competence of the teacher or of the academic setting. Frequently they lead to ridicule, disrespect, and belittlement; non-Indian students are not inclined by training or culture to view the sacred as that which has power beyond that of economics, history, or politics.

Underlying all their complexity, traditional American Indian literatures possess a unity and harmony of symbol, structure, and articulation that is peculiar to the American Indian world. This harmony is based on the perceived harmony of the universe and on thousands of years of refinement. This essential sense of unity among all things flows like a clear stream through the songs and stories of the peoples of the Western Hemisphere. This sense is embodied in these words of an old man:

> There are birds of many colors—red, blue, green, yellow—yet it is all one bird. There are horses of many colors—brown, black, yellow, white—yet it is all one horse. So cattle, so all living things—animals, flowers, trees. So men: in this land where once were only Indians are now men of every color—white, black, yellow, red—yet all one people. That this should come to pass was in the heart of the Great Mystery. It is right thus. And everywhere there shall be peace.[24]

So Hiamove said, more than fifty years ago. It remains for scholars of American Indian literature to look at this literature from the point of view of its people. Only from this vantage can we understand fully the richness, complexity, and true meaning of a people's life; only in this way can we all learn the lessons of the past on this continent and the essential lesson of respect for all that is.

Notes

1   Mythic: 1. narratives that deal with metaphysical, spiritual, and cosmic occurrences that recount the spiritual past and the "mysteries" of the tribe; 2. sacred story. The *Word* in its cosmic, creative sense. This usage follows the literary meaning rather than the common or vernacular meaning of "fictive" or "not real narrative dealing with primitive, irrational explanations of the world." 3. transrational.

2   Storm, *Seven Arrows*, p. 4.

3   Black Elk, *Black Elk Speaks*, p. 35.

4   Geronimo, *Geronimo*, p. 7.

5   McNickle, *Native American Tribalism*, pp. 12–13.

6   Marriott and Rachlin, *American Indian Mythology*, p. 39.

7   Marriott and Rachlin, p. 39.

8   Curtis, *The Indians' Book*, pp. 8, 7.

9   From a prayer of the *Night Chant* of the Navajo people.

10   I am making this inference from the account of the appearance of White Buffalo Cow Woman to Kablaya as recounted by Black Elk in *The Sacred Pipe*, pp. 67–100.

11   T. Kroeber and Heizer, *Almost Ancestors*, pp. 28–30.

12   Astrov, *American Indian Prose and Poetry*, p. 12.

13   Curtis, *The Indians' Book*, p. 356. I have reproduced this part of the chant in its entirety, although the Curtis version has only one stanza with a note regarding the proper form.

14   Astrov, p. 12.

15   Astrov, p. 50.

16   Astrov, p. 50.

17   Fire, *Lame Deer*, pp. 108–9.

18   Crazy Dog Society song of the Kiowa people. This version appears in Marriott, *Kiowa Years*, p. 118.

19   Fire, p. 115.

20   Freud, *Totem and Taboo*, p. 14.

21   Fire, p. 115.

22   Fire, p. 112.

23   '49 songs were sung (danced) just before a war party went out. They are widely enjoyed today after a powwow has officially ended after midnight. One '49 goes like this:
   When the dance is ended sweetheart
   I will take you home.
   He-ya he-he-ya
   He-ya he-he-ya.

24   Curtis, p. x.

Cycles of Appreciation

Larry Evers

Patterns of interest in American Indian oral literature have been cyclic. One indication of these cycles has been the publication of anthologies of American Indian literature.[1] Thus, a first cycle may be recognized by the publication of George Cronyn's *The Path on the Rainbow* in 1918, a second by the appearance of two anthologies around midcentury—Margot Astrov's *The Winged Serpent* and A. Grove Day's *The Sky Clears*—and a third by the anthologies that flooded bookstores in the late sixties and throughout the seventies, epitomized, I suppose, by Jerome Rothenberg's *Shaking the Pumpkin* and William Brandon's *The Magic World*.[2] As these anthologies have been the vehicles through which American Indian verbal art—narratives, prayers, and songs—has been offered to a wider American audience, their character is of special interest to those of us concerned with teaching American Indian literature. They imply a course of study that we often follow in our classrooms. At the same time, the anthologies have served as friction points around which ethnologists, folklorists, poets, and literary critics have regularly gathered to grind at critical issues the anthologies raise. Much of this discussion has been territorial and is usefully ignored, but at its best it highlights problems and issues that have remained with us through three generational cycles. I will look first at the anthologies and then sketch some problems they raise.

I

In 1883 Daniel Brinton published a wide-ranging survey of American Indian verbal art of his time, including selections intended to "engage in their presentation and publication the interest of scholarly men, of learned societies, of enlightened governments, of liberal institutions and individuals, not only in [this] country but throughout the world."[3] What followed Brinton's call, chronologically if not causally, was one of the most intense periods of collecting oral literature in anthropological history. During the last years of the nineteenth century and the first of the twentieth, Matthews,

Fletcher, Curtin, Cushing, Dorsey, Boas, and many others gathered enormous numbers of narratives and songs from tribal peoples all over this continent.

Though printed in limited scholarly editions, these translations quickly attracted the attention of many non-Indian poets and writers. The result often dismayed the anthropologists. Washington Matthews, for example, concludes his collection *Navaho Legends* with "A Last Word to Poets and Others":

> Stephen Powers, in his "Tribes of California," gives, in simple and direct language, the story of how fire came to the Karok nation. A few years after he wrote, someone worked his story into a "Poem," which appeared, most artistically illustrated, in one of our leading magazines. In this poem the Coyote, in a quandary, is represented as "stroking his goatee." Coyotes have no goatees; Indians have no goatees. The act of stroking the goatee, in thought or perplexity, is the special mannerism of a nervous American. No allusion could be more out of place in an Indian legend. Should the poet referred to ever select any of the tales in this book to be tortured into a poem, I beg that he will not, even for the sake of making a faulty rhyme, put a beard on the chin of the Navaho Coyote God. (p. 297)

Poets have let Matthews' translations stand, perhaps more in deference to their elegant simplicity than to this request. But within ten years of Matthews' "last word" a group of poets led by Mary Austin were attempting "interpretations" of anthropological translations of American Indian verbal art. The activities of Austin and other poets brought American Indian oral literature to the attention of the American literary community and provided a major stimulus for a special issue of *Poetry* magazine edited by George Cronyn in 1917 and released the following year in book form as *The Path on the Rainbow.*

The Cronyn anthology marks one of the first real efforts to offer American Indian oral literature to a general American audience as imaginative literature. Its form and editorial practice become nearly archetypal when we look at the anthologies that have followed. Similarly the critical responses it provoked—from literary critics, from poets, and from anthropologists—raise issues in regard to the appreciation of Indian stories and songs as literature that remain with us today, two generations later.

The design of *The Path on the Rainbow* is simple enough. Translations of songs from a variety of tribes done by the likes of Schoolcraft, Densmore, Matthews, and Boas were grouped into sections defined by culture areas: Eastern Woodlands, Southwest, Great Plains, and so on. The translations thus grouped appeared as the anthropologists offered them, and they were not annotated. The way those translations are framed in the anthology is telling. The book opens with an essay by Mary Austin and closes with a selection of "interpretations" of Indian songs done by Austin, Constance Skinner, Alice

Henderson, and Pauline Johnson, a Canadian poet of Indian ancestry. In her opening remarks Austin observes the remarkable likeness that some of the anthropological translations bear to the work of Imagists and goes on to suggest that a relationship seems about to develop between Indian verse and "the ultimate literary destiny of America."[4] Austin thus seems much less interested in the songs as Indian songs than she is in the possibility of reshaping the songs into poems that might redirect this "ultimate literary destiny." The introductory essay and the translations of the anthropologists are in a real sense merely preparations for the final section of "interpretations."

It is important to note that the poets did not regard these "interpretations" as attempts to translate in any strict sense. In *The American Rhythm* Austin writes:

> If forced to affix a title to my work I would prefer to call it not translation, but re-expression. My method has been by preference to saturate myself in the poem, in the life that produced it, and the environment that cradled that life so that when the point of crystallization is reached I myself give forth a poem which bears, I hope, a genetic resemblance to the Amerind song that was my point of contact. (p. 38)

In fact, Austin remarks that she was so interested in "primitive concept" that she did not bother to record the original form of the songs she encountered, "stripping them off as so much husk to get at the kernel of the experience."[5]

Such anthropological heresy brought strong response not only from anthropologists but from literary critics as well. Louis Untermeyer, in an early review of *The Path on the Rainbow*, faulted the anthology and its contributors on several counts. First he criticized their romanticism: "the pioneer's harsh estimate has been modified to a surprising degree, a good Indian, according to his students is . . . a singing one." Second, Untermeyer objected to "the arbitrary arrangement of words and a pretentious typography that is foreign to [the] native." Finally, he faulted the editing of the anthology generally for its shallow scholarship, noting that "many of these songs cry aloud for nothing so much as footnotes."[6] Untermeyer's three criticisms—of motive, of authenticity and quality of translation, and of context—were greatly developed by others in their responses to the Cronyn anthology.[7]

Just after World War II two other anthologies of American Indian verbal art were published: Margot Astrov's *The Winged Serpent* and A. Grove Day's *The Sky Clears*.[8] As I have suggested this pair of anthologies represents a second cycle in the attempt to acquaint the general American reading public with American Indian verbal art. Like the Cronyn anthology, *The Winged Serpent* and *The Sky Clears* are both organized around the notion of culture areas, and both, like the Cronyn anthology, draw their material word for word from the translations of anthropologists and folklorists. Unlike Cronyn,

Astrov and Day appear more concerned with presenting American Indian verbal art as a part of American literature than as the raw material for writing it.

The Astrov and Day anthologies thus seem better on two counts: their substantive introductions and their attempts to provide some context for the materials they anthologize. Day writes:

> Most Indian poems are not immediately comprehensible to the ordinary person today . . . and this fact has dictated the need for some explanation if a verse is to seem intelligible and pleasing. A mere "anthology" of Indian verse without any clues to the backgrounds of human needs and human emotions from which these unusual poems sprang would be worse than useless, for it would be misleading. (p. xi)

Yet, as the anthologies that marked the second cycle became more sophisticated, so, too, critical responses to them became more demanding. The most substantive response to the second cycle was one formulated by Dell Hymes in 1953 and published in 1965 as "Some North Pacific Coast Poems: A Problem in Anthropological Philology." Hymes points out that Astrov, Day, and others interested in editing American Indian verbal art share the following assumptions:

1. that the ethnologists who collected the material must be relied upon for the validity of the translations, and can be;
2. that literary versions are to be preferred to literal ones;
3. that the style, or structure, of the originals is accessible in significant part through the best translations. (p. 318)

Hymes finds these propositions misleading as he examines several song poems from the work of Schoolcraft and from collectors on the North Pacific Coast. He further observes that appreciation of American Indian verbal art has a schizophrenic quality about it in that "it insists on authenticity, but not on the original texts" (p. 333). In other words, the concern for objectivity and authenticity is displaced from the native performers and their native language texts onto the translations and the ethnologists. Hymes concludes that "the study of languages is too important to be left solely to linguistics (in the narrow sense of the term), the text too valuable to be interpreted by any who ignore linguistics" (p. 337).

Sadly, Hymes's suggestions seem to have been all but lost on editors of the third wave of anthologies of American Indian verbal art that rolled through the seventies and now appears to be ebbing. Many have regressed to editorial standards comparable to Cronyn's. Some, like Rothenberg, seem to have returned to the view that native American verbal art is nothing more than a kind of raw material to be appropriated into their own art.[9] Virtually all have continued to accept uncritically the translations of the ethnologists, a fact that is particularly disappointing when such editors are themselves American Indians.[10] And, finally, while most note the continuance of native American cultures into the last quarter of the twentieth century, few acknowledge that native languages and oral literatures continue to exist in vital ways. One recent anthologist even goes so far as to define all contemporary native oral literature out of existence. "The traditional literature," he writes, and please note the tense, "was composed in an Indian language for an Indian audience at a time when the tribal cultures were intact and contact with whites had been minimal."[11] It will come as some surprise to thousands of American Indians who continue to make songs and stories in their native tongues that they have not had a "traditional" literature for several centuries.

II

I take it that the editorial problems and decisions that anthologists have faced through the three cycles I have sketched are much like those we face as teachers. So I turn now to discuss some of the problems the anthologies raise as they may apply to our classroom practice. Three considerations seem useful: scope, context, and continuity.

Scope. A first problem facing the organizer of a course in American Indian verbal art is the assumed need to represent the breadth and variety of form, theme, and function that we find in American Indian oral literatures. The Whitman's Sampler solution used by nearly all anthologists is clearly unsatisfactory. It begs us to wrench songs and narratives from their cultural contexts and leaves us without enough time and space to develop the cultural understandings necessary to allow responsible appreciation of the material. The experience of the anthologists suggests that we should attempt to be less extensive and more intensive in our treatment of oral literatures. Given available materials, two alternate strategies may offer acceptable alternatives: a regional approach or a masterworks approach. An example of an appropriate text for a course taking a regional tack is Jarold Ramsey's rich regional anthology, *Coyote Was Going There: Indian Literature of the Oregon Country.* I have used my own *The South Corner of Time* to great advantage in teaching a course with a southwestern focus. John Bierhorst's *Four Masterworks of American Indian Literature* provides a good text for a masterworks approach.

Context. In either case, becoming more intensive and less extensive in our treatment of oral literatures would mean that we could use the time and space we gained to look at more verbal art from fewer cultures. But more than that it would mean that we could develop a more adequate context for those pieces we do use.

We respond to any work of literature by means of patterns of expectation. The patterns of expectation on which we rely when we experience American literature derive from several sources. Some are patterns of expectation that we have internalized unconsciously by virtue of having English as our first language and being raised in American culture. I have in mind my daughter's obsessive interest in charms, jump-rope rhymes, parodies, and the like, which she absorbs with an astonishing capacity and which she is constantly performing. This American childlore will unquestionably influence the way she perceives imaginative uses of language for the rest of her life.[12] In addition, I assume my daughter will gradually acquire patterns of literary expectation as her formal education proceeds. As she begins to read pieces of American literature her responses to them will derive not only from these patterns of expectation, which she has internalized unconsciously as a participant in American culture, but also from those she learned consciously through her formal training. When I speak of the necessity for gaining a context in which to appreciate American Indian verbal art, then, I mean to speak of the necessity for gaining access to those patterns of literary and cultural expectation that are assumed in the culture in which the piece exists. I mean to understand the often quoted words of Papago verbal artist Maria Chona: "the song is very short because we understand so much."[13]

Patterns of expectation and understanding of the sort Maria Chona alludes to in Papago song are not acquired easily, and they are rarely communicated in ways that can reach those of us who wish to teach native oral literatures in classrooms. We do have ways to turn for help, though. One is in the direction of those rare students who have lived in native communities, learned native languages, and troubled to understand native literatures. Gary Witherspoon's *Language and Art in the Navajo Universe* (esp. Chs. 1 and 4) is an accessible source to which we might turn to glimpse what a difference knowledge of Navajo language and culture can make in the way we perceive frequently anthologized Navajo songs. Similarly, the work of Dell Hymes with Chinookan narrative and song, Barre Toelken with Navajo legends, Dennis Tedlock with Zuni tales, and Donald Bahr with Papago orations are instances where gifted linguists have been able to describe understandings of native American linguistic form and texture in ways that promote literary appreciation.[14] A second direction in which we can turn for help in gaining a context for our appreciation of native American oral literatures is to writing by Indian people themselves. In the decade or so since the publication of N. Scott Momaday's *House Made of Dawn* a generation of Indian writers has emerged who seek in their own work to represent the content and style of the oral traditions that nurtured them. Momaday's *The Way to Rainy Mountain*, Ortiz' *A Good Journey*, Storm's *Seven Arrows*, and Silko's *Storyteller*, each in a significant way, offer us collections of oral literature framed by informed, imaginative commentary.[15] In the hands of Momaday, Ortiz, Silko, and others, such written genres as the narrative poem and the novel provide us with some of the most accurate, authentic, and accessible contexts for native American oral literatures presently available.[16]

Continuity. One of the strongest impressions that we might take away from a review of the collections of American Indian verbal art over the last century is that American Indian oral traditions are dead or dying. Time and again collectors and editors assure us that they have gathered "the last whispers of a dying race." While it is indisputable that some very substantial and complex parts of American Indian oral tradition have disappeared in the years since European contact, vital oral literatures remain in many American Indian communities.

Collectors and editors often confuse loss with change, and we should not be misled by their confusion. The nature of oral tradition includes not only conservatism and stability but innovation and change as well.[17] Oral traditions were not static when Europeans arrived. The oral traditions of some tribes have always been influenced by the oral traditions of others; indeed, tracing such influence has been one of the major tasks of scholars of American Indian verbal art. European influences have always been regarded as another matter. Nellie Barnes, for example, in an early stylistic study of American Indian oral literature considered "only forms preceding the influence of white men."[18] Yet the mere fact of European influence does not mean that native traditions are waning. In some cases just the opposite seems to be true. A classic and much noted instance is the Zuni version of the Italian folk tale "The Cock and the Mouse" published by Cushing in *Zuni Folk Tales* in 1901.[19] Whatever Cushing's role was in the translation of the Zuni version of the story, it is clear that the European story offered a new opportunity for the Zuni narrator to exercise his narrative genius, leaving his tradition enhanced rather than diminished by the European influence.[20]

It seems likely, then, that collectors' assertions that they were the last persons to have the opportunity to record narratives or songs before they were forever gone are comments on the collectors' vision of themselves and their role as preservers and saviors rather than on the tradition they are reporting. And it is plainly convenient for editors to accept such judgments. It is far easier to cut and paste from old Bureau of American Ethnology collections than to go out and gather contemporary examples of American Indian oral traditions, better to accept the denial that they are there. We must help students to see that American Indian narratives and songs continue to exist, that they are something more than museum pieces, that they continue to be a part of the fabric of contemporary American Indian life.

We should show students that American Indian oral traditions continue in three ways. First, we should point out that American Indian oral traditions continue to be sung and told in contemporary American Indian communities. In the last eight years I have worked in over a dozen American

Indian communities in Arizona and New Mexico and with Indian people from another dozen. I have yet to encounter an American Indian community in which the verbal arts do not hold an active place. Second, for those traditions that seem to have waned, we might point to the revitalization efforts of various Indian-run culture programs that are attempting to bring about a revival of the verbal arts in Indian communities where they have become weak. We might also note the parallel scholarly efforts of the likes of Dell Hymes with Chinookan material and Donald Bahr with Piman. Hymes has repeatedly said that a major purpose of his work is to restore texts and make them available to the tribal peoples of the Northwest.[21] Similarly Bahr argues in *Pima and Papago Ritual Oratory* that American Indian materials that have been collected over the last century should be taken out of cold storage and returned to Indian people in a form and with a commentary that is useful to them (pp. 3–4). American Indian verbal art can be shown then to continue through these revitalization efforts by academics and by Indian people themselves. Finally, we should show how Indian oral traditions continue in the work of contemporary Indian writers. Reference to material from oral tradition has become a major defining feature of what we consider contemporary American Indian literature, yet we have very limited understanding of just what the links are between oral traditions and the written work of Momaday, Ortiz, Silko, and others.[22] We need to know much more about the tribal traditions out of which these and other contemporary Indian writers write if we are to appreciate their work more fully.

But the place of oral tradition in the work of contemporary Indian writers goes beyond patterns of reference and allusion in stories and poems. Much of what we regard as contemporary American Indian literature seems to be more fully realized when it is read aloud, when it is performed, when, in Nia Francisco's phrase, it is "made moist with my breath."[23] It may be helpful to ask students to view contemporary American Indian writers as tellers and singers, as performers. Along the same lines, we should recognize that not all contemporary Indian verbal artists choose to publish their work in print. Barney Mitchell sings his song-poems in Navajo, as does Ruth Roessel; the Circle Film Company people prefer telling their stories to printing them; and Pueblo poets Simon Ortiz and Harold Littlebird sing many of their compositions in addition to writing. We need to help our students experience these continuing expressions of the American Indian oral tradition, not as gray masses of type on a page, but as an oral and aural experience.

In an effort to help students experience some of these performance qualities of native American literature, we developed *Words and Place: Native Literature from the American Southwest*, a series of eight videotapes of native singers, storytellers, and authors.[24] Working with narrators and singers from Hopi, Navajo, Western Apache, and Yaqui communities, we were able to record performances of story and song in the native languages of the performers and in situations closely approximating natural settings. On the tapes, tellers or singers provide commentary that constitutes a kind of oral literary criticism. Each program is available with or without English subtitles. In this way students are able to experience the sight and sounds of traditional native languages and literatures more directly than they can in conventional print formats. Other programs in the series focus on othe work of contemporary native American writers Leslie Marmon Silko, Harold Littlebird, and Vine Deloria, Jr. Each reads and comments on his or her own work and its links with native communities and oral traditions. In this way the series represents a range of performances along that continuum of imaginative verbal expression we call Native American literature. I and the others who have experimented with the series in classrooms have found it helpful in dealing with some of the problems I have sketched above.

I have been making "should" statements: we *should* become more intensive and less extensive in scope in our treatments of verbal art, we *should* work to develop adequate contexts for the songs and stories we use in classrooms, and we *should* help students to experience continuing contemporary expressions of American Indian oral literature. Making "should" statements is easy enough; moving them to actuality is not. The course designs that follow describe some possibilities, and the video project I mentioned describes another, but there are no easy answers. I am reminded of the Zuni narrator who asked Dennis Tedlock, "When I tell a story, do you *see* it or do you just write it down?" It is that vision—the kind that resides not on the printed page or the video screen but in the mind's eye—that we should try to provoke in the classroom as we circle our way through future cycles of appreciation.

Notes

1   Hobson points to the cyclic pattern of the publication of writing by American Indians in "Round Dance"; Deloria defines a similar cyclic nature of American interest in all things Indian in "A Conversation with Vine Deloria, Jr."

2   For other anthologies see Marken's bibliography, *The American Indian*.

3   Brinton, *Aboriginal American Authors and Their Productions*, quoted in Chapman, *Literature of the American Indians*, p. 223.

4   See also Alexander, "Indian Songs and English Verse."

5   *The American Rhythm*, p. 40. See Rothenberg, "Total Translation," in Chapman, pp. 292–307, for a contemporary version of this style of translating.

6   Untermeyer, Review of *The Path on the Rainbow*. See also Austin's rejoinders: "The Path on the Rainbow" and "Imagism: Original and Aboriginal."

7   Spinden, "American Indian Poetry," and Walton and Waterman, "American Indian Poetry," are exemplary.

8   Sayre notes that historically we Americans try to learn from American Indians most when our imported culture is in greatest danger—for example, during periods of war. See "A Bibliography and an Anthology of American Indian Literature."

9   See Silko, "An Old-Time Indian Attack Conducted in Two Parts," and Hobson, "The Rise of the White Shaman as a New Version of Cultural Imperialism." Two other superb critiques are

Bevis, "American Indian Verse Translations," and McAllester, "A Different Drum." Rothenberg is defended in McAllister, "The Language of Shamans."

10   See, for example, Sanders and Peek, *Literature of the American Indian.*

11   Velie, *American Indian Literature*, p. 3.

12   See Dundes' essays on American folklore collected in *Analytic Essays in Folklore* and *Interpreting Folklore* for detailed analyses of the relation between American folklore and world view.

13   *Papago Woman*, p. 51.

14   For samples, see Hymes, *In Vain I Tried To Tell You*, Toelken, "The 'Pretty Language(s)' of Yellowman: Genre, Mode, and Texture in Navajo Coyote Narratives," "*Ma'i Joldloshi*: Legendary Styles and Navajo Myth," and "Seeing with a Native Eye"; Tedlock, *Finding the Center*, "Pueblo Literature," and "Toward an Oral Poetics"; and Bahr, *Pima and Papago Ritual Oratory* and *Rainhouse and Ocean.*

15   See Momaday's *The Way to Rainy Mountain* and its prototype *The Journey of Tai-me*; Ortiz' *A Good Journey*, Storm's *Seven Arrows*; and Silko's *Ceremony*. Momaday's "The Man Made of Words" and Ortiz' "Song/Poetry and Language—Perception and Expression" also provide valuable perspectives.

16   See Roemer's "Survey Courses, Indian Literature, and *The Way to Rainy Mountain.*"

17   See Toelken, *The Dynamics of Folklore.*

18   Barnes, *American Indian Verse.*

19   The story is reprinted with a useful introduction and notes in Dundes, *The Study of Folklore*, pp. 269–76.

20   See Tedlock's "On the Translation of Style in Oral Narrative" for a discussion of Cushing's translating. Ramsey addresses the question of the reciprocity of influence in "The Bible in Western Indian Mythology."

21   See especially "Folklore's Nature and the Sun's Myth."

22   On Momaday, see my essay "Words and Place" and Watkins' chapter on Momaday in *In Time and Place*; on Ortiz, see Gingerich, "The Old Voices of Acoma"; and on Silko, see Ruoff, "Ritual and Renewal" and my "Going Along with the Story" and Evers and Carr, eds., "A Conversation with Leslie Marmon Silko."

23   The phrase is from a moving statement Francisco made at the end of a conference The Religious Character of the Native American Humanities held at Arizona State University, 15 April 1977.

24   Cinematographer Dennis Carr and I produced the series in cooperation with KUAT-TV, Tucson, and with funding from the Division of Education Programs, National Endowment for the Humanities. The eight programs are "By This Song I Walk: Navajo Song" with Andrew Natonabah; "*Iisaw*: Hopi Coyote Stories" with Helen Sekaquaptewa; "*Natwaniwa*: A Hopi Philosophical Narrative" with George Nasofotie; "*Seyewailo*: The Flower World: Yaqui Deer Songs" with Felipe Molina; "The Origin of the Crown Dance: An Apache Narrative" and "*Ba'ts'oosee*: An Apache Trickster Cycle" in two parts with Rudolph Cane; "Songs of My Hunter Heart: Laguna Songs and Poems" with Harold Littlebird; "Running on the Edge of the Rainbow: Laguna Stories and Poems" with Leslie Marmon Silko; and "A Conversation with Vine Deloria, Jr." For more detailed information see the handbook that accompanies the series. Distributor: Clearwater Publishing Company, 1995 Broadway, New York, NY 10023.

Teaching American Indian Oral Literatures

The creation of literature is the act of an imagination responsive to distinctive cultural values and to differences in the modes, whether written or oral, in which those values are expressed. Not only historically but psychologically as well, oral literature is at the root of all written literature. This suggests that the study of oral literature, both in its many forms and in its creative processes, is a useful and necessary complement to the study of American Indian written literature. It is important to explore in depth the similarities as well as the differences between written and oral modes of literary expression. The continuities between oral and written forms testify to the enduring vitality of oral art as an integral part of tribal and personal identity in contemporary Indian communities, while the written forms allow expression of the blending of Western and traditional ways. A coherent study of the differences between written and oral traditions demands special skills that must be based in great part on an understanding of American Indian aesthetic assumptions as they differ from those of the European-American critical tradition. This comparison encourages students to challenge pat assumptions and to develop new and creative critical responses to non-Western literary forms.

Methodology and Description

Context

Oral literature is a living reality whose whole existence, like that of a piece of music, exists in the performance, and, like music, this literature exists within a *tradition* of performances. Unlike the composed score for a musical piece, however, and despite the deception of the printed "text," no definitive text exists for a given piece, so that oral literature derives its form from its tradition of performances, from incorporated stylistic devices, and from the ability of the narrator to capture and hold the audience.

In the classroom, the tradition incorporates three dimensions or contexts: (1) the generating context, including the individual creator, the social milieu in which he or she works, and the tradition of prior performances; (2) the performance context, including the situation, conditions, and audience involved in the performance; and (3) the reception context, a multileveled reality involving the first audience of original auditors, the second audience of the translator/transcriber, and the final audience of the classroom presentation.

The *generating context* provides the materials and framework about and within which singers or storytellers, no less than their European counterparts, filter personal experience through the creative imagination. It then becomes doubly important for the teacher or critic to understand the cultural background from which the individual story springs, the continuo against which the counterpoint is played. Students can become familiar with some of this context by reading introductory works (Underhill, *Red Man's Religion*; McNickle, *Indian Tribes* and *They Came Here First*; Driver, *Indians*), which can lead them to more specialized works dealing with aspects of culture (Reichard, *Navaho Religion*; Parsons, *Pueblo Indian Religion*; Underhill, *Papago Indian Religion*; Benedict, "Vision" and *Concept of the Guardian Spirit*), works dealing with the relationship among culture, language, and literature (Boas, *Race, Language, and Culture*; Hallowell, "Myth"; Spencer, *Mythology and Values*; Bauman, "Differential Identity"; Witherspoon, *Language and Art*; Gill, *Sacred Words*), and those that deal with the relationship between the singer/storyteller and the community (Oppler, "Three Types"; Reichard, "Individualism"; Stern, "Some Sources of Variability"; Finnegan, *Oral Poetry*; Mitchell, *Blessingway Singer*). But as valuable as these resources may be, we should emphasize that these works are frequently written from a historically conditioned, Anglo sociological perspective. A vital step, therefore, is to check all ethnological information carefully against American Indian accounts of the given tribe before using such materials in the classroom. Finally, if students are truly to enter the living reality of oral literature, they must enter an American Indian storytelling situation, perhaps through contact with storytellers and singers in the classroom.

Understanding and analyzing the *performance context* (Bauman, *Verbal Art*) is important, but actually experiencing it is more important. Obviously, those who are in the best position to provide both the understanding and the experience are the storytellers and singers from the local Indian community. If none are available, one might employ videotaped performances such as those produced by Larry Evers (*Words and Place*), which include Navajo singing, Hopi and Apache storytelling, and Yaqui Deer Dance songs. Several scholars have attempted to recapture in part the reality of the performance (Tedlock, *Finding the Center*), but it is impossible to record all the dimensions of the performance later in an integrated manner. Nevertheless, instructors should always attempt some discussion of the performance aspects of singing and storytelling and of the many ways in which the performance defines style, form, function, and so on (Sapir, "Song Recitative"; Gayton and Newman, *Yokuts and Western Mono Myths*; Jacobs, *Content and Style of an Oral Literature*; Toelken, " 'Pretty Language(s)' "; Tedlock, "On the Translation of Style" and "Pueblo Literature"; Darnell, "Correlates"; Irvine, "Formality"). One way to do this is to discuss with the students their own personal experience with storytelling. Storytelling is not reserved only for American Indians; it is a universal process. All people have enjoyed trading stories about themselves and their experiences, their relatives, neighbors, children; all have favorite stories they ask others to tell. Though this storytelling is not called oral literature or tradition, it is an example of "performance context" that everyone understands. Such a discussion can also serve to remove the "exotic" stereotype from American Indians and place them in a universal context.

Of pressing importance to the instructor is the final *reception context*, the classroom audience. That it is an educational cliché does not diminish the importance of the principle that one must develop a teaching strategy design as much to suit the background and needs of the students as to fulfill the objectives of the course. One opening move that works well in classes composed predominantly of non-Indians is to begin with a written survey designed to discover students' knowledge, preconceptions, and expectations of Indians and their literature. In terms of actual instructional practice, one should approach with respect and humility anything touching on religion and ceremony, and the most honest thing teachers can do is to engage in a shared learning situation in which they make their own assumptions explicit and leave them open to revision. For similar reasons, wherever possible, one should not develop, teach, or evaluate such courses in isolation from an American Indian studies program and the local Indian community.

Texts

The problems involved in evaluating texts are manifold. Not all translations and transcriptions are equally valuable, their worth in many cases being limited by the purpose for which the material was collected, the linguistic competence of the translator/transcriber, the inhibitions in the transcription situation, and so on. Further, each time a story or song is printed and reprinted it becomes further removed from the performance context (Hymes, *In Vain*; Bevis, "American Indian Verse Translations"). Thoughtful discussion of translation can be found in Nida, *Toward a Science of Translation*. Texts can be located through Murdock's *Ethnographic Bibliography*, which is organized by region and tribe, and through the less extensive but generically organized bibliography by Haywood. Folkways and Canyon record companies offer recordings of Indian songs, but instructors must use them cautiously, because an understanding of the music is not easy to come by and its "foreignness" to many non-Indian students may be confusing. It is best to introduce the recordings with a competent discussion of the part music plays in cultural expression and the relationship of Indian songs to the oral tradition.

Genre

Generally speaking, folklorists (Thompson, *The Folktale*) have suffered from a perceived necessity to freeze oral performance into specific genres, when in fact so many of those characteristics that determine genre arise from the performance (Gossen, *Chamulas*; Ben-Amos, "Analytical Categories"; Frisbie, *Southwestern Indian Ritual Drama*). At the other extreme is the assumption that there are no formal characteristics, but simply thematic ones. Many American Indians, however, have evolved their own definitions, which, across the continent, show a high degree of consistency, if not uniformity. This is especially true of narrative genres, which are divided into four types based on a number of factors including the conditions under which they are told. Stories of the ancient time include:

1. creation, emergence, and migration stories.
2. stories of the Trickster, the war twins, and other early figures who transformed the world to its present order. These stories provide a natural context for ceremonial story and song.
3. stories of the remembered past include those that deal with persons and events within the lifetime of the teller.
4. general historical stories.

The events narrated in these stories constitute a good context for social and lyric song, and frequently such events are re-created in both narrative and song. These divisions and others like sacred-secular or formal genre distinctions make no pretense of re-creating reality; they are, after all, only ways of approaching a large and fluid body of material, and they are helpful primarily as a means, not as an end.

Intensiveness

The consensus of those who teach oral literature is that its radically different mode of creation and presentation demands an intensive study of fewer genres with more examples from a limited region. Nothing is accomplished by trying to illustrate all the genres from every culture area, let alone from every tribe, with a single example.

Continuity

The oral tradition is alive and well, moving and changing. This fact is central to an understanding of oral tradition. Even now, on porches, under trees, stories are being told, songs are being sung. Unlike literature from the Roman Empire, and despite the dust on almost equally ancient ethnological reports, the stories continue in time, passing from teller to teller. For this reason the instructor should emphasize some contemporary stories and songs. Instructors can use printed material (Theisz, *Buckskin Tokens*), but it is better to involve the class in storytelling with a member of the Indian community; the Evers videotapes can be valuable aids in this endeavor. The oral tradition has also developed a second kind of continuity, as many of its materials and processes have been adopted by Indian writers (Momaday, *Rainy Mountain*; Silko, *Ceremony*; Cook-Lynn, *Badger*; Vizenor, *Darkness*). Emphasizing the storytelling process illuminates these works created in the written rather than the oral tradition.

Conclusion

Understanding the American Indian oral tradition, as a discipline, demands special skills and scholarship. As a people's literature, it requires respect and cooperation, and as a living reality, care, that it may continue to grow. The courses offered here attempt to describe some approaches to oral literature while trying to adhere to these principles as far as possible within the pragmatic requirements of the academic situation. More than simply the result of curiosity, they represent the first tentative steps toward real understanding and shared learning. They spring from an experience of and deep belief in the vitality and vision of the oral tradition. As Leslie Silko writes in *Ceremony*:

> You don't have anything
> if you don't have the stories.

Course Design #1

An Introduction to American Indian Oral Traditions

Designed for juniors, seniors, and graduate students, this is a course in the forms, contexts, and creative processes of American Indian oral literatures. It is an intensive course, aimed at exploring in some depth selected genres from particular cultures, instead of extensively surveying all possible genres from every culture area. Assumptions include some familiarity, on the part of students, with Indian cultures, Indian history, and contemporary Indian literature, as well as a prior course that took a genre approach to European-American literature. The course has three emphases: the nature of the performance situation and the storytelling process, development of a sense of the continuity and vitality of the oral tradition, and an extensive study of selected genres. Each emphasis raises more specific problems such as the nature of translation and transcription, distinctive traditional and individual styles, and the use of oral materials and processes by American Indian authors working in the written mode.

Objectives

1. To introduce students to and develop their appreciation of and respect for the thematic and formal variety of American Indian oral traditions.
2. To develop in students an awareness and understanding of the viability of oral traditions.
3. To enable students to perceive the contextual, formal, and thematic relationships between oral and written Indian literatures.
4. To enable students to understand the oral "text" as only one dimension of a larger performance situation.
5. To provide students with the skills necessary to identify problems in and evaluate the adequacy of translations and transcriptions of American Indian oral literature.
6. To engage students in developing original, critical perspectives by means of which they can perceive those aesthetic and formal values in American Indian oral literature that distinguish it from both the written and the oral literatures of the European-American tradition.

Course Outline and Strategy

The course is divided into seven units, each of which emphasizes contextualization, creative process, form, and content.

Autobiography

Autobiographies can go a long way toward providing students with a sense of the wholeness of Indian experiences because they touch on almost every facet of life. They provide a good introduction to a course on oral literatures, especially if one uses an as-told-to autobiography that retains oral features. Sam Blowsnake's *Autobiography of a Winnebago Indian* retains much of the oral quality, and students can see how the teller relates his own drift away from tribal values, his dissolution, and his regeneration through the peyote religion, as an elaborate "story." Important questions arise in any such Indian autobiography. How does the narrator envision the "story"? Into what pattern(s) is it cast to integrate the personal experiences effectively? What judgments does the narrator make about the story? To what degree has the editor interfered with and altered the story?

The Nature of Oral Tradition

Introducing students to the literature in performance is best done by involving storytellers and singers from the Indian community. Then, one can reconstruct a situation in which several people, given only the barest plot outline of a story, are asked to tell the story imaginatively. One can discuss elements of performance as well as types of and reasons for variation. The class can examine a number of different texts of the same story (Reichard, "Literary Types"; Lowie, "Test Theme"; Demetracopolou, "Loon Woman"; Klievan, "Swan Maiden"; Thompson, "Star Husband"; see also the references and discussion of individual and traditional style in "Teaching American Indian Oral Literatures: Methodology and Description," above). One can also look at Indian adaptations of European stories and Bible stories, which often reveal the means by which Indian groups add new stories to their tribal literature (Thompson, *Tales*). Videotapes can also introduce students to elements of performance.

Origin Stories

Students can study in detail the two major types of origin stories, the Emergence (Wheeler-Voegelin and Moore, "The Emergence") and the Earth-Diver (Fenton, "This Island"). They can compare the text from *The Zunis* with the texts from Cushing's *Outline of Zuni Creation Myths,* Bunzel's *Zuni Origin Myths*, and Tedlock's *Finding the Center*. The four represent varying degrees of fidelity to performance: Cushing's is a paraphrased summary; Bunzel's a literal translation; *The Zunis* a free translation; and Tedlock's a close rendering of performance. Students can encounter the formal and stylistic features of the Emergence story, including the concept of physical, spiritual, and social evolution in a quest for integration. Discussion of the role of religion in Zuni life and the development of particularly meaningful clusters of symbols set the stage for a discussion of "Sayatasha's Night Chant," from Bunzel, in the ritual poetry unit. The class can use the adventures of the War Gods (*The Zunis*, pp. 150–60) to provide material for a discussion of the activities of the transformers who bring the chaotic world into order.

The Earth-Diver stories introduce students to formal and thematic elements; the Seneca version and the Maidu version, both in Thompson, provide starting points. A discussion might center on the vertical pattern in both

Earth-Diver and Emergence stories and on the means by which sacred power is brought into the world. One can also compare and contrast the activities of the Seneca Twins, Coyote and Earth-Initiate, and the Zuni War Gods and ask in what way origin stories generally establish the context for tribal identity. One might also discuss history as storytelling and storytelling as history (Eliade, *Quest*; Long, *Alpha*; White, *Metahistory*).

Trickster Stories

Radin's *The Trickster* illustrates well the necessity of reading whole cycles to appreciate the multidimensional character of the Trickster, who plays at least three roles: the aggressive Transformer (stories 48, 49), the amorous Transformer (stories 15–21, 38–39), and the classic Trickster (stories 12–14, 23–31, 32–33, 40–44). We may consider the Trickster, in the interplay of these roles, both a mirror and a mask of our humanity (Ricketts, "North American Indian Trickster"; Babcock-Abrahams, " 'A Tolerated Margin of Mess' "). Further, we can read the Hare cycle and compare it with the Twins' adventures from the previous unit. Radin's notes are necessary to understand the sociocultural context of the literature and to come to any true sense of theme. His discussion of types of tales, storytelling, and the difference in individual storytellers maintains the emphasis on the process of creating oral literature.

Comparative studies of single tales and whole cycles are suggested by Radin's outlines of other cycles (see also Boas and Tate, *Tsimshian Mythology*). These help to show how stories change (Toelken, " 'Pretty Language(s)' ").

Ritual Poetry

Since ritual poetry so clearly depends for its context on the creation stories, the instructor should select material from the same tribe or at least the same culture area as that from which he or she chose the origin stories used in class. More than any other genre ritual poetry requires a great deal of attention to context, since it usually appears on the printed page disassociated from the many ceremonial elements (setting, activities, medicines, prayers, songs, stories, etc.). For this reason it is better to settle on a single work and develop it in some detail than to try to cover too much. All published material lacks some important ceremonial elements, so there is little wonder that Indians sometimes claim that they are being misrepresented. Some works are better than others, however. The better works include Underhill, *Singing for Power*; Bahr, *Pima and Papago Ritual Oratory*; Mooney, *Ghost Dance Religion*; Kilpatrick and Kilpatrick, *Walk in Your Soul*; and Luckert, *Coyoteway*.

Because it is not possible within the scope of an introductory course to deal with entire ceremonials, the most reasonable strategy is to select a single piece that one can then place in context by referring extensively to the ceremonial of which it is a part and further by referring to patterns established in the creation story. A well-contextualized piece is the Zuni "Sayatasha's Night Chant" from the Shalako ceremonial (Wiget, "Sayatasha's Night Chant"). Bunzel supports the poem with informative and pointed introductory essays on Zuni ceremonialism, the Zuni kachinas, and the style and form of Zuni ritual poetry. She also reproduces a good translation of the Zuni origin story and provides other ritual poetry as well. Parsons' *Pueblo Indian Religion* can provide further support material.

With lengthier pieces like this one, a good strategy is to begin by providing some sense of the immediate purpose of the larger ceremony in which the piece occurs. It is helpful to establish for the student the concept of reintegration or reenactment by relating the ceremony to the origin story and to other religious stories; this enables the student to see the ceremony as ritual drama, another kind of storytelling. To this end it is useful to identify a number of ritual activities that are reflected in the chant and to discuss their function not only in the ceremony but in the chant as well. In this way, the class can have a glimpse of the performance, which includes actors, forces, activities, themes, different uses of language, and varying situations and conditions.

While "Sayatasha's Night Chant" is a considerably different type of ceremonial song than a Ghost Dance song or a medicine man or woman's curing song, it sets similar problems for a teacher, in the required emphasis on the nature and elements of the performance, the interplay of forces expressed through particular dramatic agents, and the need for larger contextualization, problems that one must face in any extensive and even partially just treatment of ceremonial literature. Consequently, this unit is likely to require more time than any other, no matter what piece the instructor selects.

Lyric and Social Song

All American Indian oral poetry is song. The words and music are distinct, but not separate, the voice being the primary musical instrument. Unlike ritual poetry, lyric poetry is free from the context of a communal religious drama, though it may have religious themes and connotations. Frequently brief and repeated for effect, its chief value is to articulate the singer's individual relationship to the world when the ordinary rhythms of spoken language fail.

Lyrics may be occasional—dance songs, death songs, lullabies, contest songs, and so on—or they may spring from a more general disposition. The principal difficulty with nonritual song lies in distinguishing between these two forms and the classes within them, a distinction that may not be possible. Some structural elements and stylistic devices such as the use of refrains and vocable syllables (Densmore, "The Use of Meaningless Syllables" and *Belief of the Indian*; Wiget, "Aztec Lyrics") are accessible in translation, and one may make analogies and craw comparisons with ideas suggested by Spinden's fine *Songs of the Tewa* and Walton and Waterman's "American Indian Poetry." Relating the poetic statement to the occasion that prompted it is a promising technique.

A substantial collection and one recommended for an intensive study is Lowenstein's *Eskimo Poems,* which includes not only a great deal of Eskimo poetry but also a judicious selection of material from Rasmussen's *Report of the Fifth Thule Expedition*, to provide a great deal of information on Eskimo culture and Eskimo concepts of poesis. Additional support material can be found in Roberts and Jenness' *Songs of the Copper Eskimo*, Carpenter's "Eskimo Poetry," and Collaer's *Music of the Americas*.

Continuity

In terms of both performance and theme, one can return to the communal dimension of storytelling from lyric song, drawing on the autobiography as the storytelling of history and on sacred stories and ritual poetry as the storytelling of the timeless and perpetual. All these dimensions—tradition and innovation, community and individual, history and myth, process and form—recur in the singing storytelling of the present moment. *The Zunis: Self-Portrayals* includes both oral historical (Secs. 2 and 3) and autobiographical material (Sec. 1, pp. 4, 5; Sec. 2, pp. 10, 14; Sec. 6, p. 42), all of which raises questions of pattern and point of view and of the ways in which contemporary storytellers are different from or similar to those of a century or more ago.

Once the sense of storytelling has been firmly reestablished, one can begin Leslie Silko's *Ceremony* and enter "a world made of stories, the long ago, time immemorial stories." Another work that is well suited is N. Scott Momaday's *The Way to Rainy Mountain. Ceremony* is not merely a novel about storytelling; it is one of the finest examples of storytelling, one in which the story's telling is in its truest sense its coming-to-be. Yet it is written. What restrictions does the written medium put on storytelling and what possibilities does it open up? How does Silko convince readers that they are *listening* to a story, not just reading one? How does she use materials from the Keresan and Navajo oral traditions and make them her own? How does she convince the reader that storytelling is alive and continuing? This kind of discussion, sparked by examples drawn from the entire course, can serve as a fine summary discussion, a fitting conclusion, and the grounds for further study.

Materials

The following works are suggested as core reading: Blowsnake, *Autobiography of a Winnebago Indian*; Lowenstein, *Eskimo Poems*; Radin, *The Trickster*; Silko, *Ceremony*; Zuni People, *The Zunis*; and any work mentioned under Ritual Poetry, such as Bunzel, "Sayatasha's Night Chant" (in *Zuni Origin Myths*). To supplement these pieces, instructors should place other materials on reserve in the library, especially Thompson's *Tales of the North American Indians*, Hymes's *In Vain I Tried to Tell You*, Jacobs' *The Content and Style of an Oral Literature*, Tedlock's *Finding the Center*, Kroeber's *Traditional Literatures of the American Indian*, and Swann's *Smoothing the Ground*.

Course Design #2

Lakota Oral Literature

Introduction

A course in the oral literature of any one people must focus on the way in which members of that community participate in the formation of their own literature. The course described here concentrates on Lakota oral literature, but the rationale for the course should have some validity for any intensive study of any tribal oral literature.

Since oral literature exists fully only as performance, a problem fundamental to curriculum design is that of how to help students respond to transcribed texts of oral genres with some understanding of how those texts come alive when performed in a community setting. Ideally a course in oral literature begins with the performance of an oral literary event that is an approximation of a true performance and that shows contemporary narrative forms.

In Lakota communities today, narratives about how people perceive the history of their own communities are perhaps the stories that most faithfully reflect the continuation of Lakota traditions and the shaping force that these traditions continue to have in the lives and art of Lakota people. Perhaps every Lakota community, urban and rural, has members who are known to have appropriated historical facts about the community and shaped these facts into an artistic form. Generally such people are willing to visit classes and give their versions of local history.

Once a group of students has shared a narrator's sense of the story of his or her own community, the students can begin to understand the imaginative and traditional stylistic features of the narrative used to introduce the course. To learn which stylistic features are significant, students must study the ways in which a narrator understands his or her own reason for sharing the narrative, understands the nature of the audience, and views the subject matter. These three dimensions of oral literature performance have affected different genres in different ways according to historical circumstances. A teacher can organize a course around the ways in which the Lakota people have used different genres in different periods of history to tell and to shape their own story. Diachronic study of oral literature is always difficult because one has to rely on the integrity of previous fieldwork. For students of Lakota literature, this difficulty is significantly reduced, because they can rely on the work of Ella Deloria. As a Sioux, she not only was a native speaker of the language but also spent years gathering material about Lakota language and literature. She collected materials that reflect the oral traditions of the early part of the twentieth century. Students can compare this material with current collections and can then see some significant reasons why oral literature continues to thrive in Lakota communities. They can examine each oral genre in an early twentieth-century context and in a contemporary one so that the older uses of narrative illuminate contemporary ones. This outline is organized according to historical period and genre so as to give a concise description of the meaning of each genre in a given historical period. The final section of the description for each genre abstracts some of the basic dynamics operating within the genre, providing an important part of the basis for continuity in oral narrative.

Methodology and Description

Winter Counts

Consisting of pictographs, the winter counts formed a system of chronology that named each year according to its outstanding occurrence. For the actual drawing of winter counts, well-qualified men were selected to narrate the events depicted. According to Oscar Howe's description of a process called "the painting of the truth" ("Theories and Beliefs," p. 69), the artist drew and painted according to aesthetic points, working from point to point toward completion of the painting. The winter counts often transmitted stories of events that the drawings recalled.

American Indians no longer use winter counts to establish chronology, but the stories that accompanied the old winter counts remain a part of oral tradition. Winter counts remain important in other ways, too. Some of the dynamics of winter-count formation live on and affect the telling of oral history in communities. Less than a century has passed since the Lakota determined and ordered time by using features of a group's experiences in a given environment to establish their chronology. Today Lakotas still feel that their experiences and local history must be the foundation for community order. Current efforts in communities to narrate local history nearly parallel the processes that surrounded winter-count formation. People of tribal repute continue to discuss events and collectively determine what will be preserved in oral tradition as community history.

The narrator of a winter count saw himself as one who by virtue of his leadership role had the right and obligation to help form the pattern of the people's continued recall of public events, saw his audience as members of the community whose very survival depended on the community's ordered continuity through time, and saw his subject as a "drawing of the truth" with the aesthetic points symbolizing the group's progress.

Personal-Experience Stories

Of all the modes of Lakota narrative, in the nineteenth and early twentieth centuries, the recounting of personal achievements was central in the daily life of the community. Individuals who narrated their deeds were signifying their earned personal prestige, which formed the invariable credentials for anyone performing a significant public action. The telling of personal-experience stories became part of both everyday and ritual activities.

In the contemporary period, community members are still expected to be able to narrate experiences that prove they are contributing community participants. Narratives about personal accomplishments must be seen as important art forms functioning in a community setting. Belief in the necessity for heroic action did not disappear with the coming of reservation life, though many opportunities for heroic action did. Today one can find stories about personal achievements in all aspects of life, and they can be analyzed as literature.

The performance conditions for personal-experience stories include the following aspects: the narrator sees himself or herself as proving that he or she possesses personal knowledge and the ability to achieve what the community requires; the narrator sees the audience as the motive for the action described (the members' continued well-being is the motive and reward for the action described); and the narrator sees the subject matter as an experience that has become part of the group's heritage.

Woyakapi (legend)

The *woyakapi* is a free-form narrative with endless possibilities for content and formal variation. Most available prereservation examples, however, show people's concern over telling stories that provide information about their environment, both physical and spiritual.

Because of the flexibility of the genre, generalizations about it are difficult, but, as in the past, contemporary subject matter includes stories about outstanding people in the community, about place names, about local beliefs that have been proven through experience (deer-woman stories, ghost stories, and so forth).

The performance conditions for *woyakapi* include the following aspects: the narrator sees himself or herself as someone conveying information about the meaning of a place or an encounter with someone or something; the narrator sees the audience as a group needing the information in order to live productively in a given environment; and the narrator sees the subject matter as an explanation of the meaning of a place or event.

Ohunkakan

Lakota *ohunkakan* are those narratives that have a definite plot and that are performed only on winter nights. The genre is subdivided, with the first subdivision corresponding closely to the general category of myth and the second to the general category of folktale. The first group consists of *ohunkakan* set in the remote past. These narratives dramatize the activities of beings very different from ourselves. The second group is set in a less remote past. The stories dramatize heroic deeds performed by people very much like ourselves.

The *ohunkakan* are formal aesthetic constructs whose thematic structures demonstrate the meanings of patterns of movement that characterize patterns of existence. For instance, Trickster tales (Iktomi tales) exemplify the results of action (movement) that established cultural order, while narratives about specific heroes (Blood Clot Boy, White-Plume Boy, Stone Boy) show patterns of action that established and maintained some dimension of cultural order. *Ohunkakan* plots can be compared intertribally to show specific tribal creative influences. Finally we must recognize the role of individual narrators in giving artistic complexity to tales. The *ohunkakan* encourage and require the most careful explication to reveal their multi-faceted life.

The narration of *ohunkakan* is decreasing in frequency because the stories no longer reflect contemporary life as directly as they once could. Nevertheless, a few narrators continue to tell and adapt *ohunkakan* to comment on modern community life.

For *ohunkakan*, the narrator sees himself or herself as someone transmitting a story that is part of the community's aesthetic heritage; the narrator sees the members of the audience as participants in the story's meaning; and the narrator sees the subject matter as belonging to a level of reality beyond everyday reality but as one that can comment on everyday reality.

Ceremonial and Ritual Literature

The transmission of ritual and ceremonial knowledge is, without doubt, central to the continuation of all facets of oral literature. Narratives about ceremonial events are certain to be included as personal experience stories and as other forms of narrative. Much ritual knowledge is inaccessible and perhaps ought not to be part of classroom analysis. Emphasis on the context of other forms of narrative should facilitate sensitive discussion of ceremonial and ritual material.

Materials

The manuscript materials gathered by Ella Deloria in the Franz Boas Collection of American Indian Linguistics, American Philosophical Society Library, Philadelphia, Pennsylvania, a collection including hundreds of pages of typescript with examples of and commentary on all genres of Lakota and Dakota oral literature, are essential background for a course in Lakota oral literature.

Useful published materials include Beckwith, "Mythology of the Oglala Dakota" (on Ben Kindle's winter count); Blish, *A Pictographic History of the Oglala Sioux*; Capps, *Seeing with a Native Eye*; Deloria, *Dakota Texts* (contains *ohunkakan* and *woyakapi* in both Lakota and Dakota, transliterated and translated with commentary on the meaning of specific semantic features of the text); Densmore, *Teton Sioux Music* (commentaries on performance conditions for music with valuable information about oral literature); Dorsey, *A Study of Siouan Cults* (background on Sioux iconography); *Ehanni Ohunkakan*; Finster, *The Hardin Winter Count*; Fire, *Lame Deer* (essential background information for understanding the dynamics of oral narrative performance); Howard, *Dakota Winter Counts as a Source of Plains History*; Howe, "Theories and Beliefs" (basic information on winter-count formation related to other aspects of Lakota aesthetics); Karol, *Red Horse Owner's Winter Count*; Mallery, *Picture-Writing of the American Indians*; and Walker, *The Sun Dance and Other Ceremonies*, *Lakota Belief and Ritual*, and *Lakota Myth*.

Course Design #3

Creation and Trickster Narratives

Designed for juniors, seniors, and graduate students with a minimum of three previous courses in American Indian studies or literature, this is a study of the distinct characteristics of American Indian oral literature through intensive analysis of selected genres and relevant literary criticism

Objectives

1. To develop an appreciation of and respect for the variety of themes and genres in American Indian oral literatures.
2. To develop an appreciation and understanding of the literatures' continuity and vitality.
3. To understand the structure of the story, the narrator's performance of the story, its reception by the audience, and the other elements necessary to understand the total context of the story.

Course Outline

This course uses various approaches to illuminate the world views of various cultures through the oral narratives produced by those cultures.

Because students may not clearly understand terms like "world view" and "myth," the course begins with definitions of these terms. The following readings present discussions of these terms from the Indian and non-Indian perspectives as well as from different critical approaches: Two non-Indian points of view are helpful: the comparative, as found in Eliade's "Sacred Time and Myths" (Ch. 2 of *The Sacred and the Profane*), and the classical, as found in Otto's "Myth and Culture" (Ch. 1 of *Dionysus*). The latter work, however, is more suited for teacher preparation than for use in the classroom. Indian perspectives on the terms can be found in Melville Jacobs' "World View" (Ch. 14 of *The Content and Style of an Oral Literature*) and in N. Scott Momaday (Kiowa), "An American Land Ethic."

After discussing the meaning of terms, the class might analyze a particular world view as expressed in a selected text, such as Genesis 1–11 (see also Leach, "Genesis as Myth").

A discussion of the general characteristics of oral narratives may be based on Kroeber's "An Introduction to the Art of Traditional American Indian Narration" (in Kroeber, *Traditional Literatures of the American Indian*, pp. 1–24). For purposes of discussion, we can divide American Indian oral narratives into two major types: sacred and secular. Others describe the same categories as supernatural and natural, true and imaginary, myth and tale. Whatever terms he or she uses, the instructor should realize that a single oral narrative may contain elements of more than one major type, that individual tribes may use more than two divisions of narratives, and that similar narratives may be categorized as different types by different tribes. The instructor should also be sensitive to the effect that the terminology may have on individual students, Indian and non-Indian. Background reading is provided by Eliade, "Structure of Myth" (Ch. 1 of *Myth and Reality*).

The discussion of the general characteristics of oral narratives and of the distinction between sacred and secular narratives may be followed by an analysis of the various elements that form the context of sacred narratives:

1. Culture of the tribe: world view, sense of place, kinship and social systems, patterns peculiar to specific narrative forms, conditions under which the story is told, and so forth.
2. Characteristics of the storyteller: his or her individual manner of structuring the story and the inclusion of himself or herself as a character in the story.
3. Performance: variations in voice and manner of the performer, impact of the collector, and so forth.
4. Audience response: structural elements in the narrative or techniques of the storyteller designed to elicit audience participation in the oral performance.
5. Language and translation: availability of a reliable oral or written text and of translations that accurately capture the particular style of the storyteller and the content of the story.

Critical readings useful for analyzing these elements include Hymes, "Discovering Oral Performance and Measured Verse"; Tedlock, "On the Translation of Style," "Pueblo Literature," and "Toward an Oral Poetics"; and Toelken and Scott (Navajo), "Poetic Retranslation and the 'Pretty Languages' of Yellowman."

The discussion of the sacred creation stories will focus on two recurrent motifs, Earth-Diver and Emergence. Background reading on the structure of the Earth-Diver story may be found in Reichard, "Literary Types and Dissemination of Myths." Texts include the following: Iroquois: "The Council Tree" and "Hah-nu-nah, the Turtle" (in *Portable North American Indian Reader*, ed. Turner, pp. 36–37); these stories combine Earth-Diver and "Fortune Fall." Cherokee: "How the World Was Made" (in *Portable North American Indian Reader*, pp. 86–88). Menominee: Skinner and Satterlee (Menominee), *Folklore of the Menomini Indians*. Ojibwe: Johnston (Ojibwe), "The Vision of Kitchi Manitou" (in *Ojibwa Heritage*, pp. 11–17). Useful critical articles are Count, "The Earth Diver and the Rival Twins"; Dundes, "Earth Diver"; and Köngäs, "The Earth Diver."

An introduction to the structure of the Emergence story can be found in Rooth, "The Creation Myths of the North American Indians." Texts include: Navajo: Matthews, *Navaho Legends*, or O'Brien and Tlo'tsi hee (Navajo), "The Creation or Age of Beginning" (in *Portable North American Indian Reader*, pp. 175–90). Supplementary Navajo texts can be found in Reichard, *Navaho Religions*; and Yazzie (Navajo), ed., *Navajo History*. Hopi:

Nequatewa (Hopi), *Truth of a Hopi*, pp. 1–10. Zuni: Tedlock, ed., *Finding the Center*, supplemented by Benedict, *Zuni Mythology*.

Often part of creation stories, the Trickster-Transformer stories are widespread among American Indian tribes, in both oral and written literatures. Trickster stories were also prevalent among the ancient Greeks, Asians, Semites, and Africans. Radin's *The Trickster* contains a full cycle of Winnebago Trickster-Transformer stories, variant versions from other tribes, Radin's analysis of the nature and meaning of the cycle, and commentary by other critics. A discussion of the characteristics of the Trickster-Transformer figure can focus on three types: (1) Heroic Transformer: frequently portrayed as a monster-slayer, aggressive hero, or creator of order, who achieves power through action. (2) Cunning Transformer: frequently portrayed as a figure (human or animal) who tries to gain power by outwitting his opponents in gambling or games or through marriage or sexual encounters. The figure often changes form to take on another identity or sex or to become an animal or an inanimate object. (3) Overreacher: usually portrayed as a figure who attempts more than he can achieve and therefore suffers humiliation or injury. Background reading may be found in Babcock-Abrahams, "'A Tolerated Margin of Mess'"; Boas, Introduction to Teit, *Traditions of the Thompson River Indians*; Brinton, *American Hero-Myths*; Kroeber, "Deconstructionist Criticism and American Indian Literature"; Ricketts, "The North American Indian Trickster"; and Toelken, "The 'Pretty Language(s)' of Yellowman." Discussion of the context of Trickster-Transformer stories should follow the outline of the various elements that form the context of sacred narratives given above.

The cycle of Trickster-Transformer stories given by Radin may be compared with other traditional cycles and stories. Instructors may wish to limit the comparison to stories from tribes from the region in which the course is taught: (1) Winnebago. "Winnebago Hare Cycle" (Radin). (2) Algonkin (Woodland and Prairie tribes located near the Wisconsin Winnebago). Fox: Jones (Fox), *Fox Texts*. Menominee: Skinner and Satterlee (Menominee), *Folklore of the Menomini Indians*. Ojibwe: Jones (Fox), *Ojibway Texts*. (3) Plains. Assiniboine: Assiniboine cycle (Radin). Blackfeet: Grinnell, "Old Man Stories" (in *Blackfoot Lodge Tales*), or Wissler and Duvall (Blackfeet), *Mythology of the Blackfoot Indians*. Sioux: E. Deloria (Sioux), *Dakota Texts*. (4) Southwest: Coyote stories. Apache: Goddard, *White Mountain Apache Texts*; or "Ba-Ts-Oosee: An Apache Trickster Cycle," narrated by Rudolph Kane (Apache), in Evers, *Words and Place: Native Literature from the American Southwest*. Keres: Boas, *Keresan Texts*. Zuni: "Coyote and Junko" (in Tedlock, *Finding the Center*, pp. 76–83). (5) Northwest Coast: Raven and Coyote stories. Oregon: Ramsey, *Coyote Was Going There* (includes Coyote tales from several tribes). Clackamas: Jacobs, *The Content and Style of an Oral Literature*. Tsimshian: Boas and Tate, *Tsimshian Mythology*.

The course can conclude with a comparison with contemporary adaptations. Performance in story, poem, and song can be seen in the videotape of Rudolph Kane cited above. Theisz, *Buckskin Tokens,* is a collection of Sioux tales retold by tribal members. Written materials include: Ojibwe: Johnston (Ojibwe), *Ojibwa Heritage,* or Vizenor, *Anishinabe Adisokan* (versions of traditional stories originally published in an Ojibwe newspaper at the turn of the century). Cree: Norman, *The Wishing Bone Cycle.* From the Southwest, both fiction and poetry are available: Silko (Laguna), *Ceremony* (a novel that utilizes creation and Trickster stories), "Coyote Holds a Full Hand" and "Toe'osh, a Laguna Coyote Story" (poem in *Storyteller*); S. Ortiz (Acoma), *Going for the Rain* (a collection of poems incorporating creation, emergence, and migration stories as well as some coyote stories), or "The Creation According to Coyote" (in Niatum, *Carriers of the Dream Wheel,* p. 144).

Personal Narrative, Autobiography, and Intermediate Literature

American Indian Autobiography

Kathleen Mullen Sands

The only American Indian most of us know at all is the public Indian: the political militant of newscasts, the warrior chief of Hollywood films, the subject of the case study or documentary, the orator and treaty maker of history texts, the creator of pottery displayed in museums. The image is slightly exotic, sometimes fearsome, and highly fragmentary. Our comprehension of Indians, despite the quantity of information available, remains superficial, because our image is a composite of diverse and sometimes contradictory traits and stereotypes, selected from various cultures and isolated from the traditions, values, and life of those cultures. Such an image can be neither harmonious nor complete, for it is anonymous.

Until we know Indians individually and intimately, they will remain merely another ethnic type—interesting, mysterious, romantic, but unknowable except as distant figures. Few channels lead beyond the stereotype, but some do exist. Personal contact, of course, is most effective, but even for those who have no such opportunity, the world of the individual Indian is not wholly closed. Fiction offers a means of knowing individual American Indians intimately, but because most literature by American Indians is relatively recent, the amount available is limited. Biography, while it offers many useful insights into Indian life, is not a true Indian genre, since most works about Indians are written by white authors. Autobiography, however, offers us an insightful, complete, and varied means of entrance into the private and public worlds of the American Indian, partly because hundreds of such works exist, but primarily because this literary form possesses intimacy and depth.

A growing interest in native cultures has resulted in increasing recognition of Indian literature as a valid element in the American tradition of letters. As Mary Austin points out in her essay in the *Cambridge History of American Literature,* aboriginal literature can no longer be considered "the product of an alien and conquered people," but must be recognized as "the inevitable outgrowth of the American environment." Unfortunately but understandably, American Indian autobiography has received little attention. In the mainstream of American literature, autobiography is at best considered a minor genre. American Indian poetry and fiction, because they are most easily associated with the greater body of American literature, have received considerable attention in recent years, while oral narratives and written autobiographies by American Indians have received almost no consideration, in part because they are sometimes difficult to find and in large measure because critics have directed little effort toward analysis of extant works.

The predominant mode of American Indian literature, though, is oral narrative, and autobiography makes up a significant portion of the body of told literature that has been preserved. The personal narrative has been collected since the colonization of Indian lands, first by military expeditions, missionaries, and historians and later, more widely and intensively, by anthropologists. The methods of collection and preservation have progressed significantly in the last three hundred years, particularly in the last century, but the essential form of the Indian autobiography has endured. It is still oral—recorded, introduced, edited, and interpreted by whites who seek to preserve and disseminate the works spoken in isolated communities, stories that are in danger of being lost to the future because they are always just one generation from extinction. Even those few autobiographies that have been written down by their subjects rather than narrated orally are heavily influenced by the whites who recorded and edited them.

The intimacy of the recorder-narrator relationship that is essential to the Indian autobiography is unusual. When this relationship is effective, the recorded narrative offers a penetrating insight into the private world of the subject, an insight that the technological expertise of documentaries, newscasts, films, and historical scholarship cannot match. By its very nature, autobiography is a personal genre that examines in depth the motives, actions, attitudes, and qualities of an individual within the network of family and tribe, while media and textbook examinations of American Indian life are limited primarily to the public Indian. Nowhere else is such direct and intense contact possible as in the works that issue from recorded autobiography.

The narrator-editor relationship has been the basis of collecting, preserving, and publishing American Indian personal narratives from the beginning. Disadvantages in the collaboration between Indian and white are perhaps most evident in eighteenth- and nineteenth-century autobiographies, but they cannot be overlooked even in contemporary works, because of their comprehensive influence on the narration of the life story. Unfortunately, many earlier collected narratives are badly marred by the bias of the collectors or by their lack of information about tribal cultures. Many early collectors were missionaries who purposely collected life stories from Christian Indians who fit the missionaries' notions of a "good" Indian because they had given up many tribal traditions in favor of white practices. Other narratives, clearly warped by the collectors' obvious romantic stereotyping, depict Indians as "noble savages." Even early anthropologists, influenced by social Darwinism, published such works. Still other stories, collected by deterministic historians, military men, or antiquarians attracted to and interested in Indian life, suffer from a lack of understanding of Indian ways or a misguided notion that they were preserving portraits of what they assumed were vanishing Americans. These works, though interesting as examples of early personal narratives, are often questionable as authentic native autobiographies because of faulty or misguided collection and editorial practices, sentiment, or blatant lack of professionalism. The later autobiographies—collected in large measure by well-trained anthropologists, folklorists, historians, and writers—are more credible, although the problematical nature of the partnership between the recorder/editor and the narrator endures.

This relationship is crucial to the validity and quality of autobiography. In almost all Indian autobiographies, the recorder/editor is the generating force who solicits the story and acts as a catalyst for the work. While this person is obviously not the subject of the work, the power he or she exerts over the presentation of the personal narrative may be and often is comprehensive. The narrator supplies the content of the autobiography, but the recorder/editor often interprets and almost always structures and edits the text. This collaboration of the narrator and recorder/editor is perhaps the most distinctive characteristic of the American Indian autobiography, but it is not the only one. Of great importance in understanding the uniqueness of this genre is the recognition of Indian autobiography as both personal and cultural narrative. That is not to say that the autobiography is simply a personalization of cultural history or ethnography. The form is literary, not anthropological, but inherent in the telling of the life story are cultural, historical, and ethnographic data, aspects of the genre that have often relegated texts to the anthropology section of archives, libraries, and bookstores rather than to literary collections. The American Indian autobiography centers on personal experience, but the subject, no matter how dominant within the culture, is a participant in his or her own family history and in the events of the tribe. Isolation of the subject from the history, traditions, and practices of the tribal culture is not only impossible but also highly undesirable. It is equally undesirable to look at such works as cultural essays and merely to extrapolate pertinent information and ignore the highly personal content and perspective and the unique mode of each narrator. That mode of narration accounts for the other distinguishing characteristic of this genre. Often the life story is told in the native language and later translated into English, and, while this can be and sometimes is a problem, it is often a clear asset in that it creates a distinctive literary style. Even when the narrator delivers the story in English, the reverence for the sacredness of the word, which marks all American Indian literature, is evident, often along with distinctive patterns of language that contribute to the persona of the subject because they establish a recognizably Indian voice in the work. The intent of the narrator determines a final characteristic of the genre. Almost universally, the subject of an American Indian autobiography tells a story, not for his or her own people, but for the world at large—that is, in practical terms, for the white audience who will read the narrative. All characteristics that aid in defining American Indian autobiography, of course, ultimately lead back to the unique form of the genre, which depends on the relationship between the narrator and recorder/editor. We must, then, approach this area of the genre first if we are to formulate critical methodology for use in analyzing and teaching American Indian autobiography.

Several degrees of intensity are possible in the recorder/editor's relationship with the narrator, and the reader can usually determine them by carefully examining introductions to autobiographies, looking not only for the information presented by the editor but also for the tone of the introduction. The most reliable recorder/editors can be counted on to give extensive information about the methodology and criteria for the work, detailing the circumstances leading to the production of the work, describing the editorial process fully, and establishing the purpose of the publication. Under the best circumstances, the recorder/editor is objective and detached, careful to let the narrator create the life story and structure it according to his or her own sense of time and emphasis.

More intrusive recorder/editors need to, or perhaps feel they have a right to, mold the work, leading the narrator during the telling and reorganizing the material later. Others see themselves as collaborators, equal partners with the narrator in the telling and presentation of the autobiography, the usual rationale being that the two have become trusted friends. Whatever the relationship, the introduction will reveal it, either through information provided by the editor or by the absence of such material. Hence, in evaluating a given autobiography, close attention to the tone and content of the introductory material is crucial, with certain kinds of information of particular importance. The reader may ask questions to elicit this information. The intent of the narrator and editor is of prime importance to the reader's comprehension of the work. Does the narrator wish to preserve a portion of a vanishing way of life? Does the narrative emphasize prereservation times, thus implying that either editor or narrator values modern times less or even repudiates them? Is this a study of personality or culture change from ancient to contemporary times? Such questions will reveal the intent of both narrator and editor or any disparity in intentions. Equally important for full understanding of the autobiography is information about the cultural era and the geographic area from which the work springs as it relates to the author's purpose. Is the work a nostalgic memoir of things past, perhaps even a statement of cultural despair? Does it center on spiritual values or secular life, or does it combine the two? What tribe and landscape does it focus on and what are the effects on the subject's life and narrative? Also basic to evaluating the work is some indication of the status of the subject in his or her culture. Is the narrator a famous man—a spiritual leader, warrior, civil leader, artist? Or is he an ordinary man, representative of his culture? Is the subject a woman? Is she extraordinary in some way or representative? Finally, the reader should pose some questions about the original narrative and the subsequent structuring. Is the text a translation from a native language or a transcription of English narration? Either may be laboriously careful, very loose, or somewhere between the two. Is the ordering of the material associative, chronological, or thematic? Does it focus on pivotal events or on problems?[1] All these questions, of course, presume that the role of the recorder/editor is inherently critical in nature, and they attempt to determine just how judicious and delicate the judgment and editorial practice of the recorder/editor are in relation to the narrator's story.

That is not, however, to say that the narrator's story need be wholly untouched. The narrator may find some editorial intrusion desirable in overcoming obstacles that might otherwise inhibit the telling of the life story: language inadequacy, avoidance of self-aggrandizement or claim to too much authority, reluctance to expose sacred information, a tendency toward excessive repetition, difficulty in remembering and ordering events, or the simple failure to recognize the value to others of his or her life experiences and narrative skills. The recorder/editor who is sensitive to the responsibility in undertaking such a task does, in fact, greatly facilitate the process of narration and certainly the production of a publishable text. The editor's principal duty is to establish an accurate text and to preserve the integrity of the narrative within the bounds of publication requirements. This requires not only a thorough knowledge of the narrator's culture but also a sensitivity to Indian perceptions of language, landscape, time, reality, and the nature of the cosmos. There are further indicators to the reliability of the narrator in several areas. Does the text retain the subject's view of the universe, or does it denigrate that view? Is there a sense of unity between the subject's life and culture, or does the disunity reflect a disintegrating world? Is there consistency in the narrator's tone, persona, language usage, sentence structure? Does the narrative retain certain characteristically Indian literary devices such as repetition? Is an extensive editorial apparatus necessary to help the reader make sense of the narrative? Does the editor interrupt the text or in other ways shift the focus away from the subject? The sensitive editor will avoid violating the integrity of the subject's autobiography, aware that the personal narrative is an act of creative imagination with an aesthetic quality deserving respect and preservation in as pure a form as possible.

Even good autobiographies—well narrated, carefully recorded, and responsibly edited—will probably not meet the criteria implied in the above questions. Autobiography is a very human form of literature and must be approached humanely by scholars, teachers, and critics. Perfection is desirable in any genre, but it is not often achieved. Still, one may find a work valuable and valid despite its flaws—and even sometimes because of them—as long as one recognizes the flaws and evaluates them judiciously in terms of the overall worth of the work.

The autobiography, while seeming to be wholly factual and straightforward, is an imaginative work of literature, thus posing a second area for critical examination. It is easy to accept autobiography as simply personal history, a rather detached and objective memoir of previous experience, but that is vastly to underrate the creative process at work in the telling of a life story. In fact, according to Roy Pascal, autobiography "imposes a pattern on life, constructs out of it a coherent story." The narrative is not a haphazard compilation of facts and events, because consciously or unconsciously it "establishes certain stages in an individual life, makes links between them, and defines, implicitly or explicitly a certain consistency of relationship between the self and outside world." This coherence assumes a narrative stance on the part of the teller, who narrates from the "standpoint of the moment at which he reviews his life, and interprets his life." It is the present that allows the narrator to "see his life as something of a unity," something that has an inherent order he or she recognizes and conveys or something on which he or she imposes order and meaning. The process of autobiography "means, therefore, discrimination and selection of facts, distribution of emphasis, choice of expression." This process, of course, depends heavily on memory, which interrelates the narrator and the events, leading to "facts in the making" as the story is told; this is a decidedly creative process, "not just reconstruction of the past, but interpretation." The narrative contains an element of developing self-knowledge; not everything is understood from the onset. Thus, it reveals a wholeness of personal identity that goes far beyond the public significance of the teller. Granted, it is a story of life in the world, but the events are symbolic and provide a way of knowing life through imagination. The symbols are not imagined, as in fiction, but are chosen and arranged. Autobiography is, in fact, "a judgment on the past within the framework of the present," dependent on and inextricably linked to language and the act of remembering that generates the work.[2] Moreover, the process takes place in the context of all experience previous to and following each reconstructed event. It is a creation of the imagination, not a fiction, but factual experience molded by time, intention, emotion, and ability to recall detail and nuance. These qualities of the personal narrative are not set out to question the reliability of the narrator—that is the job of the recorder/editor—but to point out the creative quality of the work and facilitate competent critical attention to the work as literature rather than as sociological case history. It is these qualities that make American Indian autobiographies fascinating literary texts to which we may apply narrative and stylistic analysis in much the same manner as we do to other genres of American Indian literature.

The emphasis given in this essay to American Indian autobiography as an intensely personal form of literature should not, however, mislead the reader into assuming that the reliance on and re-creation from memory signifies that the autobiography is a confessional form. Drawn from memory, inevitably it is to some degree emotionally charged, since the process of recall imposes response to event, but unlike European and mainstream American autobiography, both grounded in the Romantic tradition, it does not focus on every nerve tingle, nor does it analyze every quiver of the psyche. It tends to be retrospective rather than introspective; thus, the narrative may seem understated to the reader unaccustomed to the emotional reserve of Indian people. There is little self-indulgence on the part of Indian narrators; events occur and the subjects articulate them in words conservative in emotional connotation. They are likely to describe even moments of crisis without much intensity of language, or to imply the emotional pitch, or to state it metaphorically rather than directly. Such understatement is not an indication of repression or absence of emotion, but often it is evidence that the narrator simply takes the emotion for granted, that he or she sees the events as speaking for themselves dramatically and emotionally. A narrator may sum up a feeling "in such colorless phrases as 'I liked it,' 'I did not like it.' For one not deeply immersed in the culture, the real significance escapes."[3] Where articulation of feelings does enter the work, it may well be that the recorder/editor has asked for amplification of the narrator's feelings, and the response is often vivid and metaphorical as in "Fear went through me like a snake."[4] The Indian autobiography tends to look outward toward the world rather than inward to the person telling the story, and this focus has an effect beyond understated expression of feeling that may be equally puzzling to non-Indian readers—the apparent lack of motivation in the characters in the narrative.

In the narratives, the emphasis is on the event, and the interrelationship of events is sometimes only implied, primarily because the tribal consciousness of the narrators and their comprehensive understanding of their own cultural traditions and values makes expression of the rationale for specific actions unnecessary. Again, in the best examples of the genre, the motivation is discernible, perhaps because of the narrators' consciousness of their nontribal audience or because the recorder/editor has solicited amplification. In some cases, the motivational information is added to the narrative in the editorial process, as in *The Autobiography of a Winnebago Indian*, where Paul Radin has supplied a thorough footnote apparatus for describing tribal customs and the reasons for the narrator's seemingly puzzling actions. Integrating such crucial information into the text of the narrative is, however, preferable since it supplies a continuity and depth to the portrait of the subject.

Like all other types of literature, American Indian autobiographies vary in aesthetic value. Those with the least literary value tend toward case history, sometimes because they are brief and lacking in detailed event and sometimes because the narrative technique of the teller is flat and unimaginative. Or the relationship between the narrator and the recorder/editor may be unsatisfactory. The works are useful because of the data they contain, but the treatment is neither full nor rich enough to support extended critical analysis. Most, however, are respectable literary works that will support analysis of both style and content, and some, like *Black Elks Speaks* and *Papago Woman*, are extraordinarily fine, revealing the sensitive responses of their narrators to their culture and experiences, creating a living reality of individual and tribal life in a form that is unified and innovative and a style that is rich in metaphorical language, often lyrical, and sometimes poetic.[5] Becoming familiar with the genre of American Indian autobiography is a demanding task, since the canon is extensive, but the process is generally pleasurable and immeasurably informative. Most teachers and scholars in the field of American Indian literature can simplify the job somewhat by focusing on works that relate to a particular course emphasis, since there are many different reasons for including autobiography in American Indian literature courses and many possibilities for using these works.

Perhaps the most persuasive reason for including autobiographies in American Indian literature courses is that these oral narratives demonstrate, as no other native genre can, the transition from traditional oral literature to contemporary written literature. The autobiographies are oral in inception and frequently include traditional myths, tales, and songs, thus drawing forward into a contemporary mode of written literature elements of the oral tradition. This incorporation of traditional tribal literature and, often, of description of ceremonial and ritual events richly enhances the literary quality of the narrative and provides a context for the literature so that it may be viewed within the cultural matrix where it is performed, thus providing a life-connected view of traditional forms. Autobiography affords a continuity between the old ways and the new, not as an artificially infused bridging of forms, but as an integral part of the genre itself. Like traditional stories and contemporary fiction, it is a genre shaped by narrative event and focused on characterization and the relationship of protagonist to the community and the land. These qualities of autobiography make it a particularly good genre to include in an introductory course on American Indian literature, not only to offer students a sampling of a major genre but to lend unity and continuity to the course as well.

The inclusion of Indian autobiography, of course, is also appropriate in courses focusing wholly on the oral tradition, since, like almost all oral literature taught in the classroom, Indian autobiography has been transcribed into print. It might be related to oratory, another form usually connected with the impact of the white world on Indian culture.

There are as well a number of possibilities for developing courses focused exclusively on American Indian autobiography. A chronologically designed course might present a survey of works, beginning with early texts and progressing to recent life stories, or it might focus on texts depicting prereservation narratives in contrast to reservation and contemporary autobiographies. Regional focus on woodlands, plains, or southwestern narratives is another possible method for course development, as is tribal focus. For courses centered on the various genres from one tribe, Winnebago, Hopi, Sioux, Papago-Pima, Apache, and some other tribes have sufficient numbers of autobiographies in print to make them a substantial portion of a course. An especially rich area of autobiography is that of American Indian women's narratives, since there are many life stories to choose from in creating such a course, and these authentic portraits are particularly valuable in correcting erroneous notions about the inferiority of women in Indian societies in the past and today. Another approach might be a thematical course; correcting stereotypes might be a good place to start, since autobiography by its variety of subjects and experiences negates the possibility of simplistic categorizing. A course on the sense of place in Indian literature could be significantly enhanced by the personal narration of subjects' relationships to particular landscapes, a distinct characteristic of most autobiographies. Equally valuable might be a course centered on analysis of sacred and secular elements in autobiography and the interrelation between the two, or perhaps a course could be developed to analyze the individual in relation to the community.

For interdisciplinary programs, autobiographies might be included in courses in American Indian history, cultural history of specific regions or tribes, women's studies programs, oral history courses, and other courses related to ethnic or American studies programs.

Scholars, teachers, students, and critics of American Indian literature should not overlook American Indian autobiography. It offers many generally neglected insights into both life and literature. Its complexity and problematical nature are not unique to autobiography. Techniques and methodologies for evaluating these autobiographies can be applied to all oral literature, and the demands of judging these works inevitably sensitize the reader to contemporary written Indian literature as well, while at the same time providing a context and a sense of continuity in the total volume of American Indian literature. The autobiography's appeal is enduring because the work is personal, detailed, and intense, and these narratives open a way into the private world of American Indian men and women, which might otherwise be quite inaccessible.

Notes

1   I am indebted to R. D. Theisz for his analysis of American Indian autobiography introductions included in a paper he read at a seminar Teaching Modern American Indian Literature during the Modern Language Association meeting in New York City in December 1979. Theisz calls the genre "bio-autobiography" and categorizes degrees of narrator–recorder/editor relationships in his text.

2   Pascal, *Design and Truth in Autobiography*, pp. 9, 10, 19.

3   Chona, *Autobiography*, p. 33.

4   Chona, p. 33. See Smith, "American Indian Autobiographies," for discussion of nine autobiographies.

5   See Smith, "American Indian Autobiographies," for discussion of nine autobiographies.

A Selected Listing of American Indian Autobiographies

Anauta (Eskimo). *Land of Good Shadows.*

Apes, William (Pequot). *A Son of the Forest.*

Bennett, Kay (Navajo). *Kaibah.*

Black Elk (Sioux). *Black Elk Speaks.*

Black Hawk (Sioux). *Black Hawk.*

Blowsnake, Sam (Winnebago). *The Autobiography of a Winnebago.*

Campbell, Maria (Métis). *Halfbreed.*

Chona, Maria (Papago). *The Autobiography of a Papago Woman.*

Copway, George (Ojibwe). *The Life, History, and Travels of Kah-ge-ga-gah-bowh (George Copway).*

Crying Wind (Kickapoo). *Crying Wind.*

Cuero, Delfina (Dieguero). *The Autobiography of Delfina Cuero.*

Cuffe, Paul (Pequot). *Narrative of the Life and Adventures of Paul Cuffe.*

Eastman, Charles Alexander (Sioux). *From the Deep Woods to Civilization.*

———. *Indian Boyhood.*

Fire, John [Lame Deer] (Sioux). *Lame Deer, Seeker of Visions.*

Forbes, Jack D., ed. *Nevada Indians Speak.*

Geronimo (Apache). *Geronimo.*

Griffis, Joseph K. [Chief Tahan] (Osage). *Tahan.*

Hopkins, Sarah Winnemuca (Paiute). *Life among the Piutes.*

Hungry Wolf, Beverly (Blackfeet). *Ways of My Grandmothers.*

Johnson, Broderick H., ed. *Stories of Traditional Navajo Life and Culture by Twenty-Two Navajo Men and Women.*

Left Handed (Navajo). *Left Handed, Son of Old Man Hat.*

Long, James Larpenteur [First Boy] (Assiniboine). *The Assiniboines.*

Lowry, Annie (Paiute). *Karnee.*

Mathews, John Joseph (Osage). *Wah'Kon-Tah.*

Michelson, Truman. *The Autobiography of a Fox Indian Woman.*

———. "Narrative of an Arapaho Woman."

———. "Narrative of a Southern Cheyenne Woman."

Mitchell, Emerson Blackhorse (Navajo). *Miracle Hill.*

Moises, Rosalio (Yaqui). *The Tall Candle.*

Momaday, N. Scott (Kiowa). *The Names.*

Mountain Wolf Woman (Winnebago). *Mountain Wolf Woman, Sister of Crashing Thunder.*

Nowell, Charles James (Kwakiutl). *Smoke from Their Fires.*

Nuñez, Bonita [Wa Wa Calachaw] (Luiseno). *Spirit Woman.*

Old Mexican (Navajo). *Old Mexican.*

Plenty Coups (Crow). *Plenty Coups.*

Pretty-Shield (Crow). *Pretty-Shield, Medicine Woman of the Crows.*

Qoyawayma, Polingaysi [Elizabeth O. White] (Hopi). *No Turning Back.*

Sanapia (Comanche). *Sanapia, Comanche Medicine Woman.*

Savala, Refugio (Yaqui). *The Autobiography of a Yaqui Poet.*

Sekaquaptewa, Helen (Hopi). *Me and Mine.*

Shaw, Anna Moore (Pima). *A Pima Past.*

Standing Bear, Luther (Sioux). *My Indian Boyhood.*

Stands in Timber, John (Cheyenne). *Cheyenne Memories.*

Steward, Julian H. "Two Paiute Autobiographies."

Stewart, Irene (Navajo). *A Voice in Her Tribe.*

Talayesva, Don C. (Hopi). *Sun Chief.*

Two Leggings (Crow). *Two Leggings.*

Waheenee [Buffalo Bird Woman] (Hidatsa). *An Indian Girl's Story.*

Webb, George E. (Pima). *A Pima Remembers.*

White, Leslie A. "An Autobiography of an Acoma Indian."

Whitewolf, Jim (Kiowa-Apache). *Jim Whitewolf.*

Whitman, William. "Xube, a Ponca Autobiography."

Winnie, Lucille [Jerry; Sah-gan-de-oh] (Seneca-Cayuga). *Sah-gan-de-oh, the Chief's Daughter.*

Yava, Albert (Tewa-Hopi). *Big Falling Snow.*

Young, Lucy (Wailaki). "Out of the Past: A True Indian Story."

Zuni People. *The Zunis: Self-Portrayals.*

Intermediate Forms between Oral and Written Literature

Elaine Jahner

In literature, any literature, we find the vigor and sheer excitement that is the fallout from someone's vision—a cluttered vision, perhaps, or a partial one, but a vision nevertheless, an explosion into human consciousness that alters the tedium of day-to-day existence. And the very concept of literature requires, of course, that the volatile stuff of visions find some proper and enduring linguistic form. What is proper and how the form endures through time, though, admit of immense variety of interpretation with the most fundamental distinction being between the oral and the written modes of composition and sharing. Because the profound differences between the two derive from epistemological as well as purely artistic grounds, people whose imaginative vision has been predominantly shaped by one or the other may have difficulty understanding and appreciating what is outside their primary mode of perception. Naturally these differences have led to scholarly speculations about how the one evolves into the other, with the Russian formalists leading the way through studies of the syncretistic origins of poetry.[1]

In American Indian literature the two modes exist side by side, the one nourishing the other. The relationship between the two is an important reason for the particular place American Indian literature has in the body of world literatures, and critics have not been slow to develop commentaries that emphasize how the oral and written traditions interact in major and undeniably important works of literature.[2] But some writing is neither major nor obviously important according to the criteria that grant worldwide recognition to certain works. Yet I argue that the vitality of these writings is so fundamental that it represents its own phenomenon with its own criteria for judgment and its own place in literary history. I want to demonstrate the particular strength of these works by describing two very different authors who publish as a husband and wife team. They are Gilbert and Montana Walking Bull. But before demonstrating some of the strengths of their work, I feel it necessary to suggest what kind of phenomena I believe they illustrate.

The best way to characterize what the Walking Bulls and others like them are doing is to say that they are creating intermediate forms between the oral and the written modes of literature. Although these artists present themselves through the written form, the underlying epistemology and aesthetic assumptions derive more from the oral than from the written tradition. The poet Simon Ortiz has published an essay that, in its entirety, is a superb description of oral literature as a way of knowing as well as expressing. Part of his description of how a song functions can help to explain the kind of experience and aesthetic energy that the writers I am describing try to preserve and share:

> You not only feel it, *you know*. The substance is emotional, but beyond that, spiritual, and it's real and you are present in and part of it. The act of the song *which you are experiencing* is real and *the reality is its substance*. A song is made substantial by *its context*—that is its reality, both that which is there and that which is brought about by the song. . . . The emotional, cultural, spiritual context in which we thrive—in that, the song is meaningful. The context has to do not only with your being physically present, but it has to do with the context of the mind, how receptive it is and that usually means familiarity with the culture in which the song is sung (emphasis added).[3]

Inherent in Ortiz' statement are descriptions of the qualities that help to define the literature I am studying. The mental attitudes that characterize the work—"the context of the mind," in Ortiz' words—are directly related to a specific tribal tradition as it lives today. Often the piece itself (the song or the story or the belief) is a personal performance of a traditional form. The artist writes a traditional piece in such a way that we know how he or she experiences that piece. The writer has known the piece in its totality but cannot bring the audience into a shared performance context; hence the written mode.

Measured against the criteria by which we judge literary works, these examples of shared oral experience often fall short. Their importance and vitality have an indirect relationship to written literature. People who write down, and perhaps publish through some small press, their sense of the reality of the oral tradition are generally documenting their belief that the visionary strength inherent in the oral images has the power to order the perplexing and sometimes destructive aspects of a world radically different from the communal one that generated the oral tradition. Often these writers are trying to show the healing power inherent in traditional images. Insofar as they succeed in showing how they have genuinely adapted the context of the oral tradition, they are adding to the vitality of that tradition, and their work has aesthetic as well as social and personal value. Of course the degree of aesthetic value can vary. The best examples can and do enter the canon of world literature,[4] but I want to argue that we need to pay some attention to all points on the continuum.

Gilbert Walking Bull is a member of the Oglala Sioux tribe; his wife Montana is a Cherokee from Oklahoma. They live in Oregon, and their books have been published by the Itemizer-Observer Press in Dallas, Oregon. Together they have published three books, the titles of which are significant. One is *Mi Ta-ku-ye*, which they translate as "about my people" but which can also be literally translated as "my relatives." Another is entitled *O-hu-kah-kan*, the Lakota word for stories of times before the present world order. The third is entitled *Wo Ya-ka-pi*, the Lakota word for stories of historic time. All three books are compendia of Lakota and Cherokee traditions, and all three are intensely personal in that implicit in the telling of an old tale or belief is the teller's sense of immediate participation. This, I believe, is an important distinguishing mark of this type of literature. The texts of old stories that Gilbert records are far from the sterile texts, divorced from any context, that one finds in archives and in ethnographic transcriptions of old tales. In *Wo Ya-ka-pi*, Gilbert begins his first story by telling of his experiences the first time he heard the tale. "When we were youngsters, many animal stories were told to us during the evening time and it seemed as though I couldn't wait for the evening to come around in those days. 'Here's a story told to us by a relative of ours who came for a visit one evening. He started like this. . .'" (p. 16).

Not only do we sense the learning process whereby Gilbert appropriated in a personal way the context (using that word with all the meaning Ortiz attaches to it) of his stories but we gradually gain some sense of how the context continues to function in changed surroundings, and it is this aspect of the collections that gives them depth. One story that I particularly appreciate is Gilbert's retelling of the Stone Boy story. (No doubt my own appreciation is enhanced by the fact that I have studied dozens of versions of this story in both Lakota and English and can therefore sense something of what Gilbert appears to have done with the story.) The feature of the story that endures through time and countless tellings has to do with buffalo attacking Stone Boy's home on a stormy day. The hero manages to protect his home. In many versions of the story he asks his uncles (whose lives he has previously saved) to build walls about the home, often four of them, often of wood. From atop the walls, he kills the buffalo.

Gilbert's version, while retaining all the traditional details, is unique among the ones I have found. No doubt it is the version he heard from his relatives, but its features relate more directly to Gilbert's life and beliefs than any other versions could. First of all, the uncles make no appearance in this story. When the time comes to defend the home, Stone Boy and his grandmother work together to make two thousand arrows. The precise number emphasizes the amount of work he is willing to do. Instead of having his uncles build walls around the home, Gilbert's Stone Boy chooses a stone and throws it on the ground. It begins to grow. He and his relatives stay atop the rapidly growing stone and kill the buffalo as the storm rages. Given the meaning of all Gilbert's tales and what I know of his life, it is not going too far to see this image of Stone Boy taking stone, the substance of which he himself is made, and using it as a defense, as an implicit commentary on discovering one's own resources and drawing on them in time of need.

The example of the Stone Boy story can also show another aspect of the dynamic at work in this collection of traditional pieces. As a child Gilbert learned many stories about the powers of stone, but their meaning only gradually became clear to him. The collection enables us to perceive how this meaning became part of his adult daily consciousness. He expresses some of his perceptions, purely personal responses to his tradition, in a form that has the visual aspects of poetry but really is more closely related to the traditional oration, which uses ordinary images to remind people of the meaning of daily affairs. It even reflects patterns of folk speech. The "poem" entitled "Rocks Not Happy in Sacks" is an example of how beliefs about stone were translated into ordinary action:

> My dog Gimo knows rocks not happy in sacks.
>
> I met my friend the rock man, in Redmond.
> He was from Indiana, and we talked about thunder eggs.
> Next thing I know when I get home,
> he sends me a sack of rocks.
>
> These rocks stay in sacks long time,
> and I forget I have them
> until Gimo tears at the sack.
> He knows rocks not happy there.
> He growls and pulls at the sack,
> and it comes to my mind
> that rocks are sacred to my people,
> that rocks *are* people and belong to the earth.
> So I pick up the sack and look around
> for a place for them to rest where they can be seen.
>
> Now rocks are settled and happy on the earth
> not closed up in dark sack anymore.
> I put them in the flower bed near the window
> where I can look out to see them,
> and anyone else can see them getting the sun, the wind,
> and the rain. Each day they look happier.
>
> (*O-hu-kah-kan*, p. 4)

The clause "and it comes to my mind" is the key to all the collection, including Montana's work. Both Gilbert and Montana wanted and needed to write about the occasions on which the conditions of ordinary life were transmuted into enduring bonds with their communities, physically far away.

Such occasions were possible because they knew and understood tribal oral traditions. Sometimes these memory bonds proved healing guides; sometimes their effect was surgical, cutting away bitterness and fear. Both Gilbert and Montana used their memories of the oral traditions, but each used them in different ways.

In the sections written by Gilbert, most of the material is recognizably traditional Lakota lore recorded from a personal standpoint with occasional brief sections devoted to personal reflections. Montana's sections contain few direct references to readily identifiable Cherokee tradition. This difference is important. The two of them represent the two poles of contemporary American Indian experience. Some American Indians share in a direct line of transmission of an oral tradition. For many, though, that direct line has been broken. Parents and even grandparents adopted a cultural stance with all the outward marks of assimilation. They remained Indian, however, and, in claiming their Indian heritage, their children often try to revitalize old traditions that have no direct link to present times. This is an interesting process, worthy of study, but it is not the route that Montana chooses.

If we use Ortiz' language to describe what Montana has chosen to do, then we would say that although the elements of the act itself (the song or whatever) are rarely traditional Cherokee, the context of the mind (the attitudes) shows the adaptability of Cherokee traditions. Montana's work shows how she has personally created a relationship between the old and the new. As she explains in the Foreword of *Wo Ya-ka-pi,* "Her Cherokee mother was Mary Ann Cadow Hopkins, from Little River County, Arkansas, and her father, Benjamin Franklin Hopkins from Anna, Illinois, was a minister in the Methodist Episcopal Church South in Oklahoma for thirty years."

Montana's long poetic commentary on her childhood catches the details of a way of life that few have been able to recognize as Indian but that reflects a reality shared by many contemporary American Indian people, and it is, in its way, every bit as Indian as the more easily defined traditions. A few quotations can show how the relationship between change and an Indian identity operates:

> I remember my long black curls made
> by mama's wrapping my hair in rags,
> and I remember my black nurse who
> cared for me. She once took me to
> town and had a photo made of us.
> (*Wo Ya-ka-pi,* p. 110)

In a very real sense, the remembering itself, the power of associated reverie, is a traditional act, and the free flow of detail finally leads to a clue as to what role her own Indian tradition has played in an ostensibly non-Indian environment:

> That's about when mama bobbed her hair
> and papa exploded, but she was Cherokee
> and did as she pleased. She wore black
> crepe dresses that had long panels and
> the dresses were beaded all over.
>
> (*Wo Ya-ka-pi*, p. 112)

Being Cherokee gave her mother a particular kind of self-definition that she carried into everything she did, and Montana clearly carries on that tradition. Like her husband, Montana perceives as a part of her Indian tradition a particular way of acting, responding, and relating to the natural world. But unlike her husband, Montana cannot use her own life and personal experience as a source for many discrete and specific traditional tales and stories. She does not pretend to traditional knowledge that did not come to her through the traditional means of transmission. In her work, there is no retelling of a story learned from a book found on a library shelf. Rather she maintains a consistent honesty by being true to her own almost-assimilated past. This gives particular value and strength to her work, enabling it to speak to those who know they are Indian but have few easily identifiable cultural traits that enable them to fit into a contemporary Indian scene.

What Montana has from her Cherokee tradition is a context, an attitude, that enables her to see modern society in her own way, a way that is a gift from her Cherokee ancestors. One especially humorous example is the poem entitled "New Form," which contrasts what is natural with a particularly non-Indian and commercial way of attempting to achieve contrived form:

> Artificially lifted, the softness
> Of white flesh is caught and encircled
> By bonds of wire or bone and padded covering
> To become firm pointed tight molds
> Of hard-bosomed loveliness.
>
> (*Wo Ya-ka-pi*, p. 68)

Several of Montana's comments show that the ability to notice the basic reality of something derives from her heritage, which presented her with alternatives. Sometimes the basic reality is humorous, sometimes it shows the conflict in race relations, and sometimes it involves self-criticism. Always, though, one senses Montana's own personality. She chooses to be like her mother—Cherokee and determined to make her own decisions.

Another fairly subtle theme seems to activate Montana's comments, and this may be the most deeply traditional theme of all. An ancient reverence suggests a boundary between the area that the human intellect can and must explore and the point at which the intellect must stop and accept something as part of another level of reality that one must not reduce to the terms of human logic. This extraordinarily traditional aspect of Montana's work comes through in a poetic commentary called "Unseen Hands upon the Clippers," which is about, of all things, clipping dead gladiola stems:

> Dull shears snap at the dead gladiola stems
> while the sun shines hot upon my head
> I pile the dry stems upon the dead grass
> and push on to finish the bed.
> It is noon and the time is short,
> For I have to get back to work.
> Suddenly the shears begin to snap
> and crack. The handle moves
> without my power, though my hands
> are still upon the wood.
> Under a considerable power
> the shears move across the
> gladiola bed on their own
> as though they were automated.
> I am simply the amazed spectator.
>
> What unseen powerful hands
> grasp those handles
> and cut those stems?
>
> Finally deciding I cannot
> believe this thing that is happening,
> I lift the clippers to examine
> the bolt that holds the blades together.
> Surely there is some logical explanation.
> At the moment of examination the power stops,
> and I return to clipping
> with the dull shears.
>
> (*O-hu-kah-kan*, p. 70)

Other tellings in her collection show Montana's sensitivities to aspects of life usually identified with Indian traditions. She tells of finding a sandwich at a picnic and being startled to find a large spider on it with a circle of small gray ones facing her. She titles that poem "Grandmother Spider" and immediately suggests thoughts about southwestern Indian traditions.

Because her tribal tradition includes much that has been assimilated from non-Indian cultures as well as other tribal traditions, Montana uses non-Indian and pan-Indian imagery in many of her poems. She seems to trace her links with her past primarily through ways of feeling and observing, and she herself must find the right forms in which to tell about her feelings. One should not judge Montana's poetry on the basis of the same criteria that one would apply to the writer who is attempting to write poetry for its own sake. Montana is finding a way to tell what has been Indian and what has been a source of strength in her past, and the process of telling validates the past for her.

The intermediate forms between the oral tradition and the written are, I believe, of crucial importance in our study of American Indian literature. If, on the one hand, we apply to them exactly the same criteria that we apply to the work of artists working more consciously within the written traditions of world literature, then we are unfair to both. On the other hand, neither can we treat the intermediate forms as oral literature, since the performance elements so crucial to oral literature are not present. The absence of performance elements does not mean, though, that such writing is without standards. Some people are clearly contributing more to our understanding of the vitality of specific traditions than others are. I believe that there are some specific criteria by which we can judge these works.

First of all, the epistemological basis of the works should derive directly from the oral tradition. That is, evidence of the personal process of learning and appropriating a tradition must somehow be present. A person who sets out to write down old traditions without showing his or her own relationship to them is not fulfilling this requirement. Second, the defining qualities of oral literature that require some kind of interaction between a teller and an audience must somehow be reflected in the intermediate genres. There are various ways of achieving this interaction. Most of the time, the artist employs some form of juxtaposition as a primary technique. The writer may, for example, juxtapose a mundane incident and a traditional idea, and the reader can see how the ordinary (the audience experience) relates to the tale. The artist does not always seek clever or brilliant ways to show the relationship between the two. Instead the juxtaposition often functions in much the same way as the teller-listener interaction functions in the oral literature. The listeners bring their trivial, or perhaps traumatic, concerns to a telling, and the hearing of a familiar event retold in a new way sheds light on the immediate concern to which the traditional element is juxtaposed.

The entire process that informs the oral tradition assumes that as one passes through the challenges of a lifetime and gradually recognizes the meaning of what one has heard over and over again, one gradually becomes a teller and a teacher. If the process begins genuinely and then ends abortively, it leaves the listener with a sense of potentiality left unfulfilled. Many young people have begun the process in a community of relatives and neighbors bound by like problems and ideals, then moved into a totally different world of neon-lighted streets, universities, offices, and challenges worthy of one of their culture heroes. Sometimes the disjunction between the reservation and the contemporary city proves devastatingly destructive, and sometimes, in their struggle to find a way to survive in a world utterly different from what they first knew, the young people turn again to the traditions of that first world and find in them more answers than they would have dared to seek originally. People who find such answers may be great human beings; they sometimes are good writers; sometimes they are merely adequate writers; but like the Walking Bulls, they often turn to writing to make up for the absence of the original community. I do not believe that we can ignore the work of these people just because it falls outside the realm of our literary criteria. If the work shows a valid tradition growing and adapting, then it is worthy of our careful and gentle attention.

Notes

1   Veselovsky describes the origins of poetry in an evolutionary sequence moving from the singer to the poet and from the group to the individual. See *Three Chapters from Historical Poetics* in *Collected Works*, I. An English summary of his thought can be found in Sokolov, *Russian Folklore*, pp. 100–10.

2   A fine example of this kind of criticism is Evers' "Words and Place: A Reading of *House Made of Dawn*."

3   S. Ortiz, "Song / Poetry and Language."

4   Momaday's *The Way to Rainy Mountain* is an example of an intermediary form of the highest literary quality.

Teaching Personal Narratives and Autobiography

Course Design #1

American Indian Personal Narratives

As a genre, the personal narrative provides a means of approaching both the oral and the written process of creation and transmission in American Indian literature. Because these narratives incorporate other American Indian literary forms such as songs, tales, origin stories, and dream visions, they provide an opportunity to study forms, functions, stylistic devices, and techniques characteristic of American Indian literature.

A distinctly personal mode, the first-person narrative weaves history, traditions, beliefs, and life ways of individuals living in tribal societies into unified works that allow the reader to share the cultural and literary perception and expression of a people. Like the broader body of both traditional and contemporary American Indian literatures, personal narratives are acts of the imagination, artistically structured recollections, a transition between oral literature and modern written forms. For a broad critical overview of the genre, see W. Smith, "American Indian Autobiographies."

In order to place the personal narrative in the context of the American Indian literary tradition, some discussion of traditional oral forms is necessary. Since such materials are abundant and various, however, focusing on pictographs—the Walum Olum, winter counts, wampum belts—and similar forms created to illustrate the life stories of individual Indians would also be useful. The following works are especially appropriate in that they demonstrate the evolution of the pictograph from a material work of art accompanied by an oral narrative to a material work with written text: Stirling, "Pictograph Autobiographies of Sitting Bull"; Vistal, Warpath; and White Bull (Sioux), The Warrior Who Killed Custer.

Methodology and Description

Personal narratives may be divided into three types: oral narratives, written narratives, and memoirs. The oral, as-told-to narrative requires a recorder/editor, and, while this method may create an unreliable text as a result of the intermediary between narrator and audience, the resultant problem is useful in discussing the performer-audience relationship inherent in oral literature. The following works are representative of the genre; the instructor may wish to use works from one region as a means of narrowing the focus and simplifying cultural background reading: Black Elk (Sioux), *Black Elk Speaks*; Blowsnake (Winnebago), *The Autobiography of a Winnebago*; Chona (Papago), *The Autobiography of a Papago Woman*; Fire (Sioux), *Lame Deer*; Geronimo (Apache), *Geronimo*; Hopkins (Paiute), *Life among the Piutes*; Left Handed (Navajo), *Left Handed*; Mountain Wolf Woman (Winnebago), *Mountain Wolf Woman*; Sekaquaptewa (Hopi), *Me and Mine*; Talayesva (Hopi), *Sun Chief*; Two Leggings (Crow), *Two Leggings*. Useful critical resources include Bierhorst, "American Verbal Art"; Sayre, "Vision and Experience"; and Tedlock, "On the Translation of Style" and "Pueblo Literature."

Despite its apparent similarity to Euro-American autobiography, the American Indian first-person written narrative is distinguished by an absence of concern with self-analysis. It is occupied primarily with the authors' observations of tribal values and ways. Since it is a direct form, the author has more control than in the as-told-to form, but editing procedures may be of concern in evaluating individual works. Editorial bias can be problematic when non-Indian editors interject their conceptions of Indian life into the material supporting the narrative (prefaces, introductions, footnotes, and so on). A comparative study drawing on several sources, including, when possible, narratives by living members of the same tribe (in person or on videotape), will flesh out the study and foster a truer understanding of American Indian life, history, and literature. Instructors might approach the following texts in chronological order or choose supplementary texts to develop a regional or tribal focus: Eastman (Sioux), *Indian Boyhood*; Griffis (Osage), *Tahan*; Lowry (Paiute), *Karnee*; Mitchell (Navajo), *Miracle Hill*; Moises (Yaqui), *The Tall Candle*; Plenty Coups (Crow), *Plenty Coups*; Qoyawayma (Hopi), *No Turning Back*; Standing Bear (Sioux), *Land of the Spotted Eagle*.

While innovative in structure, the memoir, a contemporary outgrowth of the autobiography, continues to reflect the focus and elements characteristic of the genre. The following texts might be studied: Momaday (Kiowa), *The Names* and *The Way to Rainy Mountain*; Zuni People, *The Zunis*.

Instructors should supplement each work with ethnological texts and collections of traditional literature pertinent to the narrator's tribe. For example, the background reading for Maria Chona should include: Bahr, *Staying Sickness* (on Papago curing ways); and Underhill, *Hawk over Whirlpools* (a novel that incorporates Chona's material), *Papago Indian Religion*, *Papago Indians of Arizona*, and *Singing for Power* (Papago song). Similarly, a study of *The Zunis* should include Benedict, *Zuni Mythology*; Cushing, *Zuni Folk Tales*; and Tedlock, *Finding the Center.*

APPROACHES

The following questions may suggest strategies for approaching the materials.

What is the purpose of the narrative?
Was it solicited or spontaneous?
How reliable is the narrator?
What elements of humor are evident?
What oral techniques are evident in the work? What is their effect?
How are other literary genres incorporated into the text? Is it possible to compare the incorporated tales, songs, and other forms to other versions of the same material to see what changes the narrator has made?
How do published texts compare with original manuscripts?
What characteristics identify the American Indian personal narrative as a distinctly Indian literary form?

Course Design #2
American Indian Autobiographies: Historical Perspectives

This three-hour course has as its objective the study of the personal and historical experiences of American Indian people through an examination of autobiographies.

Autobiographical materials are an essential and rich source of information about the experiences of American Indian people. By examining the memories and recollections of individuals, students can develop a deeper understanding of the dilemmas and choices that all Indian people face. Most of these materials are not autobiography in a Western literary sense. Rather, they are transcriptions of oral narrative in which the recorder/editor has shaped, consciously and unconsciously, the structure and content of the autobiography. Nevertheless, the narratives of American Indians have evolved from traditional oral techniques. A constant tension exists, therefore, between the cultural and personal needs of both the narrator and the transcriber. In addition to the as-told-to autobiographies, a number of Indians have written autobiographies in English that directly reveal the relation between their lives and the experiences of their people.

One may approach this selection of autobiographies partly in chronological order. One should keep in mind, however, that the historical experiences of a tribal people in large measure are determined by the dates of initial contact with and subsequent domination by Europeans. Also, the personal memories of the narrators remain clearly within the context of tribal history and culture. Such works as *Black Elk Speaks, Geronimo: His Own Story*, and *Plenty Coups* focus on the last years of tribal independence and the early years of reservation life. In such accounts certain themes and perspectives clearly emerge: renditions of personal exploits, ideas about the proper relation between the people and the land, and reflections on military defeat and the loss of tribal freedom. In addition, one must remember that the authors of these works are reluctant to discuss the painful realities of life on the reservation.

Autobiographies narrated or written by Indians who had little, if any, experience of prereservation days tend to reflect other concerns. They enunciate changes in tribal life as a consequence of the tribes' necessary adjustments to U.S. policies regarding land use, education, and cultural assimilation. Some autobiographies, written by Indians educated at off-reservation boarding schools or at eastern and midwestern universities, suggest a profound ambivalence toward white and Indian life-styles. The lives of such writers as Charles Eastman, Luther Standing Bear, and Anna Moore Shaw have been ineluctably shaped by their contact with white culture, and their resulting bicultural posture has influenced their rendition of tribal experiences as well as their assessment of white and Indian relations in a way that often makes non-Indians uneasy. More recent autobiographies, especially those written or recorded since the 1940s, reflect the increased opportunities Indians now have to participate in the overall society and often clearly illustrate the determination of contemporary Indians to maintain their tribal heritage.

Materials

Required readings include both transitional reservation autobiographies and reservation and postreservation autobiographies. Transitional reservation: Black Elk (Sioux), *Black Elk Speaks*; Geronimo (Apache), *Geronimo*; Plenty Coups (Crow), *Plenty Coups*. Reservation and postreservation: Betzinez (Apache), *I Fought with Geronimo*; Eastman (Sioux), *From the Deep Woods*; La Flesche (Omaha), *The Middle Five*; Qoyawayma, *No Turning Back*; Shaw (Pima), *A Pima Past*; Standing Bear (Sioux), *My People, the Sioux*; Talayesva (Hopi), *Sun Chief*. Optional readings include: Transitional reservation: Eastman, *Indian Boyhood*; Black Hawk (Sioux), *Black Hawk*; Pretty-Shield (Crow), *Pretty-Shield*; Two Leggings (Crow), *Two Leggings*.

Reservation and postreservation: Blowsnake (Winnebago), *Autobiography of a Winnebago*; Campbell (Métis), *Halfbreed*; Cuero (Dieguero), *Autobiography*; Left Handed (Navajo), *Left Handed*; Mountain Wolf Woman (Winnebago), *Mountain Wolf Woman*; Sekaquaptewa (Hopi), *Me and Mine*; Sewid (Kwakiutl), *Guests Never Leave Hungry*; White Bull (Sioux), *The Warrior Who Killed Custer*; Whitewolf (Kiowa-Apache), *Jim Whitewolf*.

Course Design #3

People, Culture, and Land: American Indians in the Southwest

This three- or four-credit upper-division course is intended to explore American Indian literature of the Southwest using ethnohistorical and geographic materials to bring out the relations among peoples, cultures, and land.

Social scientists often approach the study of American Indian cultures by way of specific regions, since groups in a given geographical region interact with a common environment. The special meaning this interaction has for American Indians is evident in their literature as it has never been in anthropological studies. The unity of past and present is not in the sentimentalization of landscape or the celebration of natural beauty alone, as many Europeans have supposed, but in the dynamic relation among people, culture, and land. (See Momaday's "Native American Attitudes to the Environment"; and Vine Deloria's *God Is Red,* especially "Thinking in Time and Space," Ch. 5; "The Concept of History," Ch. 7; and "The Spatial Problem of History," Ch. 8; and Paula Allen's "The Feminine Landscape of . . . *Ceremony*" and "The Sacred Hoop," in this volume.) An interdisciplinary course designed around these themes not only can give students a more complete understanding of American Indian literature but also can place that literature in its proper cultural context.

To begin at the beginning, as understood by the various tribes, is to underline the importance of the connection between people and place. (Slides of southwestern landscapes and American Indian architecture are appropriate here.) Alfonso Ortiz' *Tewa World* and the first volume of Ethelou Yazzie's *Navajo History* were written in part to transmit oral traditions to future generations, and those works thus have a distinctive place in American Indian literature. For classroom use, a comparison with earlier transcriptions of these origin accounts would stimulate discussion of the differences between the oral literary tradition and the written.

The relation among people, culture, and land was never a static one; as other groups arrived in the Southwest, all three elements were modified. Meinig's *Southwest* concentrates on a series of interactions among cultures and their effects on land-use patterns, settlement, and transportation networks. Spicer's *Cycles of Conquest* studies the effects of Spanish and Anglo incursions on the American Indian societies of the region.

That the people-culture-land relationship remained viable is most apparent when one studies a series of literary works from a specific group—the Navajo, for example. The *Navajo Stories of the Long Walk Period* (ed. B. H. Johnson) graphically illustrate the traumatic breaking of the people-land connection. *Left Handed, Son of Old Man Hat* is the personal history of a man whose culture has reinstated itself in the Navajo country, with its vitality intact. Kay Bennett's experience, as told in *Kaibah*, is of a culture that more and more is forced to cope with Anglo-American interference, of which the school and the sheep reduction campaign of the 1930s are two examples.

From the beginning the Pueblo people of the Rio Grande valley had a different kind of connection to the land than did the Navajo. Earlier generations had chosen to adopt some aspects of Spanish culture that the Navajo rejected. Recent generations of all American Indian tribes in the Southwest have been affected by social forces that originated in the dominant society, among them urbanization and the dislocation that results from military service. Leslie Silko's *Ceremony*, Simon Ortiz' *Going for the Rain*, and Paula Gunn Allen's *Coyote's Daylight Trip* deal with the theme of dislocation and the return to union with the land and tradition.

All the themes so far mentioned will be found in *The Zunis*. This collection presents, in translation, the works of several contemporary storytellers of Zuni Pueblo. One might also use selections from Tedlock's *Finding the Center* to expose students to the Zuni narrative style.

So far, we have traced the connection between people and land in literature. The connection is made visible in sand paintings, pottery, and other southwestern art forms, best presented through slides, museum visits, and talks with native artists.

Materials and Methods

If this course is to be taught in the Southwest, there will be no need for many of the books. Instructors there can let the American Indian people speak for themselves. Elsewhere, instructors should make the maximum possible use of videotapes, slides, films, records, and, especially, knowledgeable people. Required readings include: Allen (Laguna-Sioux), *Coyote's Daylight Trip*, "The Feminine Landscape of *Ceremony*," and "The Sacred Hoop"; Bennett (Navajo), *Kaibah*; Deloria (Sioux), *God Is Red*; Hobson (Cherokee), *The Remembered Earth*; Johnson, *Navajo Stories of the Long Walk Period*; Left Handed (Navajo), *Left Handed*; Meinig, *Southwest*;

Momaday (Kiowa), "Native American Attitudes to the Environment"; Alfonso Ortiz (San Juan), *The Tewa World*; Simon Ortiz (Acoma), *Going for the Rain*; Silko (Laguna), *Ceremony* and *Storyteller*; Spicer, *Cycles of Conquest*; Witt and Steiner, "Hopi Prophecy" (in *The Way*); Yazzie (Navajo), *Navajo History*; and Zuni People, *The Zunis*.

Suggested additional readings include: Bahti, *Southwestern Indian Arts and Crafts*; Begay, *Sacred Mountains of the Navajo in Four Paintings*; Boas, *Keresan Texts*; Clark, *They Sang for Horses*; Concha, *Lonely Deer*; Klah (Navajo), *Navajo Creation Myth*; Marriott, *Maria, the Potter of San Ildefonso*; McNickle (Salish) and Fey, *Indians and Other Americans*; Nequatewa (Hopi), *Truth of a Hopi*; O'Bryan, *The Diné*; and Sando (Jemez), *The Pueblo Indian*.

This course concentrates on Pueblo and Navajo experiences, without distinguishing among different Pueblo people and without including other important groups in the Southwest. This intensive, rather than extensive, approach might give students deeper understanding. Those who wish to teach a more comprehensive course, however, may find the following alternative selections useful: Pima-Papago: Chona, *Autobiography*; Shaw, *A Pima Past*; Webb, *A Pima Remembers*. Apache: Betzinez, *I Fought with Geronimo*; Cochise, *First Hundred Years of Nino Cochise*; Geronimo, *Geronimo*. Hopi: Qoyawayma, *No Turning Back*; Sekaquaptewa, *Me and Mine*; and Talayesva, *Sun Chief*.

American Indian
Women's Literature

Transformation of Tradition: Autobiographical Works by American Indian Women

Gretchen Bataille

> A nation is not conquered
> Until the hearts of its women
> Are on the ground.
> Then it is done, no matter
> How brave its warriors
> Nor how strong its weapons.[1]
> (Cheyenne)

Shirley Hill Witt, in quoting the Cheyenne people, is speaking for Indian women of all times and in all tribal communities. But if we were to read and listen to others who have written about American Indian women, we would come away with a view much different from this age-old belief in the power of the Indian woman. Those who until recently assumed the inferiority of all women did not spare the American Indian woman. The notion that Indian women were and are inferior to Indian men permeates early writings about native societies, and even some recent writers have perpetuated this belief. John C. Ewers and Valerie S. Mathes both suggest that Indians regard women's duties (caring for home and children, preparing food and hides, etc.) as less important than male duties such as hunting and waging war. One of Mathes' conclusions about Indian women of the seventeenth, eighteenth, and nineteenth centuries is that they were seen as inferior to men by such writers as George Catlin, Lewis Henry Morgan, Edwin T. Denig, and Washington Irving.[2] Mathes, however, points out that contrary to many published accounts, Indian women were accorded a number of economic, social, and political opportunities within tribal society.

The popular view of American Indian women, however, assumes that women's work is by nature inferior to that done by men. John C. Ewers offers a generalization about Indian men and women:

The Indian Country of the Upper Missouri was a man's world before the white man's civilization penetrated that remote portion of the interior of our continent. Indian men were the hunters and warriors. As partisans they led war parties. As chiefs they deliberated in tribal councils and negotiated intertribal peaces. They were the seekers of visions, the makers and manipulators of powerful medicine bundles, and the conductors of prolonged and involved religious rituals. Women, on the other hand, were the diggers of roots and collectors of berries, the carriers of firewood and drawers of water, the dressers of hides and makers of tipis and clothing. As homemakers and housekeepers they performed scores of tasks necessary to the welfare of their families. But their role was a humble one. The Indian woman's inferior status. . . .[3]

Current views contradict the stereotypes, however. Clara Sue Kidwell argues convincingly that "the positions of women in European societies, largely derived from Judaic and Christian ideals of womanhood, led European men to overlook the power that Indian women could wield in their own societies." Kidwell further asserts that "the idea of the roles of Indian women in their own societies that emerges from the literature in which women tell their own stories contradicts the usual stereotypes of the subservient and oppressed female."[4] Support for this view comes from other American Indian women today. Bea Medicine, Sioux anthropologist, has repeatedly said in lectures and in writing that Indian women do not need liberation, that they have always been liberated within their tribal structures.

Given what appear to be conflicting views on the roles of women in American Indian communities, a logical move would be to examine this contradiction in perspective. One way to know a people is through the individual lives of the members of the group. Biography and autobiography have through the ages illuminated history by focusing on those persons who changed the course of events or who achieved notoriety or fame because of circumstances. The best-known American Indians and those whose lives were early chronicled tended to be men such as Geronimo or Black Hawk, who distinguished themselves in warfare, or Chief Joseph, whose military strategies gained him respect. Similarly, early semifictional accounts of Squanto, Sequoya, and Powhatan focused on men who had been leaders, who had befriended settlers and who had attempted to adopt some European ways. The two women most remembered from childhood books or history texts are Pocahontas and Sacajawea, Indian women who, some historians suggest, sought to become "white." Of Indian women we know far less than we do of their male counterparts throughout history, and what writers from Catlin through Ewers have accepted as fact does not appear to be substantiated by Indian women's life stories or by the accounts of Indian women today.

The autobiographies of American Indian women have undergone significant changes during this century. Most obvious is a change of attitude on the part of the subject. A self-consciousness is apparent in early life stories told by an informant, who often remained anonymous, through a translator to an anthropologist, but this self-consciousness has changed as women have become more aware of their white audience and the pressures toward acculturation. As Indian people became more a part of the dominant society, the autobiographies began to reflect this movement toward acculturation and integration. Recent autobiographies reflect a far more conscious attempt to present a story of an individual Indian woman and her relation with the tribe, with other native people, and with non-Indians.

Ethnographers had a distinct reason for wanting to hear the stories; they were after anthropological data to round out field reports. The material these editors chose to include represented what they thought was significant. Today Indian women writing their own stories are choosing the material *they* wish to include.

This paper will trace these changes in attitude and will also focus on the forces that have influenced the writers or informants. The changes have resulted from the writer's perception of the audience, the writer's purpose in revealing her life, the role of the editor, and the economic and/or political climate of the period of recording.

At the end of the nineteenth century and early in the twentieth century a rising interest in Indian customs and an increasing desire "to salvage the remains of a culture" led anthropologists and ethnologists to record life stories. Their purpose was not to focus on an individual life but rather to "use" a single life to illuminate a culture. Interestingly, the women whose lives were recorded during that period were not princesses but the mothers and wives of tribesmen. Their stories differ from the stories of their male contemporaries in that they tell, not of war exploits, but of the gathering of herbs. They speak of preparing rather than of hunting buffalo. They tell of raising children rather than of racing horses. These differences reflect the division of roles in the cultures. More important than any other feature of these stories is the extent to which they reflect the relations between women and men within a tribe.

As autobiographies moved from the traditional mode of oral literature, many of the elements of storytelling were inevitably lost. When the stories were written down, facial expressions, hand movements, and pauses disappeared on the printed page. Editors decided what events were significant in a woman's life or, more often, significant to field research on a given tribe. Indian women recognized that they could not communicate their entire lives in a foreign language and that the events they considered significant might appear to be naive or unimportant to their white interviewers. Taboos were broken; for example, to tell the life story of the family, women were often forced to speak the names of the dead. In the best tradition of contemporary storytelling, Mountain Wolf Woman told Nancy Lurie a short version of her life. Then, recognizing that this was not acceptable, she carefully told the longer version that she knew Lurie wanted.

The contradictions inherent in recent analyses of the role of American Indian women necessitate a closer look at the modes of expression as well as the content in American Indian women's autobiographies. When one looks at continuities in the autobiographies, one may be tempted to say there has been little change. Some Indian women are still transmitting life stories through interpreters and editors much as they did at the turn of the century. A closer examination, however, reveals some gradual changes in purpose, attitude, and the role of the editor.

If we turn first to the earliest materials and the views of the collectors, we find men who perceived themselves as performing a necessary task, salvaging what would otherwise soon be lost:

> It is evident that aboriginal manners and customs are rapidly disappearing, but notwithstanding that disappearance much remains unknown, and there has come a more urgent necessity to preserve for posterity by adequate record the many survivals before they disappear forever.[5]

The notion that American Indians were the "white man's burden" predominated in the earliest recorded autobiographies. Early ethnologists considered the life stories only a small part of the total field report on a given group, however. Kroeber quotes Franz Boas, who described autobiographies as being "of limited value, and useful chiefly for the study of the perversion of truth by memory." In his article on the use of autobiographical evidence he continues to say that

> among nonliterate tribal folk some normal elderly persons are likely to feel their life not as something interesting in its individuation and distinctiveness, but as an exemplification of a socialization. Such a person is conscious of himself first of all as a preserver and transmitter of his culture.[6]

This assumption is borne out by some of the earliest autobiographies and also by accounts for publications such as Elsie C. Parsons' *American Indian Life*, a collection of twenty-four vignettes composed by anthropologists based on their research. Presented as nonfiction, they are, however, fictional accounts. It is impossible to know how much was deleted by editors interested more in the culture than in the individual. Kroeber cites Michelson's "Narrative of a Southern Cheyenne Woman" and "Narrative of an Arapaho Woman" as examples in which the narrator submits individuality and personal feeling in order to express the accepted social standards of the group. Although the bulk of Michelson's reports discloses familial relationships, courtship and marriage, and some ritual, both the informants and the editor make it clear that there are omissions. In speaking of the "Tipi Decorators," for example, the Southern Cheyenne Woman says, "I was very carefully instructed never to disclose the ceremony in the presence of males. So I shall be obliged to discontinue the subject."[7] Michelson himself tells us in the preface to the Fox Woman's autobiography, "It may be noted that at times the original autobiography was too naive and frank for European taste, and so a few sentences have been deleted."[8] And Frank B. Linderman, writing of his translation of Pretty-Shield's life story comments, "Such a story as this, coming through an interpreter laboring to translate Crow thoughts into English words, must suffer some mutation, no matter how conscientious the interpreter may be."[9]

In 1936 Ruth Underhill published the story of an old Papago woman, Maria Chona. Taken through an interpreter, the words expressed Maria's thoughts, but Underhill arranged the material in chronological order. Underhill expresses her attitude toward the material in her analysis:

> Indian narrative style involves a repetition and a dwelling on unimportant details which confuse the white reader and make it hard for him to follow the story. Motives are never explained and the writer has found even Indians at a loss to interpret them in older myths. Emotional states are summed up in such colorless phrases as "I liked it," "I did not like it." For one not deeply immersed in the cultures the real significance escapes.

Her choice of words—"unimportant details" and "colorless phrases"—and her earlier admission that she omitted repetitions and emphasized points Maria had not exemplify the ability of the editor to change the original story in significant ways. Underhill says, in fact, "It is an Indian story told to satisfy whites rather than Indians."[10] In the story itself Maria tells the reader she was "different" because she had husbands who took her places and she knew cures and songs. She was also independent enough to leave her husband when he took another wife. The contemporary reader must wonder at the independence and mobility that marked Maria Chona's life, especially in light of the stereotype of the Indian woman. Maria told her story at age ninety, so it is possible that her memory was not as sharp as it once had been. Nevertheless, despite the intrusion of a white editor, Maria comes across as an individual Indian woman who was aware of her skills and position within the tribe. She was also aware of the changes that were taking place within her society. She refers, for instance, to liquor and Catholicism and their influence on the people. She points out, too, that her father was buried instead of being put in a cave and that her people no longer slept on mats but had started using blankets and pillows. Throughout the autobiography Maria is aware of her audience—"white people" —and often relates events in her life to experiences with which the audience can identify. But certain elements in the work identify Maria's life as one that certainly did not fit any stereotype. She recognized that as a songmaker and visionary she was not typical of the tribe, and she also had powers to cure and skills at basketmaking that set her apart from most men and women.

Looking closely at the earliest autobiographies, one sometimes finds clear statements of the woman's personal thoughts and purposes for telling the story. Even when the statement is veiled, the impact of the thought is clear. Waheenee, telling her story in 1921, reveals her sadness:

> I am an old woman now. The buffalo and black-tail deer are gone and our Indian ways are almost gone. Sometimes I find it hard to believe I ever lived them. . . . I cannot forget our old ways. Often in summer I rise at daybreak and steal out to the cornfields; and as I hoe the corn I sing to it, as we did when I was young. No one cares for our corn songs now. Sometimes at evening I sit, looking out on the Big Missouri. The sun sets, and dusk steals over the water. In the shadows I seem again to see our Indian village, with smoke curling upward from the earth lodges, and in the river's roar I hear the yells of the warriors, the laughter of little children as of old. It is an old woman's dream. Again I see but shadows and hear only the roar of the river; and tears come into my eyes. Our Indian life, I know, is gone forever.

Her editor, because of a different perspective of the past, brushes these deep thoughts away: "Conservative and sighing for the good old times, she is aware that the younger generation of Indians must adopt civilized ways."[11]

Michelson's Arapaho woman says that she won't tell private or personal experiences out of respect for her male relatives, but she subtly reveals the differences between the present and the past:

> There were no briar weeds, or stickers, or burrs; so the children as well as their parents were nearly always barefooted. All that one could see on the prairies was grass, buffalo grass, and blue stem. When camps were pitched we would make our beds on the ground with grass for undercushions. The air was always fresh. We wore no head-shade; in fact we didn't mind the weather in those days.[12]

Pretty-Shield's reluctance to talk about the changing conditions of her people and her admission, "I am trying to live a life that I do not understand," suggest deep and yet unclear feelings about the life she is relating. She is not ambivalent, however, in her statement about the changes the men in the tribe have experienced:

> Our men had fought hard against our enemies. . . . Our men, our leaders, began to drink the white man's whiskey, letting it do their thinking. . . . Our wise ones became fools. . . . But what else was there for us to do? . . . Our old men used to be different.[13]

Lucy Young may have spoken for all the women whose life stories were "corrected" and "grammatically improved" by white editors. She told her brief story in 1939 when she was over ninety years old. She lived through the same period as did the previously mentioned women, and she explains why her story needed to be told: "I hear people tell 'bout what Inyan do early days to white man. Nobody ever tell it what white man do to Inyan. That's reason I tell it. That's history. That's truth. I seen it myself."[14]

All these women's lives come to us through at least one intermediary, often several. Their stories provide little specific information about the role of Indian women, but careful reading suggests that their status was neither subservient nor inferior. These women emphasize the roles of both males and females, the familial relationships, the material culture, and, above all, a regret for the changes from the old ways.

A collection that was published in 1974 but had been gathered during the 1940s is Elizabeth Colson's *Autobiographies of Three Pomo Women*. Colson intended the life stories to supplement the ethnographies on Pomo culture and to provide some insight into the lives of the Pomo women who had grown up during the period of acculturation. Perhaps Mrs. Martinez' comments best epitomize the pulls on women during this period. When asked what she wanted for her granddaughter, she answered, "I think if she stayed home with me and made baskets that would be good. And I want her to go to school and learn something. That would be good too" (p. 82). The pulls toward tradition and the pushes toward acculturation are apparent in the autobiographies of these three women.

The next major group of life stories reflects this dilemma and in part provides the response with which many Indian women felt comfortable. Following the period when autobiography was collected for ethnographical study came a period during which Indian women chose consciously to write their own life stories, sometimes with the aid of an editor, but often independently. Nancy Lurie writes of this period: "By the 1930s Indian women seemed to have held up better under the stresses of reservation life than men and were often in the forefront of work in tribal councils and business committees. . . . Women were said to have suffered less 'acculturation stress.'"[15] Lurie comments also that during the period of acculturation and indoctrination Indian men were learning vocational and technical skills that often were of no use on the reservation. Women, however, were being trained in teaching, nursing, and office work, skills they could put to use on the reservation. Despite their fears of losing the old ways, the women survived and continued to provide direction for the people. What was this direction and what do the autobiographies during this period suggest were the prevailing attitudes? Generally the autobiographies reflect the Indians' acceptance of white culture, of Christianity, and of public education in place of traditional tribal education. The old ways are not forgotten, but they are seen as unworkable in a new social order.

Anauta, an Eskimo woman from Baffin Island, traveled widely, speaking throughout the country. She recognized the difficulty of adjusting and said of the book *Land of Good Shadows*, which tells her life story, "It's all my life. . . . I live more myself in that book than I do any time now in this new life of adjusting myself to a new world" (p. xv). There was during this period a conscious attempt to correct the misinformation about Indians as savages and to bring the Indian and white worlds closer together. Polingaysi Qoyawayma says that her autobiography is an attempt to "span the great and terrifying chasm between my Hopi world and the world of the white man." When the author decided to go to school, her mother admonished her:

> You have taken a step in the wrong direction. A step away from your Hopi people. You have brought grief to us. To me, to your father, and to your grand-parents. Now you must continue to go to school each day. You have brought this thing upon yourself, and there is no turning back. (p. 26)

Her grandmother warned her of the loss of Hopi beliefs and culture, but she also reminded her of her responsibility as a member of the coyote clan to provide a bond between the Bahana (white man) and the Hopi people. She does not reject her heritage, but she assumes that many of the traditional ways will indeed be lost. She realizes that the education of the children is now in the hands of teachers and public schools rather than in the hands of mothers or grandmothers, and she advises the educators to "help [the chil-dren] to realize the value of their own heritage" (p. 174).

Other women in this generation of writers accepted white ways and Christianity. Helen Sekaquaptewa, for example, adopted the Mormon reli-gion and white attitudes, and her life story reflects this perspective. And Anna Shaw, whose parents had converted to Christianity and who herself was unique among Indian women in receiving a high school diploma in 1920, is described by Edward Spicer as a "culturally assimilated Presbyterian Pima."[16] Her own view of Indian life is a result of her experience: she moved from the reservation to the white world and finally back to a blend of the two. She describes her experiences naively, however, saying that she did not experience discrimination at school, that discrimination did not exist at the American Railway Express Company where her husband worked, and that there was no prejudice in her Phoenix neighborhood. Such experiences must certainly not have been the norm for Indian people in Arizona, a state that did not allow American Indians to vote until 1948. Anna Shaw's story is an Indian version of the Horatio Alger myth: "Minority people can climb the ladder of success by hard work" (p. 166). Although she recognizes what was traditionally a part of her culture, she has adapted to and adopted an alien way of life.

Florence Shipek in her comments about Delfina Cuero recognized the dilemma that American Indians faced in the 1930s, 1940s, and 1950s:

> This autobiography is typical of life stories of most of the Indians who had no place to call their own. . . . All relate the same search for a place to live and the

same terrible struggle to feed and clothe the children, whom they loved dearly. . . . They hold no bitterness about the past and are only looking for the chance to work and to earn enough to feed and clothe their children. They feel that they have survived through the crises and that there will be a future for their children as the children are learning the new ways.[17]

Shipek describes Delfina's life as typical of the "destruction of Indian self-sufficiency on the land, of Indian society, culture, and religion." The recognition of the loss is a bitter one, for the lessons taught by the grandmothers and through the stories don't work in the society anymore. Delfina and her children become victims of her men's anger, and the changes in the culture result in disintegration of family ties as well as the loss of the traditional ways.

Sah-gan-de-oh speaks for herself and for others of her generation when she remarks that her story is similar to those of "many other American Indians of today who are completely integrated in the American way of life."[18] Yet she sees a greater purpose in sharing her experiences:

It is my hope that those of you who read this will better understand us. We are not refugees from another world, feathered and warlike as the TV and movies depict us but a proud race who love our heritage and are striving to keep alive our own culture. (p. 7)

Although she wishes to keep alive her culture, she accepts the philosophy taught at Haskell, a Bureau of Indian Affairs school: "They all helped us to become better citizens and adjust to a better way of life" (p. 58). In her own teaching she adopts the attitude of an outsider: "We had the most adorable little papooses. . . . I thought it a shame those babies had been taken away from their homes at so early an age but they didn't seem to be the least bit unhappy or homesick" (p. 56). She accepts the policy of termination as inevitable and ends her book with a diatribe against her own people, blaming them for whatever problems they have. She criticizes Indian parents for not making public education compulsory, blames tribal politics for internal problems, says parents use welfare checks at local bars, and finally says the housing situation could be improved "with a little extra work and a few less 'six-packs' of beers." In her simplistic analysis she divides all Indians into three groups: those working as professionals, those making a good living, and those addicted to "firewater" (p. 185). Perhaps more than any other Indian woman writing at this time, Sah-gan-de-oh represents the assimilated Indian woman who believes wholeheartedly that the only way to survive is to assimilate into white society. Her analysis of the economic situation ignores the realities of prejudice and rejection Indian people have experienced. She appears to be too far from the memories of "what used to be" to recognize the traditional values and their place in her life.

The women's movement has focused on the role of women in society and has helped to bring about significant changes in individual lives as well as in society's perception of women's roles. During the past decade we have scrutinized the family, marriage, parent-child relations, and career opportunities. We have also examined the role of minority women and debated the relative importance of ethnicity and feminism. Indian women repeatedly deny their interest in or need for "liberation," saying they cannot afford the luxury of feminist goals because they must devote their energies to keeping families intact, getting jobs, and fighting the political battles of their people. This attitude does not mean that Indian women have not achieved recognition, however. Ada Deer, Bea Medicine, Annie Wauneka, LaDonna Harris, Liz Cook-Lynn, Leslie Silko, Buffy Sainte-Marie, and numerous other Indian women have achieved success in politics, education, medicine, and the arts. Throughout the country Indian women serve on tribal councils and Title IV committees. The belief that Indian women do not need the feminist movement is consistent with the role Indian women have played in their societies through the years. Recent autobiographies reaffirm this belief. An examination of the roles of Indian women in traditional societies reveals the power that many contemporary Indian women allude to in autobiographies. These writers show how that power has been corrupted or diminished during this century.

Looking at contemporary life stories one finds that the old methods of obtaining autobiographies are still in use today: Nancy Lurie edited Mountain Wolf Woman's story; David E. Jones recorded the story of Sanapia; Don Barnett and Rick Sterling edited Bobbi Lee's story. The editors' awareness of Indian perspectives is generally higher now than in the past, however, and is reflected in the methods of presentation as well as in the editorial comments. Nancy Lurie, for example, explains why Mountain Wolf Woman told her story—her niece requested that she do so—and explains her own purposes—to provide a literary document as well as an anthropological source. She provides extensive explanatory footnotes for the reader, thus enabling Mountain Wolf Woman to tell her own story as free from intrusion as possible. Nancy Lurie focuses on the role of the Winnebago woman and compares Mountain Wolf Woman with her brother Crashing Thunder:

> Mountain Wolf Woman's autobiography is a predictable reflection of greater self-confidence enjoyed by women in comparison to men in a culture undergoing rapid and destructive changes. As was true of many American Indian groups, the roles of wife, mother, and homemaker for which the Winnebago girl was prepared could be fulfilled in adulthood despite the vagaries of acculturation. . . . Winnebago boys were prepared for traditional roles as warriors, hunters and shamans long after these roles stood little chance of effective fulfillment. (p. 100)

Just as Mountain Wolf Woman adapted, Sanapia adjusted to Christianity and peyotism, while maintaining the traditional patterns of Comanche culture.

Her purpose is clear: to pass down necessary information to the next eagle doctor. Ironically, despite the almost seventy-year span since the first recorded women's autobiographies, Jones comments, "Women occupied an inferior position in society, though they were respected for their full share in the food quest" (p. 9). Sanapia, however, in the narrative clearly states that she considered herself equal to a male (p. 4). In this narrative the purpose again is to document a life in such a way as to illuminate a culture's history and patterns. In this regard the story is similar to those collected by the earliest ethnographers.

The most recent autobiographies differ substantially from those we have already discussed. Indian women are beginning to record their own autobiographies in English without interpreters or editors to restructure the material. Bobbi Lee, although she tells her story with the help of editors, is telling the story not to provide ethnographic material but rather to describe the oppression of her people from a political perspective. She recognizes the three responses to oppression that have characterized Indian experience of this century and that are reflected in most autobiographies. The first, the submission and integration response, led many Indian people to assimilate and adopt the dominant society's values, aspirations, and world view. Another response to oppression in this century has been through internalized violence, manifested in drug and alcohol abuse, prostitution, and physical abuse. Bobbi Lee sees a third and more positive response for her generation: self-determination, Red Power, and a spate of political movements and causes. The 1970s brought Wounded Knee, the Trail of Broken Treaties, the Longest Walk, fish-ins, and numerous other expressions of Indian power. This renewal of interest in Indian experience is reflected in the recent autobiographical works. Bobbi Lee's ancestors earlier in the century responded to oppression by submitting and integrating, by accepting an inferior status within a dominant culture. She details the violence that has often characterized Indian experience, a violence that the writers in the 1940s and 1950s sought to explain away as a result of too much "firewater." She recognizes finally the role of contemporary Indian women within a society still operating according to traditional values:

> Most of the militants there [at a demonstration in Olympia, Washington] were women and three of them did most of the speaking. . . . They were traditionalists so there was nothing unusual about women acting as spokesmen for the group. In fact, they told me they were having trouble getting the men involved. The only man who spoke was Hank Adams, who'd been to university and wasn't traditional. (pp. 91–92)

Canadian Indian women, perhaps because of a double dilemma of identity in a country that quite arbitrarily categorizes women according to their heritage and their husbands' identity, have written a great deal about their position in contemporary society. Maria Campbell, in *Halfbreed*, states that the purpose of her book is to explain "what it is like to be a halfbreed woman in our country. I want to tell you about the joys and sorrows, the oppressing poverty, the frustrations and the dreams" (p. 8).

And Emma LaRoque, having experienced the contemporary struggle for identity, describes her dilemma and that of other women by saying that native people are faced with two choices: they may choose to remain Indian, a move that many believe associates them with the reservation, or they may choose to join the dominant society, a choice that some erroneously link with trying to "be white." Her concern is that non-Indians mistakenly regard Indian existence as frozen in time and assume that Indian culture cannot change (p. 10). Paula Gunn Allen has written of the alienation of the half-breed. She writes of biculturation today, but this biculturation is not new. The dilemma has existed from the moment of first contact.[19] When the first Indian women began allowing the stories of their lives to be committed to paper—to be edited and analyzed by those from another culture who did not understand the taboos, the rituals, or the roles—the differences in culture became apparent. For a brief period at midcentury Indian women tried to fit the mold of white society, to condemn those Indians who clung to tradition, who did not accept the new ways. But even then these women did not stray far from their heritage, recognizing always from whence they came and at the same time not being sure how to cope with that heritage.

Although the changes pointed out in this paper might indicate that the autobiographies of American Indian women have progressed in a linear manner, close examination reveals that the elements that appeared in the earliest recorded life stories continue to appear in the most recent works. Above all, the desire to preserve the heritage is apparent in nearly all materials reflecting the lives of American Indian women. Family ties continue to be important. Especially significant as a strong force in native cultures is the grandmother, both mythical and real. The grandmother is often the storyteller, the preserver of the past and the strength for the future. Her role as storyteller emphasizes the importance of the oral tradition and the significance of the stories. This emphasis on the role of the grandmother highlights another significant subject covered in most of the autobiographies: the emphasis on sex roles and division of labor. In earlier autobiographies and in earlier times the division of labor was far more explicit, and roles were defined and understood by the tribe and by individuals. Recent accounts, however, emphasize the disintegration that has resulted from the lack of defined roles. In contemporary accounts the female is responsible for holding the family together, getting a job, and raising the children. The most significant transition in the autobiographies reflects this blurring of defined sex roles. Society, political movements, and the people themselves are now questioning roles that once were defined by the tribe and by tradition.

One recent collection of profiles of Indian women, Katz's *I Am the Fire of Time*, reflects concerns that have existed in the minds of Indian women through the years. In the interviews Katz conducted with contemporary Indian women, she heard such comments as the following:

> They will have to learn to live in a society that doesn't fully accept them. . . . Indian women have always been strong. . . . They've kept families together. It is becoming necessary to be modern in order to preserve the old ways. . . . Within each of us there is a struggle between traditional values and new life-styles.[20]

The Indian woman is and has been strong within her culture. The evidence from the women themselves supports this statement. The trappers who desired Indian women, the missionaries whose religion dictated that women be regarded as inferior, the painters who saw Indian women as romantic figures—all were viewing Indian women from a decidedly ethnocentric position. The life stories of Indian women contradict these images and support the view that the role of the Indian woman was and is defined within American Indian cultures as important and essential.

Notes

1 Witt, "The Brave-Hearted Women," p. 17.
2 Mathes, "A New Look at the Role of Women in Indian Society," p. 131.
3 Ewers, "Mothers of the Mixed-Bloods."
4 Kidwell, "Bright Eyes," pp. 118, 122.
5 Fewkes, *40th Annual Report of the Bureau of American Ethnology* (Washington, D.C.: GPO, 1925), p. 1.
6 Kroeber, *The Nature of Culture*, pp. 320, 324.
7 Michelson, "Narrative of a Southern Cheyenne Woman," p. 9.
8 Michelson, *Autobiography of a Fox Indian Woman*, p. 298.
9 Pretty-Shield, p. 11.
10 *Autobiography of a Papago Woman*, pp. 3, 4.
11 Waheenee, *An Indian Girl's Story*, pp. 175–76, 189.
12 Michelson, "Narrative of an Arapaho Woman," p. 609.
13 Pretty-Shield, pp. 24, 251.
14 Young, "Out of the Past," p. 358.
15 Lurie, "Indian Women," p. 33.
16 Shaw, *A Pima Past*, p. 8.
17 Cuero, *The Autobiography of Delfina Cuero*, p. 15.
18 Winnie, *Sah-gan-de-oh*, p. 7.
19 Allen, "A Stranger in My Own Life."
20 Katz, *I Am the Fire of Time*, pp. 11, 122, 154, 162.

American Indian Women's Autobiographies

Anauta (Eskimo). *Land of Good Shadows*.
Bennett, Kay (Navajo). *Kaibah*.

Campbell, Maria (Métis). *Halfbreed.*
Carius, Helen Slwooko (Eskimo). *Sevukakmet.*
Chona, Maria (Papago). *The Autobiography of a Papago Woman.*
Colson, Elizabeth, ed. *Autobiographies of Three Pomo Women.*
Crying Wind (Kickapoo). *Crying Wind.*
Cuero, Delfina (Dieguero). *The Autobiography of Delfina Cuero.*
Hopkins, Sarah Winnemucca (Paiute). *Life among the Piutes.*
Hungry Wolf, Beverly (Blackfeet). *The Ways of My Grandmothers.*
Kegg, Maude (Ojibwe). *Gii-Ikwezensiwiyaan/When I Was a Little Girl.*
Kelley, Jane Holden. *Yaqui Women.*
Landes, Ruth. *The Ojibwa Woman.*
Lee, Bobbi (Métis). *Bobbi Lee.*
Little Bear, Mary (Cheyenne). *Dance around the Sun.*
Lone Dog, Louise (Mohawk-Delaware). *Strange Journey.*
Lowry, Annie (Paiute). *Karnee.*
Martinez, Maria (San Ildefonso). *The Story of an American Indian.*
Michelson, Truman. *The Autobiography of a Fox Indian Woman.*
———. "Narrative of an Arapaho Woman."
———. "The Narrative of a Southern Cheyenne Woman."
Mountain Wolf Woman (Winnebago). *Mountain Wolf Woman.*
Nuñez, Bonita [Wa Wa Calachaw] (Luiseno). *Spirit Woman.*
Pitseolak (Eskimo). *Pitseolak.*
Pretty-Shield (Crow). *Pretty-Shield.*
Qoyawayma, Polingaysi [Elizabeth O. White] (Hopi). *No Turning Back.*
Sanapia (Comanche). *Sanapia.*
Sekaquaptewa, Helen (Hopi). *Me and Mine.*
Shaw, Anna Moore (Pima). *A Pima Past.*
Silko, Leslie Marmon (Laguna). *Storyteller.*
Stewart, Irene (Navajo). *A Voice in Her Tribe.*
Waheenee [Buffalo-Bird Woman] (Hidatsa). *An Indian Girl's Story.*
Winnie, Lucille (Seneca-Cayuga). *Sah-gan-de-oh.*
Young, Lucy (Wailaki). "Out of the Past."
Zitkala-Sa [Gertrude Bonnin] (Sioux). "Impressions of an Indian Childhood."
———. "An Indian Teacher among Indians."
———. "The Schooldays of an Indian Girl."
———. "Why I Am a Pagan."

Additional Resources on American Indian Women

Anderson, Lynn. *Medicine Woman.*
Brand, Johanna. *The Life and Death of Anna Mae Aquash.*
Braudy, Susan. "'We Will Remember' Survival School."
Brown, Judith K. "Economic Organization and the Power of Women among the Iroquois."
Cameron, Anne. *Daughters of Copper Woman.*

Christensen, Rosemary A. "Indian Women."
Cruikshank, Julie. "Native Women in the North."
Ewers, John C. "Deadlier than the Male."
Fisher, Dexter, ed. *The Third Woman.*
Foreman, Carolyn Thomas. *Indian Women Chiefs.*
Foster, Mrs. W. Garland. *The Mohawk Princess.*
Green, Rayna. "The Pocahontas Perplex."
Gridley, Marion E. *American Indian Women.*
Hammond, Dorothy, and Alta Jablow. *Women.*
Heizer, Robert, and Albert B. Elsasser. *Original Accounts of the Lone Women of San Nicholas Island.*
Jacobs, Sue-Ellen. *Women in Perspective.*
Jahner, Elaine. "A Laddered Rain-Bearing Rug"; "Woman among the Wolves."
Johnston, Verna Patronella. *I Am Nokomis, Too.*
Jones, Louis Thomas. "Eloquent Indian Women." In *Aboriginal American Oratory.*
Kidwell, Clara Sue. "The Power of Women in Three American Indian Societies."
LaRoque, Emma. *Defeathering the Indian.*
Lewis, Claudia. *Indian Families of the Northwest Coast.*
Lurie, Nancy Oestreich. "Indian Women."
Marriott, Alice. *Maria, the Potter of San Ildefonso.*
Mathes, Valerie Shirer. "American Indian Women and the Catholic Church."
Mathur, Mary E. Fleming. "Who Cares That a Woman's Work Is Never Done . . . ?"
Medicine, Bea (Sioux). "Role and Function of Indian Women."
Metoyer, Cheryl A. "The Native American Woman."
Miller, Dorothy I. "Native American Women."
Niethammer, Carolyn. *Daughters of the Earth.*
O'Meara, Walter. *Daughters of the Country.*
Smithson, Carma Lee. *The Havasupai Woman.*
Spindler, Louis S. "Menomini Women and Culture Change."
Terrell, John Upton, and Donna M. Terrell. *Indian Women of the Western Morning.*
United States Department of Labor. *Native American Women and Equal Opportunity.*
Waltrip, Lela, and Rufus Waltrip. *Indian Women.*
Witt, Shirley Hill. "Native Women Today."
Women of All Red Nations.

Grandmother Spider's Lifeline

Susan J. Scarberry

Threading her way through space, Grandmother Spider spins her thoughts into existence. According to many origin stories, she first made creatures appear on earth and light appear in the sky, and even now she looks after her children when their well-being is threatened. In old and new stories of American Indians, Grandmother Spider's web is an expression of her love for the people, binding various life forms together. Her web is a woven structure suspended between earth and sky, at once real and symbolic of the coherence of all experience.

Whereas most non-Indian cultures have stressed the negative power of Spider Woman, seeing the web as a net or weapon that she uses to entrap unwary men and her loom as a symbol of fate and death, many Indian cultures have stressed her positive life-creating power, recognizing that she uses her powers to protect her people. In the dual role of creator and protective deity, Grandmother Spider or Thought-Woman serves as an archetype for poets and storytellers.

For Grandmother Spider, thought and action are one. All her thoughts are realized, affirming the creative power of the word. Being maternal and responsible, she never abandons her creations; usually she saves those in distress. After the example of Grandmother Spider who spins and weaves the threads of life, American Indian poets weave verbal images into verse for the good of their people. In a sense, Grandmother Spider provides the inspiration for this task.

Contemporary American Indian poets such as Paula Gunn Allen, Leslie Silko, Simon Ortiz, and Joseph Bruchac incorporate traditional mythic stories about Grandmother Spider into their poetry and fiction, as they imagine new adventures for her. In this way her existence as a potent supernatural being is honored and the people remain blessed. Grandmother Spider's belly-spun lifeline connects her children to her now as always.

Like most powerful deities, Grandmother Spider has multiple identities, takes on many forms, and has various names. This ancient earth deity, the original earth mother, is widely known throughout the Southwest as Spider Woman. To the Navajo she is Na'ashjé'ii 'Asdzáán; to the Hopi she is

Kokyanwuhti; and to the Keres she is Tse Che Nako, Thought-Woman. Elsewhere she is known, too, as among the Kiowa and Cherokee, even though she does not figure in all native tribal cosmogonies. Those who know her, however, affectionately call her Grandmother Spider. This tiny creature is actually an aspect of the supreme intelligence of the universe. Some societies see Spider Woman as a cocreator. The Hopi, for instance, say that she assisted Taiowa and Sótuknang by creating beings on earth. The Keres, however, say that she herself is the highest deity from whom all else has emanated.

One can think of Grandmother Spider as the consummate conceptual artist and of her creation of the earthworks as her finest live "performance." Understanding art as thought or idea, "the piece" becomes dramatically realized, even as she conceives of it. For Grandmother Spider, like the contemporary poets, has long been interested in the process of composition. Because she is aware of the aesthetic dimension of the experience, she has carefully designed the lighting, the sounds, and the creatures that move across the landscape. There is no acting in this real situation; Grandmother Spider is merely performing a necessary task with her usual imaginative flair and impeccable good taste. In the Hopi story, when she raises the woven blanket of creative wisdom, over which she has sung the creation song, the Twins underneath draw breath to praise her work and to participate in the spectacle of new life—life that is constantly being recreated.[1]

Of course, Grandmother Spider thinks of everything. She knows that the cosmos needs light, since light is indispensable to life. She is responsible for the distribution of light and darkness in the world. Traveling upward from her home in the underworld, she moves toward the light. Cherokee creation stories say that Grandmother Spider is a "sun-catcher" or bringer of light who ventures east to fetch a tiny bit of the sun to carry homeward, along a thread.[2] Through this benevolent act she helps the crops grow and keeps the animals from bumping into one another. The gift of light provides consciousness, nourishment, and warmth.

Spider Woman often gives of herself in other ways, too. Having the power to alter events, she frequently intervenes in human affairs. If the people are threatened, she can rescue those in danger. Spider Woman also protects the people in more subtle ways. As a keeper of sacred traditional knowledge, she is a powerful transmitter of culture. By teaching the young their traditions, she practices "preventive medicine." Through her good advice and knowledge of the old ways, she enables the people to help themselves. They respect her age because it testifies that she knows the secrets of survival. Spider Woman teaches the young how to hunt and how to sing, equally valuable survival skills. She teaches them how to live a full life.

The people emulate the original creative act in many ways, especially through playing with language and working with basic art forms. Grandmother Spider gave the people the skills of weaving, pottery, and basketry, in order that they might delight in these activities and survive more easily. Pots and baskets, vessels roughly resembling the shape of female parts, have long been associated with the feminine. Generally, pottery and weaving have been women's arts. The Cherokee say that Spider Woman fashioned a little clay bowl to carry the sun fragment in, to bring light home for the people:

> And from then on pottery making became woman's work, and all pottery must be dried slowly in the shade before it is put in the heat of the firing oven, just as Grandmother Spider's bowl dried in her hand, slowly, in the darkness, as she travelled towards the land of the sun.[3]

This explanation of the coming of light and the origin of pottery reveals that imagination is a survival tool. Once Grandmother Spider has done things in a certain way, human beings continuously create beautiful useful objects, inspired by her love of design. Just as she has given the arts to her people as an expression of maternal love, so too have the people learned to share their talents with one another. Weaving knits the people together.

In its most rudimentary sense, weaving brings something into being. Weaving, molding, speaking, and singing are the essential processes of creation. To weave is to interlace, to form a fabric or design, a story or a poem. To weave is to construct in the mind or the imagination. No wonder then that weaving has always been, in most cultures, the central metaphor for creation and for the activity of life itself. Weaving signifies motion and order, and it is only fitting that the great web-weaver, Spider Woman, is the highest creative deity. Moving in and out, from side to side, she throws the shuttle in order to weave the world. The fabric or web is the "child" of the mother weaver. The image of a child encased in a web is an image of a child protected and blessed.

Ordinarily weaving goddesses in Indo-European mythology are said to weave the web of life and spin the threads of fate. The Nordic Norns, among others, have traditionally decided the destinies of men and women. But in American Indian cultures Grandmother Spider is said to weave the web of life and spin the threads of the old ways, which, in turn, bear upon the new ways. Although the spider by its spinning and killing symbolizes the alternation of the forces of creation and destruction on which life depends, the web itself represents wholeness, balance, and beauty. The web in its circularity and durability suggests the continuity of a living tradition.

Industrious Spider Woman weaves meticulously, patterning her fabric after the master plan in her mind. Her web is susceptible to subtle vibrations, finely tuned into the nuances of her thought. The close connection between weaving and thinking is especially apparent in Navajo rug workmanship. As Noël Bennett says about the Navajo in *The Weaver's Pathway*, "The weaver's thoughts and ideas become woven into the fabric and form the pattern" (p. 34). Simon Ortiz develops his poem "Two Women" in terms of parallel images of a Navajo woman and Grandmother Spider. The poem begins, "She is a Navajo woman sitting at her loom." The second stanza reads, "Quickly, Grandmother, / the Spider spins, / quick flips and turns, / the colors."[4] These women are reflections of each other.

Weaving, basketry, and string games are parallel activities. String figures can become very complex and difficult to execute. During an interview with a Navajo family, folklorist Barre Toelken learns that the string figure designs come from Spider Woman. A daughter says, "The Spider Woman taught us all these designs as a way of helping us think. You learn to think when you make these. And she taught us about weaving, too." A son adds, "If you can think well, you won't get into trouble or get lost."[5] Spider Woman can always help you find your way home, or your way out of a difficult situation. Threads cross, like paths, but you can easily untangle them or differentiate them from one another.

Spiders have a good sense of direction and adapt remarkably well. They are survivors, possessing the ability to regenerate damaged legs and spinnerets. Some can balloon or sail along on their own draglines for thousands of feet. The *Nephila clavipes* spider spins a silk that is the "strongest natural fiber known."[6] If damaged, a spiderweb shudders but will usually hold, with one strand dangling. A daddy longlegs will deliberately shake his web, if he is frightened; this action renders him and the web invisible. In many old stories Grandmother Spider disappears when those around her least expect it. Perhaps this trick explains why the spider has long been thought of as a weaver of illusions.

Poets, like spiders, spin strong lines. They are interested in maintaining vital connections. To an extent all artistic impulses are patterned after those of Spider Woman, but the poet's interest in shaping language most closely coincides with Grandmother Spider's own concerns. All poems could be said to exist because of her, but some poems expressly owe their existence to her. Numerous contemporary Indian poets have drawn on traditional oral tales about her, in an effort to make a new poetic statement about the nature of the relationship that she maintains with the people. Some poets mix materials, giving us a composite portrait of Spider Woman as we know her from several traditions and through the poets' own special perceptions of her. The weaving motif, which emphasizes relationship, has probably been a poetic metaphor since time immemorial.

Weaving imagery is common in contemporary American Indian prose, too. Leslie Silko's short story "Lullaby," for example, opens with these words: "The sun had gone down, but the snow in the wind gave off its own light. It comes in thick tufts like new wool—washed before the weave spins it."[7] The setting draws reference to the world of Grandmother Spider. Words like "sun," "light," "wool," "weaver," and "spins" remind us of the old stories. Ayah, an old Navajo woman, remembers her childhood: "While she combed the wool, her grandma sat beside her, spinning a silvery strand of yarn around the cedar spindle." The grandmother spins, the mother weaves, and the little girl cleans the wool. Generations of women carry on the legacy they have received from Grandmother Spider. The "silvery strand of yarn" that grandma spins in this story may be the same magnificent silk dragline that Spider Woman spins. The liquid spittle that she spurts out dries instantly, full of magic power.

One of Grandmother Spider's greatest gifts to the people is clothing. Woven fabric fashioned into clothes protects the people by keeping them warm and reminds them that she, the giver, is with them all the time. Simon Ortiz in "To Insure Survival," written for his newborn daughter Rainy Dawn, says:

> Grandmother Spider speaks
> laughter and growing
> and weaving things
> and threading them
> together to make life
> to wear;
> all these, all these.[8]

Linda Hogan, writing in *Shantih*, describes Spider people as "weaving dog hair into cloth, / webbing ladders together to climb to the air / tying their life to the wind."[9] Here the images reinforce the sky-earth connection that Spider Woman maintains.

The web symbol, suggesting a knitting of kinship and tradition and a point of connection between spiritual and mundane realities, is usually positive in Indian poetry, as we have seen. An orb web represents the interdependent structure of life patterns balanced in a dynamic whole. In "A Poem for Diane Wakowski," Ray Young Bear chastizes her for her lack of perception of this cosmic architecture and for her bloodlessness: "your blood does not flow, not even a little. / the spinning of fathers is useless— / you weave no patterns, not even a word."[10] According to Young Bear, she lacks the sensitivity and skill that any good poet should possess. If she weaves at all, she probably weaves cobweb, signifying the fragmentation and messiness of her view of the world. The image of a well-ordered web remains positive but elusive.

Usually the image of a cobweb is negative, indicating confusion, madness, or death. In "Pure Country" Carter Revard graphically describes the eerie beauty of black widows' webs down in an outhouse hole.[11] In "Women's Day 1975," Paula Gunn Allen talks of cobweb air that "hangs brown and sullen."[12] And Leslie Silko in *Ceremony* tells us that Tayo occasionally slipped into "the black gauzy web where he could rest in silence," a dangerous retreat into the realm of death (p. 175).

The most prevalent image of the spiderweb, the orb web, is an orderly arrangement of threads radiating out from a central hub and linked to one another in a spiral. Just as there is good power in a circle, so is there power in a web of this sort. In "Affirmation" Allen says: "The power of spider thoughts / so small, / mount, thread by thread."[13] In *Ceremony* Silko describes the weather near Mount Taylor: "The wind came up from the west, smelling cool like wet clay. Then he could see the rain. It was spinning out of the thunderclouds like gray spider webs and tangling against the foothills of the mountain" (p. 100). Here the sky images remind us of the sky deity Grandmother Spider who is pleasing the people, the plants, and the animals by wetting down the land.

To retain Grandmother Spider's goodwill, the people must show her respect. They must love her and offer her gifts, as she has done for them. These are the basic conditions of the relationship. Ortiz, in a retelling of a very old story, says that even Coyote describes Grandmother Spider as "a wonderful helpful person."[14] The narrator in *Ceremony* tells us that "She waited in certain locations for people to come to her for help" and that long ago she helped Sun Man recapture the stormclouds from the Gambler (p. 98). For all of these deeds and many more, the people owe Grandmother Spider gratitude. Unfortunately though, some neglect her, causing an imbalance in the great scheme of things. Joseph Bruchac's poem "The Grandmother Came Down to Visit Us" treats this problem. He describes an incident during a party:

> When the spider dropped down from the ceiling
> Only Phil and I moved to save it
> in a room full of people fearing
> the shadow-weaver, the oldest gift giver.[15]

The last stanza begins, "The grandmother came down / to visit us and they all want to hurt her." People have fallen away from their original relationship with Grandmother Spider. Things are in a bad way when there's no love, no spirit of reciprocity. The people's relationship with Spider Woman is a good indication of the healthiness of the culture.

Even when others have neglected Grandmother Spider, the poets have not. They see themselves in relation to her, as a direct reflection of her. Silko in the beginning of *Ceremony* shares an intimacy with her. The narrator says of Thought-Woman, "I'm telling you the story / she is thinking" (p. 1). The novel, a prodigious creation itself, begins with the Laguna creation account, which establishes the foundation of truth for the culture. Silko pays her respects by weaving her own stories. Liz Sohappy Bahe, too, speaks of the connection between women as maintained by the weaving/storytelling tradition in "Talking Designs."[16] We learn of the old lady weaver who works the life story of the people into her cloth, and in "Grandmother Sleeps" we learn that the poet, too, will weave and bead after her, in her manner, with her tools.

"Self-Portrait" by Judith Ivaloo Volborth extends the comparison between the poet and Spider Woman:

> Crooked Old Woman
> sits, composes shadows,
> weaves tapestries
> of dust and cobwebs,
> sings to the lines
> in her face.[17]

The identity of the poet and that of the original creator merge. This old woman is still actively composing poetry of her own flesh.

The special Native American issue of *Shantih* contains a prose work by Paula Gunn Allen entitled "Ephanie." Grandmother Spider appears in the narrative, revealing the author's absorption with this figure. Ephanie says, "The way back is the self-extruded thread of beckoning Grandmother Spider, she who is the guardian of my life, that takes me into mind, memory: not betrayed that beckoning."[18] Grandmother pulls her children back when the time is right. Allen's most eloquent poem about the poet's relation to Spider Woman is simply entitled "Grandmother":

> Out of her own body she pushed
> silver thread, light, air
> and carried it carefully on the dark, flying
> where nothing moved.
>
> Out of her body she extruded
> shining wire, life, and wove the light
> on the void.
>
> From beyond time,
> beyond oak trees and bright clear water flow,
> she was given the work of weaving the strands
> of her body, her pain, her vision
> into creation, and the gift of having created,
> to disappear.
>
> After her,
> the women and the men weave blankets into tales
>   of life,
> memories of light and ladders,
> infinity-eyes, and rain.
> After her I sit on my laddered rain-bearing rug
> and mend the tear with string.[19]

"After her," the archetype of creation, the poet works. After the visionary— the weaver—the poet mends. The poet repairs the shattered patterns, the ragged web, by weaving words that bind all of Grandmother Spider's children together. James Welch's poem "Snow Country Weavers" resonates with yet another image of this shared reality:

> I saw your spiders weaving threads
> to bandage up the day. And more,
> those webs were filled with words
> that tumbled meaning into wind.[20]

Weaving can be a metaphor for healing.

Through experimentation with language, whether oral or written, the oral tradition is enriched and expanded. Many other American Indian writers such as Maurice Kenny, Geary Hobson, and Carol Lee Sanchez have threaded spider images through their poems, giving a new vitality to the old stories. People now have just that many more stories to tell. Grandmother Spider's own story is a story about shaping thoughts, feelings, and language, about articulating experience and truth. The care she has taken in her craft and with her people continues to influence the poets' perceptions of the world. By extending the possibilities for creative thought, she suggests that meaningful connections already exist; we just have to see which way the warp runs. The shimmering lifeline holds.

Notes

1 Waters and Fredericks, *Book of the Hopi*, p. 4.
2 Marriott and Rachlin, *American Indian Mythology*, p. 47.
3 Marriott and Rachlin, p. 50.
4 S. Ortiz, *Going for the Rain*, p. 21.
5 Toelken, *The Dynamics of Folklore*, p. 95.
6 Walther, *A Spider Might*, p. 39.
7 In *Southwest*, ed. Kopp and Kopp, p. 242.
8 Ortiz, *Going for the Rain*, pp. 10–11.
9 *Shantih*, 4, No. 2 (1979), 28.
10 Niatum, ed., *Carriers of the Dream Wheel*, p. 297.
11 *Shantih*, 4, No. 2 (1979), 34.
12 Allen, *Coyote's Daylight Trip*, p. 22.
13 Allen, *Coyote*, p. 20.
14 S. Ortiz, *A Good Journey*, p. 41.
15 Niatum, *Carriers*, p. 31.
16 Niatum, *Carriers*, p. 10.
17 *Shantih*, 4, No. 2 (1979), 38.
18 *Shantih*, 4, No. 2 (1979), 44.
19 Allen, *Coyote*, p. 50.
20 Welch, *Riding the Earthboy 40*, p. 47.

Ain't Seen You Since: Dissent among Female Relatives in American Indian Women's Poetry

Patricia Clark Smith

I

Until very recently, I think it was relatively easy for a casual reader to tell if a poem was American Indian in origin, whether the poem was traditional or contemporary, and even if the author's name was something sneaky like Johnson instead of Running Wolf.* A reader could almost certainly identify such a poem by its subject matter, and often by its diction and sound as well. A quick flip through most anthologies of American Indian poetry compiled before ten or more years ago will prove the point.[1]

The American Indian poet—usually presumed to be a male, a "brave," unless the song in question happened to deal with corn grinding or child soothing—was most given to speaking of nature or praising the gods or urging them to do something, like bring rain, or simply desiring them to continue in their cycles of existence. The poet might—rather touchingly, considering what we know in retrospect of his romantic destiny to fade away—boast of the prowess of himself and his people in hunting and warfare, of the beauty of his woman, or of his whole way of being. Sometimes he gave voice to sorrow over death or a reluctant lover, but his stance was almost always nobly resigned. He was never crabby or depressed about the vagaries of human life. Even granted that there was and is a genuine American Indian cultural tendency away from what A. Grove Day calls "the soul cry of the impassioned individualist," it does seem especially remarkable, and not at all in accord with the '49ing spirit of his present-day descendants, that the poet's hard times never seemed to arouse in him either wit or satire.[2] If we rely on most of the anthologies and Bureau of American Ethnology (BAE) collections, we will conclude that the American Indian poet's emotional world is always either joyous or solemn. For all we know from what has come down to us through the work of anthropologists and translators, the

Indian did not in any form of literature save oratory—and, later, autobiography—concern himself with contemporary conditions of soldiers and forts, boarding schools and treaties, trading posts and removals.

As far as form is concerned, if we are to believe English translations and "renditions" of the songs, we must assume that American Indian poets of all tribes were inclined to a quaint archaic diction sprinkled with *Lo!*'s and *thou*'s and awkwardly inverted sentence order, as in this Omaha ritual chant for the sick:

> Aged one, eçka
>
> He! The small grasses grow about thee, eçka,
> Thou sittest as though making of them thy dwelling place, eçka,
> He! Verily thou sittest as though covered with the
>   droppings of birds. . . . [3]

Most popular poetry in English was a long time catching up with Wordsworth's plea for "language really used by men," but the unusually archaic poetic language assigned to the American Indian poet in translation seems in keeping with the.fading-into-the-twilight quality of the entire culture. Finally, the poems, as they appear in the old collections, are marked by a strongly rhythmical and repetitive character, not because a recorder or editor made a concerted attempt to reproduce the intricacies of a given rhythm, the particular pattern made by a given phrase repeated with slight variations, but because *any* use of rhythm or repetition served to give the effect of primitiveness, for that is what all primitive peoples do with their language—speak simply and carry a big drumstick.

I have been mocking the worst Anglo versions of traditional American Indian poetry, and of course I have exaggerated at the expense of some fine early scholars who did what they could and did some things well and with great sympathy for another culture and an alien language. I apologize to their bones. But certainly those early collectors missed a great deal. Their expectations influenced what they asked to hear, what they chose to record, and especially how they rendered what they heard into English. The astounding thing to me is how many characteristics of the old BAE collections, and how many more marks of the sentimental "renditions" fashioned from them, appear in the sort of American Indian poetry that has until very recently been most widely anthologized. The kind of poetry I am speaking of, often written in workshops at schools like the Institute of American Indian Arts in Sante Fe, is very close in its technique and tone to many nineteenth- and early twentieth-century versions of Plains love songs and Woodlands laments. It is strongly biased toward American Indian themes, and it is conventional, as opposed to traditional; that is, cradleboards and dances and spirits of one stripe or another are rife, but if there is, say, a dance, that dance seems to have little connection with the Gallup ceremonial or the powwows and '49s, or even with a dance occurring in its natural setting and sequence at an active pueblo. The poet appears to have written the work, not after experiencing something firsthand or reaching back into personal or family memory, but rather after being tied down in a dark room with a headset strapped on and forced to listen to tape after tape of the works of Natalie Curtis and Alice Corbin Henderson. A friend calls such works "eagle feather poetry." Perhaps these poems come about because teachers find it difficult not to voice, aloud or silently, expectations of what an "Indian poem"—or a fourth grade poem or a Chicano poem, for that matter—should be about. But I am not sure this is necessarily the cause, any more than I know why my freshmen on the University of New Mexico campus, who are certainly not readers of scholarly journals, often write critical prose that reads like a parody of the dreariest paragraph in *Dissertation Abstracts*. Perhaps all beginning poets find it difficult not to sense the world's expectations of what their poems should be about. In any case, my point is that for the general public not in touch with certain small presses, American Indian poetry has probably meant, if it meant anything, something like this:

> Thus it was I heard the feet beat—
> My ear down,
> On the ground—
> Yea, I put my lips to thee and drank song,
> My mother,
> O, ho!

or this Sigmund Rombergian lyric:

> August is laughing across the sky
> Laughing while paddle, canoe and I,
> Drift, drift,
> Where the hills uplift
> On either side of the current swift.
>
> . . . .
>
> Dip, dip,
> While the waters flip
> In foam as over their breast we slip.

or these contemporary poems:

> Sun dancers
> Whirling, twirling madly—
> Feet churning Mother Earth
> Until clouds weep.
>
> An eagle wings gracefully
>   through the sky.
> On the earth I stand
>   and watch.
> My heart flies with it.[4]

Only during the last ten years or so, largely through the work of a few editors and a few small presses, has poetry appeared that is both genuinely American Indian and genuinely fresh contemporary poetry.[5] This is not to say that American Indians have not written such poetry before now; they have, but their work has seldom seen print. The latest and most inclusive source of good American Indian poetry is Geary Hobson's *The Remembered Earth*, and, as Hobson remarks in his introduction, many recent poems share subjects with the larger culture, and are not exclusively devoted to American Indian themes (pp. 9–10). Of course, many poems do deal freshly with traditional culture, but a great number concern themselves with contemporary life on and off the reservation; in these works one finds bars and anthropologists, '49s and soybean fields, and, as the title of a book by one poet, nila north-Sun, suggests, Diet Pepsi and Nacho cheese. Moreover, there are poems on themes important to anyone living in America these last years— Vietnam, outer space—and themes that have always been important to people in all places and circumstances—youth and age, love and death, nature and loneliness.

The American Indian poet, then, is no longer writing inside a box fashioned of birchbark or woven willow. But, as Hobson also suggests, even if a poet shares themes and techniques with other poets, "emphases may differ." I think we have come to a time when it is both possible and compelling to ask whether there is something that might be called a contemporary American Indian "way" of writing poetry—if, despite their undisputed citizenship in the world at large, these American Indian poets do share something. I want to talk about a relatively narrow category—poems by contemporary American Indian women about female relatives—to see what these poets are saying, how they say things, whether these poets, different as they are, have anything special in common, and whether they differ in any marked way from Anglo women poets also writing about mothers and daughters and grandmothers.

II

I do not pretend to be an expert on the emotional landscapes of either Anglo or American Indian women, and one needs to be especially wary of generalizations, given the great differences not only among American Indian tribal cultures but among the wide variety of Anglo groups as well. Instead of starting with pronouncements about the nature of relations between female relatives in any group, I prefer to work with the poetry itself. I want to begin with a brief, nonstatistical survey of an anthology convenient to the purpose—Lyn Lifshin's *Tangled Vines: A Collection of Mother and Daughter Poems*. Save for the works of a few black writers like Lucille Clifton and

Nikki Giovani, Lifshin's selection presents the works of contemporary white American poets and is, to my mind, an excellent representative collection of poetry on the subject of mothers and daughters.

Browsing through these poems, one is of course aware of the diversity of what the poets choose to emphasize about mother-daughter-grandmother-aunt relations, and one also notices the wide variety of tone and technique. But if one happens to have read a good deal of American Indian women's poetry on the same subject, one is also likely to notice certain things these Anglo poems share that are simply not to be found in American Indian women's writing. Most strikingly, a surprising number of the Anglo poems in Lifshin's anthology—a good half—center on a woman seeing a woman relative as an alarming, alien creature. I would like to discuss this characteristic Anglo imagery at length and to ask what American Indian women poets use in place of such imagery.

In the Anglo poetry, the image of the woman relative as alien can range all the way from seeing the other woman as suddenly unfamiliar in some way to seeing her as a monster. The alien creature, be she daughter or mother, is at best disquieting, at worst genuinely life-threatening, in her estrangement. Mothers may see their daughters as usurping, draining, devouring strangers who have somehow invaded their lives; daughters see mothers as ogres out to mold, reshape, and imprison them and thwart their growth. A few passages from these Anglo poems will provide examples of the kind of imagery I am speaking of. Here are mothers on the subject of daughters:

> Her feet
> are bare. I hear her breathe
> where I can't get in. If I
> break through to her, she will
> drive nails into my tongue. . . .
>> (Shirley Kaufman,
>> "Mothers and Daughters,"
>> p. 12)

> My daughter has no teeth. Her mouth is wide.
> It utters such dark sounds, it cannot be good. . . .
>> (Sylvia Plath, "Three Women," p. 2)

> I think, although I fear to know for certain,
> that she becomes a cat at night.
> Just yesterday, I saw tiger shadows
> on the wall of her room. . . .
>> (Judith Minty,
>> "Waiting for the Transformation," p. 8)

And daughters on mothers:

> Like small crazed animals
> we leaped before her
> knowing there was no escape
>
> She had to consume us utterly
> over and over again
> and now at last   .
> we are her angels
> burned so crisp
> we crumble when we try to touch
>   (Judith Hemschemeyer,
>   "The Survivors," pp. 60–61)
>
> My mother
> the magician
> can make snakes appear in her hand.
> My ovaries appear in her hand,
> black as figs and
> wrinkled. as fingers on washday. . . .
>   (Sharon Olds, "Tricks," p. 74)
>
> she turned to stone
> and her curly hair to snakes
> trying to escape her children. . . .
>   (Kathleen Spivak,
>   "Daughterly," p. 53)
>
> I had about as much chance, mother,
> as the carp who thrashed
> in your bathtub on Friday,
> swimming helplessly back and forth
> in small hard pool you made for me. . . .
>   (L. L. Zeiger, "The Fish," p. 59)

From wider reading, I feel safe in saying that the profusion of imagery in these examples does not simply reflect a bias on the part of this particular anthologist. In my culture, or at least among the woman poets of my culture, it does seem common for daughter to regard mother, mother to regard daughter, as some sort of stranger—unreachable, unknowable, and threatening to her identity. Whether unknowingly or by intent, whether by her actions or by her mere presence, the mother inspires fear and wonder. Perhaps there is among us an arrested fixation on the stage of our development when, as Nancy Friday puts it in her popular book on mothers and daughters, we realized with amazement and rage that "we could not control Mother, that she was *not* us, that she could go away and leave us," or that she could do things to us that showed us plainly that our desires and hers were not in harmony.[6] In the works of mothers writing about daughters, the moment that takes great hold on our imaginations seems to be the time when a woman perceives that the life she has borne, once part of her own body, is now a separate and quite willful entity. (It may be that this moment makes mothers more uneasy if the child is a daughter; perhaps women *expect* men, and hence a manchild, to be different.)

The image of mother or daughter as *other* is central to a good many Anglo women's poems that are positive in their tone; because such imagery is used does not mean that the poem is not about loving. Often, the climax of a poem is a resolution of the sense of otherness. Daughter or mother finally acknowledges the humanity or mortality of the other woman; accepts her as simply a person rather than as a mythical figure of frightening, unpredictable power; begins to see human connections and resemblances between herself and the other woman; or comes to some adult and freeing perception about the nature of mother-daughter alienation:

> Dear clown, dear savage daughter,
> So different from me and yet
> So much like me, I know
> sharpening your claws on me
> is how you begin to grow.
> > (Patricia Goedicke,
> > "Circus Song," p. 18)

> I have made hot milk
> & kissed you where you are.
> I have cursed my curses.
> I have cleared the air.
> & now I sit here writing,
> breathing you.
> > (Erica Jong,
> > "Mother," p. 49)

The image of a woman relative as an alien being simply does not appear in American Indian women's poetry. I don't mean to say that dissent between women is absent from that poetry; it is not, although its occurrence is far rarer than in mainstream poetry. But when an American Indian woman poet speaks of separation between female relatives, she does not depict it as a mythologized personal struggle between two individual women. What separates the two is not a quest on the part of one or both for power or ascendancy, nor is it a sense that the antagonist is somehow of another order of being altogether. Instead, American Indian women poets see personal discord between women as a matter of cultural alienation.[7] A female relative—a mother, for example—may seem strange, not because she is a Medusa or a harpy or a killer of her hapless carp-child, but because the daughter literally cannot speak to her, since the mother's language and ways are literally, not just metaphorically, different from the ways of the daughter. Language, custom, and geographical environment, rather than psychological barriers, effect the separation between the generations.

One might raise the possibility that American Indian women are not psychologically sophisticated enough, or poetically honest enough, to deal strongly and directly with conflict between women relatives in their poems. But surely this is not so; we are talking about poets who display great honesty and sophistication in writing about other matters, and it seems unlikely that relationships among women would be the single subject they would all choose to sentimentalize, to sidestep. It seems far more likely that for all the diversity of American Indian tribal backgrounds and circumstances, there is something here that might be called a genuine cultural tendency, a tendency to see conflict between women as not totally a personal matter but, rather, as part of a larger whole, as a sign that one of the pair has lost touch not with just a single individual but with a complex web of relationships and reciprocities. The tendency to see family conflict as inevitable, natural, even healthy and worthy of being encouraged in some measure is a mark of Anglo culture. We may regret certain things; for instance, we may speculate, as Friday does, that a greater sexual honesty between mothers and daughters might ease our estrangement from one another.[8] Nonetheless, we accept separation, rebelliousness, alienation between the generations of women as the not entirely regrettable norm. This is not at all the sense of family one finds in American Indian women's poetry.

Of all American Indian women poets, Marnie Walsh (Dakota) and nila northSun (Shoshone-Chippewa) are probably the sharpest depictors of the breakdown of family. Both write in a tragicomic tone, often in first-person narratives flatly presented in a colloquial reservation English that rings wonderfully true. Their comic sense is both bitter and wise; as Carter Revard remarks, Walsh tells these grim stories of reservation life in Coyote's voice, a Trickster's and survivor's voice.[9] To tell stories of separation and fallings away with such wit and perspective is to survive, to go on, to surmount pain.

When Walsh and northSun speak of the separation between women relatives, they refer to a *cultural* separation, precisely the kind of gap that exists, as northSun puts it in the title of one of her poems, between "the way and the way things are."[10] Walsh's "Bessie Dreaming Bear: Rosebud, So. Dak. 1960" pares the story about mothers and daughters down to its barest bones:

> we all went to town one day
> went to a store
> bought you new shoes
> red high heels
>
> ain't seen you since[11]

northSun's stories, too, have to do with separations brought about in large part by the lure of a larger culture that offers plastic shoes and Diet Pepsi. In an entire cycle of poems, she describes with greater leisure than Walsh the gaps and connections between a number of women in a single family.[12] The alienation in these poems happens not all in a moment, after one Saturday morning purchase at Woolco, but over three, perhaps even six, generations. Most poems in the group treat with affection, humor, and poignancy the granddaughter-speaker's maternal grandmother, "gramma." The speaker's parents and siblings, who come into the poems very little, are obviously West Coast urban; we learn that gramma's children have married Anglos and moved away. But, for the speaker, to return to gramma's house on the Paiute-Shoshone reservation is to return to the center of something, if not precisely the center of her own being. There, "the way" at least temporarily envelopes her, even if she is always slightly an outsider at heart; her cousin, not the speaker, can talk Indian and must translate when gramma isn't in the mood to speak English or feels the need to "Say indian words / when the english ones embarrassed her / quithup for shit / moobee-ship for snot" (p. 11).

The grandmother's world is touched by the larger culture in that those around her drink Kool-Aid, smoke Salems, and watch Lawrence Welk. But these are small encroachments. This gramma still prefers to "talk Indian." Her ancestors built brush shelters in summer; she moves her bed outside under the shade of the trees during the high heat. Spirits, at least of one sort, are still real for her: the affectionate, attention-demanding ghost of grandpa plagues her at night. The social controls of tribe and family are something she has felt strongly, even if she has not always complied with them; she lives where she does because she had to move away from home after violating a marriage custom by running off with the fiancé of her sister, who, as eldest, was supposed to marry first; she respected her mother-in-law enough to bear twelve children, trying for the male child the mother-in-law had hoped for. And, above all, this gramma tells stories. northSun's poems about her early years in gramma's house abound with circular, reciprocal imagery of shared food, space, talk, activity:

> on hot summer days gramma laid
> on a bed under one of the trees
> she'd visit with my mother in the shade
> drinking kool-aid
> smoking salems
> talking indian
> we made mud pies
> dozens and dozens of mud pies
> . . . .

when evening started to come
so did the mosquitoes and
we all went into the house
grandpa would come home
                    ("what grandpa said," p. 8)

we would whisper from our beds
"gramma tell us stories"
we all slept in the big living room
my cousin
us 3 kids
& gramma

. . . .

late at night
she'd whisper back from her bed
                    ("what gramma said
                    late at night," p. 11)

The night comes when, asked for another story, she whispers that she has no more stories to tell: "ask your mother / she can tell you more" (p. 12). But exactly what more the speaker's mother can tell is not clear. She can "talk Indian," although she has not taught her own children to do so. And although she has elected only occasionally to visit gramma's bed under the tree—that radiating center—the mother is clearly closer to "the way" than her daughter; she is less a dweller in the world of Diet Pepsi and Nacho cheese. In the title poem of northSun's book, the mother reminds her speaker-daughter, perhaps wistfully, that when the daughter was a child she ate with relish foods nourishing and natural, foods that suggest a rich and earth-connected life, foods that the poet makes seem valuable in more than a nutritional sense:

my mother says when I was little
i liked it all
crab crayfish ketchup cauliflower
asparagus pumpkin pie rabbit deer
quail pheasants prawns rice rudding. . . . (p. 26)

This urban-born daughter has, by now, limited her menu to convenience foods—"it makes / it easy to figure out"—and by implication her life, too, is limited, less nourishing than it once was, poorer than her gramma's has been. As she says in another poem, "moving camp too far":

i don't know what it
was to hunt buffalo
or do the ghost dance
but
. . . .

> i can eat buffalo meat
> at the tourist burger stand
> i can dance to indian music
> rock-n-roll hey-a-hey-o
> i can
>   & unfortunately
>   i do
>   (p. 14)

The grandmother, for all her warm sense of family, with which northSun
endows her in other poems, is at a loss to understand her pizza-eating grandchildren; perhaps this is why she feels that she has "no more stories to tell"
and that her daughter, the speaker's mother, can tell more useful stories. In a
cultural sense, the grandchildren she loves have become strangers:

> gramma thinks about her grandchildren
> they're losing the ways
> don't know how to talk indian
> don't understand me when
> i ask for tobacco
> don't know how to skin a rabbit
> sad sad
> they're losing the ways
>
> but gramma
> you told your daughters
> marry white men
> told them they would have
> nicer houses
> fancy cars
> pretty clothes
> could live in the city
>
> gramma your daughters did
> they couldn't speak indian anymore
> how could we grandchildren learn
> there are no rabbits to skin
> in the city
> we have no gramma there to
> teach us the ways
>
> you were still on the reservation
> asking somebody anybody
> please
> get me tobacco
>   (p. 13)

The granddaughter accuses gramma of having begun the process of alienation. For all her warmth and strong identity, she has urged her own daughters down a road from whence there is no turning back, though none of them may have anticipated that.

One interesting thing about this poem is northSun's attitude toward the grandmother's failure as a teacher. Anglo poets often show a marked fear of the older woman who will insist on telling others what to do:

> She thinks of my life
> as a bed only she
> can make right
> > (Lyn Lifshin, "My Mother
> > and the Bed," in Lifshin,
> > pp. 56–57)

> you would
> pull me from my element
> scrape away the iridescence
> chop me into bits and pieces
> to simmer in your special broth
> > (L. L. Zeiger, "The Fish,"
> > in Lifshin, p. 59)

northSun's poetry, however, expresses regret and longing for missed instruction, for someone to "teach us the ways." The speaker's wry self-examination shows that she knows what she has lost, what it means not to speak Indian, to eat Nacho cheese instead of rabbit. But, with brilliant honesty, she makes it equally plain that she is unable or unwilling—probably both—to return to the old ways, to graft those ways on to herself and play at being old-time Indian. Her strength is that she knows who she is and what has happened to her; she knows that she cannot go back, and she's out to survive. That, in the old stories, is Coyote's strength. No matter how many poses he may strike before others—and in these days one of those poses is surely to pretend to be exactly as one's ancestors have been in the past—at the bottom line he does not fool himself. Neither does northSun. She values "the way," but she also acknowledges, and even celebrates a little, "the way things are."

Self-knowledge, shrewd judgment, and an eye for irony are not the strengths the grandmother herself possesses. Another poem, "what gramma said about her grandpa," suggests the origins of the gulf between gramma and her grandchildren, as the gramma's voice relates without a trace to conscious irony the story of her own white grandpa:

> he was white grandpa
> his name jim butler
> he's good irish man

he was nice talk our
language
big man with moustache
boss of town
tonopah
he found silver mine
we still on reservation they
come tell us 'your grandpa
found mine' so
we move to tonopah
he say 'buy anything you want
don't buy just little things
don't buy just candy
buy something big'
that's what he used to say
4th of july he make
a great long table
put sheet over it
then put all kinds of food on it
he say 'get your plate &
help yourselves'
he fed all the indians
he was good man
but then
he marry white woman
and we go back to reservation

(p. 6)

Grandpa Jim Butler remains in gramma's mind a nice man because he, like a number of the Irish who made successful Indian scouts and fighters and traders, possesses certain qualities valued highly by most American Indian cultures. He has the gift of tongues, "can talk our language," and he is generous when it suits him, sharing expansively his table and his possessions. That he is inconstant seems not to register on gramma; perhaps it is just that his leaving the family flat is so much a given of "the way things are" in the world of Indian-white relations that she considers it all too unsurprising for comment. The important thing is that she seems to make no distinction between two very different kinds of giving. One kind is Jim Butler's too easy Celtic generosity, which is a western version of the picnic-sponsoring generosity of Tammany Hall bosses, the generosity of the boss of the town who intends that his gifts will reflect well on himself. The other kind of giving is well described by the Navajo medicine man who said

> I can travel all over the Navajo Reservation and never be without a home. Each clan has a history and we are all of one family. When I am miles from my hogan, I introduce myself to a stranger, name my clan. He asks me to stay with him and eat.[13]

This generosity is an integral part of American Indian cultures, the sharing that takes place because that is what nature does for men and women, what they do for nature, what they do for one another unthinkingly. This generosity is not for show but is a traditional way of living in the world. But gramma seems not to notice the vital difference between these two kinds of giving. She remembers the past plenitude without emotionally recalling the cost, and the result, generations later, is that her own grandchild must remain something of a visitor, however loving a one, in her grandmother's house.

This maternal grandmother has suffered a certain amount of cultural alienation, and yet she and her family make as many connections between the generations as love can accomplish and distance will permit. The maternal grandmother's world remains relatively intact, always there for her urban descendants to enter into as fully as possible. This is not true of the speaker's "other gramma," the paternal grandmother, a cheerful urban alcoholic who is far less recognizable as a relative:

> she staggers down streets
> and maybe somebody think
> there go somebody's gramma
> yeah well i spose she my
> gramma
>
> she old indian wino
> big toothy smile
> like the one my dad wears
> like mine
> ("my other grandma,"
> p. 20)

The genetic connection must be acknowledged, but beyond facial structures there are few links between this gramma and her family. Though originally from a culture where tribal and family history and the reckoning of kinship are vital, she is even uncertain of her grandchildren's names. A visit to her is not a time of sharing food and talk in crowded intimacy, but a time to exchange hurried token greetings in a bleak neutral zone:

> when we go visit gramma we
> don't go to her house
> she only sleep there
> we head straight for bar
> us kids wait in car
> it's a short visit
> it always is
> she staggers out tries to guess
> who's who
> (p. 20)

But what makes this poem about the family drunk different from Anglo poems on the same subject—Anne Sexton's poems about her father, for example—is the real nature of the grievance, the source of the alienation:

> gramma's got a world of her own
> just her a few old cronies the
> bartender oh yeah and her
> husband who wears the beer can
> hat . . .
>
>   (p. 21)

It is not this gramma's drunkenness per se that sets her apart. Other members of the family do not regard her as a monster who degrades and shames them; rather, they regard her with a patient affection. The trouble is that she has chosen not just to abandon her old-time native culture but also to abandon almost completely the web of relationship in favor of the exceedingly private culture of the alcoholic. Exclusivity, as opposed to sharing, marks her "world of her own," and that world, unlike the maternal gramma's, is certainly not accessible for restorative visits. But the mere fact of her alcoholism need not make a difference. In another poem, northSun acknowledges drinking as well as a toothy smile as part of her "heritage"—the title of the poem—and imagines the possibility of a coming-together with this other gramma, of them drinking together. But that cannot take place on gramma's narrow turf. The speaker imagines forging for herself a "way" that is possible for her to live within "the way things are," and invites the wino gramma to join her there:

> no gramma i won't be like you
> i don't like cheap wine
> i won't wear jersey print dresses
> & fake pearl earrings
> or hang out on the edge of the
> bar in oakland
> not for me gramma
> i'll get drunk from tequila
> sitting in my trailer
> on a montana reservation
> wearing blue jeans & buckskin
> no gramma i'm not exactly like you
> but come visit
> let me be your shugur
> and we'll have anuthur
>
>   (p. 22)

This vision is not comparable to life lived under a shade tree within a close family circle, where even such everyday actions as the drinking of Kool-Aid seem nearly ceremonial because they are shared. But it isn't a bar in Oakland, either. It is an imaginative attempt to envision a way of life that would enable the speaker to maintain some connections with "the way"; it is a vision of the speaker established and at ease in a kind of halfway place where, perhaps, either grandmother might join her.

I have dealt so extensively with northSun because of the tough excellence of her poetry and because, of all contemporary American Indian women, she writes most extensively of the estrangements between women in a family. But other American Indian women also write of the problem of alienated women as a cultural rather than a personal affair. Janet Campbell Hale (Coeur d'Alene) writes of returning to her father's wake where she feels a stranger to the old people, not because of her youth or because the relatives are presented, as in many Anglo poems, as faintly grotesque and morbid living specimens, but because

> I
> Don't speak
> The language
> And so
> I listened
> As if I understood
> What it was all about[14]

Again, Joy Harjo (Creek) in "White Sands" writes of driving to her sister's wedding:

> my sister is getting married
> in a white dress in Tulsa
> the way my mother knew it would be
> with her daughters
> > (a December wedding
> > under a pure sky)
>
> but i am the one
> who lives alone with two children
> in the desert of a place
> > in New Mexico
> and she never saw me in a white gown
>
> when i drive to Oklahoma for the wedding
> i will be dressed in
> the clear blue sky
> that burns the silvery white sand
> near Alamogordo
> and my mother won't see this
> my eyes burning
> > behind my darkened glasses
> > (p. 68)

This time it is perhaps more the mother than the child who has forsaken a traditional way of life for the ideals of Norman Rockwell paintings and *Modern Bride*; because of those adopted values, she is disappointed in her daughter. The speaker herself has moved away from the Creek country of Oklahoma. Much as northSun imagines creating for herself a compromise world, drinking tequila in a reservation trailer, the speaker lives by herself, but in at least one sense she preserves the older ways: her connection with the earth is so close that land becomes garment and body, flesh of her flesh. Harjo holds out not even a fantasy, as northSun does, of making connection with her mother; she just assumes that the mother will not see her daughter with clear eyes. The affirmation of the poem lies not in the possibility of a renewed relationship with the mother, but in the daughter's unbroken and radiant connection with something larger and more important than a single individual.

The difference between the Anglo poet's emphasis on personal, psychological alienation between women and the American Indian poet's emphasis on cultural alienation between them may come about simply because the difference between "the way" and "the way things are" is something most American Indians are troubled by daily. Many of their parents and a great number of their older relatives still speak the old tongues, dwell in the old communities where people still follow, in some measure, the older ways of life, behaving in certain ways toward mothers-in-law, for example, or being wary of contact with bears, even if there is a tv set in the hogan. But the great waves of European immigration, the great changes in language and behavior and belief that marked so clearly the differences between first and second and third generations in this country, lie farther in the past for most white Americans. (Even in that past, most Europeans came voluntarily, and many with the idea that it was desirable for their children to leap gladly into the melting pot. European immigrants had fewer ways to give up and gave them up more easily than did American Indians.)

If the daughters of turn-of-the-century immigrants had had more leisure time in which to write, and if writing poetry about family conflict had then been in vogue, American literature might contain more poems about cultural alienation in the kitchen. Interestingly, the only contemporary Anglo poet I can name offhand who touches on mothers and grandmothers in a way similar to that of American Indian poets is Carolyn Forche, who, in her *Gathering the Tribes*, explores her connections and disconnections with her Eastern European grandmother. Perhaps, too, something of this sense of cultural mother-daughter alienation can be found in the work of Jewish women poets of the first half of the century. But for most of us now, the question of what it means to be Irish or Estonian isn't much of a question any longer, and we have the leisure to focus on personal conflicts, to create for ourselves personal instead of tribal mythologies. Intramural rivalries become most intense when there is no longer any possibility of being a member of a varsity team.

The sense of the family unit as being only a part of a very real and much larger entity, a people, still remains, I think, with American Indian women and emerges in their poetry in the absence of one-on-one battles between women. The phenomenon that marks Anglo women's poetry—the mother or daughter seen as private and personal enemy and the bitter relish with which both often regard such conflicts—is, unlike cradleboards or Vietnam or Tastee-Freez stands, simply not an American Indian theme; the monster-mother and the usurper-daughter are not American Indian images. But the pain and conflict caused for women by the gap between "the way" and "the way things are" and the attempts women make to build bridges over that ravine are among the most vital stories American Indian women poets have now to tell.

Notes

* I would like to thank Gerri Rhoades for making me start to think about this subject, and William McGlothing for the check and balance of his sharp criticism.

1 Readily available anthologies of translations of traditional native American poetry include *American Indian Poetry: An Anthology of Songs and Chants*, ed. Cronyn; Astrov, *American Indian Prose and Poetry*; Day, *The Sky Clears*. For some examples of the kind of contemporary poetry I am speaking of in the introductory section, see *The Whispering Wind*, ed. Allen, and *Voices From Wah'Kon-Tah*, ed. Dodge and McCullough. The last two volumes do contain a number of strong poems, especially those by Paula Gunn Allen, Simon Ortiz, and Marnie Walsh in *Voices from Wah'Kon-Tah*.

2 Day, *The Sky Clears*, p. 2.

3 "Ritual Chant for the Sick (Omaha)," trans. Alice Fletcher, in Cronyn, *American Indian Poetry*, p. 57.

4 "Earth Mother," trans. Frank Gordon, and "The Song My Paddle Sings," trans. Pauline Johnson, in Cronyn, *American Indian Poetry*, pp. 234, 241; "Sun Dancers," by Patricia Irvina, and "Eagle Flight," by Alonzo Lopez, in Terry Allen, *The Whispering Wind*, pp. 80, 7.

5 A partial list of these periodicals and presses would include *South Dakota Review, Cimarron Review, Blue Cloud Quarterly, Sun Tracks, Greenfield Review, Scree, Akwasasne Notes, Pembroke*, Indian Historian Press, Strawberry Press, A Press, Red Earth Press, Yardbird, Cold Mountain Press, the Crossing Press, the Rio Grande Writer's Association Press, Puerto del Sol.

6 Friday, *My Mother, My Self*, p. 113.

7 For a supporting discussion of mother-daughter relations among women in southwestern tribes as reflected in other literary genres, especially autobiography, see Bannan, "Spider Woman's Web."

8 Friday sounds this note throughout much of her book.

9 Revard, "Deer Talk, Coyote Talk, Meadowlark Territory."

10 northSun, "the way and the way things are," *Diet Pepsi and Nacho Cheese*, p. 13.

11 Walsh, "Bessie Dreaming Bear: Rosebud, So. Dak. 1960," *A Taste of the Knife*; rpt. in Hobson, *The Remembered Earth*, p. 369.

12 northSun's cycle of family poems in *Diet Pepsi and Nacho Cheese* includes "what gramma said about how she came here," "what gramma said about her grandpa," "what gramma said about her kids," "what grandpa said," "what happened to grandpa," "what

gramma said after," "what gramma said late at night," "what gramma said in the last story," "the way and the way things are," "how my cousin was killed," "shadow knew nothing was my cousin," "my other grandma," "grandma and burgie," "heritage," "babe," and "little red riding hood."

13   Popovi Da, "Indian Values," p. 26.

14   Hale, "Desmet, Idaho, March 1969." For Anglo women poets' portrayals of mourners, see, for example, two poems in *Rising Tides*, ed. Chester and Barba: Carolyn Stoloff, "For the Suicide's Daughter," p. 167, and Sylvia Plath, "Last Words," p. 217.

The Feminine Landscape of Leslie Marmon Silko's *Ceremony*

Paula Gunn Allen

There are two kinds of women and two kinds of men in Leslie Marmon Silko's *Ceremony*. The figures of Laura, Night Swan, Grandmother, Betonie's Grandmother, and Ts'eh represent one kind of woman, while to some extent Auntie, Betonie's grandfather's wives, and grandfather's mother represent the other. Josiah, the Mountain Spirit, Betonie's grandfather, Ku'oosh, Betonie, Robert, and Tayo represent a kind of man associated with the first category of women, while Rocky, Emo, Pinky, Harley, and the witches represent men associated with the second. Those in the first category belong to the earth spirit and live in harmony with her, even though this attunement may lead to tragedy; those in the second are not of the earth but of human mechanism; they live to destroy that spirit, to enclose and enwrap it in their machinations, condemning all to a living death. Ts'eh is the matrix, the creative and life-restoring power, and those who cooperate with her designs serve her and, through her, serve life. They make manifest that which she thinks. The others serve the witchery; they are essentially inimical to all that lives, creates, and nurtures.

While *Ceremony* is ostensibly a tale about a man, Tayo, it is as much and more a tale of two forces: the feminine life force of the universe and the mechanistic death force of the witchery. And Ts'eh is the central character of the drama of this ancient battle as it is played out in contemporary times.

We are the land, and the land is mother to us all. There is not a symbol in the tale that is not in some way connected with womanness, that does not in some way relate back to Ts'eh and through her to the universal feminine principle of creation: Ts'its'tsi'nako, Thought Woman, Grandmother Spider, Old Spider Woman. All tales are born in the mind of Spider Woman, and all creation exists as a result of her naming.

We are the land. To the best of my understanding, that is the fundamental idea that permeates American Indian life; the land (Mother) and the people (mothers) are the same. As Luther Standing Bear has said of his Lakota people, "We are of the soil and the soil is of us." The earth is the source and the being of the people, and we are equally the being of the earth. The land is not really a place, separate from ourselves, where we act out the drama of our isolate destinies; the witchery makes us believe that false idea. The earth is not a mere source of survival, distant from the creatures it nurtures and from the spirit that breathes in us, nor is it to be considered an inert resource on which we draw in order to keep our ideological self functioning, whether we perceive that self in sociological or personal terms. We must not conceive of the earth as an ever-dead other that supplies us with a sense of ego identity by virtue of our contrast to its perceived non-being. Rather, for American Indians like Betonie, the earth *is* being, as all creatures are also being: aware, palpable, intelligent, alive. Had Tayo known clearly what Standing Bear articulated—that "in the Indian the spirit of the land is still vested," that human beings "must be born and reborn to belong," so that their bodies are "formed of the dust of their forefather's [sic] bones"—he would not be ill. But if he had known consciously what he knew unconsciously, he would not have been a major agent of the counter ceremony, and this tale would not have been told.

Tayo's illness is a result of separation from the ancient unity of person, ceremony, and land, and his healing is a result of his recognition of this unity. The land is dry because earth is suffering from the alienation of part of herself; her children have been torn from her in their minds; their possession of unified awareness of and with her has been destroyed, partially or totally; that destruction characterizes the lives of Tayo and his mother, Auntie and Rocky, Pinky and Harley, and all those who are tricked into believing that the land is beyond and separate from themselves.

The healing of Tayo and the land results from the reunification of land and person. Tayo is healed when he understands, in magical (mystical) and loving ways, that his being is within and outside him, that it includes his mother, Night Swan, Ts'eh, Josiah, the spotted cattle, winter, hope, love, and the starry universe of Betonie's ceremony.

This understanding occurs slowly as Tayo lives the stories—those ancient and those new. He understands through the process of making the stories manifest in his actions and in his understanding, for the stories and the land are about the same thing; perhaps we can best characterize this relation by saying that the stories are the communication device of the land and the people. Through the stories, the ceremony, the gap between isolate human being and lonely landscape is closed. And through them Tayo understands in mind and in bone the truth of his and our situation.

Tayo is an empty space as the tale begins, a vapor, an outline. He has no voice. "He can't talk to you. He is invisible. His words are formed with an invisible tongue, they have no sound," he tells the army psychiatrist (p. 15).

Invisible and stilled, like an embryo, he floats, helpless and voiceless, on the current of duality, his being torn by grief and anger. Love could heal him—love, the mountain spirit Ts'eh, the "wonder" being, who was the manifestation of the creator of the waters of life that flow from a woman and bless the earth and the beloved with healing, with rain. It is loving her that heals Tayo, that and his willingness to take up her tasks of nurturing the plant and beast people she loves. And he had loved her from "time immemorial," unconsciously. Before he knew her name, he had given her his pledge of love, and she had answered him with rain:

> So that last summer, before the war, he got up before dawn and rode the bay mare south to the spring in the narrow canyon. The water oozed out from the dark orange sandstone at the base of the long mesa. He waited for the sun to come over the hills. . . . The canyon was full of shadows when he reached the pool. He had picked flowers along the path, flowers with long yellow petals the color of the sunlight. He shook the pollen from them gently and sprinkled it over the water; he laid blossoms beside the pool and waited. He heard the water, flowing into the pool, drop by drop from the big crack in the side of the cliff. The things he did seemed right, as he imagined with his heart the rituals the cloud priests performed during the drought. Here the dust and heat began to recede; the short grass and stunted corn seemed distant. (p. 93)

As Tayo completes his prayer and begins to descend the mountain, he sees a bright green hummingbird and watches it as it disappears: "But it left something with him; as long as the hummingbird had not abandoned the land, somewhere there were still flowers, and they could all go on" (p. 96). Forty-eight hours after Tayo makes his prayer, the sky fills with clouds thick with rain. The rain comes from the west, and the thunder preceding it comes from the direction of Mount Taylor, called Tse-pi'na in Laguna (Woman Veiled in Clouds), a mountain that is blue against the sky, topped in white when it rains or snows. Having prayed the rain in, Tayo must experience its power personally as the next step in the ceremony. The rain makes it necessary for Josiah to miss his date with Night Swan, so he sends Tayo to the nearby village of Cubero with a message for her. He writes the message on "blue-lined paper" (p. 96).

Night Swan is a mysterious and powerful woman. We know that she is associated with Ts'eh by her circumstances and the colors with which she surrounds herself. Many signs indicate that she is associated with the ceremony of which Tayo was an integral (though unknowing) part: the color of her eyes, her implication in the matter of the spotted (half-breed) cattle, Auntie's dislike of her, and her mysterious words to Tayo when he leaves her. Additionally her room is filled with blue: a blue armchair, curtains "feeling colored by the blue flowers painted in a border around the walls," blue sheets, a cup made of blue pottery painted with yellow flowers. She is dressed in a blue kimono when Tayo enters her room, and she wears blue slippers (p. 98). Most important, she is associated with a mysterious power that Tayo associates with whatever is behind the white curtain:

> He could feel something back there, something of her life which he could not explain. The room pulsed with feeling, the feeling flowing with the music and the breeze from the curtains, feeling colored by the blue flowers painted in a border around the walls. He could feel it everywhere, even in the blue sheets that were stretched tightly across the bed. (p. 98)

This woman, who appeared out of the southeast one day and took up residence in Cubero, on the southern slope of the mountain, and who disappears as mysteriously after Josiah is buried, is surrounded with emblems of the mountain rain. She takes Tayo to bed. This is not an ordinary coupling, for nothing about Tayo's life is ordinary while the counter ceremony moves toward resolution:

> She moved under him, her rhythm merging into the sound of the rain in the tree. And he was lost somewhere, deep beneath the surface of his own body and consciousness, swimming away from all his life before that hour. (p. 99)

The encounter with Night Swan sets the seal of Tayo's destiny in those moments. Through her body the love that Ts'eh bears for him is transmitted. Night Swan is aware of the significance of her act and tells Tayo, "You don't have to understand what is happening. But remember this day. You will recognize it later. You are part of it now" (p. 100).

These passages tell of the ceremonial nature of man and woman; they embody the meaning of the action of the relation between the characters and Thought Woman that is the basis of Laguna life:

> In the beginning Tse che nako, Thought Woman, finished everything, thoughts, and the names of all things. . . . And then our mothers, Uretsete and Naotsete, said they would make names and they would make thoughts. Thus they said. Thus they did.
>
> (Laguna Thought Woman Story)

From the foregoing it is clear that the Lagunas regard the land as feminine. What is not so clear is how this might be so. For it is not in the mind of the Laguna simply to equate, in primitive modes, earth-bearing-grain with woman-bearing-child. To paraphrase grandma, it isn't that easy. If the simplistic interpretation was accurate to their concept, the Lagunas would not associate the essential nature of femininity with the creative power of thought. The equation is more like earth-bearing-grain, goddess-bearing-thought, woman-bearing-child. Nor is ordinary thinking referred to here: that sort of "brain noise" that passes for thinking among moderns. The thought for which Grandmother Spider is known is the kind that results in physical manifestation of phenomena: mountains, lakes, creatures, or philosophical-sociological systems. Our mothers, Uretsete and Naotsete, are aspects of Grandmother Spider. They are certain kinds of thought forces if you will. The same can be said of Ts'eh, indeed, must be said of her if the tale that Silko tells, that Spider Woman *thinks* all into being is to have its proper significance. Psychoanalytically, we might say that Tayo's illness is a result of the repression of his anima and that through his love of Ts'eh he becomes conscious of the female side of his own nature and accepts and integrates feminine behavior into his life. This Jungian interpretation of the process of Tayo's healing is accurate enough, though it misses an essential point of the story: Tayo's illness is connected to the larger world. The drought-stricken land is also ill, perhaps because the land has also repressed its anima.

Silko illustrates this nexus with the metaphor of the witchery and the ceremony used to contravene its effects. Through the vehicle of the story, Ts'its'tsi'nako's thought, Silko explains how the witchery could be responsible for sickness in individuals, societies, and landscapes simultaneously:

> Thought-Woman, the spider
> named things and
> as she named them
> they appeared.
>
> She is sitting in her room
> Thinking of a story now.
> I'm telling you the story
> she is thinking. (p. 1)

After Tayo completes the first steps of the ceremony, he is ready to enter into the central rituals connected with a ceremony of cosmic significance, for only a cosmic ceremony can simultaneously heal a wounded man, a stricken landscape, and a disorganized, discouraged society.

He becomes a warrior, thus dissociating himself from the people. A warrior in a peace-centered culture must experience total separation from the tribe. He has been prepared for his role by the circumstances of his birth and upbringing: Auntie was especially forceful in propelling him away from the heart of what he was. By virtue of his status as an outcast who, at the same time, is one of the Laguna people in his heart, he is able to suffer the ritual of war and dissolution. Only total annihilation of the mundane self could produce a magic man of sufficient power to carry off the ceremony that Tayo is embroiled in.

At the opening of the story, Tayo is still experiencing this stage of the ceremony. He is formless, for his being is as yet unshaped, undistinguished from the mass it sprang from. Like rainless clouds, he seeks fulfillment—a ceremony, a story about his life that will make him whole. He has the idea that if he had died instead of Rocky or Josiah, the land would be full of rain. This "story" of his is inappropriate. Perhaps because of his status as an outcast, he does not understand the nature of death, nor does he know that it is not in the deaths of two individuals that the prosperity or the suffering of the people rests. Perhaps no one has told him that the departed souls are always within and part of the people on earth, that they are still obligated to those living on earth and come back in the form of rain regularly (when all is well), so that death is a blessing on the people, not their destruction. What Tayo and the people need is a story that will take the entire situation into account, that will bless life with a certain kind of integrity where spirit, creatures, and land can occupy a unified whole. That kind of story is, of course, a ceremony such as Betonie performs with Tayo as the active participant, the manifester of the thought.

After Tayo walks through Betonie's ceremony, finds the cattle, and puts them in a safe pasture, after he has confronted the witchery and abandoned all thought of retaliating against it, after he has been transformed by these efforts and his meeting with Ts'eh from isolated warrior to spiritually integrated person, after he has taken on the aspect of unity termed *naiya* (mother) in Laguna, he is free to understand the whole thing:

> He would go back there now, where she had shown him the plant. He would gather the seeds for her and plant them with great care in places near sandy hills. . . . The plants would grow there like the story, strong and translucent as stars.

"But you know, grandson, this world is fragile," old Ku'oosh had told Tayo, and having entered the ways of unification of a fragmented persona, Tayo is free to experience that fragility directly:

> He dreamed with his eyes open that he was wrapped in a blanket in the back of Josiah's wagon, crossing the sandy flat below Paguate Hill. . . . the rumps of the two gray mules were twin moons in front of him. Josiah was driving the wagon, old Grandma was holding him, and Rocky whispered "my brother." They were taking him home. (p. 254)

The fragility of the world is a result of its nature as thought. Both land and human being participate in the same kind of being, for both are thoughts in the mind of Grandmother Spider. Tayo's illness is a function of disordered thinking—his own, that of those around him, and that of the forces that propelled them all into the tragic circumstances of World War II. The witchery put this disordered thinking into motion long ago and distorted human beings' perceptions so that they believed that other creatures—insects and beasts and half-breeds and whites and Indians and Japanese—were enemies rather than part of the one being we all share, and thus should be destroyed. The cure for that misunderstanding, for Tayo, was a reorientation of perception so that he could know directly that the true nature of being is magical and that the proper duty of the creatures, the land, and human beings is to live in harmony with what is. For Tayo, wholeness consists of sowing plants and nurturing them, caring for the spotted cattle, and especially knowing that he belongs exactly where he is, that he is and always has been home.

The story that is capable of healing his mind is the story that the land has always signified:

> The transition was completed. In the west and in the south too, the clouds with round heavy bellies had gathered for the dawn. It was not necessary, but it was right, even if the sky had been cloudless the end was the same. The ear for the story and the eye for the pattern were theirs; the feeling was theirs; we came out of this land and we are hers. . . . They had always been loved. He thought of her then; she had always loved him, she had never left him; she had always been there. He crossed the river at sunrise. (p. 255)

So Tayo's initiation into motherhood is complete, and the witchery is countered for a time, at least for one human being and his beloved land. Tayo has bridged the distance between his isolated consciousness and the universe of being, because he has loved the spirit woman who brings all things into being and because he is at last conscious that she has always loved them, his people, and himself. He is able at last to take his normal place in the life of the Laguna, a place that is to be characterized by nurturing, caring for life, behaving like a good mother. Auntie can now treat him as she treats the other men, not as a stranger, but as a friend whom it is safe to complain about, to nag, and to care for. Even Grandmother knows that he is no longer special after he returns from the Paguate hills, where he became simply a part of the pattern of Laguna life and the enduring story within the land, and she comments that "these goings-on around Laguna don't get me excited any more." Perhaps she is also implying that ordinariness can replace the extraordinary nature of life while the ceremony is being played out. Tayo has come home, ordinary in his being, and they can get on with serious business, the day-to-day life of a village, which is what the land, the ceremony, the story and time immemorial are all about.

Teaching American Indian Women's Literature

Except for some classic ethnographical studies such as Ruth Landes' *The Ojibwa Woman* or biographies such as *Mountain Wolf Woman*, edited by Nancy Lurie, Indian women receive little attention in the classroom. This is not a result of the unavailability of materials, but suggests, instead, that teachers and researchers have made selective use of the literature. Ruth Underhill summarizes the Indian woman's place as described in early monographs:

> The ceremonial spotlight caught them briefly at their high points of puberty, childbirth and widowhood and the economic spotlight when their marriages were arranged and paid for. Otherwise they formed, in most cases, an undifferentiated mass of workers, excluded from council and often from ceremonies.

Such assumptions about the role of women in American Indian cultures misrepresent reality. The apparent neglect of the Indian woman has sometimes worked to her advantage. She escaped the humiliation of being characterized as foolish Tonto or brave Little Beaver; when she was presented, however, she was often portrayed as one who helped the army against her own people or as a Pocahontas figure who saved the life of a white captain. Both portrayals are equally inaccurate. Although American Indians regard the popular notions of the Indian woman as ludicrous, the rest of society has come to identify the Indian woman in these negative and inaccurate ways.

So, too, have some modern literary treatments of Indian women presented them as simple and childlike. As a result of these unrealistic Indian women characters and the disproportionate number of male Indian characters presented by white writers from Cooper and Melville up to Hemingway and Faulkner, many students cannot find works that present Indian women as positive characters. Such characters, however, do exist. The following course outline suggests materials and methods useful in introducing the literary records of the American Indian woman. The course is offered for one semester in three units, but it could also form three separate courses to be presented in sequence. Alternatively, each section could be incorporated into a general women's studies course, a genre course, or a survey of American literature, biography, or autobiography. This flexibility allows for maximal use of the literature of American Indian women in a university curriculum.

To understand the American Indian woman, one needs to look to American Indian literary and religious traditions and recognize that in none of them does the concept of women created from man occur. Indians believe that human beings were created, that both sexes were present in the original creation; this idea underscores their pervasive belief in the ontological necessity for balance in every aspect of universal being. Male supremacy, like any other idea of one-sidedness, is uncongenial to traditional American Indian thought or social systems. Men and women complement each other, and Indians regard women as active participants in the cultural group, not as outsiders in a male-dominated society.

Indian women have traditionally held positions of power in their tribes. The power, however, has diminished as tribal governments have reorganized and adopted "white" ways. Still, the role of the Indian woman is, as it was traditionally, one of stability and importance. As the giver of life, woman is perceived as a creative force, one with Mother Earth, the ultimate living deity. As teacher, the woman is the link between one generation and the next; thus, if she fails to teach her children, she has failed herself and her tribe. Women represent continuity and completeness. If women fail to pass on their contributions, they cause the circle to be broken, the sacred tree to die. Because they perform this important function in the perpetuation of the tribe, women are recognized as worthwhile contributors; indeed, they are necessary to the life of the tribe.

One can approach the subject of the American Indian woman in literature chronologically, beginning with the appearance of the female image in the myths and legends. The earth is generally seen as a mother image. The sun, sky, wind, stars, and clouds are often designated as masculine powers that nourish the earth and make it fertile. In the Cherokee cosmogony, however, the sun, *seln,* is feminine. Many of the deities in these early literary works are women who possess both the creative and the destructive forces of the universe. This literature has traditionally been passed on orally to a select audience, but now such material is being included with increasing frequency in anthologies. More accessible also are the early ethnographic biographies. Poems and stories that first appeared in publications of the Indian Historical Society and newspapers such as *Akwesasne Notes* and *Wassaja* are now appearing in collections. Major publishers, as well as the long-enthusiastic small presses, continue to produce the poetry and prose of American Indian women.

Contemporary writers use much of the language and symbolism of the ancient oral traditions, but they create new images from them, images that reflect contemporary experience or embody past experience and breathe into it new life. Despite tribal differences in tradition and ceremonies, much contemporary Indian literature evokes similar themes: nostalgia for the old ways, the frustration of being part of two worlds, the beauty of a vital and living culture that everyone, except old relatives, said was dead. The literature of the contemporary Indian woman returns full circle to the images, structures, and characters of the oral traditions that have always existed and that still form the basic meaning and structure of life for tribal peoples. Some songs and poems reflect humorous tribal gossip while others are serious personal statements; such variety reflects the totality of Indian experience. Some writers choose to adopt the rhetoric of protest literature, and others maintain connections with the past by employing structures used in oral literature. Apparent throughout most of the literature, however, is the presence of the Indian woman as a storyteller and bearer of meaning and tradition. Methods and forms have changed, but the tradition remains. Through the dynamic process of creation the American Indian woman continues to define herself.

Course Design #1

Female Figures in American Indian Ceremonial and Ritual Literature

In a sense, one might say that myth is culture; it is the roots of the people, their coherence, their significance, and their map for living. Ceremonial literatures of the tribes provide each with self-definitions and social definitions of the most fundamental sort, giving the person's relationship to being in its various forms. Myth is perhaps central to a person's and a people's sense of reality. It helps one know who one is, why one is, and what one is to express in one's life. Myth is, in literary terms, the controlling metaphor, from which all meanings are derived, all perception and sensation are ordered, all relationships are defined, and all experience is assimilated and understood.

In order to construct a conceptual framework that will allow understanding of the place of women in the American Indian literary tradition, one must look at the place those women occupy in their own tradition. That place becomes more evident through a study of the ceremonial literature of a given tribe. Such a study is also important for understanding the themes and symbols with which the American Indian woman works when she articulates her experience in written modes and when she tells the stories and sings the songs of her people.

The course materials will enable students to place individual pieces of literature within a context that constitutes the broader base of the pieces and to view them as part of a living tradition that is as pertinent to an Indian woman's life today as it has been to the long life of her people. In beginning a course with a survey of ceremonial literatures (also known as myths and legends, though most available materials are actually derivative or personal accounts of the mythic cycles), one should draw from sources that will illuminate the course materials. In this way, students can read the work of the individual writer with understanding of the themes, symbols, motifs, and structures that form it. This will enable students to deal with contemporary novels, stories, poetry, and special works such as Cook-Lynn's *Then Badger Said This.*

For example, an instructor who focuses on the Southwest might draw on the myths and legends of the Keres (Pueblo), using especially those that deal with Spider Woman. The creation stories and associated ceremonial practices center on her, and understanding Spider Woman, her relation to the people, and her various guises—Iyetiko, Uretsete, Naotsete, and the Irriako—is central to understanding poems by Silko, Allen, and Sanchez as well as Silko's novel, *Ceremony.* In conjunction with some ethnographic texts (like that of Boas), one can draw from sources such as Gunn's *Schat-Chen*, Purley's "Keres Pueblo Concepts of Diety," and Hunt's *Dancing Horses of Acoma.* These can be supplemented with studies of other pueblos, such as Waters and Fredericks' *Book of the Hopi* and Tyler's *Pueblo Gods and Myths.* The theme of woman as creative power in southwestern American Indian literature can be further followed through autobiographies, ethnological biographies, and the contemporary works of Mrs. Walter K. Marmon (Laguna), Leslie Marmon Silko (Laguna), Paula Gunn Allen (Laguna-Sioux), Carol Lee Sanchez (Laguna-Sioux), Wendy Rose (Hopi), and Louise Abeita (Isleta). This study can be accompanied by slide presentations of the artwork of southwestern women such as Linda Lomahaftewa (Hopi), Pablita Velarde (Santa Clara), Helen Hardin (Santa Clara), Maria (San Ildefonso), Carol Lee Sanchez, and Lucy Lewis (Acoma). The varieties of traditional and contemporary art materials by women in the southwestern American Indian traditions are, of course, too numerous to cover completely. In accordance with the theme of woman as a creative power in literature and society, one might make a similar study of Changing Woman (and her multiple forms and guises), relating this myth to the work of Navajo women writers such as Nia Francisco, and artists such as Emmi Whitehorse.

The point to emphasize is that the themes, symbols, motifs, and basic understandings with which American Indian women in any native culture have traditionally worked are exactly those that first appear in the oral and ceremonial literatures. A study of these primary materials is basic to an understanding of the literary works of the writers in those traditions.

Course Description

This course is designed as a three-hour lecture/discussion course for juniors and seniors. It has as its primary objectives: to familiarize the student with traditional oral materials of the Keres (Laguna), the Hopi, and the Navajo; to demonstrate the interlocking nature of contemporary written literatures, the oral tradition, and contemporary life among these tribes; to enable the student to apply critical techniques to the preparation of essays and papers on American Indian contemporary literatures; and to acquaint the student with alternate images of American Indian women through the study and examination of traditional and contemporary texts by and about them.

To these ends, instructors will select readings for their pertinence to the stated objectives, and student work will center on meeting those goals. Students will write two short critical papers and one long one.

(A similar course can be developed for the Lakota using the work of Ella Deloria, Lowie, Underhill, and the De Malley-Jahner volumes now being prepared by the University of Nebraska Press, in conjunction with the prose and poetry of Elizabeth Cook-Lynn, Gertrude Bonnin, nila northSun, and Marnie Walsh.)

Course Outline

The oral materials, autobiographies, biographies, and historical works will form the basis for discussing the contemporary works. We have found that introducing accessible contemporary materials—"Yellow Woman" by Silko, for example, along with one or two Yellow Woman narratives from *BAE*—works better than attempting to teach oral tradition and history and then contemporary work. A teacher of these materials needs to be well versed in the history and contemporary life of the people whose literature is under consideration. An understanding of "Yellow Woman" depends to some extent on familiarity with the location of Laguna, on the realization that the oral tradition includes jokes and gossip, and on the Laguna's present beliefs about morality. (See Evers and Carr, "A Conversation with Leslie Marmon Silko"; *This Song Remembers,* ed. Jane B. Katz; *The Third Woman,* ed. Dexter Fisher; and Silko's *Ceremony.*)

Both instructor and student must remember that these women live in contemporary America much, if not most, of the time. Their work moves from the traditional writing of Nia Francisco to the highly urban poetry of Wendy Rose.

In considering the writing of these women, one needs an understanding of the urbanization process, relocation programs, and radical politics in Indian America. The films *The Exiles* and *The Pride and the Shame* can aid in conveying the poverty and alienation of many contemporary American Indians. A look at *OHOYO,* a newsletter produced by the National Women's Program Development, Inc., at the OHOYO Resource Center can help in understanding the conditions in which the contemporary American Indian woman lives.

Keres (Laguna-Acoma)

After students have examined shorter works and background materials, they should be prepared to read *Ceremony*. The novel's important themes include the place of women in the tribe; the relations among land, people, and rain; the dualities of Western civilization; and the position of the half-breed. The transformation of Tayo from a soldier to a nourisher is central to Laguna ceremonial life as well as to the book.

Readings: creation and emergence stories from Purley, Boas, Parsons, White, Benedict, or Stirling; Yellow Woman story from Bureau of American Ethnology; background information from Parsons, Boas, Stirling, Gunn, White, Malinowski, Hewett, and Dutton; Silko, "Yellow Woman," "The Man to Send Rain Clouds," and selected poems; Allen, *The Woman Who Owned the Shadows* and poems from *Coyote's Daylight Trip* and *Shadow Country*; Sanchez, poems from *Message Bringer Woman* and *Conversations from the Nightmare*; Abeita, *I Am a Pueblo Indian Girl*; and Silko, *Ceremony*, and *Storyteller*. (Poems by Silko, Allen, and Sanchez, along with those of Veronica Riley, can be found in Hobson, *The Remembered Earth*; Fisher, *The Third Woman*; and Katz, *I Am the Fire of Time*.)

Hopi

Readings: creation and other stories from Waters, Fewkes, Nequatewa, and Wallis; background information from Parsons and Tyler; Rose, *Lost Copper, Academic Squaw*, and *Long Division*; Qoyawayma, *No Turning Back*; Smith, *Hopi Girl*; and Sekaquaptewa, *Me and Mine*.

Navajo

Readings: creation stories, ceremonial literature, and oral tradition materials from Bierhorst, Haile, Wyman, Kluckhohn, and Matthews; poetry by Francisco, Yazzie, Natoni, Chato, and Topahonso (in Hobson, *The Remembered Earth*; and Fisher, *The Third Woman*); Topahonso, "Snake Woman" (in *The Remembered Earth*); and Bennett, *Kaibah*.

Materials

The list of materials that follows is not definitive, nor is it meant to be a rigid list of sources. It is offered as a guide to the subject. The sources an instructor chooses will depend in part on the length of time available for this study and on the materials that he or she has selected for the rest of the course or sequence of courses.

Background and oral literature: Benedict, *Tales of the Cochiti Indians*; Boas, *Keresan Texts*; Eggan, *Social Organization of the Western Pueblos*; Gunn, *Schat-Chen*; Haile and Wyman, *Beautyway*; Hewett and Dutton, *The Pueblo Indian World*; Katz, *This Song Remembers*; Kluckhohn and Leighton, *The Navaho*; Nequatewa, "Dr. Fewkes and Masauwu" (in *Hopi Customs, Folklore and Ceremonies*) and *Truth of a Hopi*; Niethammer, *Daughters of the Earth*; Parsons, *Hopi and Zuni Ceremonialism*, *Notes on Ceremonialism at Laguna*, and *Pueblo Indian Religion*; Tyler, *Pueblo Gods and Myths*; Underhill, *First Penthouse Dwellers of America* and *Red Man's Religion*; Wallis, "Folktales from Shumopovi, Second Mesa"; Waters, *Masked Gods*; Waters and Fredericks, *Book of the Hopi*; White, *The Acoma Indians*; and Wyman and Kluckhohn, *Navajo Classification of Their Song Ceremonials*.

Anthologies: Fisher, *The Third Woman* (Allen, Francisco, Rose, Silko, Harjo, Walters, among others); Hobson, *The Remembered Earth* (all poets in this course); Katz, *I Am the Fire of Time* (Allen, Silko); Milton, *Four Indian Poets* (Allen); Niatum, *Carriers of the Dream Wheel* (Silko, Rose); Rosen, *The Man to Send Rain Clouds* (Silko; also Opal Lee Popkes and Anna Lee Walters).

Primary Sources: Allen, *The Blind Lion*, *Coyote's Daylight Trip*, and *Shadow Country*; Rose, *Academic Squaw*, *Hopi Roadrunner, Dancing*, *Long Division*, and *Lost Copper*; Sanchez, *Conversations from the Nightmare* and *Message Bringer Woman*; and Silko, *Ceremony* and *Storyteller*.

Autobiographies and personal narratives: Abeita, *I Am a Pueblo Indian Girl*; Bennett, *Kaibah*; and Qoyawayma, *No Turning Back*.

Course Design #2

Life Stories and Native Traditions

In developing a course on American Indian literature, we must keep in mind the continuity between oral expressive forms (myths, legends, stories, songs, mnemonic rituals) and written literary expression (poetry, essays, prose fiction). We can observe the continuance of the oral tradition in the works of a writer like Ella Deloria, who consciously attempts to record that tradition and its importance to her tribe in *Dakota Texts*. As a writer, Ella Deloria extends the tradition of the American Indian woman as repository and purveyor of culture. We have seen how the position of the woman in the mythic structure of tribal cosmologies has allowed her historically to develop a storytelling function within her community. What may not be so apparent, perhaps, is the process by which she emerges as a conscious writer. We can chart the transition from reliance on primarily oral forms to the conscious transformation of those forms into literary genres by examining ethnographic biographies, life stories, and native traditions.

The value of this kind of analysis is twofold: (1) it articulates links between oral and written forms, thereby establishing a literary tradition for American Indian women writers, and (2) it provides us with important information about the historical and cultural development of women within American Indian societies. This discussion will focus on ways in which we can teach life stories and ethnographic materials as literature and treat them as the precursors of the generic prose narrative.

Storytelling is a ritual act of re-creation and generation. It is a way of establishing historical and metaphorical connections between individuals and their universe.

Indian women began to emerge as literary chroniclers of native traditions in the nineteenth century by writing down their life stories for a primarily white audience or by telling the stories to anthropologists or ethnographers. Both of these functions are important in the development of the American Indian woman as writer. In the first instance, American Indian women modeled their stories on the sentimental novels of the day and wrote semifictional accounts of their lives. Two such writers are Sarah Winnemucca Hopkins, author of *Life among the Paiutes* (1883), and Zitkala-Sa, author of ''Impressions of an Indian Childhood'' (1900). While works of this type may strike us as overly romanticized accounts of Indian life, they raise the important literary question of audience. Who is the audience for the American Indian woman writer? In many instances, audience dictates form, and one can easily see that some of the first literary exercises of Indian women may be imitations of Anglo-American literary forms, especially since the oral tradition by definition provides no written models.

The relationship of the author to her material is another important issue. The writers often use English to describe a life story within a community that is quite distinct culturally and linguistically from Anglo-American society. This convergence of English and American Indian traditions raises the literary problems of voice and point of view. How does the author authenticate her story when she has removed the storytelling process from its oral context? This conflict may well be the first literary example of the dilemma of every author who writes out of both Anglo-American and American Indian traditions. While the narrative forms are not fully developed in the literature of the women writers, we do see the beginnings of a conscious effort to transform American Indian oral forms into written forms.

Ethnographic biographies, however, raise other issues. The autobiographies told by women to anthropologists were influenced by the cultural orientation of the anthropologists, whose questions could shape the response of the storyteller, inhibiting both narrative flow and content. The question of authenticating the text becomes crucial. One way to approach the ethno-graphic biographies is to view them in relationship to the frames in which they are set. Just as white abolitionists supposedly established, in their prefaces, the verity of slave narratives by testifying to the "blackness" of the narrators, so too do anthropologists and ethnographers, through their introductions and footnotes, unwittingly create a context of values. The major literary question in the autobiographies, then, is that of authorial control over the text. Who is telling the story and, again, to whom and for whom? In what way does the author find her own voice, and can we identify this voice in terms of diction?

Another literary problem is the development of narrative. How does the storytelling process change when external influences, such as the presence of outside examiners, are introduced? How does context change process? We can see this question more clearly when we compare one life story, such as *The Autobiography of a Fox Indian Woman* (ed. Michelson, 1925) to another, such as *Mountain Wolf Woman* (1961). We see several levels of narrative at work in various forms of refinement. First, the relation between the ethnog-rapher and the storyteller forms one narrative—what we might call a narra-tive of intent; that is, the dialectic between the two voices articulates the purpose of the autobiography and defines the audience. Second, there is the narrative of process, or the actual telling of the life story in which the teller establishes her own voice through the process of selecting what material she will communicate. This is often determined by audience, since a good storyteller must create audience interest. Finally, the relation of the preface and the supporting ethnographic materials to the life story itself forms a third level, the narrative of authentication, or the attempt to establish the ethno-graphic biography as a true representation of the customs and history of a given tribe.

Seen in this way, autobiographies become the link between the oral tradition and written literary forms. They also become a vehicle for self-definition of the woman writer. It is interesting to note that autobiography has continued to develop in contemporary literature and may well reflect the desire of the American Indian writer to gain authorial control over her mate-rial. Certainly, the life stories illuminate the process by which the oral tradi-tion informs and structures narrative, providing a transition to contemporary writers such as Leslie Silko and Paula Gunn Allen whose work reflects and extends the oral tradition through the coherence of several levels of narrative.

Viewing ethnographic materials in literary terms should not detract from their importance as documents of historical and cultural change. In fact, the autobiographer's art in shaping her material stands out in clear relief when one compares the life stories with anthropological descriptions of American Indian traditions. With these thoughts in mind, one might include in a section on autobiography examples of romanticized life stories, ethnographic biog-raphies, and essays on American Indian traditions. Students can examine and compare these materials in terms of levels of narrative, diction, point of view, and authorial control of text. Most important, perhaps, autobiography gives us insight into the values of the American Indian woman writer and the process by which she identifies herself and extends and shapes her art to express her particular cultural heritage. (See the extensive lists of autobiographies on pp. 64–65 and 97–98.)

Course Design #3
Contemporary Voices and Literary Craft

Until quite recently the primary literary output of contemporary American Indian women was limited to fine poetry. The publication of Janet Campbell Hale's *Owl Song* and Leslie Silko's *Ceremony*, however, added a new genre to the body of literature by American Indian women. Elizabeth Cook's *Then Badger Said This* introduced yet another approach, a combination of poetic and prose traditions. As contemporary Indian women writers begin to reshape the traditional literature, they no longer express themselves exclusively in tribal forms, nor do they choose to explain their lives through interpreters. Instead, they are reworking ancient beliefs and traditional structures as they continue the process of articulating American Indian experience. Indian women of the twentieth century are speaking in their own voices and out of living cultures.

The culmination of the accumulated years of traditional storytelling can be seen in the work of contemporary women writers such as Leslie Silko. In her short fiction, especially "Storyteller" and "Yellow Woman," Silko provides brief glimpses into the world of the imaginative experience. Her novel *Ceremony* relies essentially and significantly on the oral heritage. Leslie Silko passes on the story of Tayo from Thought-Woman—"I'm telling you the story she is thinking"—and in the process she illuminates the unity of the past and the present.

Poetry by women appears in virtually every recent anthology of American Indian literature. *Voices from Wah'Kon-Tah* (ed. Dodge and McCullough), *The Third Woman* (ed. Fisher), *The Remembered Earth* (ed. Hobson), and *The First Skin around Me* (ed. White) contain, among them, the works of some thirty women poets. Collections such as *Coyote's Daylight Trip* and *Shadow Country* by Paula Gunn Allen, *Academic Squaw* and *Hopi Roadrunner, Dancing* by Wendy Rose, *Conversations from the Nightmare* and *Message Bringer Woman* by Carol Sanchez, and *Laguna Woman* by Leslie Silko provide in-depth studies of the poetry of southwestern Indian women.

Cook combines poetry and prose in *Then Badger Said This*, and the result is a literary form similar to that of Momaday's *The Way to Rainy*

Mountain. Such a work omits the element of romance essential to the novel and focuses instead on the quality of the imagination, the sounds of the language, and the perdurance of traditional form.

Many women are writing nonfiction and providing thought-provoking inquiries into the nature of the literature. Critical articles have appeared in *Indian Historian* as well as *College English, College Composition and Communication, Journal of Ethnic Studies, American Indian Quarterly, Minority Voices, MELUS,* and *Journal of American Indian Culture and Research.* Such articles outline the problems of defining and describing American Indian literature and discuss the symbols and motifs that are prevalent in the literature.

In presenting contemporary literature by American Indian women, an instructor must take note of some fundamental differences between the perspectives presented by American Indian women and those expressed by non-Indian feminist writers of this century. Although some American Indian women articulate feminist views, generally the references to Mother Earth, Spider Woman, Changing Woman, Thought-Woman, and other female principles and deities arise from the oral tradition and not from a political stance. The relation of American Indian women to American Indian men has varied, depending on tribal organization and/or traditions, but both men and women recognize that their separate roles in society are necessary in order for the group to be made whole. Indian women were not and are not the stereotypical followers of the men. Their traditional sense of power comes through clearly in much of the contemporary literature as an expression of the cultural heritage of American Indians, not as political rhetoric. The values expressed throughout the contemporary writing reflect a continuation, not a corruption, of the past.

Modern
and Contemporary
American Indian Literature

Old Traditions and New Forms

A. LaVonne Brown Ruoff

Most of us have been taught that American literature began after the landings at Jamestown and Plymouth Rock. Long before the British landed, however—charter in one hand and Bible in the other, determined to tame both the land and its pagan inhabitants—the natives of North America had developed a richly complex body of oral literatures. What did begin after these landings was the body of American literature written in English. Although the first contributions to this literature were made by British settlers, later contributions were made by American Indians, former slaves, and immigrants from many lands, after they had mastered a new language and unfamiliar literary forms. This article will survey the major works written by American Indians from 1772 to 1959.[1]

The early history of American Indian literature written in English reflects the religious education the Indians received in missionary schools. Among the first to publish in English was Samson Occom (Mohegan, 1723–92). A former pupil of the Reverend Eleazar Wheelock, Occom later served as schoolmaster and minister to various eastern Indian tribes. In 1772 Occom preached a sermon at the execution of Moses Paul, a Mohegan Indian convicted of committing murder while intoxicated. The sermon, with its forceful plea for temperance and its description of the effects of liquor on Indians, was enthusiastically received; temperance sermons were rare in those days, and those addressed to Indians were virtually nonexistent. Issued under the title *A Sermon Preached at the Execution of Moses Paul, an Indian* (1772), this first sermon published by an American Indian became a best-seller and was reprinted in at least nineteen editions. Occom also published *A Choice Collection of Hymns and Spiritual Songs* (1774), which contained several of his own compositions.

David Cusick (Tuscarora, d. c. 1840) was the first Indian to publish a history of his people based on oral traditions, a form incorporated by many later Indian writers into their books. His *Sketches of Ancient History of the Six Nations* may have been published as early as 1825, the date of the preface, but probably was published in 1827. A few paragraphs were added to this twenty-eight page history in the editions of 1828 and 1848. Cusick divides his history into discussions of the myths of the origin of the universe and of North America; the settlement of North America by Indians; and the origin of the kingdom of five nations, wars against fierce monsters, and wars against other tribes.

The earliest major Indian writer of the nineteenth century was William Apes (Pequot, b. 1798). Descended from King Philip, Apes was one quarter white. His *Son of the Forest* (1829) is the first full autobiography published by an Indian. Apes gives a moving account of the abuse he suffered as a child at the hands of his alcoholic grandparents. He uses his experience to introduce an attack on Indian alcoholism, for which he holds whites responsible. After a severe beating, Apes was taken in by a white family and later bound out from age five to a series of masters. He later ran away to join the army during the War of 1812, became a convert to Methodism, and was ordained in 1829. His defense of Indian causes is foreshadowed by his comments on the white image of the Indian, a term he deplored: "But the proper term which ought to be applied to our nation, to distinguish it from the rest of the human family, is that of 'Natives'" (p. 21). Apes attributed his own childhood fear of Indians, developed after living in the white world, to the stereotypical stories of atrocities told him by whites. To educate his audience in Indian history, Apes appends to his autobiography numerous excerpts from historical accounts of Indian-white relations. The autobiography and the appended history established a model followed by subsequent Indian writers—that of combining personal reminiscence with history.

Apes also published *The Experience of Five Christian Indians of the Pequod Tribe: or, the Indian's Looking-Glass for the White Man* (1833). His *Indian Nullification of the Unconstitutional Laws of Massachusetts, Relative to the Marshpee Tribe* (1835) is a well-documented account of the grievances of this tribe, which Apes joined and encouraged in its fight for justice. Apes's *Eulogy on King Philip* (1836) demonstrates his oratorical power.

Like Occom, Elias Boudinot [Galagina] (Cherokee, c. 1803–39) was educated at a mission school. In 1824 he was appointed editor of the new *Cherokee Phoenix*, and the Reverend Samuel A. Worcester became his assistant. Written primarily in English and partly in Cherokee, this weekly newspaper was published between 1828 and 1835, when it was suppressed by the Georgia authorities for its unfavorable remarks about the state. Boudinot also translated into Cherokee a short fictional work entitled *Poor Sarah*, published in 1833. A staunch proponent of the necessity of Cherokee removal to Indian Territory, Boudinot was assassinated by Cherokee enemies in 1839. Another Indian author of this period was Paul Cuffe (Pequot), who in 1839 published a brief account of his thirty years at sea and in foreign travels: *Narrative of the Life and Adventures of Paul Cuffe, a Pequot Indian*.[2]

By mid-nineteenth century, Indians from the woodland areas of the Midwest and Canada had begun writing and publishing. The most prolific writer of this period was George Copway [Kahgegagahbowh] (Ojibwe, 1818–69). A convert to Methodism, Copway had only three years of formal schooling at Ebenezer Academy in Jackson, Illinois. His *Life, History, and Travels of Kah-ge-ga-gah-bowh* (1847), the first book written by a Canadian Indian, was so popular that it went through six editions in a single year. The revised edition appeared under two titles: *The Life, Letters and Speeches of Kah-ge-ga-gah-bowh, or, G. Copway* (1850) and *Recollections of a Forest Life: or, The Life and Travels of Kah-ge-ga-gah-bowh, or George Copway* (1850). In this book, Copway echoes Apes's condemnation of liquor and its effect on Indians. He also emphasizes his commitment to Christianity and education as the salvation of the Indian: "I loved the woods, and the chase. I had the nature for it, and gloried in nothing else. The mind for letters was in me, *but was asleep*, till the dawn of Christianity arose, and awoke the slumbers of the soul into energy and action."[3] The book contains several powerful descriptions of Ojibwe life, including the family's near starvation one winter. Copway also describes the importance of the dream in Ojibwe religion and in his own experience. He includes one of his own poems expressing his sorrow at the departure of many of the Indians who once roamed the land, lamenting, "Where have my proud ancestors gone?" (p. 96). He demonstrates his oratorical style and his commitment to the Indian cause in his attack on the government's treatment of American Indians and on its emphasis on money rather than on education: "I would now ask, what are millions of money without education? I do not mean that an *equivalent* should not be given for lands ceded to the government. No; but I do mean that this equivalent should be appropriated in such a way as to produce the greatest benefits and the happiest results" (p. 127). The book closes with a discussion of why the Indian population has diminished and what should be done to help these suffering people—themes repeated often in his books and speeches. Copway attributes the Indians' decline to alcohol, disease, inability to pursue a new course of living, and broken spirit. To combat these, he urges education and the establishment of a separate Indian nation—the major political cause for which he fought for many years (pp. 140–41).

Copway's *Traditional History and Characteristic Sketches of the Ojibway Nation* (1850; 1851) is the first history of that tribe to be published by an Indian. It later appeared under the title *Indian Life and Indian History* (1858). In addition to describing the topography of traditional Ojibwe territory, Copway traces his people's migrations as contained in their legends and discusses their wars with such perpetual enemies as the Iroquois, Huron, and Sioux. He also describes the tribe's religious beliefs, forms of government, language and pictograph writings, modes of hunting, and games. His inclusion of a selection of traditional myths and stories served as a model for later Indian writers. Copway's *Running Sketches of Men and Places, in England, France, Germany, Belgium, and Scotland* (1851) contains his impressions of his tour of Europe on his way to serve as a delegate to the Peace Congress at Frankfurt. He begins with a tribute to his native land:

> My heart can but *One* native country know
>   And that, the fairest land beneath the skies.
> America! farewell; thou art that gem,
> Brightest and fairest in earth's diadem. (p. 15)

Copway describes the ocean in Byronic terms: "Here too are objects of terror—shoals and quicksands that lie treacherously concealed, waiting the behests of Fate, and the manic fury of the Ocean to give their desolate bosoms the treasures of which they are forever bereft" (p. 21). He pays tribute to Great Britain, which he finds "not so large in extent of territory as some countries, but large in point of population and the intelligence of the people" (p. 84). He includes brief character sketches of such luminaries as Disraeli, Lord John Russell, and Baron de Rothschild, as well as an enraptured account of a concert by Jenny Lind.[4]

Copway's following among such intellectuals as Longfellow, Cooper, Irving, Morgan, Schoolcraft, and Parkman enabled him to establish a weekly, *Copway's American Indian*, published between July and fall 1851. His continued financial appeals, however, and his supporters' declining confidence in his credibility gradually caused them to abandon him. Little is known of his activities from 1851 to 1867, when he advertised himself in Detroit as a healer. He renounced Methodism, returned to his Indian religion, and finally converted to Catholicism shortly before his death in 1869.

During this period, other Ojibwes were recording their personal experiences and the history of their nation. Peter Jones [Kahkewaquonaby] (1802–56), a Methodist missionary, wrote his *Life and Journals of Kah-ke-wa-quo-na-by*. Published in 1860, four years after Jones's death, this book contains a brief autobiography and a description of his mission among the Ojibwes and other tribes between 1825 and 1855. His *History of the Ojebway Indians* was published in 1861. Though this book and Copway's history cover some of the same material, Jones also gives an analysis of Ojibwe marriage customs, the structure of the language, a fervent defense of Indians' morality and ability to learn, and accounts of Indian affairs in which he participated. Another Ojibwe Methodist missionary, Peter Jacobs [Pahtahsega] (1805–90) wrote a brief journal of his activities, together with a history of the Wesleyan Mission in the Hudson Bay Territories: *Journal of the Reverend Peter Jacobs . . . Commencing May 1852* (1853).

The best and fullest history of the Ojibwes written by a member of that nation was completed in 1852 by William Whipple Warren (1825–53) and entitled *History of the Ojibways, Based upon Traditions and Oral Statements*. Though Warren was unable to find a publisher before he died, the book, together with a memoir, was published in 1885 in the Collections of the

Minnesota Historical Society. Warren's work as an interpreter enabled him to learn much about Ojibwe life and culture. Highly respected by Indians and non-Indians, he was elected to the Minnesota State Legislature in 1850 and was its only Indian member. The success of some earlier sketches about Ojibwe life published in a Minnesota newspaper encouraged him to complete a book-length history. After a general introduction to the Algonkins and to the Ojibwe nation, Warren gives a detailed history of their origin and migration legends, their movement westward, and their battles with enemy tribes. Because he was able to obtain from Ojibwe elders the stories of both the mythic and the historical past, the book is an invaluable guide to general Ojibwe culture and to the histories of various bands.

The publication of these personal and tribal histories stimulated other American Indians to do likewise: Peter Dooyentate Clarke (Wyandott), *Origin and Traditional History of the Wyandotts, and Sketches of Other Indian Tribes* (1870); Chief Elias Johnson (Tuscarora), *Legends, Traditions and Laws of the Iroquois, or Six Nations, and History of the Tuscarora Indians* (1881); and Chief Andrew J. Blackbird [Mackawdebenessy] (Ottawa), *History of the Ottawa and Chippewa Indians of Michigan; A Grammar of Theirr* [sic] *Language, and Personal and Family History of the Author* (1887).

Sarah Winnemucca Hopkins (Paiute, c. 1844–91) was the only Indian woman writer of personal and tribal history during most of the nineteenth century. Born near the Sink of the Humboldt River in Nevada, Sarah was the granddaughter of Truckee, whom she claimed was chief of all the Paiutes, and the daughter of Old Winnemucca, who succeeded his father as chief. Because Sarah and her family followed Truckee's policy of peaceful coexistence with whites, she spent much of her life serving as a liaison between the Paiutes and whites in her people's native Nevada and in Oregon, where they moved to escape white encroachment on their Pyramid Lake Reservation. After the end of the Bannock War of 1878, in which many Paiutes participated after leaving the Malheur Reservation in Oregon, Sarah accompanied her father and her brother Naches to Washington, D.C., to obtain from Secretary of the Interior Carl Schurz permission for the Paiutes to return to the Oregon reservation. Unfortunately, the government provided neither supplies nor transportation for the tribe's return.

Sarah's disillusionment with federal Indian policy and with its agents aroused her to take the Paiute cause to the public. Encouraged by the success of her first lecture in San Francisco in 1879, she toured the East delivering more than three hundred lectures. Both her lectures and her book *Life among the Piutes* (1883) strongly supported the General Allotment Act, then under consideration by Congress.[5] By the time the bill was passed, in 1887, much of the land on the Malheur Reservation to be allotted to the Paiutes had already been seized by whites. Sarah, who had earlier witnessed white seizure of lands at the Pyramid Lake Reservation, lost faith in the power and desire of the government to protect Indian land. Consequently, in 1884 she returned to Nevada to found a school for Paiute children that was located on her brother's farm near Lovelock. Forced by ill health and lack of funds to abandon the school in 1887, she died four years later.

Life among the Piutes is among the most imaginative personal and tribal histories written in the nineteenth century. Though contemporary critics questioned whether Sarah, who was largely self-educated, actually wrote the book, scholars today generally agree that internal evidence and the statement by Mrs. Horace Mann that her editorship was minimal substantiate Sarah's authorship. The book vividly portrays young Sarah's paralyzing fear of the whites her grandfather so respected. Especially moving is her description of her terror while being buried alive temporarily by her parents to hide her from whites who were reputed to be cannibals. With a sharp eye for detail, Sarah re-creates scenes and dialogue that give her descriptions an immediacy missing in many other histories of the period. Her chapter on the domestic and social moralities of the Paiutes offers valuable insight into the tribe's world views.

Most of the book, however, is devoted to description of the Paiute-white conflicts. Though she admires white achievements, Sarah eloquently attacks the religious hypocrisy of white Christians determined to take all Indian land and exterminate its inhabitants. Though they covenant with God to make this land the home of the free and the brave, they rise to seize the welcoming hands of the land's owners: "your carbines rise upon the bleak shore, and your so-called civilization sweeps inland from the ocean wave; but, oh, my God! leaving its pathway marked by crimson lines of blood, and strewed by the bones of two races, the inheritor and the invader; and I am crying out to you for justice" (p. 207).

Although autobiography, history, and reinterpretations of oral stories overwhelmingly dominated the writing by American Indians during the nineteenth century, John Rollin Ridge (Cherokee) directed his talents to journalism, fiction, and poetry. Ridge (1827–67) was the half-Cherokee grandson of Major Ridge, one of the most influential leaders of the tribe before removal. Both Major Ridge and his son John were assassinated for their role in bringing about the sale of Cherokee lands. John Rollin Ridge was only twelve at the time of the forced walk to Indian Territory. Late in his teens, he shot a man—probably in self-defense—and fled in 1850 to the California gold fields, where he worked as a clerk. Writing under the name "Yellow Bird," a literal translation of his Cherokee name Cheesquatalawny, Ridge became a regular contributor to such San Francisco periodicals and journals as *Gold Era, Hesperian,* and *Pioneer.* His most famous work is his fictional biography, *The Life and Adventures of Joaquín Murieta, the Celebrated California Bandit* (1854). Though the novel made him no money because the publisher absconded with the firm's profits, it established the image of

Murieta as a folk hero and precipitated a flood of stories, dramas, and films that made Murieta a popular figure in Mexican and California legend. Ridge portrayed Murieta as a Robin Hood figure, driven to evil deeds by circumstances but always willing to aid a fair damsel in distress. To strengthen the credibility of his fiction masquerading as fact, Ridge created imaginary dialogue. As the following passage illustrates, the novel races at a breathless pace, filled with derring-do and punctuated by gunfire:

> He dashed along that fearful trail as if he had been mounted upon a spirit-steed, shouting as he passed:
> "I am Joaquín! kill me if you can!"
> Shot after shot came clanging around his head, and bullet after bullet flattened on the wall of slate at his right. In the midst of the first firing, his hat was knocked from his head, and left his long black hair streaming behind him.[6]

Although he never published another novel, Ridge did continue to write for journals. One year after his death, his wife published his collected *Poems* (1868), most of which were written before he reached twenty. The volume also contained an autobiographical account of his life to age twenty-three. Only two poems reflect his Indian background: "A Cherokee Love Song" and "The Stolen White Girl." Although most of the poems are sentimental, his "The Arkansas Root Doctor" is an interesting character sketch showing his ability to develop a narrative and to use dialect. The best poem is "The Humboldt River," a moving description of the agonies suffered by a group crossing the Nevada alkali flats.

The first American Indian novel devoted to the subject of Indian life is Simon Pokagon's *O-gî-mäw-kwĕ Mit-i-gwä-kî (Queen of the Woods)* (1899). Pokagon (Potawatomi, 1830–99) was the son of Chief Leopold, whose territory near South Bend, Indiana, encompassed present-day Chicago. Educated at Notre Dame high school, at Oberlin, and in Twinsburg, Ohio, Simon Pokagon was often described as the most educated full-blooded Indian of his day. Andrew Blackbird was his classmate at Twinsburg. In his semiautobiographical novel, Pokagon uses himself as the narrator, gives his wife's name, Lonidaw, to the chief character, and includes some details of their backgrounds. The dramatic deaths suffered by the character Lonidaw and her daughter, however, are fictional. The novel, published a few months after Pokagon's death, contrasts the idyllic forest life of the Potawatomi with the destructive forces introduced by the white man.

The novel opens with Pokagon's expressing his desire to return to the wild life after attending school. When he does return, he meets Lonidaw, a kind of woodland nymph completely in tune with nature. Perfect in mold and make of body, with dark eyes full of soul, she is accompanied by a snow-white deer (sacred in Potawatomi mythology). Though Pokagon returns to school, the power of Lonidaw and the woodland life call him back so that the two can be married. In a highly romanticized scene reminiscent of Chateaubriand's *Atala* or the Haidée episode in Byron's *Don Juan,* Lonidaw decorates Pokagon's hair with evergreens and calls to wild pigeons with "musical chattering": "It was a most endearing sight to behold these beautiful flowers of the animal creation in their native state close by, with their brilliant coloring of gold and royal purple intermixed, outrivaling the beauty of the rainbow."[7] After the couple marries, the white deer, jealous of Pokagon, departs forever. Pokagon and Lonidaw abandon the white world for the beauties of forest life, rearing their two children in solitude.

When their son reaches twelve, however, Pokagon sends him off to school against Lonidaw's wishes, only to see him return three years later as an adolescent drunk. The destructive effects of alcohol on Indians dominate the last part of the novel. Shortly after the boy's return, Pokagon's daughter is killed when her canoe is run down by a boat operated by two inebriated whites. Lonidaw almost drowns in a vain attempt to save her daughter. Weeks later, while dying of a broken heart, Lonidaw urges Pokagon to dedicate his life to fighting alcohol, which claimed first her father and then her children. The novel ends with a strong attack on liquor and other vices and a powerful description of delirium tremens. The novel is of interest as an idealization of the Indians' carefree life in the forest before the coming of the whites and as a vivid illustration of how white vices destroy innocent Indians. It is also of interest for its introductory essay on the Potawatomi language and for its incorporation of Potawatomi dialogue into the fabric of the plot.

At the turn of the century, Indian writers continued to devote their energies to autobiography and to histories and portrayals of Indian culture in conflict with white authority. Among the best-known autobiographies of this period is *The Middle Five* (1900) by Francis La Flesche (Omaha, c. 1857– 1932), which describes the experiences of La Flesche and his Indian friends at a Presbyterian mission school in Bellevue, Nebraska. La Flesche's goal was to reveal the true nature and character of the Indian boy. His autobiography emphasizes the adjustments faced by the boys when they entered school and their happiness when living the old life—a recurrent theme in the autobiographies of the period. Most of La Flesche's writing, however, was devoted to the new discipline of anthropology, to which he and Alice Fletcher contributed such important studies as *The Omaha Tribe* (1911) and *The Osage Tribe* (1924–28). Indians contributed significantly to the collection, translation, and interpretation of American Indian oral literature between the 1890s and 1930s. Among these anthropological writers were William Jones (Fox), Ella Deloria (Sioux), John N. B. Hewitt (Tuscarora), William Morgan (Navajo), Archie Phinney (Nez Perce), and Arthur C. Parker (Seneca).

The most influential and widely read American Indian writer of the first part of the twentieth century was Charles Eastman [Ohiyesa] (1858–1939). In his lifetime, Eastman moved from the nomadic tribal life of the Santee Sioux to the drawing rooms and lecture halls of America and England, meeting such illustrious people as Matthew Arnold, Henry Wadsworth Longfellow, Ralph Waldo Emerson, Francis Parkman, and Theodore Roosevelt. Though often described as a full-blooded Sioux, Eastman was at least one-quarter white. His mother's grandfather was Seth Eastman, a New Englander, and her mother was at least one-fourth French. The 1862 Minnesota Sioux uprising determined the direction of Eastman's early life. His father, Jacob Eastman (Many Lightnings), was imprisoned as a result of his participation in the conflict. Eastman was taken at age four by his grandmother and uncle first to the northern Dakota Territory and later into Manitoba as the Sioux fled the white backlash. Until he was fifteen, Eastman led the life of a traditional Santee Sioux boy and was isolated from contacts with whites. The return of his father ended this free life. Convinced by his experiences during imprisonment that Indians must take up the book and the plow if they were to survive, Jacob Eastman took his son to Flandreau, Dakota Territory, and insisted that the boy begin school. For the next seventeen years, Charles Eastman attended a series of schools, including Dartmouth College (class of 1887) and Boston University Medical School, from which he received his M.D. in 1890 at age thirty-two.

Eastman assumed his first position as agency physician at Pine Ridge in November 1890, just as the Ghost Dance religion swept through the reservation. He tended the survivors of the Wounded Knee massacre, which occurred the same year. During this period he met and married Elaine Goodale, a Massachusetts writer and teacher on the Great Sioux Reservation. Although Eastman returned to Pine Ridge with his bride, he soon left because of policy disputes. After an unsuccessful attempt to establish a medical practice in St. Paul, he spent the next two decades in a variety of positions pertaining to Indian affairs. During World War I, the Eastmans purchased a summer camp in New Hampshire, for which Eastman served as director. Different world views, increasing incompatability, years of financial strain, and the death of a beloved daughter in 1921 took their toll on the Eastmans' marriage. That year Elaine and Charles went their separate ways. Elaine remained in the East. Charles moved to Detroit to live with their only son, eventually purchasing a small wooded property near Desbarats, Ontario, where he built a cabin. During the last decade of his life, he depended on generous friends for financial support. In 1939, after a tepee in which he had been living caught fire, Eastman suffered smoke inhalation and a short time later contracted both pneumonia and a heart condition. He died on 8 January 1939.

Eastman's literary career began in 1893, when an autobiographical sketch was published. During their years together, Eastman and his wife collaborated on his books, as he acknowledged in *From the Deep Woods to Civilization*: "The present is the eighth that I have done, always with the devoted cooperation of my wife. Although but one book, 'Wigwam Evenings,' bears both our names, we have worked together . . ." (pp. 185–86). Elaine Goodale Eastman, a talented and published writer before her marriage, confirms this, emphasizing that she collaborated on all of his nine books.[8] The extent to which Elaine Goodale Eastman was essential to Charles Eastman's productivity as a writer is indicated by the fact that after their separation he never published again, while she continued to publish poetry, essays, and fiction.

Eastman began his first book, *Indian Boyhood* (1902), for his children. The opening lines express the spirit Eastman hoped to transmit to his readers: "What boy would not be an Indian for a while when he thinks of the freest life in the world? This life was mine. Every day there was a real hunt. There was real game."[9] The book combines personal experiences with history, tales, descriptions of Sioux customs, and character sketches. Eastman introduces his reader to such traumatic episodes in his boyhood as having to sacrifice his dog—though he does not tell his young readers that the dog was to be eaten as part of a ritual. The book ends with the arrival of his father after release from prison.

In 1916 Eastman published the second part of his autobiography, *From the Deep Woods to Civilization*. Here he is far less conscious of the need to convince his audience of the validity of the Indian world view and customs. The book shows the deepening of his own sense of Indianness experienced during his 1910 field work with the Ojibwe in the dense forest of northern Minnesota. He openly questions the superiority of the white way and reveals some of his frustrations in facing and overcoming the midwestern fear of the Sioux. He expresses some of this in his account of his years at Dartmouth (1883–87): "It was here I had most of my savage gentleness and native refinement knocked out of me. I do not complain, for I know that I gained more than their equivalent" (p. 67). The autobiography contains some forceful criticisms of government policy, particularly its indifference to the hunger and protests of the Sioux, which Eastman felt led to the spread of the Ghost Dance religion: "Never was more ruthless fraud and graft practiced upon a defenseless people than upon these poor natives by the politicians! Never were there more worthless 'scraps of paper' anywhere in the world than many of the Indian treaties and Government documents" (p. 99). Eastman closes the book by stating that his object has been to present American Indians in their true character before non-Indian Americans.

In all his works and lectures, Eastman attempted to serve as a bridge between Indian and white cultures—to reveal to his white audience the world views, customs, literature, and history of the Indians so that non-Indian Americans might appreciate and emulate American Indian virtues. He makes his most fully developed statement of his concept of Indian ethics in *The Soul of the Indian* (1911), in which he describes the worship of the "Great Mystery" as "silent, solitary, free from all self-seeking" (p. 4). He stresses that the Indian faith was not formulated in creeds or forced on those unwilling to receive it. There were no temples and no shrines except those of nature. In *The Indian To-day* (1915), Eastman surveys Indian history, contributions to America, achievements, reservation life, and problems, and he discusses government policies toward the Indian. His *Indian Heroes and Great Chieftains* (1918) is a collection of short biographies, primarily of Sioux leaders. The book is among his most interesting works because of its anecdotes, which the leaders or their contemporaries told to Eastman.

Eastman's books for children were extremely popular. In *Red Hunters and the Animal People* (1904), he combined traditional legends with adventure and animal stories based on common experiences and observations of Indian hunters. *Old Indian Days* (1907), even more explicitly imaginative than the earlier book, is divided into stories about the warrior and those about the woman. *Wigwam Evenings: Sioux Folktales Retold* (1909) contains traditional stories rewritten to hold the attention of young children; the authors altered the Trickster stories to eliminate offensive elements. This book was also issued in 1910 under the title *Smoky Day's Wigwam Evenings: Indian Stories Retold.*

Eastman's reinterpretations of Indian stories and his autobiographies stimulated the publication of similar works by other Sioux writers. In 1916 Marie McLaughlin published *Myths and Legends of the Sioux*, with a short autobiography. Zitkala Sa [Gertrude Bonnin] (1876–1938) published two collections: *Old Indian Legends* (1901), her re-creation of Sioux legends, and *American Indian Stories* (1921), which includes her short stories about her people (two of which were printed earlier by *Harper's Magazine*) and her autobiographical essays published in 1900 and 1902 by the *Atlantic Monthly*. These were her only literary works; she spent most of her life as a dedicated worker for Indian rights.

Next to Eastman, the most widely read Sioux writer was Luther Standing Bear [Ota K'te] (c. 1868–1939), a member of the Teton or Western Sioux. Though he claimed to be an Oglala, Standing Bear may actually have been a Brule. Like Eastman, Standing Bear belonged to the generation of Sioux who witnessed the end of the old wild life and the beginning of reservation life. He joined the first class at the Carlisle Indian School, established in 1879 by Richard Henry Pratt, an army officer, to educate and civilize young Indians. By 1884 Standing Bear had returned to the reservation to teach and eventually to marry. Frustrated by agency restrictions and by the difficulties of earning a living on the reservation, Standing Bear eagerly signed up with

Buffalo Bill's Wild West Show, which toured the United States and England in 1902. Severe injuries suffered in a 1903 train wreck prevented him from joining a second tour. By 1907 he found life on the reservation so intolerable that he left to appear in shows in the East. His experiences made him decide to sell his allotment and seek citizenship, which he did in 1907. Five years later, he had settled in California, where he became a movie actor, lecturer, and volunteer for Indian causes.

Standing Bear's career as an author began late in life when he was persuaded to write his popular autobiography, *My People, the Sioux* (1928). Assisted by E. A. Brininstool, Standing Bear gives a simple but straightforward account of the life of the Western Sioux and their adjustments to reservation living. Especially moving are his descriptions of his early experiences at Carlisle. In 1933 Standing Bear published *Land of the Spotted Eagle*, assisted by Melvin Gilmore and Warcaziwin (or Wahcaziwin). Though enlivened by personal anecdotes, this book focuses far more on Sioux beliefs, customs, and life than did *My People, the Sioux*. The conditions Standing Bear found on the Pine Ridge Reservation in South Dakota, after an absence of sixteen years, so shocked him that he was spurred to write his second book. He forcefully criticizes federal Indian policy and describes his Carlisle experiences with great bitterness. In the last two chapters, "Later Days" and "What the Indian Means to America," Standing Bear powerfully states his feelings about the damage done to Indians by whites and about the need for the country to recognize the contributions of American Indians. In addition to these two books, Standing Bear also wrote *My Indian Boyhood* (1931), directed to children, and *Stories of the Sioux* (1934), a collection of stories.

Writers of other tribes also followed Eastman's example. The most adventure-filled autobiography to appear during World War I was Joseph Griffis' *Tahan: Out of Savagery into Civilization* (1915). Griffis was born around 1854 to a white father, the famous scout California Joe, and a half-Osage mother, Al-Zada. When Griffis was four, Kiowas captured him and killed his mother. A Kiowa stepfather and a Cheyenne stepmother adopted him, and he lived with them until 1868. That year, while young Griffis and his stepmother visited relatives at the Washita River, Custer attacked, massacring 103 women and children. Both Griffis and his stepmother were taken prisoner by the troops, for whom his own father served as chief scout. Identified as a white captive, Griffis was placed on a ranch, from which he quickly escaped. He subsequently engaged in a series of daring escapades as a member of a ragtag Indian band, an outlaw, an army scout, a hobo, and a petty thief. After eventually making his way to Canada, Griffis converted to Christianity, joined the Salvation Army, and married a white woman. After becoming a Presbyterian minister in the East, Griffis moved to Oklahoma, where he left the ministry to become a lecturer. Aside from the description of

Griffis' exploits, the autobiography contains material on Kiowa life as well as a vivid account of the Washita massacre. In addition to this book, Griffis also wrote *Indian Circle Stories* (1928), a collection of tales from various Oklahoma tribes.

The only Pueblo Indian to write a book during this period was James Paytiamo, whose *Flaming Arrow's People, by an Acoma Indian* appeared in 1932. This beautifully illustrated book describes Paytiamo's childhood as well as Acoma culture and beliefs. It also contains several myths.

The most widely read and published writer among American Indian women of the turn of the century was Emily Pauline Johnson [Tehakionwake] (Mohawk, 1861–1913), the daughter of G. H. M. Johnson [Onwanonsyshon], chief of the Six Nations Indians, and his English-born wife Emily S. Howells. Though she had only two years of formal schooling, Johnson read avidly. Her career as a poet and professional reader began in Toronto in 1892 when she recited her poem "A Cry from an Indian Wife." The recital was such a success that the next day all the Toronto newspapers wondered why she was not a professional reader. In 1894 she began a career as an interpreter of her own works. Always wearing Indian dress and using her Indian name, she continued to perform for the next sixteen years to enthusiastic audiences in Canada and England. Her first engagements in England created a demand there for the publication of her first volume of poems, *White Wampum* (1895). This was followed by *Canadian Born* (1903), published in her native country. Her collected poems were printed in *Flint and Feather* (1912), which included the contents of the first two poetry volumes, miscellaneous poems, and a biographical sketch.

Almost half of the poems in *White Wampum* utilize Indian themes. "Wolverine," "As Red Men Die," and "The Cattle Thief" are strong outcries against the white man's mistreatment of the Indian. In these and in other narrative poems, Johnson uses melodramatic episodes and romanticized diction, reflecting her youthful absorption of Scott, Byron, and Longfellow. *White Wampum* also contains her most famous lyric, "Song My Paddle Sings," which describes the power of the West Wind on the river the speaker traverses with her canoe. Although *Canadian Born* has fewer poems on Indian themes, it does include one of her better Indian character sketches. In "The Corn Husker," Johnson ends her description of an Indian woman who has "Age in her fingers, hunger in her face, / Her shoulders stooped with weight of work and years," with the following stanza:

> And all her thoughts are with the days gone by,
>   Ere might's injustice banished from their lands
> Her people, that to-day unheeded lie,
>   Like the dead husks that rustle through her hands.
>
>   (*Flint and Feather*, p. 95)

Today Johnson is better known for her *Legends of Vancouver* (1911) than for her poetry. Most of the stories were told to her by Chief Joe Capilano (Squamish) of Vancouver, whom she met in London in 1906. Johnson opens each story with a description of a specific scene that figures in the legend. She achieves a casual, conversational tone by telling how she learned the tale and by using dialogue between herself and Chief Capilano to introduce the legend. Her volume is among the most successful of the period in its reinterpretations of oral literature and was the first attempt to record the mythology of the Indians of the north Pacific Coast.

Her final books were entitled *The Shagganappi* and *The Moccasin Maker*, both published in 1913 to raise funds for her care while she was dying of cancer. *The Shagganappi* is a collection of boys' adventure stories, in which the Indians, ranging from the Northeast to the Northwest Coast, are always loyal, protective, and courageous in their relations with whites. The title story (which means "buckskin cayouse" in Cree) describes the triumph of a young mixed-blood named Fire Flint over the prejudice among the boys at his school. Johnson was one of the earliest American Indian writers to introduce the mixed-blood as a central character. "A Red Girl's Reasoning," published in *The Moccasin Maker*, is among Johnson's best works of fiction. In it, the mixed-blood heroine firmly and finally rejects her new husband, who argues that her parents were not married because they had an Indian rather than a church or civil ceremony. Johnson celebrates the deep love that could result from a mixed marriage in her account of her mother's life and marriage to her Mohawk father, entitled simply "My Mother." This tribute to her parents, who married despite family objections, is fictional only to the extent that Johnson changed the participants' names. The story also emphasizes the theme of strong maternal love, which appears in other Johnson stories as well.

At this time, Emily Pauline Johnson was among the very few American Indians whose books of poetry were published. Another was Alexander Posey (1873–1908), a Creek journalist. Posey's father Lewis claimed to be one-sixteenth Creek. His mother, whose English name was Mary Phillips, was a full-blooded Creek and a member of the old and powerful Harjo family. Raised as a Creek, Posey did not learn English until he was twelve. After attending Indian University at Bacone, Posey held a number of educational and journalistic posts in Indian Territory. Because of his knowledge of both Creek and English and because of his integrity, he served as a delegate to almost every council or convention held in that territory. His poems were published by his wife after his death from drowning: *The Poems of Alexander Lawrence Posey* (1910). Most were written between May 1896 and October 1897, after he settled on a farm with his new wife. Although most of Posey's poems are romantic evocations of nature, his "When Molly Blows the Dinner-Horn" celebrates the coming of evening in the spirit of Robert

Burns's "Cotter's Saturday Night." The volume includes one rhetorical protest poem, "On the Capture and Imprisonment of Crazy Snake, January
1900," an allusion to the Creek leader Chitto Harjo, who strongly opposed
allotment. The poem opens:

> Down with him! chain him! bind him fast!
>   Slam to the iron door and turn the key!
> The one true Creek, perhaps the last
>   To dare declare, "You have wronged me!"
> Defiant, stoical, silent
>   Suffers imprisonment! (p. 88)

   In 1901 Posey edited the *Indian Journal* at Eufaula, Oklahoma, in which
his "Fus Fixico Letters" originally appeared. Fixico dutifully reports in his
letters, written in Creek-style English, his friends' opinions on corruption and
politics in Indian Territory after allotment. Posey heightened the humor of the
letters by including well-known Creek elders as characters. An accomplished
satirist, Posey was influenced by Burns, whom he greatly admired. He no
doubt was also influenced by Finley Peter Dunne, whose fictional Mr.
Dooley and Mr. Hennessey first began their political commentaries in the
1890s. Posey's satires and his witty newspaper columns, which received
national recognition after they were widely reprinted, established an Indian
model for political humor. Some years later, a fellow Oklahoman, Will
Rogers, would receive even greater recognition as a political satirist.
   Like Posey, Rogers (Cherokee, 1879–1935) was a member of a family
prominent in Indian Territory. Young Will, however, chose not to follow the
path of his father Clement Vann Rogers, who was a prosperous rancher and
banker as well as a tribal senator. Instead Will left school in 1898 to become
a cowboy and eventually an entertainer, performing rope tricks. By the
beginning of World War I, Rogers had become a regular on the vaudeville
circuit, reaching his greatest successes as a stage performer in the Ziegfield
Follies of 1916–18 and later in 1922 and 1924–25. Rogers' famous line,
"All I know is what I read in the papers," became the preface for his witty
commentaries on the national scene, which endeared him to his audiences.
His first two books, both published in 1919, consisted of these commentaries
plus other material: *Roger-isms: The Cowboy Philosopher on the Peace Conference* and *Roger-isms: The Cowboy Philosopher on Prohibition*. The popularity of Rogers' humor led to a weekly column, which the *New York Times*
began syndicating in 1922. Four years later Rogers accidentally developed
what was to be his most influential written medium—the daily telegram.
These brief reports to the nation began with a cable to the *Times* during a
London trip in 1926. Rogers' trenchant remarks in his short telegrams eventually ran in 350 newspapers. During the 1920s, Rogers published a series of
books based on these columns and on his observations during his many trips

abroad: *Illiterate Digest* (1924), *Letters of a Self-Made Diplomat to His President* (1926), *There's Not a Bathing Suit in Russia* (1927), and *Ether and Me* (1929).

In his writing and in his stage and movie performances, Rogers adopted the role of the wise innocent—a semiliterate cowboy whose bad grammar and hyperpole gained him instant rapport with average Americans. Rogers represented to them the embodiment of an American hero, unabashed by president or prince, always ready to do verbal battle with the hypocrites of big business or government in order to defend the underdog. Rogers never betrayed their trust. In return, the American public made him the most popular humorist of his age, a popularity that continued after his tragic death in a plane crash during a tour of Alaska in 1935.

During the 1920s American Indian writers also produced novels. In 1927 Mourning Dove [Humishuma; Cristal McLeod Galler] (Okanogan, 1888–1936) published *Co-ge-we-a, the Half-Blood,* which she wrote in collaboration with Lucullus McWhorter. Her career as a writer is especially remarkable because she completed only the third grade, plus a brief stint in a business school, where she learned to type. She left school to care for her family and spent much of her adult life as a migrant worker in Washington state.

Co-ge-we-a introduces the theme of the mixed-blood's attempt to find his or her place, a concern that dominates much of the fiction written by American Indians in the 1930s and in the 1970s. The heroine Cogewea becomes infatuated with a "crafty Easterner," whose fancy ways draw her away from a mixed-blood cowboy suitor until she realizes that the city man is only after her money. Though she initially rejects her mixed-blood suitor because accepting him would mean "living Indian," she gradually recognizes the importance of the values both he and her aged Indian grandmother represent. After her white lover absconds with some of her savings, she returns to her cowboy. The dilemma faced by mixed-bloods like Cogewea is vividly portrayed in an incident that occurs during a Fourth of July celebration. Dressed as a white woman, Cogewea enters and wins a "ladies' horse race," only to be denied the prize by a judge who calls her a squaw. When she then enters the race for Indian girls, she is told that she has no right to be there because this is a race for "Indians and not for *breeds!*" (p. 66).

Following the publication of this novel, Mourning Dove turned to collecting the legends of the Okanogans, which were printed in *Coyote Stories,* edited by Heister Dean Guie (1933), and in a revised version called *Tales of the Okanogans,* edited by Donald M. Hines (1976).

The most published American Indian writer of the 1920s was John Milton Oskison (1874–1947). One-eighth Cherokee, Oskison was born in Indian Territory. He graduated from Stanford in 1898, when he also won *Century Magazine*'s prize competition for college graduates with the short story "Only the Master Shall Praise," published in January 1900. After doing graduate study in literature at Harvard, he worked for the *New York Evening Post* and for *Collier's Magazine* as an editor and feature writer. He was also a free-lance writer on finance and Indian affairs. Oskison served with the American forces in France during World War I. During the twenties he published the novels *Wild Harvest* (1925) and *Black Jack Davy* (1926), as well as the fictional biography *A Texas Titan: The Story of Sam Houston* (1929). Both novels, "southwesterns" set in Indian Territory just before statehood, are concerned with the new surge of white settlers into Cherokee land near a town called Big Grove. In *Brothers Three* (1935) Oskison perceptively evaluates these two novels when Henry Odell, a fictional version of Oskison, describes his own two early novels: the first is "a mess, misty, sentimental, badly knit, with impossible situations and caricatures of human beings"; the second is somewhat of an improvement, "amateurish, but at least I put into it the people and the country I knew" (pp. 343–44).

Oskison's best novel is *Brothers Three*. Here he demonstrates an ability to develop character and to sustain plot, characteristics missing from his early novels. The book is a history of the Odell family's efforts to establish and hold on to the farm started by the father, Francis, and his quarter-Cherokee wife, Janet. While the father put his trust in the land and its ability to produce if properly respected, the sons use the capital Francis created to finance unsuccessful investments. Each of the three parts of the novel describes the struggle by one of the brothers (Timothy, Roger, and Henry) to break away from farming and the failure of the family's efforts. By the end of the novel, the farm is in debt and the third son, Henry, returns from his New York life as a writer and stock investor to help reestablish it.

Like his two previous novels, Oskison's *Brothers Three* is set in Indian Territory and includes Indians as minor characters. In this novel, however, major characters are also part Indian. Nevertheless, the novel focuses, not on Indian life, but on the importance of honesty, loyalty, hard work, and thrift, represented by Francis and Janet Odell, and on the economic and social history of Oklahoma from the turn of the century through the depression. Janet and Francis Odell's firm character is contrasted with the shiftless character of the poor whites who come to live on land leased from the Indians after allotment and who look down on the Odell boys and any child "however slightly 'tainted' by Indian blood" (p. 55). Oskison's growing interest in his own Indian heritage is evident in the preface to *Tecumseh and His Times* (1938), which is dedicated to "all Dreamers and Strivers for the integrity of the Indian race, some of whose blood flows in my veins; and especially to the Oklahoma Shawnee friends of my boyhood" (p. iii). Oskison believed that Tecumseh symbolized more clearly than any other Indian apostle and warrior "the red man's hope for a paradise regained" (p. viii).

The most accomplished American Indian writers to emerge in the 1930s, John Joseph Mathews and D'Arcy McNickle, became known more for their historical and biographical works than for their fiction. Mathews

(c. 1894–1979) was one-eighth Osage, a descendant of the union between a trader and an Osage woman. His grandmother, born of this union, and her husband John Mathews settled in 1872 on what was then the Osage Reservation, where both Mathews and his father were raised. Mathews served in the aviation branch of the U.S. Signal Corps during World War I. After graduating from the University of Oklahoma in 1920, Mathews completed a B.A. at Oxford University in 1923. He returned to the area of his childhood, near Pawhuska, Oklahoma, to ranch and to write. While a member of the Osage Tribal Council, on which he served for many years, Mathews was instrumental in establishing the Osage Museum. His first book *Wah'Kon-Tah* (1932) is an account of Osage life from 1878 to 1931. Using the journal of Major Laban J. Miles, the first government agent for the Osage, Mathews colorfully portrays Miles's frustrated attempts to guide the tribe down the white man's road and the Osage's determined struggles to retain the old ways while adapting to the new. The concluding chapter introduces the prototype of the hero of *Sundown*: a young, jazz-age Osage, ashamed of his backward parents but dependent on them for money.

Sundown (1934) is the only novel Mathews published. The protagonist, Challenge Windzer, is the son of a full-blooded Osage mother who is a quiet traditionalist and a three-quarter-blooded father who is a strong advocate of allotment and an avid reader of Byron. Challenge Windzer is a passive hero who rejects his ancestral past without feeling at home in the white-dominated present. As such, he is the forerunner of similar heroes created by Momaday, Welch, and Silko. Although Windzer occasionally feels in adolescence the urge to cast off his clothes and run free, he has become too separated from the life he led as a boy to give in to such urges. His white education has cut him off from his Indian roots. This cultural separation is completed by a brief stint at the University of Oklahoma and by service in the armed forces during World War I. When he returns home after the war, Windzer inherits enough money from the family oil leases to destroy his desire for either education or work. Though he dreams of becoming a lawyer at the end of the novel, he rejects his mother's suggestion that he return to flying. Instead, he falls asleep to dream of glory, rather than accept the challenge of working toward it. Neither Windzer nor his two boyhood Indian friends, who dropped out of the university, one to become an alcoholic and the other a peyote ritualist, have been able to bridge the gap between the two cultures successfully.

Talking to the Moon (1945) is a Thoreauvian account of Mathews' return to the blackjacks region of Oklahoma, where he was raised, to build a cabin and to live in harmony with his environment. Mathews uses the Osage divisions of time by moons as a framework for his highly imaginative blending of myth, history, and personal experience. The book contains some beautifully wrought descriptive passages and some memorable character sketches of the Osage people. Following this book, Mathews published a biography entitled *Life and Death of an Oilman: The Career of E. W. Marland* (1952). Mathews' major work is *The Osages: Children of the Middle Waters* (1961), a lengthy history of the tribe that is a primary source for information about the Osage.

The best-written and most polished novel by an American Indian in the 1930s is D'Arcy McNickle's *The Surrounded* (1936). Half Flathead, or Salish, McNickle (1904–77) attended government boarding school in Oregon, graduated from the University of Montana, and attended Oxford and Grenoble. In *The Surrounded*, his first book, McNickle focuses on the identity crisis faced by Archilde Leon and the violent consequences of the conflict between two cultures. The protagonist is half Flathead and half Spanish, the son of an Indian woman renowned for her Catholic piety and for her refusal to abandon Indian ways and a Spanish father who, after forty years of living among Indians, has no insight into their world view. Though he now feels close to his mother, who lives in a small cabin separate from her husband, Archilde remembers when as a boy he was ashamed of her. The circle of events that will entrap Archilde begins with his promise, after his return home for a brief visit, to take his mother on a last ritual hunt before she dies. His firing a shot into the air during the hunt brings his brother Louis, a horse thief hiding in the mountains who has killed a deer out of season. The game warden confronts the party and kills Louis. The mother then strikes down the warden with a hatchet. A second circle of violence enchains Archilde when his lover Elise LaRose later persuades him to escape to the mountains. There, Archilde is again a passive onlooker as Elise shoots the sheriff who finds them. The female characters are central to the plot because their actions make it impossible for Archilde to leave the reservation. As Archilde tells Elise when she wants to escape, "you can't run away nowdays" (p. 287).

McNickle's next novel is *Runner in the Sun: A Story of Indian Maize* (1954), written for readers of middle school age. Set in the precontact Southwest, the novel describes the culture of the cliff dwellers and the adventures of Salt, a teenage boy who journeys to Mexico to find a hardy strain of corn that his people can grow to save themselves from starvation.

McNickle did not publish another novel until *Wind from an Enemy Sky*, which appeared posthumously in 1978. Here McNickle moves from the clash of two cultures within the individual to that between groups. The plot contrasts the values of the non-Indian culture, symbolized by a dam that cuts off the Indians' water and violates a holy place, with those of the Indian culture, symbolized by the tribe's sacred Feather-Boy medicine bundle. The plot also contrasts the responses of two brothers to government pressure to alter the traditional Indian life-style. Bull, a fierce conservative, keeps his people as far away from white contact as possible. Henry Jim, the elder brother, left the tribe thirty years ago when his younger brother was selected

principal chief, gave the tribe's medicine bundle to a local priest, and became a successful but lonely rancher regarded by the government as its
"masterpiece."

The dying Henry Jim returns to tribal ways, however, and persuades Bull
to get government help in retrieving the medicine bundle. The murder of a
dam engineer by a young Indian sets off the chain of events that ends in
tragedy. The owner of the dam construction company promises to return the
bundle, unaware that it has rotted away from neglect in his museum of
Indian artifacts. When he attempts to substitute a South American Indian
golden statue, Bull kills him and the government agent. An Indian police
officer then kills Bull. Once more the clash of cultures has ended in the death
of the participants. McNickle's forty years of experience in Indian affairs
since the publication of *The Surrounded* have strengthened his belief in the
continuing inability of the representatives of the two cultures to communicate their vastly different world views to one another.

With the exception of his biography *Indian Man: A Life of Oliver La
Farge* (1971), McNickle's other books have been histories: *They Came Here
First* (1949); *The Indian Tribes of the United States* (1962); *Indians and Other
Americans*, with Harold E. Fey (1970); and *Native American Tribalism*
(1973). In addition to being an author, McNickle cofounded the National
Congress of American Indians and served as the first director of the Newberry
Library Center for History of the American Indian.

The only Indian dramatist to achieve critical acclaim during the 1930s
was [Rolla] Lynn Riggs (1899–1954). Descended from Cherokees on his
mother's side, Riggs was born on a farm near Claremore, Oklahoma, which
was then Indian Territory. After graduation from the Oklahoma Military
Academy in 1917, Riggs entered the University of Oklahoma in 1920, where
he continued to write poetry and began to write plays. *Cuckoo*, his first play,
was produced at the university in 1921. To recover from an illness, Riggs
subsequently went to New Mexico. His second play, *Syrian Knives*, was
produced there in 1925.

In 1926 Riggs moved to New York to devote himself to writing. His first
play to be produced on Broadway was *Big Lake* (1927), which was not a
success. Two of his best plays were folk dramas set in Oklahoma and written
during a 1928 Guggenheim fellowship year in Paris: *Borned in Texas*, produced under the title *Roadside* (1930), and *Green Grow the Lilacs* (1931).
The comedy *Roadside* deals with the attempts of a high-spirited cowboy on
the run from the law for his brawling to win the love of a sharp-tongued but
warm-hearted Oklahoma woman. The play was a greater critical than financial success. *Green Grow the Lilacs* achieved both. Full of down-to-earth
humor and lively cowboy songs, this play has been etched into American
consciousness through its adaptation into the hit musical *Oklahoma!* (1943)
by Richard Rodgers and Oscar Hammerstein. Though the musical follows

the play closely, Riggs did not collaborate in its preparation. Both plays demonstrate Rigg's ability to capture Oklahoma dialect and folk culture. Critics have praised his feeling for atmosphere and period as well as his ability to evoke a natural lyricism.

Of particular interest is Riggs's tragedy *Cherokee Night* (1936), which deals poignantly with the sense of loss faced by the mixed-bloods growing up around Claremore as they grow away from their Cherokee heritage during the period 1895–1931. Rigg's first attempt to write a play with a contemporary setting was *Russet Mantle* (1936), produced in New York. A satirical comedy that examines the dilemma faced by modern couples choosing between financial security and romantic love, *Russet Mantle* was praised as a human comedy. Called wise, fresh, and incorrigibly ridiculous, the play was considered by critics to be the best thing Riggs had written. Though Riggs continued to write plays, he did not equal the success achieved by his earlier work.

During his writing career, Riggs also published a volume of poetry entitled *The Iron Dish* (1930) and served as a free-lance screenwriter on such films as *Garden of Allah* and *The Plainsman*. In 1942, he enlisted as a private in the U.S. Army. After the war, Riggs settled in New Mexico. In addition to his work as a writer, Riggs also served as a guest author and director of drama at Northwestern University and the University of Iowa.

During the 1940s and 1950s, the few Indians who published books returned to the genres of cultural history and autobiography used by earlier authors. Among the writers of this period were Ella Deloria (Sioux), *Speaking of Indians* (1944); Ruth Muskrat Bronson (Cherokee), *Indians Are People Too* (1944); and Lois Marie Hunter (Shinnecock), *The Shinnecock Indians* (1950). In 1959 Jason Betzinez (Apache) published his *I Fought with Geronimo*, edited by Wilbur S. Nye. Betzinez wrote this fascinating combination of oral history and personal experience when he was almost one hundred years old. The end of the 1960s saw the evolution of a new generation of American Indian writers who were to publish in numbers unprecedented in the history of American Indian literature in English.

This new period of contemporary American Indian literature began with the publication of two novels by N. Scott Momaday (Kiowa): *House Made of Dawn* (1968) and *The Way to Rainy Mountain* (1969). *House Made of Dawn* brought Momaday more critical acclaim than any previous American Indian novelist had received. Through his emphasis on the problems of Indians in contemporary society, the importance of oral tradition and ritual, and the use of memory to structure plot, Momaday provided an example that several American Indian novelists later followed. *The Way to Rainy Mountain* drew the attention of non-Indian audiences to the interrelationship of oral literature, history, and personal experience. By moving back and forth across the mythic, historical, and recent past, Momaday showed that the identity of the individual grows out of the totality of experiences transmitted from one generation to another. His descriptions of places sacred to the Kiowa in the legends of their origin and migration, of tribal life in Oklahoma, and of his life as a child emphasized the importance of specific locations and of landscape in Indian life.

American Indians have always had a tradition of creativity in story and song. As they were introduced to the written word, Indians used it as a tool both to help preserve their oral traditions and to share them with others. They also used the written word to extend the boundaries of their own creativity into nontraditional genres. From the beginnings of this literature written in English by men like Samson Occom and William Apes to the publication of Momaday's *House Made of Dawn* and *The Way to Rainy Mountain*, American Indian authors have developed an impressive body of written literature. Because most of their works have been out of print until very recently, however, few contemporary American Indian writers had the opportunity to read the work of their predecessors. This impressive body of literature has too long been allowed to languish unread in research libraries. This significant contribution to American literature must no longer be ignored.

Notes

1   Because of space restrictions, this survey is limited to books written by American Indians. I have omitted translations of parts of the Bible and of hymns. Available biographical information is given for authors whose works are discussed.

Research for this article was supported by a fellowship in the Native American Studies Program, Dartmouth College, funded by the Education Foundation of America.

2   Cuffe's father and namesake, the son of a former slave and an Indian mother, became well known as a merchant captain and advocate of Negro exodus to Africa.

3   *The Life, Letters and Speeches of Kah-ge-ga-gah-bowh, or G. Copway* (New York: Benedict, 1850), p. 1; all citations are from this edition.

4   Although the epic poem *The Ojibway Conquest* (1851) was published under Copway's name, it was actually written by Julius Taylor Clark, who allowed Copway to publish it under his own name to raise funds to aid his work among the Ojibwe. It was published under Clark's name in 1898. See Elisha Williams Keyes, "Julius Taylor Clark."

5   The General Allotment Act of 1887 was designed to break up the Indian reservations—a goal supported by both reformers and opportunists. Under this act, Indians who took their land in severalty became citizens of the United States and were subject to all its obligations. Far from turning Indians into prosperous owners of private land, the Allotment Act introduced an era in which Indians lost their land by fraud and by force. By 1934 sixty percent of the land owned by Indians in 1887 had passed out of their control. See Washburn, *The Indian in America*, pp. 242–43.

6   [John Rollin Ridge] [Yellow Bird], *The Life and Adventures of Joaquín Murieta*, p. 87.

7   *O-gî-mäw-kwe Mit-i-gwä-kî*, p. 127.

8   Elaine Goodale Eastman to Mr. Winn, 7 April 1939, A.L.S. in Archives, Baker Library, Dartmouth College. Cited with permission.

9   *Indian Boyhood*, p. 20.

Who Puts Together

Linda Hogan

> I am he who puts together, he who speaks,
> he who searches, says. I search where there
> is fright and terror. I am he who fixes, he who
> cures the person that is sick.[1]

N. Scott Momaday, in his novel *House Made of Dawn*, draws on the American Indian oral tradition in which words function as part of the poetic processes of creation, transformation, and restoration. Much of the material in the novel derives from the Navajo Night Chant ceremony and its oral use of poetic language as a healing power. The author, like the oral poet/singer, is "he who puts together" a disconnected life through a step-by-step process of visualization. This visualization, this seeing, enables both the reader and Abel, the main character, to understand the dynamic interrelatedness in which all things exist and which heals. By combining the form of the Navajo healing ceremony with Abel's experience, Momaday creates harmony out of alienation and chaos, linking the world into one fluid working system.

Momaday is able to achieve this harmony because of his awareness of the language and poesis used in Navajo Chantway practice. The Night Chant is a complex ceremony for healing patients who are out of balance with the world. Its purpose is to cure blindness, paralysis, deafness, and mental disorders by restoring the patient to a balance with the universe, through symbolic actions and through language in the form of song or prayer. Words used to paint images and symbols in the minds of participants evoke visual and imaginative responses from and in the hearer. By multiplying, through speech, the number of visual images in the mind of the hearer, the ceremony builds momentum. Language takes on the power of generation. Various forms of verbal repetition intensify the rhythm, and as description and rhythm build, words become a form of internal energy for the listener.

With knowledge of how language and creative visualization work, a capable singer or writer is able to intensify and channel this energy that derives from words. Sound, rhythm, imagery, and symbolic action all combine so that the language builds and releases, creating stability and equilib-rium. John Bierhorst regards this buildup and release of tension as a form of charged energy: words are positively and negatively charged and resemble electricity. The plus and minus charges allow a transmission of force: "Their ceremonial method is twofold; on one hand the ritual repulses 'evil,' on the other it attracts 'holiness.' Accordingly, each of its separate rites may be categorized as either repulsive or attractive, as either purgative or additory."[2]

This verbal and symbolic accumulation and exorcism have a parallel effect on the body. The mind produces sympathetic responses within the organism. In *The Seamless Web*, Stanley Burnshaw discusses the physiologi-cal effects of language. He claims that "the sources of an artist's vision involve aspects of biological responses and processes of accumulation and release to which no investigation has yet found access" (p. 3). Although Burnshaw is concerned more with the creative act as a release, he finds that the biological organism responds to the suggestion of words and images. In this way, healing can occur as a result of the proper use of language—language as a vehicle for vision, as a means of imagination.

Momaday makes use of accumulation and release in various sections of *House Made of Dawn*. Before Abel can be returned to balance, he is undone in many ways by language. In the exorcistic sections, Abel is broken down by language, his own as well as that of others. We see him taken apart by the words of those who rely on the destructive rather than on the creative capa-bilities of language: "Word by word by word these men were disposing of him in language, *their* language" (p. 95).

The word stands for what it signifies. It has both the power of creation and the power of destruction. For those who do not understand this potential of language, words lack power. Words degraded and overused are capable of destruction. Using language without knowledge of its functions diminishes its creative power. And there is a difference between the understanding that Navajos and other Indian people have of language and the way in which white people use language:

> The white man takes such things as words and literatures for granted. . . . He has diluted and multiplied the word, and words have begun to close in upon him. He is sated and insensitive; his regard for language—for the Word itself—as an instrument of creation has nearly diminished to the point of no return. It may be that he will perish by the Word. (p. 89)

Abel's muteness is a form of paralysis. He is unable to put the past together in his mind, to make use of his own language to make himself whole:

> He had tried in the days that followed to speak to his grandfather, but he could not say the things he wanted; he had tried to pray, to sing, to enter into the old rhythm of the tongue, but he was no longer attuned to it. And yet it was there

still, like memory, in the reach of his hearing. . . . Had he been able to say it, anything of his own language—even the commonplace formula of greeting "Where are you going"—which had no being beyond sound, no visible substance, would once again have shown him whole to himself; but he was dumb. Not dumb—silence was the older and better part of the custom still—but inarticulate. (p. 57)

Abel's inability to articulate, to form a song or prayer, keeps him from achieving wholeness. Without language, his own or that of others, he is unable to visualize. Remembering imprisonment, he realizes the need for imaginative vision and knows that his own lack of seeing narrows the world even more than did the walls of his cell: "After a while he could not imagine anything beyond the walls except the yard outside, the lavatory, and the dining hall—or even the walls really" (p. 97). But after he gains a full awareness of language, vision opens up to him. In "The Priest of the Sun" section, Abel recalls several incidents that reveal the importance of language. He remembers Tosamah's sermon on the Word, Benally's recitation of the Night Chant, Francisco's chanting and praying, and Olguin's discussion of "acts of the imagination" and legal terminology. After this awareness, this memory of language, occurs, Abel's vision takes place. It descends on him like a miracle of health. He sees the runners, "the crucial sense in their going, of old men in white leggings running after evil in the night. They were whole and indispensable in what they did; everything in creation referred to them . . ." (p. 96). And Abel, at this turning point where memories begin to piece together, sees the division and loss of balance that have affected him:

Now, here, the world was open at his back. He had lost his place. He had been long ago at the center, had known where he was, had lost his way, had wandered to the end of the earth, was even now reeling on the edge of the void. (p. 96)

Imagination and vision follow language. Description allows seeing. The potential of language to heal and restore lies in its ability to open the mind and to make the world visible, uniting all things into wholeness just as the runners are whole and indispensable.

That Abel is divided is obvious. He is a person incapable of speech, one who "could not put together in his mind," or imagine (p. 25). Momaday, in his essay "The Man Made of Words," addresses this contemporary division of self from the world and the problem of how the inability to visualize, to imagine, keeps us from harmony with the rest of creation:

We have become disoriented, I believe; we have suffered a kind of psychic dislocation of ourselves in time and space. . . . I doubt that any of us knows where he is in relation to the stars and to the solstices. Our sense of the natural order has become dull and unreliable. Like the wilderness itself, our sphere of instinct has diminished in proportion as we have failed to imagine truly what it is.[3]

The imaginative experience, inspired by the images and symbols of language, becomes a form of salvation. Just as language takes apart and distances, it can also put together. When this crisis of imagination is healed, restoration takes place. Those who understand the potential of words as accumulated energy, as visualization of the physical, can find balance and wholeness. Words used properly and in context, whether in written prose or in the oral form of prayer and incantation, return us to ourselves and to our place in the world. They unify the inner and outer. In this respect, for Abel and for the reader, *House Made of Dawn* works much like the Night Chant. It focuses the imagination, creates a one-pointedness of mind through concrete images. It breaks down and then builds momentum, using the two forces to restore balance.

Language as accumulation is a means of intensifying the power of words. This accumulation combined with the exorcistic, or release, sections of the book takes Abel on a journey of healing, a return to the sacred and to the traditional. When words take on these powers, one is careful with them, careful not to dilute and diminish their meanings as white people have done. Each word needs to carry weight, and this is central to Momaday's understanding of language as a distillation where meaning is intensified by careful use of words. When Tosamah speaks of his grandmother, he shows an understanding of both the healing function of condensed language and the importance of the imaginative journey, guided by words:

> She was asking me to go with her to the confrontation of something that was sacred and eternal. It was a timeless, *timeless* thing. . . . You see, for her words were medicine; they were magic and invisible. . . . And she never threw words away. (pp. 88–89)

Tosamah is able through language to reach some "strange potential of Himself" (p. 85). The ability to say, in poetic form, that which is unspeakable, to create and hold an image in the mind, gives language its power. What is spoken is seen. Words draw images and symbols out of the mind. They take hold of the moment and make it eternal. Tosamah, who in a sense speaks for Momaday, reaches that "strange potential" by experiencing the language he has spoken. He speaks as an inspired poet. As mythically the word created the earth, Tosamah's language creates vision. He is inspired by the language that speaks through him and by its capacity to recover, mentally, the world from which people have become divided. As Octavio Paz says of the poet, "Through the word we may regain the lost kingdom and recover powers we possessed in the far-distant past. These powers are not ours. The man inspired, the man who really speaks, does not say anything personal; language speaks through his mouth."[4]

Language, speaking through Tosamah, restores him to unity with the world. After his speech, he steps back from the lectern, and "In his mind the earth was spinning and the stars rattled around in the heavens. The sun shone, and the moon" (p. 91). He recognizes that a single star is enough to fill the mind and that the value of language lies in its ability to operate on the mind.

Abel also realizes his potential through language, through Benally's recitation of the Night Chant and through Francisco's memories that are "whole." As in the Night Chant, order is achieved through an imaginative journey: Benally takes Abel through this step-by-step process of visualization, singing parts of the Night Chant ceremony. Understanding the power words hold and the sacred action they contain, he sings quietly:

> Restore my feet for me,
> Restore my legs for me,
> Restore my body for me,
> Restore my mind for me,
> Restore my voice for me.
>   (p. 134)

This excerpt from the Night Chant allows the hearer to visualize each part of the body being healed, from the feet up to the voice. The purpose of describing health is to obtain health. This purpose is furthered by taking the patient on an imaginative journey and returning him, restored to himself. Sam Gill, talking about the nature of Navajo ceremonials, points out that "The semantic structure of the prayer is identical to the effect the prayer seeks, the restoration of health."[5] Benally continues, and his singing returns Abel home to his grandfather, Francisco:

> Happily I go forth.
> My interior feeling cool, may I walk.
> No longer sore, may I walk.
> Impervious to pain, may I walk.
> With lively feelings, may I walk.
> As it used to be long ago, may I walk.
> Happily may I walk.
>   (p. 134)

Francisco's dying memories continue the journey, completing the ceremony for Abel. The memories are similar to those Abel experiences in the first section of the book, and they symbolically connect the two men, using identification, which is also an important function of the language in the Night Chant, where the patient and singer identify with the holy ones. Because "the voice of his memory was whole and clear and growing like the dawn," Francisco's words finally restore Abel. Abel, running, at the end of the book, is finally able to sing, and the words he hears are from the Night Chant: "House made of pollen, house made of dawn" (p. 191).

Momaday's use of the journey derives from oral tradition, in which the journey is used as a symbolic act that takes the hearer out of his or her body. The journey is an "act of the imagination" fired by language. In *The Way to Rainy Mountain*, Momaday defines the psychic potential of the mental, or symbolic, journey as a miracle of imagination made up of mythology and legend, an idea in itself:

> It is a whole journey, intricate with motion and meaning; and it is made with the whole memory, that experience of the mind which is legendary as well as historical, personal as well as cultural. (p. 2)

He says that the imaginative recalling of the journey reveals the way in which "these traditions are conceived, developed, and interfused in the mind." It is this interfusion with which we are concerned. The interfusion of things in the mind acts as a catalyst, merging myth, history, and personal experience into one shape, to reassemble the divisions of the self.

Healers and singers from other nations or tribes are also familiar with this traditional use of language as journey, as interfusion. The Mazatec Indians in Mexico use a similar oral technique to cure disease. A medicine woman says of the patient, "Let us go searching for the tracks of her feet to encounter the sickness that she is suffering from."[6] And the healer goes, imaginatively, out of her own body:

> She is going on a journey, for there is distanciation and going there, somewhere without her even moving from the spot where she sits and speaks . . . and the pulsation of her being like the rhythm of walking.[7]

The healer follows the footprints of the patient, looking for clues to the cause of disease in order to return the patient to balance.

Just as the symbolic journey in the Night Chant and the journey in *House Made of Dawn* have their physiological components, so the Mazatec healing ritual has an organic, biological parallel: "it is as if the system were projected before one into a vision of the heart, the liver, lungs, genitals and stomach."[8] Through seeing, through visualizing, the words interact with the nervous system. In traditional oral literature as well as in *House Made of Dawn*, speaking is healing.

Momaday's imaginative, visual creation and fusion of myth and history with the present returns us to the idea of positively and negatively charged language. For what takes place within the mind, acted on by language, also takes place within the body. Language conceived as accumulation and release is language that can pass the reader/hearer across a threshold into equilibrium. Burnshaw, in a discussion of creativity, focuses on the transformational qualities of words used in this capacity:

. . . a creative artist inhales the surrounding world and exhales it. Whatever is taken in is given back in altered condition or transformed into matter, action, feeling, thought. And in the cases of creative persons, an additional exhalation: in the form of words or sounds or shapes capable of acting upon others with the force of an object alive in their surrounding worlds.

Such an object arises out of characteristic cycles of accumulation and release. . . . (p. 33)

A singer, writer, or healer is able to unite the internal with the external. This unity of word with the force of an object is the theoretical framework for *House Made of Dawn*. The structure of the book replicates the progression of the Night Chant, making use of mythology, history, symbolism, and creation to stimulate response in the reader. Just as the Night Chant ceremony seeks to duplicate the universe in the mind of the hearer, Momaday creates a model of the universe in the book. Each section contains repetitions of images and symbols of the universe that are fragmented and need to be united again into one dynamic system.

These repetitions are important in channeling the energy of language. In Navajo Chantway practice, according to Gladys Reichard, the more often something is repeated, the more power it has to concentrate the mind and focus attention.[9] Through this concentration, through a balance brought about by accumulation and release, the union of time, space, and object takes place within the imagination. The words of prose or poetry function like an opening of the self into the universe and the reciprocal funneling of the universe into the self.

This repetition and the replication of the universe assist seeing, or vision. Language in this poetic function, which resembles the oral traditions, "provides a double system of images and forms for the body and mind to work with in seeking to understand one system by another."[10] It is as though two universes, or systems, one internal and the other external, act simultaneously upon the hearer and fuse together. Inner and outer merge and become the same. Words are linked with the objects they designate. Past and present merge. This comes about through the circular organization of the book, the expansion and contraction and the order that give the book its sense of poetic presence and immediacy.

These methods are characteristic of oral tradition, in which the word and the object are equal and in which all things are united and in flux. The distinctions between inner and outer break down. Momaday, making use of these oral techniques in his poetic language, returns Abel, along with the reader, to an earlier time "before an abyss had opened between things and their names."[11]

This return gives to words a new substance and power not unlike that of oral ritual. The life of the word and the fusion of word and object, by means of the visual imagination, return the participant or reader to an original source that is mythic, where something spoken stands for what is spoken about and there is "no difference between the telling and that which is told."[12] It is a form of dynamic equilibrium in which all things are assembled into wholeness and integrated and in which persons can "name and assimilate" (p. 111).

Speaking or hearing becomes a form of action. Reichard comments, "The Navajo believe, in common with many American Indians, that thought is the same or has the same potentiality as word. To thought and words they add deed, so that there is no use trying to differentiate."[13] Words are actions that have the ability to align and heal. This concept is the basis for the Night Chant, in which the patient identifies with the gods, goes on a symbolic journey, and is made holy. By the patient's visualizing the action, the action takes place and the patient is restored. The ceremony consists of "words the utterance of which is actually the doing of an action."[14] Abel's ability to see, to concentrate his being, at the end of the book is the result of language.

Words, therefore, are a materialization of consciousness. And deeds are the manifestation of words. By evoking in the hearer or reader a one-pointedness of mind, the poem, song, or prayer becomes more than just expression. It is a form of divine utterance that moves us to action, that is action itself. It is an extension of the internal into the external.

Language used in this way becomes a form of dynamic energy, able to generate and regenerate. Attention, focused by language, has the power to give existence to something imagined. Words, sung or written, cast off their ordinary use and become charged with a luminous new energy. They accumulate the power to return us to a unity of word and being, linking the internal with the external. As in the Orphic tradition, language creates the world and lets the world return through the song or the word.

The song or word in oral tradition is responsible for all things, all actions. According to Navajo accounts, the universe was created by the word. According to Reichard, the Navajo say that in prehuman times the original state of the universe was one word.[15] Tosamah, a Kiowa, also acknowledges this creative ability of the word and understands that through this creation (which was the word) all things begin and are ordered:

> Do you see? There, far off in the darkness, something happened. Do you see? Far, far away, in the nothingness something happened. There was a voice, a sound, a word, and everything began. (p. 90)

Language perceived as creation and as a unity of word and being has the power to heal. Combining the oral elements of word energy created by accumulation and release, imaginative journey and visualization, Momaday restores Abel to his place within the equilibrium of the universe. Momaday assumes the traditional role of speaker as healer by permitting Abel and the reader to see the order of the universe. He speaks as a poet, combining the verbal and the visual. Language restores the poet to this role as the primordial speaker "whose power of language undergirds the world, thus to provide man with a dwelling place."[16] When the world is engaged and all things are seen and understood as one great working system, balance and healing take place, and this is beyond language.

The ability of the word to control visualization and therefore unite all things is the concept behind *House Made of Dawn* and the Navajo Night Chant. The speaker understands that the "Magic of the Word lies in the fact that it is capable through image and symbol of placing the speaker in communion with his own language and with the entire world."[17] The healing that takes place beyond language comes of the resonance, the after-image of speech in the imagination. The visual energy remains, having been sparked by words. In literature, whether oral or written, it is that which allows us to "put together" in the mind. Restoration follows language and results from the figurative aspects of words and their ability to open out the imagination and thereby affect the physiological. As energy, language contains the potential to restore us to a unity with earth and the rest of the universe. Accumulation, repetition, and resonance all unite to tie us, seamlessly, to the world.

Notes

1   Munn, "The Mushrooms of Language," p. 113.
2   Bierhorst, *Four Masterworks of American Indian Literature*, p. 282.
3   Momaday, "Man Made of Words," in Hobson, *The Remembered Earth*, p. 166.
4   Paz, *Alternating Current*, p. 48.
5   Gill, "Prayer as Person," p. 152.
6   Munn, "The Mushrooms of Language," p. 91.
7   Munn, "The Mushrooms of Language," p. 94.
8   Munn, "The Mushrooms of Language," p. 97.
9   Reichard, *Navaho Religion*, p. 118.
10 Sewell, *The Orphic Voice*, p. 39.
11 Paz, *The Bow and the Lyre*, p. 19.
12 Momaday, "Man Made of Words," p. 172.
13 Reichard, *Prayer*, p. 9.
14 Gill, "Prayer as Person," p. 143.
15 Reichard, *Prayer*, p. 9.
16 Bruns, *Modern Poetry and the Idea of Language*, p. 67.
17 Gill, "The Trees Stood Rooted," p. 7.

Bear and Elk: The Nature(s) of Contemporary American Indian Poetry*

Kenneth M. Roemer

I

The study of contemporary American Indian literature poses a frustrating problem, one that forces readers to define the limits of the diversity and the unity of new voices in American literature. Even a passing glance at modern Indian essays, fiction, and poetry—especially poetry—reveals "a wide variety of styles and tones."[1] The spectrum ranges from literal translations of traditional chants and myths to protest essays, stream-of-consciousness fiction, and poems that, unless included in an anthology of American Indian literature, would probably not be considered American Indian poetry.[2] And yet there are recurring patterns. For example, one often finds certain types of *narrators*, particularly young, first-person narrators; similar *settings*: reservations, bars, highways, urban ghettos; familiar *characters*: respected grandparents, white policemen, priests, government officials, enduring mothers, the Indian returning from the white man's war; recurring *episodes*: how Indians trick non-Indians, how non-Indians cheat or misunderstand Indians; and often-used *themes*: the traditional religious Indian facing non-Indian secular ways, members of "dead" cultures trying to revitalize empty modern lives, and the power of words. One also notices the authors' commitment to give themselves "up to a particular landscape in [their] experience, to look at it from as many angles as [they] can, to wonder about it, to dwell upon it."[3]

But are these patterns pervasive and cohesive enough to justify making valid generalizations about contemporary American Indian literature as a separate and distinct literary "movement"? Several recent anthologies of contemporary American Indian literature, especially the most comprehensive collection (Geary Hobson's *The Remembered Earth*), imply at least a partial answer to the question: modern Indian literature consists of anything written recently by any American Indian. But Hobson is quick to point out in his useful introduction that Indianness is difficult to define. One can use several different criteria, including the "tribe's or community's judgment," "the neighboring non-Indian communities' judgment," "the federal government's judgment," or, of course, "the individual's judgment." Even if we could all agree on how to determine just who is or is not an American Indian, we would find that some critics have raised another question: to be admitted into the Indian literary scene must an author write about Indian subjects? Hobson answers, "To insist that Indians write only 'Indian' poems or books is as myopic as wishing Joseph Conrad had written 'Polish' novels." Thus, not surprisingly, Hobson includes in his anthology the work of full-bloods as well as that of writers who "probably would have difficulty producing . . . a tribal enrollment number," and he includes poems and stories about both Indian and non-Indian topics. This approach seems much more sensible than the attempts of some critics to prescribe what subjects can and cannot be regarded as American Indian literature.[4]

Still, nonprescriptive approaches may suggest tentative perimeters for this new literature. (The literature is new only in the sense that large publishing houses, awards panels, and scholars have actively encouraged American Indian authors for only about a decade. As Hobson makes clear in his introduction, Indian literature written in English is certainly nothing new.) I offer one tentative approach in this essay. I will begin with a brief survey of one type of American Indian literature, contemporary poetry. A detailed, comparative interpretation of two poems follows the overview. I selected these two works because together they suggest some obvious similarities and striking diversities in modern American Indian poetry. This two-step approach is limited, of course. A brief window-shopping tour of one contemporary genre combined with a microscopic probe of two short poems will not provide the key to modern Indian literature, but it may help us to get beyond both all-inclusive approaches and overly restrictive generalizations about an exciting literary phenomenon.

II

The volume and diversity of contemporary American Indian poetry contains a broad spectrum of styles and themes. Poems such as Alonzo Lopez' "Direction" or Simon Ortiz' "Smoking My Prayers," for example, draw heavily on traditional oral Indian literature in both form and content, whereas others examine traditional subjects or experiences but employ modern free-verse forms as do, for instance, Grey Cohoe's "The Folding Fan," Duane Niatum's "Indian Prayer," and Norman H. Russell's "Two Circles." Identity-quest poems and historical comparisons span the past and the present: Fred Red Cloud's "A Tale of Last Stands," Emerson Blackhorse Mitchell's "The New Direction," Bruce Ignacio's "Lost," Linda Hogan's "Heritage," Robert J. Conley's "Self-Portrait," and Joy Harjo's "3 AM." Then there are distinctly modern poems. Some focus on contemporary settings: one finds reservation poems such as the monologues of Marnie Walsh's personae, Lew Blockcolski's "Reservation Special," Archie Washburn's "Hogan," and Ray Young Bear's "February's Children"; urban poems such as Simon Ortiz' "Relocation" and his poems about Gallup and San Francisco; and bar poems such as Joseph Bruchac's "Three Poems for the Indian Steelworkers in a Bar Where I Used to Drink" and Ortiz' "I Like Indians." Another distinctly modern form is the protest poem. Examples range from satiric critiques—such as James Welch's "Man from Washington," Wendy Rose's "Three Thousand Dollar Death Song," and Ortiz' "Ten O'Clock News"—to more explicit outcries: "I, the Fake Made Bomber and Walking It Home Again" by Byron Black, "Homage to Andrew Jackson" by Carroll Arnett, and "Boom the Explosion" by Gary White. Finally, there are poems that transcend time and ethnic boundaries, though some relate to subjects often associated with American Indians. Many concentrate on real or symbolic landscapes or animals: Ortiz' "Dry Root in a Wash," Ramona Carden's "Tumbleweeds," Dana Naone's "Girl with the Green Skirt," Peter Blue Cloud's "Wolf," N. Scott Momaday's "Angle of Geese" and "The Bear," and Leslie Marmon Silko's "Snow Elk" (retitled "In Cold Storm Light") and "Story from Bear Country." Others focus on religion: Momaday's "Before an Old Painting of the Crucifixion" and Janet Campbell's "Our Friend, the Virgin Mary"; on memories: Ronald Rogers' "Kindergarten"; on life stages: Russell's "I Do Not Wish to Be Old"; on poets, poetic experimentation, or the power of words: William Jay Smith's "The Tall Poets," Ted Berrigan's "Presence," and Welch's "Snow Country Weavers."[5] In spite of this diversity, the recurring patterns mentioned earlier appear throughout the poetry. The personae are often young, reflecting the youth of many of the poets; the allusions are often personal (in the best poems this adds intensity to the poetry; in the lesser poems it adds only obscurity); the characters, settings, subjects, and episodes are frequently similar to those found in contemporary Indian fiction; the poets tend to avoid rigid rhyme and meter; and certain themes—the conflicts between cultures, the endurance and revitalization of oral traditions and ancient spiritual views, and the importance of the landscape—permeate these new songs.

Up through the late 1960s, few scholars appreciated the harmonies and diversities of this poetry, because the works were scattered and sometimes difficult to discover. Those interested had to hunt through individual issues of *South Dakota Review, New Mexico Quarterly,* and other regional magazines, the publications of the Institute of American Indian Arts at Santa Fe, and copies of Indian newspapers such as *Akwesasne Notes.* Needless to say, this situation made it difficult for teachers to present collections of contemporary American Indian poetry in the classroom. Fortunately, John Milton's first two collections of contemporary Indian literature and art, *The American Indian Speaks* (1969) and *American Indian II* (1971), and the

American Indian issues of *Nimrod* (Spring-Summer 1972) and *Dakotah Territory* (Winter 1973–74) paved the way for Hobson's anthology and for more special issues such as "Dreams and Drumbeats," *Indian Historian*, 9 (Spring 1976), *New America: A Review*, 2 (Summer-Fall 1976), and *Shantih*, 4 (Summer-Fall 1979); and for American Indian literary magazines, such as *Blue Cloud Quarterly* and *Sun Tracks*; for bibliographies, especially Angeline Jacobson's *Contemporary Native American Literature* (1977), which focuses on poetry; and for several anthologies of Indian poetry. These anthologies range from inexpensive paperback collections—such as *The Whispering Wind* (1972), edited by Terry Allen and Mae Durham; *Arrows Four* (1974), edited by Terry Allen; *Voices from Wah'Kon-Tah (1974), edited by Robert Dodge and Joseph B. McCullough; and The First Skin around Me* (1975), edited by James L. White—to more elaborate cloth volumes such as Kenneth Rosen's *Voices of the Rainbow* (1975) and Duane Niatum's *Carriers of the Dream Wheel* (1975), the fifth book in Harper and Row's Native American Publishing Program. Good collections by individual poets are also now available; these include Momaday's *The Gourd Dancer* (1976), Welch's *Riding the Earthboy 40* (rev. ed., 1975), and Ortiz' *Going for the Rain* (1976).[6]

So now one has no excuse for ignoring contemporary Indian poetry; to do so would be to miss an excellent opportunity to destroy many stereotypes: such caricatures wilt before the diversity of the modern poetry. And considering the quantity of contemporary Indian poetry and the quality of many of the poems, it is not surprising that the most celebrated Indian novelist, N. Scott Momaday, calls himself a poet and that the most famous Indian essayist, Vine Deloria, Jr., claims that modern Indian poetry can "tell you more about the Indian's travels in historical experience than all the books written and lectures given."[7]

III

A valuable complement to any survey of contemporary American Indian poetry, including the foregoing thumbnail sketch, is an intensive study of specific poems. A comparative examination of similar poems can illuminate the unity and diversity of modern Indian literature. For instance, many contemporary Indian poems focus on nature; one subcategory of this type of poetry is the animal poem. Just a glance at recently published anthologies reveals that at least 126 poems by Indian authors either concentrate on descriptions of animals or depend heavily on animal names or imagery.[8] Animal poems especially seem to captivate two poets: N. Scott Momaday (b. 1934), the Kiowa Pulitzer Prize-winning author of *House Made of Dawn* (1968), and Leslie Marmon Silko (b. 1948), a writer whose heritage combines Laguna, Mexican, and Anglo cultures. Her talents are ably displayed in her collection of poetry, *Laguna Woman* (1974), in Kenneth Rosen's collections of fiction and poetry, *The Man to Send Rain Clouds* (1974) and *Voices of the Rainbow* (1975), in her novel, *Ceremony* (1977), and in her collection of fiction and poetry, *Storyteller* (1981). In 1981 she received one of the MacArthur Foundation awards. Several brief episodes in Momaday's entrancing prose poem, *The Way to Rainy Mountain* (1969), focus on animals; Chapter 1 of *The Names* (1976) begins, "The names at first are those of animals . . . "; and one third of the poems in his chapbook, *Angle of Geese and Other Poems* (1974), and several poems in *The Gourd Dancer* (1976) describe animals. One of Silko's most interesting poems is "Snow Elk" (retitled "In Cold Storm Light"); ten of her eighteen contributions to *Voices of the Rainbow* and a fascinating poem—"Story from Bear Country"—published in *Wanbli Ho* (Spring 1976) and reprinted in Hobson's anthology depend heavily on animal imagery, as do ten of the poems in *Storyteller*. I will limit the following comparative interpretation to "The Bear" and "Snow Elk." Both are good poems. I single them out here because the close parallels and equally obvious differences between them reveal as much or more about the unity and diversity of contemporary Indian literature as do general surveys of many works.

Momaday's "The Bear" was originally published in the *New Mexico Quarterly* (Spring 1961). It is frequently anthologized and is the opening poem in *Angle of Geese*. Yvor Winters, in his study of the short poem in English, *Forms of Discovery*, praises "The Bear" as a rare example of successful syllabic verse characterized by the careful selection and juxtaposition of details (pp. 289–90). The *New York Times Book Review* also called it a "very fine poem."[9] Silko's "Snow Elk" first appeared in *Quetzal* (1972), a publication of the Southwest Poets Conference. It was reprinted with a new title, "In Cold Storm Light," in Rosen's *Voices of the Rainbow* and in *Storyteller*.[10] At the MLA Summer Seminar on Native American Literature (Flagstaff, 1977) Silko gave one of her rare public readings of "Snow Elk." She paired the poem with the first poem she ever wrote, "Prayer to the Pacific," and explained that the earlier poem expressed the need for summer rain, while the later poem expressed the need for "lots of snow" in winter. She went on to explain the origin of the poem: "I watch the sky a lot. One afternoon in Chinle [Arizona] I was looking out the window. . . . there's an uplift out where Canyon de Chelly begins. It was in the wintertime. This is what I saw."

The Bear

What ruse of vision,
escarping the wall of leaves,
rending incision
into countless surfaces,

would cull and color
his somnolence, whose old age
has outworn valor,
all but the fact of courage?

Seen, he does not come,
move, but seems forever there,
dimensionless, dumb,
in the windless noon's hot glare.

More scarred than others
these years since the trap maimed him,
pain slants his withers,
drawing up the crooked limb.

Then he is gone, whole,
without urgency, from sight,
as buzzards control,
imperceptibly, their flight.

Snow Elk
[IN COLD STORM LIGHT]

In cold storm light
I watch the sandrock
    canyon rim.

    The wind is wet
        with the smell of piñon.
    The wind is cold
        with the sound of juniper
            And then
                out of the thick ice sky
                    running swiftly
                    pounding
                    swirling above the treetops
                The snow elk come,
            Moving, moving
                white song
                    storm wind in the branches.
And when the elk have passed
    behind them
        a crystal train of snowflakes
        strands of mist
            tangled in rocks
            and leaves.

The similarities in topic and structure are obvious. Both poems attempt to capture the impact of experiencing the appearance of two of nature's grandest creations in the context of imposing settings. Furthermore, Momaday and Silko present these experiences in parallel stages. The first two stanzas of each poem build a sense of expectation for the arrival of the animal named in the title. The second stage (stanzas three and four of "The Bear," the long third stanza of "Snow Elk") captures the appearance—"a pantheistic incarnation" might be a better description, since the bear and the herd of elk become visible manifestations of natural forces. Finally, in the last stanza of each poem, the animals disappear as suddenly and as mysteriously as they appeared.

The reader is left with a sense of having experienced a divine visitation, an effect achieved in part by the three-part structure that transforms linear time into a stop-frame drama. The "normal" chronological transitions of approach and withdrawal are missing; hence the appearance is isolated, "dimensionless" in the way a vision is dimensionless, an event that steps out of time. Thus the structure becomes ironic: the poets use a conventional three-part time sequence to frame an event that transcends such a sequence.

Of course the treatment of animals and time in these poems is not unique to American Indian literature. Nevertheless, both the association of certain animals with divine forces and the association of certain earthly events with visitations of holy beings have deep roots in many Indian oral traditions and beliefs. The roles animals play in numerous creation narratives and in traditional ceremonies designed to invoke the power and presence of holy beings attest to that.[11] One can also find the attitudes toward nature and time suggested by "The Bear" and "Snow Elk" in other examples of contemporary Indian literature. They certainly are reflected in *The Way to Rainy Mountain* in Momaday's re-creations of Kiowa legends about bears, Grandmother Spider, horses, and buffalo and in the dynamic relationships between contemporary experience and ancient myth. On a more general level, the sense of standing in awe of nature that appears in the animal and wilderness descriptions in "The Bear" and "Snow Elk" recurs in the animal and landscape descriptions in Momaday's *House Made of Dawn*, James Welch's *Winter in the Blood*, Gerald Vizenor's *Darkness in Saint Louis Bearheart*, and in the stories in *The Man to Send Rain Clouds* and *The Remembered Earth*. We can make similar observations about modern poetry; there is much more variety in nature description, however, primarily because there is more poetry than fiction. (Of course in both the fiction and the poetry the awe of nature is mixed with a realistic awareness of the harshness of nature, as in, for example, the Montana cold of *Winter in the Blood*.) The time sense of the finite present momentarily merging with dimensionless realms is an important element of modern fiction writers' thematic treatment of the ways in which ancient beliefs impinge on and transform the present. Some of Silko's own stories—"Tony's Story," "Yellow Woman," and "Humaweepi, the Warrior Priest," for example—exemplify this pattern. ("Humaweepi" even includes the dramatic appearance of a sacred bear in the form of a rock formation.) Thus, the similarities between "The Bear" and "Snow Elk" help to illuminate certain characteristics of the treatment of nature and time in contemporary American Indian fiction and poetry.

From the differences between the two poems we can infer an equally important lesson: watch out for hasty generalizations about the unifying characteristics of American Indian literature. Both these poems were written by southwestern Indians, and in them the two poets express similar attitudes about nature and time. But "The Bear" is a dense Faulknerian reading experience: Momaday is as concerned with the powers and limitations of perceptions and words as he is with nature. "Snow Elk" is a haikulike, sensory reading experience: sensory images are stripped down, isolated, mixed, and arranged typographically so as to create an appropriate visual effect. The impact of one poem is so different from that of the other that it seems almost irrelevant and definitely misleading simply to note that they are both "about" animals.

The differences between the two poems are apparent right from the opening lines as the poets anticipate the coming of the animals mentioned in the titles. Momaday builds suspense by asking a complex rhetorical question that appears to enumerate, in opaque Latinate diction, several characteristics of the bear while simultaneously questioning the ability of human beings to understand the bear. The first stanza indicates power, even violence, as suggested by the harsh-sounding "escarping," the surgical "rending incision," and the fractured image of "countless surfaces." The second stanza more than hints at a decline: a drowsiness and a life that has "outworn valor."

But the apparent enumeration in the first two stanzas is ambiguous; these stanzas raise as many questions as they answer. In part this is due to Momaday's avoidance of anything concrete with the marginal exception of "wall of leaves." There is not much here to grasp on to; hence the reader must grope and wait. Another reason for groping is that the first and second stanzas suggest different characteristics (power and decline), and in the second stanza contradictory characteristics becloud any precise image of the bear as a consistent, one-dimensional entity. This creature of nature may be "sleepy" according to Webster's definition, but "somnolence" implies a grand drowsiness. Then too, "outworn valor" suggests endurance, and there is still "the fact of courage." Furthermore, one must remember that Momaday presents the entire introduction in the form of a question. The characteristics of the bear may be the result of a trick played by the senses (or by the senses in league with nature) on the viewer. This trick may shape, select, and color what the viewer perceives as the bear. Thus Momaday feeds the reader's expectations by shrouding the subject of the poem in a complex haze—a haze that challenges the reader to guess what will appear and how he or she will perceive what appears.[12] Approached in this way, the first stage of "The Bear" seems closer to Ralph Waldo Emerson's later nature poems— "Maia," for instance—than to any re-creation of a Kiowa experience in the Southwest.

The experience of the Southwest dominates the introductory stanzas of "Snow Elk." Here, instead of a "ruse of vision" we find the icy clarity of a detached first-person persona viewing a canyon landscape. As Silko said before her 1977 reading, "It was in the wintertime. This is what I saw." First, the persona's view is associated with the tense, clear atmosphere of "cold storm light." If this is the lull before the outbreak of the storm, and the mood suggests that it is, there is certainly no haze; there is not even the distortion of the "noon's hot glare." The focus is on the precise horizon of a "canyon rim." In the next stanza this line of rock is colored, not by a visual trick, but by a combination of synesthesis and repetition with variation. The persona's sensitivity to the mixtures of the wet touch, piñon smell, and juniper sound of the wind indicates an intense state of anticipation and a confidence in concrete perceptions. The repetition with variation, a very common characteristic of southwestern ceremonial chants,[13] together with the alliteration, expresses a pounding, a building before an exciting event. Therefore, even though Momaday uses a regular rhyme scheme and consistent syllabic line measurement[14] and Silko uses free verse, the sounds of the repetition in "Snow Elk" play a more important role in the buildup to the appearance than do the rhymes and syllable measurement, which, because of the unstressed final syllables and the complexity of Momaday's question, do not capture the reader's attention in the first stanzas of "The Bear."

The next stage in both poems is the climax. The poets build on the language and assumptions of their introductions, and the primary literary source of Momaday's bear further emphasizes the differences between the poems.

The contradictions continue and multiply in the third stanza of "The Bear." The animal is "Seen," but this may be another "ruse of vision," since the bear seems to appear out of nowhere: "he does not come." He does "move" but is as still as the lovers on Keats's urn. He is "dimensionless" yet constricted by the blunt, four-letter "dumb." All these apparent contradictions are consistent with the tenor of the opening rhetorical question because they question our ability to perceive and capture certain types of experience, while they attest to an honesty that refuses to simplify or reduce complex phenomena. And this attitude toward language and experience recalls another writer's attempts to capture ungraspable experiences. The following

passage appears in the last paragraph of the third section of William Faulkner's "The Bear":

> Then he saw the bear. It did not emerge, appear: it was just there, immobile,
> fixed in the green and windless noon's hot dappling, not as big as he had
> dreamed it but as big as he had expected, bigger, dimensionless against the
> dappled obscurity, looking at him.[15]

This obvious source also helps to explain the dense Latinate com-
plexities of the first two stanzas, a type of language that permeates *Go Down,
Moses*, the collection in which "The Bear" appears. The passage from
Faulkner also helps us to understand Momaday's fourth stanza, which adds a
personal, almost pathetic dimension to the bear. Like Faulkner's Old Ben,
Momaday's bear is scarred and maimed; each has a "trap-ruined foot."[16]
Like Melville's white whale, these old-timers are both godly cripples; their
power and endurance are legendary, but they are also pitiable victims of the
human conquest of nature. After reading the final details of the fourth stanza
(which are especially moving because the concreteness of the description
seems even more humiliatingly painful as contrasted with the ambiguities of
the opening stanzas), one realizes that Momaday's poem is as much a tribute
to Faulkner's Old Ben as it is a memorial to nature's bears.

Nature is still in the forefront in Silko's climax. The scene is an icy
tempest as opposed to a Faulknerian "windless noon's hot dappling." After
the announcement, "And then,"[17] the indented third stanza becomes an
imaginative continuation and expansion of the sensory impressions, repetition, and typography of the first two stanzas. The snowstorm and the elk rush
together. As the persona watches the high canyon rim, the appearance of the
elk and the arrival of the snow are indivisible; both come out of the sky—the
elk coming over the horizon and merging with the windswept snow. The
persona's line of sight follows the elk and the snow as they swirl down
through the branches combining to become the dramatic crescendo of the
"white song." Silko emphasizes the rhythm by using indented and separated
lines, "running swiftly / pounding / swirling above the treetops." By stacking
these short lines on top of one another, Silko achieves a visual effect that
corresponds to the sight of the running-falling elk-snow. Similarly, the power
and movement of the storm and the herd are suggested by the repetition,
indentation, and extension toward the right margin in the last three lines. As
in "The Bear," the climactic section emphasizes more than one dimension of
the experience perceived. But in "Snow Elk" this complexity is still purely
experiential: as Silko's comments at her 1977 reading indicate and as the
opening and closing of the poem confirm, "Snow Elk" is as much a poem
about snow as it is about elk. Thus, the new title, "In Cold Storm Light," is
quite appropriate.

Silko stresses this dual perception in the imagery and typography of the last stanza. The final signs of the visitation are the "crystal trail" and the "strands of mist," a natural aftermath of both storms and herds of elk. Silko achieves a denouement not only by the description of the gentle motion and settling of the snow but also by the trailing of the last lines toward the right margin. A sense of closing is attained because the action is closer to the persona. Instead of the grand scale of events perceived as emanating from a canyon rim or "Out of the thick ice sky," the passing is small enough and near enough to be seen tangling the rocks and gracing the leaves.

The denouement of "The Bear" begins with another echo of the first appearance of Faulkner's Old Ben. Faulkner's "Then it was gone" becomes the more personal "Then he is gone"; "without haste" becomes "without urgency."[18] These borrowings from Faulkner continue the ambiguous treatment of the bear. He, for no apparent reason ("without urgency") and with no transition (he disappears "whole"), vanishes back into the wilderness.[19] This description of the bear's withdrawal is, of course, realistic, since the thick foliage and dappled light of a forest can obscure enough of an animal to make him seem to appear or disappear suddenly. But the omission of such an explanation and the juxtaposition of "gone, whole" preserve the magic of the initial "sight." Then in the last two lines Momaday interjects a new comparative method of viewing the bear: he compliments the bear's grandeur and power by offering an image of soaring grace and control, a buzzard's flight. But, as with all the other perceptions of the bear, these godly qualities are tinged with ambiguity. The image of the buzzard's masterful flight is shaded by the bird's reputation as a scavenger that hovers over sick and aging beasts ready to prey on their carcasses. Eventually this crippled old god of the wilderness will be a buzzard's dinner. What Robert Zoellner has identified as the "universal thump" in *Moby-Dick*,[20] sounds throughout Faulkner's *Go Down, Moses* and Momaday's "The Bear." We begin to perceive the complexities and the brotherhood of nature only when we see that "all creatures great and small" are subject to the primeval forces of natural process.

IV

A comparison between "The Bear" and "Snow Elk" (or "In Cold Storm Light") is bound to be an exercise in the obvious, in spite of the complexities of both poems. Why should anyone expect identical outlooks and poems from poets as different as Leslie Marmon Silko and N. Scott Momaday? Nevertheless, there are important similarities between the two poems, just as there are recurrent patterns throughout contemporary Indian literature. And now that enough good modern Indian poetry and fiction are readily available, scholars and critics will face a great temptation to emphasize common denominators. Hence, in the initial studies of this "new" American literature we must be careful to establish appropriate perimeters. There are lines to be drawn, but the boundaries must be flexible enough to include the tremendous diversity of American Indian cultures and experiences. If critics simplistically delineate unifying characteristics of contemporary Indian literature, they will repeat the sins of the fathers by manipulating new stereotypes to suit their concepts of "ethnic" or "minority" literature. Fortunately, there is evidence that several students of contemporary Indian poetry are avoiding this temptation and are instead offering provocative studies of patterns discovered in the work of individual poets (for example, Patricia C. Smith's "Coyote Ortiz")[21] and patterns that characterize the work of several poets (for instance, James Ruppert's "The Uses of Oral Traditions in Six Contemporary Native American Poets").[22]

Of course, the literature itself will undermine most attempts to devise new stereotypes. Clearly there are disadvantages to compiling anthologies unified primarily by the authors' claims to American Indian racial or cultural identities. This approach to modern Indian literature will never ensure consistent quality or that illusive anthropological bugaboo, "authenticity," but it should ensure diversity. Maintaining simplistic stereotypes about "the Indian way" will be quite difficult for readers confronted with collections that include the stream-of consciousness poems of Ted Berrigan, the taut brevity of Norman H. Russell, the long narrative poems of Carter Revard, the personal tones of Paula Gunn Allen, the complex imagery of Wendy Rose and Ray A. Young Bear, the blunt protests of Byron Black, the voices of tradition from the Institute of American Indian Arts, the wit and surrealism of James Welch, the storytelling voices of Leslie Marmon Silko, and the changing voices of Simon Ortiz and N. Scott Momaday.

Actually, "The Bear" and "Snow Elk" alone deflate the stereotypes. Indians were once and are still sometimes pigeonholed as "children of nature." "The Bear" and "Snow Elk" demonstrate Momaday's and Silko's devotion to nature, but they also prove that Momaday and Silko are not "primitives" or children and that their perceptions of nature spring from different origins and from having traveled different paths.

Notes

*This essay is a revised version of an article that first appeared in *Journal of Ethnic Studies*, 5, No. 2 (1977), 69–79. Reprinted by permission of the editor.

1   Rosen, Preface, *Voices of the Rainbow*, p. xvii.

2   Possibly the best quick introduction to the diverse essays, fiction, and poetry is Chapter 7 of *Literature of the American Indian*, ed. Sanders and Peek, of which an abridged paperback edition (Beverly Hills: Glencoe, 1976) is available. One advantage of this comprehensive col-

lection is that it allows the reader to see contemporary Indian literature within the context of many other types of traditional oral Indian literature (Chs. 1–6), though this anthology has received some valid criticism for poor editing. See Sayre, "A Bibliography and an Anthology of American Indian Literature," and a review by Evers in *College Composition and Communication*. Another more recent anthology is Velie's *American Indian Literature*. Unfortunately this attractive volume is also flawed. See Evers' review in *Studies in American Indian Literatures*.

3   Momaday, *The Way to Rainy Mountain*, p. 83.

4   Hobson, ed., *The Remembered Earth*, pp. 8, 9. Buller comes dangerously close to the prescriptive approach in "New Interpretations of Native American Literature." Another recent anthology that includes contemporary Indian literature is Fisher, ed., *The Third Woman*.

5   Many of the poems mentioned in this paragraph can be found in Milton's collections, in Sanders and Peek, in Hobson, and in *Voices from Wah'Kon-Tah*, ed. Dodge and McCullough. (1975). See also the collections edited by Allen and Durham, Rosen, and Niatum.

6   The Harper and Row program is much less active now than it was during the mid-1970s. Several other less available collections include *Four Indian Poets*, ed. Milton; *Come to Power*, ed. Lourie; and *Sweetgrass: An Anthology of Indian Poetry*, ed. Keon. Several general anthologies of Indian literature contain sections on modern poetry, and several other poets—notably Allen, Blue Cloud, Bruchac, Cook, Niatum, Rose, Russell, Silko, and Vizenor—have published collections of their poetry. See also *Indian Historian* (Spring 1976), which focuses on student poetry,.and James L. White's magazine, *Angwamas Minosewag Anishinabeg* (*Time of the Indian*), which is designed to encourage creative writing by children in tribal communities in the Minneapolis area. A good way to keep up with these new collections and with old and new anthologies is to read the reviews and bibliographies in *Studies in American Indian Literatures*, the newsletter of the Association for the Study of American Indian Literatures, edited by Karl Kroeber at Columbia University.

7   Foreword, Dodge and McCullough, p. 13.

8   The following list of the 126 poems is arranged alphabetically by the poet's last name. Minerva Allen, "Returning from . . . "; Paula Gunn Allen, "4 (The Dead Spider)," "Snow-goose"; Carroll Arnett, "The Old Man Said: Two," "Tlanuwa," "*uwohali*"; Jim Barnes, "Wolf Hunting near Nashoba," "The Last Chance," "Tracking Rabbits: Night"; John Barsness, "Deer Hunt 1971," "Crazy Woman Rode a Dead Horse," "Walking in a Bear's Tracks," "Branding Spring"; Duane Big Eagle, "What Eagle Saw in the West"; Peter Blue Cloud, "Bear," "For Rattlesnake," "Wolf," "Hawk Nailed to a Barn Door," "Sweat Song," "Death Chant," "Composition"; Joseph Bruchac, "First Deer," "Birdfoot's Grandpa," "The Dolphin Burial"; Janet Campbell, "Red Eagle"; Gladys Cardiff, "Leaves like Fish," "Dragon Skate"; Robert J. Conley, "The Rattlesnake Band"; Elizabeth Cook-Lynn, "The Bare Facts"; Anita Endrezze-Danielson, "Raven/Moon," "In the Flight of the Blue Heron: To Montezuma," "Shaman/Bear"; Nia Francisco, "She-Bear"; Phil George, "Eagle Feather, IV," "Coyote's Night"; Raven Hail, "The Tiger"; Joy Harjo, "Watching Crow . . . "; Lance Henson, "impressions of strong heart song cheyenne dog soldier," "portrait in february," "Flock," "Among Hawks," "Moth"; Geary Hobson, "Deer Hunting," "Buffalo Poem #1"; Linda Hogan, "Blessings," "Mosquitoes," "Celebration: Birth of a Colt," "After Fish," "Thanksgiving"; Maurice Kenny, "Akwesasne," "Cold Creek"; Chiron Khanshendel, "Grebs at Sunset"; King Kula, "Dream Seeker"; Harold Littlebird, "December 22, 1977"; Alonzo Lopez, "Eagle Flight," "The Lavender Kitten"; Winston Mason, "The Raven"; N. Scott Momaday, "The Bear," "Buteo Regalis," "Pit Viper," "Angle of Geese," "Mammedaty, 1880–1932"; Dana Naone, "Thought of Going Home"; Duane Niatum, section 3 of "No One Remembers Abandoning the Village of White Fir," "Street Kid," "Owl Seen in Rearview Mirror," "Runner for the Clouds and Rain"; William Oandasan, "Natural Law"; Calvin O'John, "Song and Flight"; Simon Ortiz, "To Insure Survival," "The Boy and Coyote," "My Father's Song," "The Creation: According to Coyote"; Ted Palmanteer, "Pass It on Grandson"; Thomas Peacock, "Six Eagles"; W. M. Ransom, "Critter"; Carter Revard, "The Coyote"; Ronald Rogers, "Jicarilla in August"; Rokwaho (Daniel Thompson), "i dream . . . "; Norman H. Russell, "old men climbing," "a great mosquito dance," "i have many friends," "the great way of man"; Leslie Marmon Silko, "Snow Elk" ("In Cold Storm Light"), "Deer Song," "Helen's Warning at New Oraibi," "Cotton Wood Part Two: Buffalo Story," "Aunt Alice told my sisters . . . ," "Estoy-eh muut and the Kunideeyahs," "Deer Dance/For Your Return," "A Hunting Story," "Skeleton Fixer," "Where Mountain Lion Lay

Down with Deer," "He Was a Small Child," "Coyotes and the Stro'ro'ka Dancers," "Story from Bear Country," "Four Mountain Wolves," "Hawk and Snake," "Horses at Valley Store," "Indian Song: Survival," "Preparations," "Sun Children," "The Time We Climbed Snake Mountain," "Toe-osh: A Laguna Coyote Story"; Mary Tallmountain, "The Last Wolf"; Jim Tollerud, "Bird of Power"; Gerald Vizenor, "An Old Spiderweb"; Judith Ivaloo Volborth, "Black-Coat Meets Coyote"; Marnie Walsh, "John Knew-the-Crow 1880," "June the Twenty-Second," "The Red Fox"; James Welch, "Magic Fox," "Snow Country Weavers"; Ray A. Young Bear, "For the Rain in March: The Blackened Hearts of Herons," "Black Dog," "These Horses Came." See also the nine animal poems by students in *Arrows Four,* ed. Allen, pp. 84, 86, 92, 100, 101, 102, 126, 139, 141.

9   Bromwich, "New Poetry Made a Little Less Private," p. 7. See also Trimble, *N. Scott Momaday*, pp. 16–17.

10   I would like to thank N. Scott Momaday, Leslie Marmon Silko, Harper and Row, and Seaver Books for permission to reprint the two poems.

11   The Cheyenne creation story, readily available in the Signet edition of Marriott and Rachlin's *American Indian Mythology*, offers several good examples of the importance of animals. An excellent example of this type of ceremony is the Navajo Night Way. If the singer performs the ceremony properly, a holy being will enter the ceremonial hogan and inhabit the person sung over.

12   Reviewers often misunderstand this haze in Momaday's poetry and fiction. See the reviews of *House Made of Dawn* by William James Smith and by Sprague. For an answer to this criticism see Sanders and Peek, p. 448.

13   The Navajo Night Way provides some of the best-known examples of this technique. Excerpts from this ceremony or other traditional southwestern chants using repetition with variation are available in almost every general anthology of Indian literature.

14   "The first and third lines of each stanza contain five syllables apiece, the second and fourth contain seven." Winters, *Forms of Discovery*, p. 289.

15   Faulkner, *Go Down, Moses*, p. 209. Winters observes that Momaday's poem "owes something to Faulkner," but he does not follow up his observation. See *Forms of Discovery*, p. 289.

16   *Go Down, Moses*, p. 193.

17   In the 1972 and 1975 printings of the poem Silko capitalized every letter in "And then," made the separation between the second and third stanzas equal to the space between the first and second, and aligned the "A" beneath the "th" in "the sound of juniper." In the 1981 printing, reproduced above, she eliminated the melodramatic spacing and capitalization and placed the "A" beneath the "o" in "sound of juniper," so that the third stanza extends further to the right on the page. This visual effect enhances the excitement of the poem's climax.

18   *Go Down, Moses*, p. 209.

19   Momaday even omits some of Old Ben's withdrawal: "It crossed the glade without haste, walking for an instant into the sun's full glare and out of it, and stopped again and looked back at him across one shoulder. Then it was gone." *Go Down, Moses*, p. 209.

20   *The Salt-Sea Mastodon*, esp. Ch. 4.

21   Smith, "Coyote Ortiz: *Canis latrans latrans* in the Poetry of Simon Ortiz."

22   Ruppert's essay appears in an issue of *AICRJ* devoted to American Indian literature. For a brief examination of how several other contemporary Indian authors use oral traditions see the concluding section of my essay "Native American Oral Narratives: Context and Continuity" and my review of Vizenor's *Darkness in Saint Louis Bearheart*.

Coyote Ortiz: *Canis latrans latrans* in the Poetry of Simon Ortiz

Patricia Clark Smith

Coyote, old wanderer: a ragged, four-legged verb, always in motion, busy, going somewhere. That's what you notice first—motion, the main attribute of living creatures, creatures who persist in staying alive despite the odds. Coyote: Simon Ortiz knows him:

> Oh yes, last time . . .
> when was it,
> I saw him somewhere
> between Muskogee and Tulsa,
> Heading for Tulsy Town I guess,
> just trucking along.[1]

I surprised Coyote once on New Mexico 53 headed south out of Grants, not far from Simon Ortiz' Acoma. I couldn't figure out why he should be trotting down the middle of a highway until I saw that he was alley-trapped by the high fencing on either side of the road for a few miles. I idled behind him for a while as he loped along, panicked but somehow still self-possessed, planning, veering off the pavement now and again to try another jump at the fences. He was a fine-looking coyote, big, with a thick reddish pelt. I looked at the gun racks on pickups impatiently passing me and hoped I wouldn't spot his hide slung over the fence or carpeting the road when I returned. I didn't. I think he made it:

> . . . hope it don't rain,
> hope the river don't rise.
> He'll be back. Don't worry.
> He'll be back.

(p. 18)

Of course, Coyote's never really been gone, but never mind that. He's here. He's here as a literary figure most fully in the poetry of Simon Ortiz, and that is mainly what I want to talk about. But I might just as well say at the beginning that Coyote's been showing his face these last ten years and more in a lot of other people's poems, too, especially west of the big rivers. There's a whole debate going on about the legitimacy of these sightings, about whether Anglo poets have the reason and the right to appropriate Coyote as their own. That they do so, of course, is not surprising; for better or worse, Coyote has always been as he is in the traditional Pueblo and Navajo oral tales, too striking a presence not to attract attention, whether envious or scornful.

In his essay "The Incredible Survival of Coyote," Gary Snyder talks eloquently about Coyote's appeal for him and his contemporaries. First, he is for Snyder the "protector spirit," the genius of western place that Anglo latecomers lack in their own myths and texts. (Presumably, we brought in our trans-Missouri baggage no creature of our own that could adapt to the mesas and dry washes as easily as the East African little hare and the Gold Coast spider did to the woods and farmlands of the American South—little hare evolving into Brer Rabbit, Anansi the Spider into Aunt Nancy.) Snyder says Coyote gives non-Indians a fix on the place, not just on the West as it exists in Anglo history, but back into "myth time, into the eternal now of geological time."

Second, says Snyder, Anglo poets growing up radical and disenchanted throughout the fifties and sixties are drawn by antiheroic, nondualistic Coyote, who operates distinctly for neither good nor evil but who simply *operates*, with joyous, indiscriminate energy—a Dean Moriarty of the mesas, perhaps.

Snyder writes perceptively about the wonderful appeal of Coyote, but his essay is far more sensitively drawn than most of the Coyote poetry he quotes or alludes to in support of his point—that Coyote's rank native presence is a natural and envigorating addition to contemporary Anglo western American poetry. In a lot of those poems Coyote figures as a stand-in for the poet as he perceives himself: Rabelaisian hipster, saloon philosopher with a course in Eastern religious thought behind him, con man in a good cause, braggart warrior against polite society. The poems are sometimes engaging, often funny. But while there are exceptions—I would cite especially John Milton's Coyote in his *The Blue Belly of the World*—the Coyote figure in much contemporary poetry, as in the Lewis MacAdams poem Snyder quotes, comes off as far more one-dimensional, far less warmly fleshed, and far less moving than Snyder's essay would suggest.

Because his presence is supposed to lend a sense of place, too often poets don the Coyote mask too self-consciously, utter the coyote cry too automatically, too much on cue, to give any real sense of native westernness. This seems to me another instance of what we might call the yucca phenomenon in regional poetry: stick some yucca in a poem and call the poem southwestern; trot out Coyote and call the poem a work of native wisdom and humor. More than anything else, I am put off by the poets' glib eagerness to fuse cultures, *all* cultures, even when they do so lightly and wittily, making easy, hip-shot allusions to suggest that good old nondualistic Coyote is only another Buddhist in a fur coat (or "a *friend* of the Buddhist," as MacAdams would have it).[2] The borrowed Coyote persona in many poems seems exactly that: borrowed, recycled, not earned through any real knowledge of and sympathy for either coyotes or Coyote.

I don't really want to enter the lists here, as Geary Hobson has done with wit and energy, on the subject of one person's right to borrow another's medicine bag.[3] Right or wrong, poets have always borrowed, and often with rich results. Yeats wasn't Celtic, after all, any more than Pound was Chinese, and perhaps how well poets borrow is partly a matter of how secure they are in their own skins. In any case, of all contemporary poets' Coyotes, Ortiz' is the most natural, the least self-conscious, the least tamed and trained to do vaudeville turns, the least given to emitting offstage howls just to provide atmosphere. Perhaps this is true because Ortiz is an American Indian; in any case, Ortiz writes out of a deep familiarity with Coyote and coyotes and is, quite simply, a fine poet. To be sure, Ortiz' Coyote also lusts and flimflams and brags, but Ortiz' art reaches beneath this popular Coyote surface to reveal depths and nuances of Coyote's character that underlie or are implied in the traditional tales of his fortunes. This Coyote is no mere con man, no stubborn self-preserver, although he knows that con games and self-preservation are important. Simon Ortiz' Coyote was present at the creation, and Ortiz reveals Coyote's profound connection with the natural world; he shows us the complex spirit that lies beneath the comic hide. If comparing Coyote to Buddha makes some of us uneasy, maybe we would come closer to the truth by saying that Coyote's antisocial and outrageous behavior, like that of Pueblo clowns, springs not merely from foolishness and conceit, but from a vision of creation so deep and true that it can make human rules for proper behavior and discreet action seem ripe for mocking. (The original Acoma Koshari clown was said to be different from other people because "he knew something about himself," and he eventually went to live with his Sun Father).[4]

In any event, the Ortiz Coyote is no one-dimensional comic; his comedy embraces tragedy and touches on high truth. Yellowman, the Navajo storyteller, told Barre Toelken that Coyote stories "are not funny stories. . . . Listeners are laughing at the way Ma'ii [the Navajo name for Coyote] does things, and at the way the story is told. Many things about the story are funny, but the story is not funny." And Yellowman also said, in explanation of Coyote's wildly inconsistent behavior, "If he did not do all those things, then those things would not be possible in the world."[5] In his myriad-mindedness, his actions silly and shrewd, Coyote establishes the range of human possibility. He is what we are and what we could be.

From one poem to another, Ortiz' Coyote reveals that range of possibilities. Sometimes he appears in his most popular incarnation—Old Man Coyote, southwestern Trickster, scruffy charmer, and chump. A number of Ortiz' poems are retellings—in which he deftly creates a sense of both storyteller and responding audience—of tales in which Coyote figures as a sort of negative behavior model, a creature delightfully uncontented to be modest, careful, chaste, and incurious. In "Telling about Coyote," from *Going for the Rain*, Coyote gambles away for all eternity his luxuriant fur coat; in "And there is always one more story," from the same book, Coyote—a female this time—suspended over a cliff from helpful Grandmother Spider's anchor skein, falls to her death because she can't resist peeking up Grandmother's dress.

Ortiz' Coyote, then, in the most popular tradition, is often self-destructive and foolish. But throughout the body of Ortiz' work, even more so than in the traditional oral tales, the emphasis is unremittingly on Coyote's survival. The old stories Ortiz chooses to retell and the new situations he records or invents all make Coyote's continuance far more prominent than his foolhardiness. Even though, as Ortiz says, there is of course "always one more story," many of the traditional tales Ortiz *could* choose from do end momentarily in indignity, injury, or death, with Coyote's restoration understood and unremarked, occurring somehow in the silence between the completion of one tale and the beginning of the next. For example, in one much-recorded story, "Coyote and Horned Toad," told at Acoma and elsewhere, a story that Ortiz does *not* use, Coyote—or Tsuushki, as he calls himself in Keresan—is enraptured by Horned Toad's singing and asks to be taught his song. Horned Toad obliges, and Tsuushki trots off singing, only to forget the song when he is startled by a flight of ducks noisily taking off. He returns to Horned Toad, who has anticipated Coyote's scatterbrained forgetfulness and has casually slipped out of his skin and wrapped it around a sharp flint. When the skin doesn't respond to Coyote's four ritual requests for a reprise of the song, Coyote grows angry, snaps the skin up, and swallows it, and "the sharp flint within cut his stomach and throat, and he died."[6]

Significantly, Ortiz' Coyote stories never end in this way; Coyote always gets up and brushes himself off and trots away *within* the narrative itself, perhaps not quite as good as new, but alive, in motion, surviving. In the gambling tale, for example, mice take pity on Coyote's naked body and patch together a substitute pelt out of old fur scraps and pitch; after Grandmother Spider has indignantly let Coyote Lady plunge to her death, Skeleton Fixer happens upon her dried remains at the foot of a mesa and by his magic makes the dry bones live. In the sequence from *A Good Journey* that begins, "Like myself, the source of these stories is my home . . . ," an Acoma man, an in-law invited along on a rabbit hunt, kills Coyote even though the Laguna field chief has already warned him to avoid shooting Coyote at all costs for the sake of the Laguna Coyote clan people. The Coyote clansmen, of course, chase the culprit, hollering what Ortiz translates as "you confounded no-good dirty Acoma," but "Coyote suddenly jumped up and he ran away," and the Acoma gets a reprieve (pp. 29–30). In Ortiz' stories, you never need to worry; Coyote will indeed be back, and you don't have to wait around long for his resurrection.

Even in one teller's stories, Coyote is never quite the same, even in stories that turn on the same theme. Movingly, Ortiz assumes a gentler tone in his short story "Men on the Moon," as he tells of a far less jaunty Coyote, also threatened, also surviving. Faustin, an old Acoma man, watches with concern a film of a moon rocket blasting off on the new tv his daughter has given him, and then he falls asleep to dream of a terrible *mahkina*, an apocalyptic engine that reminds Faustin of drilling rigs he has seen, moving inexorably across the landscape on metal legs, crushing trees and causing streams to boil. In the dream, as Flintwing Boy watches its terrible progress, Tsushki the Coyote runs to his side, breathless and trembling with fear. Flintwing Boy soothes him, calms him, and together the two perform a ceremony, facing the east and praying for protection and guidance: "that is all we ask," says Flintwing Boy. Then he sends Coyote off to warn the people that they must come together and decide what to do, while he remains to observe: "Coyote turned and began to run. He stopped several yards away. Hahtrudzaimah, he called. Like a man of courage, Anawah, like a man."

The dream gives Faustin reassurance; like the drillers around Acoma, the misguided scientists may give up if they do not find what they are looking for, in this case, "knowledge useful in finding out where everything began and how everything was made"—knowledge, of course, in which the puzzled old man at Acoma, watching the expensive and complex rocket on tv, is already secure.[7]

The significance of Ortiz' special feeling for Coyote as resister and survivor is made explicit in this story. As an American Indian and as a lover of the natural world, Ortiz finds no fact of history more moving than any creature's survival; while whole species and whole groups of human beings have been assisted into oblivion, others have managed to persist. At a poetry reading in Albuquerque several years ago, Ortiz spoke with delight of the native flocks of crows and ravens that scrounge the yards and parks of suburban Albuquerque, unloved by indignant householders, yet still thriving and vocal. And likewise, for all the official and unofficial policies of genocide, for all the *mahkinas*, "Indians are everywhere": this is Simon Ortiz' proudest and most repeated theme. A park ranger in Florida may tell him that "This place is noted for the Indians / That don't live here any more," and yet a "big Sioux" walks unexpectedly into a bar in Flagler Beach ("Christ's sake, how's relocation, Brother?"). The owner of a hot dog stand in Pensacola can direct him to the home of big Chief Alvin McGee in Almore,

Alabama, whose face reminds the poet of the face of his grandfather, of the mountains of home, of the old Creek faces "when they bothered to put them in the history books," Chief Alvin McGee, who, out of his large vitality, will smile and bless the poet.[8] "You meet Indians everywhere," and Coyote, another American Indian who has also insisted on staying around "like a man," to the annoyance of many, is a natural embodiment of that proud Indian survival.

But Coyote is important in Ortiz' works as more than an emblem of blessed Indian chutzpah and sheer cussed Indian continuance. Ortiz' narrative strategies are interesting. Sometimes he tells *about* Coyote, as an observer, a third-person voice, most often in the poems that retell the old stories, that deal with Coyote the comic shill, the Coyote who manages to survive his own cleverness. But in other poems Ortiz draws into a closer narrative relationship with Coyote, taking on the persona himself, and he does so most often in those poems in which Coyote is something like a seer. Consider "How Close," in *Going for the Rain*:

> I wonder if I have ever come close
> to seeing the first seed, the origin,
> and where?
> I've thought about it, says Coyote.
>
> Once I thought I saw it in the glint
> of a mica stratum a hairbreadth deep.
> I was a child then,
> cradled in my mother's arms.
> We were digging for the gray clay
> to make pottery with.
>
> That was south of Acoma years back;
> that was the closest I've gotten yet.
>
> I've thought about it, says Coyote.
>
> (p. 45)

Coyote here remembers a moment of pure childhood vision when, like one of Blake's innocent augurs, he comes close to glimpsing the world, not in a grain of sand, but in a mica hairline in a bank of clay, a crack that seems to hold the possibility of opening out and permitting him to glance into the heart of creation.

The poet's deepest self lives in touch with that creation, and Ortiz' name for that self is Coyote. In the poems, Coyote is often a voice speaking straight out of the genes, out of both tribal and personal memory. In "Albuquerque Back Again, 12/6/74," Ortiz again takes on Coyote's voice as he recalls an act of communion with the mountains before a return to urban life, to

> the traffic
> and ordinary insanity
> of people going places
> they might not actually know
> the destinations of . . .

Coyote touches the mountains as some bless themselves with holy water before leaving a church, in hope that touch will sustain them in the world beyond the doors of the sanctuary:

> Yesterday, turning south
> for New Mexico at San Luis
> Coyote looked at the mountains
> and said, "We'll see you again."
> And prayed for safety, strength,
> and the ability to see beauty. . . .
> (*Going for the Rain*, pp. 79–80)

Coyote, then, draws strength from touching the earth, the natural world of which he is at once a part and a worshiper. But Ortiz sees Coyote's survival as tenuous, constantly threatened not alone by Coyote's propensity to do himself in, the main threat in the traditional Coyote stories, but also by a *mahkina* world, a world grown noisy, heedless, and hostile to coyotes and to the Coyote in the Indian, in the poet. In "The Boy and the Coyote," the speaker is confined to a veterans' hospital, a circumstance hinted at in the dedication of the poem and chronicled more fully in the hospital poems of *A Good Journey*. As he walks the saltcedar thickets beside the Arkansas River, he remembers his childhood self. If in "How Close" he remembers being the Coyote-child drawing near to seeing the infinite in a mica hairline, here he remembers and feels "lonesome" for that same child's auditory sense, a hearing so acute as to bring him into a mystic's union with the life around him. Here, he so clearly remembers the listening boy he once was that memory slides out of the past and into the present tense: "He listens to the river / The slightest nuance of sound."

Fittingly, at this moment when through memory he is united with the child in him, he comes across the prints of the animal who is the natural emblem of what lies deepest in him, a self that somehow endures despite the indignities and distractions of hospitals and exile, a self that is always there, awaiting rediscovery, and leaving signs of its continuing presence:

> Breaking thin ice from a small still pool
> I find Coyote's footprints.
> Coyote, he's always somewhere before you,
> He knows you'll come along soon.
> I smile at his tracks which are not fresh,
> except in memory, and say a brief prayer,
> for good luck for him and for me and for thanks.

This moment of discovery and integration is shattered by the reports of a shotgun. The moment widens out as the speaker, now fully one with Coyote, freezes, encroached upon and threatened, but with his senses honed once more to that childhood Coyote acuity:

> . . . even the wind holds to itself.
> The animal in me crouches, poised immobile,
> our eyes trained on the distance, waiting
> for motion again. The sky is wide,
> blue is depthless, and the animal
> and I wait for breaks in the horizon.

This is a world where shotgun blasts reverberate through Coyote's thicket, where men are confined in hospitals. And yet the speaker, for all his fear, is able to affirm his deepest Coyote-loves, his continuing desire to be the one who listens for the mystery, for the pulse of the blood's country, for what lies at the heart of things:

> Coyote's preference is for silence
> broken only by the subtle wind,
> uncanny bird sound, salt cedar scraping,
> and the desire to let that man free,
> to listen for the motion of sound.
> (*Going for the Rain*, p. 88)

But the most beautiful and moving transformation Ortiz works on the Coyote of oral tradition is to make Coyote himself into the loremaster, the preserver and teller of the stories, as well as the chief and most multifarious character in them. At the very beginning of *A Good Journey*, Ortiz quotes from an interview with himself:

Why do you write? Whom do you write for?

. . . Because Indians always tell a story. The only way to continue is to tell a story, and that's what Coyote says . . . (p. [9])

Although I know of no Acoma tradition in which Coyote himself is the teller of the tales and the one most aware of their importance, the role Ortiz gives him is a logical imaginative extension of Coyote's personality both in nature—his is the most striking natural voice of the Southwest—and in the old tales.[9] For one thing, the Coyote of these tales, while he may not be a storyteller in the sense of a keeper and passer-on of lore vital to his people, is highly verbal, to put it mildly, a storyteller in the sense that he is consummately skilled at pulling the wool over people's eyes and talking them into doing things. In the crudest sense, like any con man, he survives, he "continues," by telling stories. On the surface, at least, his credibility is low among the creatures (including human beings) who have been hanging out with him for millennia. In "Two Coyote Ones," Ortiz imagines some goats remarking:

> Better watch out for that cousin.
> He gets too sly for his ownself
> to be trusted. He'll try to sell you
> A sack of flour that's got worms in it
> that somebody probably has thrown out.
>   And
> they'd get into a certain story
> about one time at Encinal when he brought
> a wheelbarrow that was missing only one wheel
> to this auntie he liked and he had a story
> for why the wheel was missing. . . .
> And so on.
>   (*A Good Journey*, p. 101)

Still, for someone widely known as a braggart and a trickster, Coyote's batting average is not zero. In the "Like Myself" sequence from *A Good Journey*, Pehrru—Coyote in his Old Man form—with a few well-chosen laconic words convinces a troop of white soldiers that a kettle that happens to be resting on hot ashes is really a magic kettle that boils all by itself without fire, and he sells the kettle to them after much well-acted reluctance (pp. 30–32).

In the kettle story, the soldiers are gullible, and the trick is both easy and sweet. But even with a tougher audience, where Coyote's survival depends not on gulling people but rather on winning them over, Coyote can sometimes succeed, as in "And Another One," when Coyote comes across four people eating supper. They are not pleased to see him:

> One of them said
> "There comes Pehrru.
> Don't anyone invite him to sit down and eat.
> He's much of a liar."

Gradually, however, Pehrru-Coyote works the conversation around to a tale about a cow that has given birth to five calves:

> One of them, beloved, was just standing around,
> looking hungry, not feeding because
> as you know, cows usually have only four nipples.
>   (*A Good Journey*, pp. 33–34)

At that, the four invite Coyote to sit down and eat, not because Coyote has tricked them into it, but because the tale shrewdly suggests the sorrow and the pity of his own hunger and, more especially, the unnaturalness of hunger unappeased.

Moreover, Ortiz' Coyote, like Coyote in the traditional tales and like most poets, sometimes uses his verbal skills even on himself, talking himself into feeling better, giving himself a shot of flippant courage, as in "A Barroom Fragment," from *Going for the Rain:*

> He was talking,
> "I invited her to Las Vegas,
> and when we got to the hotel
> she asked for a separate room.
> I told her, 'Shit, if you want
> a room to yourself, why baby
> that's alright, have it.'
> I had brought her up there
> on a four-million-dollar airplane,
> and I told her, 'You can
> go across the street
> and take a thirty-thousand-dollar bus
> back to Burbank.' "
> That was Coyote talking.
>
> (p. 57)

You know it's Coyote talking because of his ability to turn his rejection into an epigram, a beautifully phrased put-down. The pleasure of that act will carry him through, despite the uncooperative woman. Was he really that witty when he told her to get lost? That's another matter. But at least he now has one more story to tell.

In a number of poems, Ortiz confronts the issue of Coyote's credibility and, for the most part, concludes that one must know when to trust him and have the faith to do so at those times. In "The Creation, According to Coyote," the fine poem that opens *Going for the Rain*, Ortiz begins with a reference to the problem of credibility:

> "First of all, it's true."
> Coyote, he says this, this way,
> humble yourself, motioning and meaning
> what he says.

Coyote goes on to recount the Acoma creation story, the tale of the emergence of the first people in their soft larvaelike form out of the First World:

> There was nothing to know then,
> until later, Coyote told me this,
> and he was b.s.-ing probably,
> two sons were born
> Uyuyayeh and Masaweh,

But, you know, Coyote,
he was mainly bragging
when he said (I think)
"My brothers, the Twins, then said,
'Let's lead these poor creatures
and save them.' "

And later on, they came to light
after many exciting and colorful
and tragic things of adventure;
and this is the life, all these, all these.

My uncle told me all this, that time.
Coyote told me, too, but you know
how he is, always talking to the gods,
the mountains, the stones all around.

And you know, I believe him.

                                        (pp. 3–4)

In this poem, although the speaker will ultimately believe Coyote, Ortiz, until the last line, deliberately maintains a tension between the stereotype—the Coyote we wouldn't trust as far as we could throw him—and certain facts that argue strongly for Coyote's trustworthiness on this particular matter. In the first place, Ortiz gives Coyote a story to tell that the imagined Acoma audience already knows and accepts as true, since it is the orthodox Keresan creation story. The People really *do* emerge from the lower world; hero twins really *are* born to lead them. In the second place, Ortiz here puts Coyote in impeccable company, because the story is told not only by Coyote but also by the speaker's uncle, the male relative who is his proper teacher, the child's natural external source of true stories about his own people. The story is generally accepted to be true; uncles are trustworthy in such matters; both Coyote and the uncle tell the story. The audience, then, knows that Coyote is a truthteller even before the last line certifies him as one.

Ortiz plays throughout with the shiftiness of the stereotypical Coyote—"You know how he is"—but the way he is, really, is the way good poets are: he is to be believed on the matters that count the most, to be believed from the gods' perspective, to be believed in a realm of meaning that lies beyond surface manipulative foolery. For instance, Ortiz states that Coyote "was b.s.-ing probably" when he lay claim to Uyuyayeh and Masaweh as his brothers, but probably it is a Coyote lie on only the most literal level. From the gods' point of view, the world is intended to be a place of reciprocity and mutual alliance, a world of brothers. Incredible things like creations do happen, have happened, and one loses out on something precious and life-restoring by narrowly mistrusting Coyote just because of his surface trickiness, his propensity to sell you a wormy sack of flour or to speak in

metaphor and hyperbole. On the important matters, he knows. He was there.
And so are the stylistic signals; Ortiz hems and haws parenthetically in the
lines where he is discussing Coyote's credibility, but when he switches to
retelling the story that the supposed charlatan told him, the pace alters
radically. Ortiz' narrative of the creation itself, derived from both uncle and
Coyote, is firm, rapid, authoritative, carrying with it all the emotional energy
of conviction. The questioning of credibility is almost ritual; the speaker
knows that Coyote knows, when it comes to important things.

Again, in "Two Coyote Ones," Ortiz devotes the first section of the
poem to an exuberant retelling, with understated admiration, of Coyote's
fast-talking, horse-trading, boastful antics:

> That Coyote,
> I wonder if he still has that silver buckle
> that everyone was talking about,
> or did he already pawn it
> at one of those places "up the line?"
>
> He's like that, you know, and then he'd tell
> people who ask,
>
> "Well, let me tell you,
> I was at Isleta and I was offered
> a good deal by this compadre who had
> some nice ristras of red chile. He had
> a pretty sister . . . " And so on.
> And you can never tell.

Then the poem shifts to another story, purportedly autobiographical this
time—and I have often hoped it is truly autobiographical—a tale of the
speaker and Rex, his dog, sitting beside a campfire:

> And this
> blonde girl came along, driving a truck,
> and she brought a cake.
> That was real Coyote luck,
> a blonde girl and a ginger cake.

It *is* real Coyote luck, and it is the kind of story Coyote is likely to tell,
just plain too good to be true. Still, the speaker seems to smile and resign
himself to sticking to truth, determined not to make of it the campfire boast
he might:

> Actually, we just talked
> about the goats and what I was doing
> which was living at the foot of the La Plata
> Mountains and writing.

I think I could have
done something with that gimmicky sounding
line, which was true besides, but I didn't.
It was just nice to have a blonde girl
to talk with. I had to tell Rex the dog
to cool it a couple of times. He and I
were alone a lot that summer, and we were
anxious, but we kept our cool.

In the final section of the poem, "I" suddenly switches to "Coyote," as autobiography passes into legend:

There's this story that Coyote was telling
about the time he was sitting at his campfire
and a pretty blonde girl came driving along
in a pickup truck, and she . . . and so on.

And you can tell, after all.
                    (*A Good Journey*, pp. 100–02)

Ortiz leaves the reader to wonder how Coyote might finish the story, whether he would go on to inflate it into a tale of fireside conquest or keep to the facts. I think perhaps the point is that it doesn't matter. One can say of Coyote's stories what one says of all good poetry: even if it didn't really happen, it's true. The simple facts, in this case, are as much to be marveled at as any embellishment that a storyteller might give them: a blonde girl and a ginger cake materialize out of the night, reminding us of the man—perhaps a mountain kachina or perhaps just a Navajo—who appears to the narrator in Leslie Silko's "Yellow Woman." In any event, we can trust Coyote about the heart of the matter: something strange and wonderful has happened.

Coyote, then, gets to be the storyteller and the poet in Ortiz' works for a number of reasons: because of his traditional verbal skills and his ultimate reliability and because "you know, Coyote / is in the origin and all the way / through," as Ortiz remarks in "Telling about Coyote," the opening poem of *A Good Journey* (p. 15). In mythic time, throughout historical time, in personal present-day experience, Coyote has been there and seen it all, and he is one of the best witnesses to the multiplicity, to the "many exciting and colorful and tragic things of adventure."

We should take note of one remaining affinity between Coyote and poet that Ortiz seems especially drawn to: the particular way in which both manage to continue. The central Coyote poem that sets forth this shared method of survival is "And there is always one more story," the tale of Coyote Lady and Skeleton Fixer that I referred to earlier. "It must be an old one," Ortiz says in the leisurely prose introduction, because he heard it from his mother, "who heard it from a woman who was talking about her grandson who was telling the story which was told to him by somebody else. All those voices telling the story, including the voices in the story." Ortiz is unusually concerned to establish this particular tale as ancient and well shared, as one of the stories Indians always tell in order to continue. Furthermore, of all the poems, this is the one on which he lavishes the most care in trying to create a sense of the storytelling occasion, with interjections from children's voices and familiar asides from the speaker ("I don't know why she wasn't grinding corn too—that's just in the story"), asides that break into the formal pattern of the narrative.

Tsuushki—Coyote Lady, in this one—is at work grinding with some Quail Women, who decide to take her along with them when they go to get a drink. The water is in a cistern at the top of a rock pinnacle, so the Quail Women donate some of their feathers to Coyote Lady, and all fly to the top. Coyote Lady is the last to drink, and while she is kneeling at the cistern the Quails decide to trick her by stealing the feathers back and leaving her stranded. When Grandmother Spider happens by, she agrees to help out by lowering Coyote Lady from the pinnacle in her basket, provided she promises not to "look up, not once/ not even the least little bit." Of course the temptation proves too strong, and Coyote Lady ends up as "a scatter of bones at the foot of the pinnacle": "Well, at this point, the story ends, but / as you know, it also goes on." Skeleton Fixer happens on the bones, and, wondering who has died, he rearranges them properly and sings his magic song over them. Coyote jumps up, restored, much to the disgust of Skeleton Fixer:

> Oh, it's just you, Coyote—I thought
> it was someone else.
>
> And as Coyote ran away,
> Skeleton Fixer called after her
> . . . .
> Go ahead and go, may you get crushed
> by a falling rock somewhere . . . !
> (*A Good Journey*, pp. 39–43)

Ortiz' version of the tale makes the world seem, if not downright hostile, at least mildly malicious. Coyote Lady's only real failing is the irrepressible and highly human one of giving in to curiosity. The tale seems to me unusually sympathetic to Coyote. The Quail Women are capricious in their friendship, and, while their relish of the joke may be understood to lie in their desire to get revenge for Coyote Lady's past actions, within the tale, at least, she has done nothing to provoke them. She was not even the one to bring up the notion of flying, does not ask to be what she is not naturally, although Coyote's insistence on attempting something beyond his or her native capabilities is what brings Coyote to grief in many traditional tales. In a version of this story told at neighboring Laguna, a male Coyote joins a flock of bluebirds, not quail, and they are scornful of him right from the first because he begs them to let him help grind corn, not his proper, natural occupation. Furthermore, even though, as in Ortiz, it is their idea to outfit him with feathers so he can reach the water, they really don't want him near their water supply, because, as a predator, "He always has some dirty stuff around his mouth."[10] In the Laguna version, Coyote, by his own actions and because of his nature, is clearly asking to be tricked. Ortiz, in his literary version, seems careful to be more sympathetic to Coyote, to describe what happens as a result of both a personal failing and the world's mischief; his tale invites a reader to dwell not so much on Coyote Lady's flaws or on the wickedness of the world as on simple lucklessness, on the way things often happen. The important thing is that enough remains, despite the catastrophe. As long as there are bones, they can be fleshed out anew. Never mind that the unwitting agent of Coyote Lady's restoration would not have bothered to fix this particular skeleton if he had known its identity, and never mind that he sees her off with a curse. That doesn't matter. Coyote is meant to continue, and does, as long as something of him (or her) remains. Only the bones are left, but the image of bare bone is resonant in all cultures. Bones are, after all, the indispensable foundation that remains to tell us the nature of the creature. They are the frame that supports the more destructible parts of the body, the parts of flesh that may wax and wane.

The images in Ortiz' tale of Coyote and Skeleton Fixer underlie a number of his poems about the survival of the American Indian coyote-poet. Even where they do not specifically invoke Coyote, the poems say that the poet, like Coyote, can be renewed from fragments. In the poet's case, they are fragments of his culture, not of his physical body, and the renewal comes about not through Skeleton Fixer's magic but from the miracle of his own will to remember and cherish, and so to survive.

Two poems in particular—"Fragment" and "The Poems I Have Lost," both from *Going for the Rain*—embody most explicitly this theme of the poet re-creating himself from fragments. In "Fragment," the renewal is possible, not because of bones, but rather through a small stone:

> On my way to city court
> to be judged again,
> I pick up a small stone.
>
> The month is March;
> it will be Easter soon.
> I put the stone in my pocket;
> it is that I feel the need
> for deliverance and maybe
> if I do this.

My hands are sweaty;
my fervent vain wish
is that I had never
been in jail
that first time.

I put the stone in my other hand
and caress it with my fingertips.
I find it is moist
and realize it is a fragment
of the earth center
and I know that it is
my redemption.

                              (p. 74)

The speaker tells us he is on his way "to be judged again," implying but not detailing the actions and events that have eroded his sense of himself. Easter is approaching, the Christian festival of redemption and the time of seasonal renewal for the whole natural world. It is a time to wish for a new beginning, to wish "that I had never / been in jail / that first time." The speaker knows that his wish is "vain," but the hope of finding himself again is not. The stone is the fragment that recalls for the speaker the origins, the heart of things, that which endures despite his present circumstances. It embodies what Ortiz, in the preface of *A Good Journey*, says is necessary for people to survive; it tells him something about himself that he needs to know, just as children need to know "how they were born, how they came to this certain place, how they continued." The little stone is a fragment of the earth's center, just as the mica hairline can be "the first seed, the origin"; it is a fragment from which all other things that matter may be inferred. It enables him to transcend the present circumstances of loss and self-destruction, and the story of finding it becomes, in itself, a story of how he continues. The stone is indeed a "Fragment," but it is enough.

"The Poems I Have Lost" presents a tale that is almost a contemporary analogue to the story of Coyote and Skeleton Fixer:

She said to take the L-train
to . . .

I know where I left them—
on the floor of her apartment
with five locks on Thirteenth Street,
Somewhere Else City, USA.
I don't think I'll ever go back.

A young couple picked me up
east miles out of Ashville—
had just started a poem too—
and we stopped and smoked
at a roadside table
at the edge of June tobacco fields.
I lost them somewhere
between there and the Atlantic Ocean.

I wrote Duffie a long rambling
letter, called it a poem,
from Nashville, because
I got lonesome for sunsets
in Colorado Springtime and then
dropped the letter in the mailbox.
I wonder if it ever found her
in Juneau, Alaska.

The last thing I remember
was leaning into the roots
of a piñon tree. It wasn't
the horse that had thrown me;
it wasn't McCallister either
who owned the horse. It was
all that damned beer we had
been drinking all afternoon.

I got a letter from St. Paul, Minn.
inviting me up there to read poems.
I fell off the plane in Denver,
lost my ticket and most of my poems
but managed to hold on enough
to a few remaining things.

Memories, I guess they are,
crowd me because of all the signals
I've missed, the poems that keep
coming back in pieces.

Fragments remain with me, of course;
I touch the bare skeletons, smell
the old things, and see new visages pass
many, more times.
Those are enough.

                                   (pp. 43–45)

    As in the tale of Coyote and Skeleton Fixer, Ortiz seems careful here to
present the situation as not entirely the result of either a hostile world or a
personal weakness. To be sure, he begins the poem by evoking a vision of an

impersonal urban America, where subways bewilder, where apartments need five locks, where neither letters nor poets can be certain of finding their destination. Nonetheless, it *is* a world containing friends to whom one is moved to write, where there are still sunsets, where one meets openhearted people, where even strangers ask to hear poems, and where, sometimes, the impersonal postal service *does* function, but the poet does not. Ortiz is too honest, too good a poet, to indulge in mere angry militancy, unilaterally denouncing Amerika-spelled-with-a-k. As the speaker straightforwardly admits, human fallings-off into alcohol and forgetfulness and despair do occur, and Anglo *mahkina* America and the speaker himself both seem reciprocally involved in the falls that occur here. The falls are not, in this case, from mesa tops, but from horseback, from the gangways of planes, and they are falls that are outward signs of deeper fallings away, forgetting one's origins, where one is going on the journey. Still, the important thing seems not to assign blame but to get the scattered self back together, to flesh out the bones. And, as in the old Coyote tale, there *are* bones. The speaker may fall, poems may be lost in some indefinite space, but something even more important than the poems remains, and that is the source of the poems: the bare skeletons, the old things.

Memory, then, and a sense of continuity. If the speaker can retain the old stories and traditions, nothing is really lost. Ortiz here is talking about more than the possibility of reconstructing lost manuscripts from memory. The surface of the world has altered desperately and a person can feel overwhelmed by the loss of a vital culture, of the native Coyote-self. But despite appearances, Ortiz in his poetry, like Leslie Silko in *Ceremony*, is saying that the old stories are more than cultural artifacts and childhood memories. They hold true and remain relevant as a way of understanding the world; indeed, the old stories are still going on, continuing to happen. In "The Poems I Have Lost," the "new visages pass many many times," again and again, because beneath those new visages lie old bones. In remembering what is old, one can deal with what is new. Coyote is not dead; his bones are continually being refleshed. Nor is the poet's self lost as long as he can hang on to the truth of that continuance, as long as he can remember and pass on the stories.

Flintwing Boy, then, is not just a cardboard figure in an old man's tale. He is alive in a new form and confronting old enemies. Coyote is not to be met with only in quaint stories that happened, if they ever did happen, back in "myth time." He walks Albuquerque's Central Avenue, shows up at the Laguna fiesta, hangs out around a campus in Tulsa. These days, he is even writing some pretty fine poems about himself, poems about his continuing presence that in themselves are powerful restoratives. Ask him his name, and he'll probably grin and give you some long story about how he's this and that and his name is legion. But one of his right names, surely, is Simon Ortiz.

Notes

1   S. Ortiz, "Telling about Coyote," *A Good Journey*, p. 17.
2   MacAdams, "Callin Coyote Home," *News from Niman Farm*. Quoted in Snyder.
3   Hobson, "The Rise of the White Shaman as a New Version of Cultural Imperialism." See also Evers, "Further Survivals of Coyote."
4   "The clown's mystical liberation from ultimate cosmic fears brings with it a liberation from conventional notions of what is dangerous or sacred in the religious ceremonies of men. . . . The ability of American Indian religions to allow room for the disruptive, crazy, but creative power of the clown is perhaps their greatest strength." B. Tedlock, "The Clown's Way," in Tedlock and Tedlock, eds., *Teachings from the American Earth*, pp. 105–17. Tedlock's article is especially pertinent because she deals at some length with Acoma Koshari clowns.
5   Toelken, "The 'Pretty Language(s)' of Yellowman."
6   Gunn, *Schat-Chen*, pp. 214–15. D. Tedlock also records a similar Zuni version of this tale, "Coyote and Junco: Suski Taap Silo," in *Finding the Center*, pp. 76–83.
7   Ortiz, "Men on the Moon," *Howbah Indians*, pp. 11–19.
8   Ortiz, "Travels in the South," *Going for the Rain*, pp. 34–37.
9   For an account of the zoological facts and the southwestern traditions concerning Coyote as a "singer," see Dobie, *The Voice of the Coyote*, especially the opening chapter, "The Father of Song Making."
10   "The Borrowed Feathers," in Lopez, *Giving Birth to Thunder*, pp. 48–49. In Keres tradition, Coyote is a predator because he disobeyed the orders of the first Hunt Chief to fast for four days before a hunt. See Tyler, *Pueblo Animals and Myths*, pp. 162–63.

A Critical Approach to American Indian Literature

Elaine Jahner

The momentum built by the creative efforts of American Indian writers is helping Indians and non-Indians alike to appreciate the intense vitality of individual tribal traditions whose many oral genres have kept alive compact, highly charged modes of communicating and linking past with present, generating the energy that infuses both the oral and the written genres of today. Contemporary American Indian writers seem to know very well indeed what Elizabeth Cook-Lynn means when she writes that "The spirit lives / . . . when we hang by fingernails, remote and hidden at the ridge of words."[1] The tribal oral traditions offer no secure hold on words that say once and for all what anything is all about. There are many ways of using words to understand the law of things, the forms of things, the junctures that grasp, link, and lead further so that the world can come to all who continue to hang "at the ridge of words," moving from past to future through traditional ways of understanding events.

In the living tribal traditions, many people still have an immediately experienced sense of the ways in which different kinds of narrative have to do with different ways of knowing. With such perception goes a responsibility for keeping alive the many ways of experiencing and knowing reality. Complete human knowing is far more than merely an accumulation of rational and generally predictable formulations of issues and themes; it requires an ability to use words so that they describe relations of all kinds at every level of being and becoming. Clearly, such knowing has a communal dimension that affects the balance between an author's sense of creative freedom and his or her feeling of responsibility to continue the communal traditions, whether these involve ceremonial, mythic, historical, or even fantastic narrative. This balance often comes about through the writer's efforts to relate the demands of written genres to the vitality of the oral traditions.

Transcribing an oral event is comparable to preparing sheet music. Only experience of the performed event can permit full entry to the meaning of what is transcribed. Indian literary artists themselves have not forgotten that, in spite of efforts to preserve tribal literatures by writing down the texts of oral performances, the literature remains alive only through continued performances that involve direct participation in the ways of thinking, knowing, and performing that characterize the different oral forms. A growing number of artists are trying to infuse written genres with qualities that characterize oral genres instead of merely recording the words of an oral art form. Non-Indian critics and readers must keep this in mind as they evaluate the creative efforts of today's American Indian writers. Critics need to be aware that conventional approaches and vocabulary are as likely to obscure as to illuminate the ways in which a specific tribal tradition can provide a writer with a set of optional approaches to the form and content of original creative work. The non-Indian critic is likely to assume too close a similarity between the ways in which Indian writers use their living tribal traditions and the ways in which many European and American writers use mythic traditions that have no immediate links to today's secular world.

In developing an approach and a vocabulary with which to respond to American Indian literature, critics have to remain constantly alert to the dangers of ethnocentrism, which would force American Indian literature into a non-Indian frame of reference, making the Indian works appear to be lacking. The journey toward decreased ethnocentrism in critical judgments can profitably begin with consideration of tribal aesthetics in relation to oral literature performance, because the different genres of oral literature affect the ways in which members of the tribes use language. When we isolate and examine those features of narrative that place a particular text in the tradition of a specific tribe, we can discover the features that mark a people's social life. Since the most significant aesthetic qualities of oral literature are those that are specific to a given tribe, the task of studying oral literature can seem overwhelming to the non-Indian critic or scholar who can hardly expect to find time to study in detail the aesthetic traditions of many tribes. A way out of the impasse lies in cooperation among many critics, writers, folklorists, anthropologists, and art historians, all of whom can publish sensitive descriptions of specific artistic traditions, not in the style of the once-popular "definitive" accounts of "dying" traditions, but in a way that shows both the continuity and the open-endedness of tribal ways. One foundation for such scholarship can be a renewed awareness of the dynamics of oral literature. In this essay I will point out some features of oral literature performance that are central to the way a living tradition affects people's ways of knowing and experiencing the world. I will also attempt to show how awareness of oral literary dynamics can make one aware of particular features of written literature.

Oral Literary Genres

Oral literature maintains its continuity even though it exists only in forms that accept, absorb, and organically transform new influences. It preserves traditions while it assimilates outside influences. The many facets of oral literature come into focus when we remember that those who participate in performances experience the struggle between change-resistant and change-oriented social forces. For those who perceive traditional narratives as fossils, this notion of narrative performance is difficult to accept, but participants in such events are aware that no two performances have precisely the same meaning. Each frames the motivational network that brings people together for a particular event. Each participant brings with him or her the questions, sorrows, and triumphs of life. Each person's experience induces openness to some aspects of the myth, tale, legend, or humorous story. In a very real sense the participant's life becomes one term of a metaphor while the narrative becomes the other term, and from this relationship springs the energy that is often called intuition or insight. An example can clarify the process. Recently a young woman who was attempting to learn more about her own tribe's traditional tales visited her grandmother hoping to share her grandmother's extensive knowledge of narrative. Just before the visit, the young woman had broken her engagement, but she did not feel ready to discuss the matter. Her grandmother, of course, noticed the absence of the engagement ring but respected the granddaughter's privacy and refrained from questioning her. In responding to the granddaughter's desire to learn traditional tales, she drew from her extensive knowledge of traditional motifs dozens of elements likely to touch the young woman's pain and confusion about the canceled wedding. To one unfamiliar with what the participants in the narrative event were experiencing, the grandmother's tales would have seemed unstructured, somewhat incoherent, and simplistic, but anyone who knew about the needs of the participants would be amazed at the sensitivity and subtle use of art to respond to very real but as yet unspoken needs.

The precise way in which oral literature affects the social life of small groups depends on the dynamics of specific performances. As the folklorist Dan Ben-Amos has stated, each ethnic genre is a verbal art form "consisting of a cluster of thematic and behavioral attributes."[2] In today's print-oriented academic environment, the study of thematic attributes comes more easily than the study of behavioral attributes. Yet both are so significant to the way that contemporary writers use oral literature dynamics in their work that a brief survey of outstanding behavioral attributes of these performances must preface discussion of specific uses of oral literary devices in written compositions. The interrelationships among songs, poetry, and ceremonies are basic and direct. For this reason, they are more easily and immediately understood than the relations that exist among myth, folktale, legend, and various written genres, so I will concentrate on the latter group in this essay.

Much has been written about the role of myth in culture, but not all of it can help the critic appreciate the vitality of myths in many American Indian communities. There the myths are an intimate part of ordinary daily activities, because they tell of the drama that gives meaning to the ordinary.

Several contemporary scholars have studied the profound ordering power of myth, regarding it as a component of a culture's deep structure.[3] Robert Plant Armstrong, using the term ''mythoform'' to describe the abstract, deep structural ordering power of myth, ascribes remarkable influence to it, calling it ''strong, viable, subtle, inescapable, pervasive—operating behind each possibility of man's relationship to the world, refracting through each sense and each faculty into terms appropriate to them.''[4] Myth operates at every level of life, but people are not always aware of it. As all who experience culture conflict know, people often achieve their clearest awareness of the power of myth when they are experiencing either the loss of its power in their own lives or a change in the way myth functions in their lives. People experience a sense of alienation when the terms in which they have traditionally viewed life seem temporarily or permanently inadequate, and they sometimes experience alienation as some form of illness. Recovering involves reevaluating their personal relationships with their own myth or the rather unlikely alternative of accepting some other myth. Therefore we can most easily observe the behavioral attributes related to myth when we study a society's resources for healing and for reintegration. Although the themes of specific mythic narratives may have to do with creation, the most readily observed results of the use of a vital and active myth are the recreation and reestablishment of an individual's sense of harmony with his or her society and culture. Modern American Indian writers have shown an intense and sophisticated awareness of this dimension of tribal myth.

The folktale is another important oral genre in many tribal communities. To an outsider the world of the folktale often seems only slightly less removed from ordinary reality than that of the myth. Many American Indians who still belong to communities where folktale performance occurs, however, can find in the tales the parameters of the ordinary as well as excursions into the realm of the nonordinary and supernatural. Folklorist Gyula Ortutay's comments on Hungarian folktales are equally true of those American Indian tales that still reflect the daily life of the communities in which they are told. According to Ortutay, the tale ''constituted a living part of the world of realities; not a tale, but a true and living reality, the authenticity of which was not at all inferior to that of the real experiences of the tangible world.''[5] Ortutay correctly relates two things: the sense of reality that the tale conveys and a structural coincidence between metaphysical beliefs and the order of causality in tales. The tale, even when it moves into the realm of the fantastic, shows the functioning of ways of thinking and acting that are part of a metaphysical view of the world. A particular incident in a folktale may seem unbelievable, but the way in which a hero or heroine responds to the fantastic is consistent with the metaphysical outlook of the tribal group. Furthermore, the tale keeps alive the sense of mystery and aliveness to the unknown that nourishes religious experience. In addition to the coincidence between religious and folktale behavioral qualities, I would add a structural coincidence between the stylistic development of the folktales of a particular group and the social structure of that group. A Lakota example can illustrate the main features of such a structural coincidence. Much traditional Lakota art derives from an aesthetic of movement among various spheres of being. The circle is the basic symbol of the culture, and it represents all the roles and social categories that determine how people move in the various spheres that determine their identity. The culture carefully prescribes point-to-point movement within the various interlocking circles, so that people move in accord with the way they perceive the ultimate power, or the deity, to move. Not even a folktale hero can disregard the basic structure of movements with impunity. The hero's deeds may be fantastic but his *movements* delineate a design akin to that which every person is trying to inscribe from one point to another in the various spheres of being. The folktales are aesthetic constructs that characterize each sphere of existence. They help to establish connections between heroic action and specific kinds of movement. The connections provide a metaphor for specific actions that occur in the lives of all the people. In dealing with any metaphor in modern American Indian writing, the critic or teacher should take into account the range of metaphoric reference of the community from which the work emerges.

Legend is another oral genre that the literary critic cannot afford to ignore. Studying legend formation and use can be particularly productive for the literary critic because legend formation demonstrates the process whereby vital local beliefs continue to generate new narratives. Through legend, belief (mythic energy) becomes fused with the daily life in a particular region. The thematic and behavioral attributes of the legend are all consistent with the individual tribe's world view and have to do with people's tendency to invest certain places and persons with an aura of the exceptional. Legend makes myth and history seem real to the person who lives within the limitations imposed by a particular socioeconomic environment. Although legends can be (and often are) ironic, they require a narrator who sees himself or herself as the teller of a true story about an encounter with something that, although it may be out of the ordinary, is still consistent with local belief. The narrator tends to view the audience as an informal group that must learn about every possible kind of encounter in any given environment. The legend narrator generally views the subject matter as a validation of tenets of the belief system. Both Indian and non-Indian writers often use legends to serve specific literary ends, but some American Indian writers are attempting the more difficult task of applying the dynamics of legend formation to the task of writing about a particular tribal group. Just as legend formation bestows value on particular places and people, thereby validating tribal beliefs, so can the writing of poems, short stories, and novels bestow value on places and people.

Other oral literary genres are important in determining the aesthetics of any tribal group, but myth, folktale, and legend provide the primary resources for the writer. Even so brief a survey as this can show the immense range of techniques and genres available to the contemporary American Indian writer who wants to use traditional artistic processes as the contextual matrix and the structuring force for new works of literature. Modern writers have responded in various ways to the challenge posed by their own living traditions, and in the second half of this paper I want to examine ways in which writers have used the traditions to provide structure for their consciously modern efforts.

Intermediate Genres

Some works in every literary tradition have traits that derive from both the oral and written modes. Contemporary American Indian writing presents several examples of works that occupy some kind of midpoint in the continuum between oral and written composition. N. Scott Momaday's *The Way to Rainy Mountain* is the preeminent and most instructive example of the type. Momaday's book is a carefully structured compilation of myth, legend, and personal commentary. In this intensely vital book, Momaday tries to capture the spirit of oral literature performance by using his personal commentary to complete the matching process that occurs in oral performance.

It is interesting to study the role of the narrator in this experimental narrative. Momaday's representation of himself is twofold; he presents himself as someone who tells about the mythic voice as it has functioned in his community and he shows his own participation in the development of that voice. He is both presenter and audience. As presenter of the myths he allies himself with the elders who had the responsibility of keeping the myth alive for the community and of finding points of contact between the timeless myths and time-bound action in this world. The historical sections of *The Way to Rainy Mountain* help us experience some of those points of contact. But Momaday is also the storyteller's audience recording his own responses to the myths. In so doing, he captures the dynamic features of oral performance. As he responds to his people's myth and history, he finds that the myth reveals the meaning of his own memories. For example, the third myth in the book tells of a talking dog who saved the Kiowas, and this story prods

Momaday's own memory of the dogs around his grandmother's house: "There were always dogs about my grandmother's house. Some of them were nameless and lived a life of their own. They belonged there in a sense that the word 'ownership' does not include" (p. 23). Momaday's experiences enable him to understand the myth teller's full purpose in describing how the dog once saved a Kiowa from destruction. The myth explains why, in Kiowa culture, the dog is surrounded by meanings that transcend the ordinary semantic features of the word "ownership" when that word is applied to the relationship between dogs and people. Such examples of added and culturally unique meanings help explain what Momaday means when he mentions oral tradition's "deeper and more vital context of language and meaning than that which is generally taken into account."[6] The listener must be someone whose cultural experience enables him or her to respond to the myth and, by responding, to capture some of the essential meaning of personal experience. The perception of oneself as a member of a myth teller's audience—a member who is discovering one's own context of vital meaning and therefore discovering features of one's own poetic language—is basic to understanding Momaday's role as the persona in his own work.

What is the major purpose of this complex experiment with literary form? An essential part of the answer to that question is in the Prologue to the book:

> In some sense, then, the way to Rainy Mountain is preeminently the history of an idea, man's idea of himself, and it has old and essential being in language. The verbal tradition by which it has been preserved has suffered a deterioration in time. What remains is fragmentary; mythology, legend, lore and hearsay—and of course the idea itself, as crucial and complete as it ever was. That is the miracle. The journey herein recalled continues to be made anew each time the miracle comes to mind, for that is peculiarly the right and responsibility of the imagination. (p. 2)

The poet, making the imaginative journey through a particular culture's myth and legend, can align these with personal memories and personal experience of a kind of meaning that has its essence in the culture's verbal tradition. Completion of such a journey is the prelude to further transmission of the meaning, but it can also be the prelude to a change in the mode of transmission. Once the artist lives and makes the essential idea his or her own, the miracle that Momaday talks about, that artist can continue the transmission process in the written as well as the oral mode. Since the idea itself has been nourished and kept alive orally all through the centuries, however, its continuity depends on new forms that relate intimately and precisely to the oral tradition. That is why transitional works like *The Way to Rainy Mountain* are so important and so interesting. Albert B. Lord in *The*

Singer of Tales noted the importance of such forms when he wrote that "the seeds of 'literary' style are already present in oral style. . . . We are working in a continuum of man's artistic expression in words. We are attempting to measure with some degree of accuracy the strength and mixture of traditional matters of expression" (p. 130).

Other writers have tried, far less successfully than Momaday, to adapt oral literary techniques to the written mode.[7] Each attempt is interesting theoretically, but direct reflections of the oral tradition and transitional works are necessarily artistically limited. The excitement of contemporary American Indian literature lies in the more complex adaptations of the traditional oral forms.

The Novel

The novel is particularly well suited to accommodating the diverse aesthetic energies that exist in traditional tribal communities. Because of its generic history, the novel automatically suggests contrasts between the tribal way of life with its accompanying aesthetic modes and the non-Indian way, which is so deeply linked with European tradition. Individual American Indian authors have accepted the challenge that the novel presents. By working with the tensions between two essentially different aesthetic modes, they have fashioned structures that relate as intimately to the life of the modern American Indian community as the oral forms have related to the continuing life of the community. Each new novel by an American Indian who is consciously concerned with the principles of continuity that lie at the heart of tribal life is another step in developing a new type of American novel, one that relates directly to the oldest aesthetic traditions of the Western Hemisphere.

N. Scott Momaday's *House Made of Dawn* has recently begun to receive the academic and critical attention that it deserves.[8] The novel embodies many levels of perception and reveals the complex life struggle of tribal cultures in a world that threatens all such cultures. In the novel Momaday uses the same narrative voices he employed in *The Way to Rainy Mountain,* in which the three voices—the mythic, historical, and immediate—take turns, and juxtaposition remains the major structural device of the novel, although Momaday uses considerably more interweaving of the three voices to develop the plot. The immediate voice is that of the protagonist Abel, a man who must leave the reservation when he is drafted and who cannot relate his experiences with the non-Indian world to the Indian way of life until after he has lost contact with all but the most basic realities. Then he learns that for him the roots of all meaning lie in his Indian heritage, symbolized by the ritual race that he runs at the end of the novel. The historical voice is presented through Abel's grandfather, with his memories of village life, and through the parish priest's reading of an old journal left by a predecessor. Momaday's descriptions of the land and references to rituals constitute the mythic voice. The novel's first paragraph indicates the tone that the mythic references establish:

> There was a house made of dawn. It was made of pollen and rain, and the land was very old and everlasting. There were many colors on the hills, and the plain was bright with different-colored clays and sands. Red and blue and spotted horses grazed in the plain and there was a dark wilderness on the mountains beyond. The land was still and strong. It was beautiful all around. (p. 1)

The paragraph begins and ends with references to the Navajo Night Chant.[9] The novel's title and its basic structure are derived from this healing chant. The Navajo regard sickness as lack of harmony, making no radical distinction between physical and mental illness. In the Navajo language a state of health is also a state of beauty or accord. This fact explains the reference in Momaday's first paragraph to beauty all around. Initially Momaday establishes the associations that will shape the thematic structure of the novel. Even his style is based on a traditional stylistic mode. As Gladys Reichard has observed, "associations have been suggested as the key to Navaho symbolism. . . . Though they may often seem to be peculiar, these associations are by no means 'free' but are held together in a stipulated pattern which only the details that compose it can explain."[10] Reichard's comments on Navajo symbolism could serve as well as a commentary on the style of *House Made of Dawn*. The texture of associations is carefully woven. In the first paragraph the idea of healing and myth is linked to that of one's relation to the land. In *The Way to Rainy Mountain* Momaday wrote about the impact land can have on the individual personality: "All things in the plain are isolate; there is no confusion of objects in the eye, but *one* hill or *one* man. To look upon that landscape in the early morning, with the sun at your back, is to lose the sense of proportion. Your imagination comes to life, and this, you think, is where Creation was begun" (p. 5).

All of Momaday's writing implies that creation in a very real sense does begin with the land. The perspective that the land imposes inspires the imagination to find meaning in life. Thus the land inspires stories, the first of which is a creation story, a "coming out" story. The same need to create meaning that led the tribal people of yesterday to retell myths and legends exists today; however, circumstances are such that in today's world the impulse to create must result in written literature as well as in legend and folktale.

Clearly Momaday's belief that creation begins with the land is an important part of his effort to understand how myths, legends, and tales evolve into
other forms of literature. In "The Man Made of Words," he wrote:

> I am interested in the way that a man looks at a given landscape and takes
> possession of it in his blood and brain. . . . We Americans need now more than
> ever before—and indeed more than we know—to imagine who and what we
> are with respect to the earth and sky. I am talking about an act of the imagina-
> tion essentially. (p. 53)

Momaday suggests that the American Indian people, of all Americans, are
best able to "imagine who and what we are with respect to the earth and
sky" because the Indians have a tradition of such imaginative creation of
meaning: "Storytelling is imaginative and creative in nature. . . . Man tells
stories in order to understand his experience, whatever it may be. The possibilities of storytelling are precisely those of understanding the human experience" (p. 56). The possibilities of storytelling are those of relating the
immediate to the historical by means of the mythic voice whether in oral
performance or in written literature. Such is Momaday's theory of the three
narrative voices.

House Made of Dawn gave Momaday occasion to dramatize the differences in the Indian and the non-Indian attitudes toward language, differences
that result from the Indian's close association with ancient oral traditions.
During Abel's trial he realizes that "word by word these men were disposing
of him in language, their language, and they were making a bad job of it" (p.
95). This realization is a pivotal point in the novel: "He could understand,
however imperfectly, what they were doing to him, but he could not understand what they were doing to each other" (p. 95). Abel's inability to understand what his judges are doing to each other with their words is juxtaposed
to sections of a sermon given by a priest in the American Indian church in
which the priest says of the non-Indian that "he has diluted and multiplied
the Word and words have begun to close in upon him. He is sated and
insensitive; his regard for language—for the Word itself—as an instrument of
creation has diminished nearly to the point of no return. It may be that he
will perish by the Word" (p. 89). The novel provides an alternative to perishing by the word. The alternative is making that journey toward understanding
that is an imaginative experience given form through custom, ritual, and
storytelling; in other words, through the oral tradition whereby imaginative
experience becomes part of the experience of living in a group. What was
once an unquestioned way of doing things has come, with the passing of
time and changes in culture, to be but one of many ways. Custom, ritual,
legend, and tale are no longer seen as inevitable, but they still retain their
integrity in harmonious relation to other customs and rituals and ways of
communicating. So the oral tradition evolves into literature. The person who

is conscious of the value of ancient lore and legend as a journey toward what he or she is today can employ elements of the oral tradition in order to ensure continued progress in the journey toward understanding.

One can see how Momaday employs the narrative techniques of southwestern myths, legends, and tales. But is intensive research necessary in understanding other writers who may rely less directly and obviously on oral literary precedents? I believe it is. A good test case is James Welch's *Winter in the Blood*. Welch's novel has few allusions to tribal ceremonies or customs; its straightforward and clear style makes most of the novel's meaning easily accessible to readers from any culture. But there are levels of meaning that give sonority and depth to the novel, and these can be reached only if one is willing to allow the novel's many facets—plot, character, imagery, and structure—to operate against a background of Blackfeet culture and Blackfeet oral literature.

Welch's unnamed protagonist seems a far cry from the heroes of Blackfeet myth and legend. He is at home on the Blackfeet reservation in Montana, and he is there simply because he has no reason to be elsewhere. A victim of apathy, he cannot even manage to care that the Cree woman with whom he has been living has stolen his gun and run away. The one character who has escaped apathy is the protagonist's old grandmother. Although confined to a rocking chair, she has not given up, and her very existence forces other characters to think about the continued intrusion of past events and attitudes into current life. Her imagination remains intensely alive, and she has all the vitality of a character who has been shaped by tales of immensely audacious heroes and heroines.

The same cannot be said for Welch's protagonist, who has no positive relationship to his own or his people's past and, as a result, is utterly unable to accept present realities. Like the heroes of tribal legends, Welch's protagonist needs some kind of vision that will show him his role in relation to his people. Unlike the old heroes, however, the modern man does not go to the wilderness to pray. Instead he goes to the non-Indian towns surrounding the reservation where his wanderings lead to no vision, unless the realization that he does not belong out there can be called a vision. But the well-written, sometimes hilarious, sometimes incredibly sad town scenes are merely preparation for the real epiphany, comparable to a vision, that occurs near the end of the book. The meaning of the protagonist's crucial insight is never made explicit. After finishing the novel, the perceptive reader realizes that a complex thematic structure has been guiding the entire book and that an intricate texture of references to that thematic structure has been woven through the story, but that is as far as the reader can get without placing the novel in its traditional context and realizing that the epistemological basis for *Winter in the Blood* is every bit as Indian as George Bird Grinnell's *Blackfoot Lodge Tales*, even though the immediate experience of the protagonists is entirely different, and the contemporary novel shares some of the basic dynamics that gave vitality to the tales.

In Welch's book, as in many other American Indian novels, the thematic properties of the text can be decided only on referential grounds. We have to rely on ethnological information to interpret the metaphorical structures and their thematic import. Frequently, as in the book in question, metaphorical references are related to the cultural metaphors. The entire cultural system of the nomadic plains and mountain tribes depended on systems of meaningful movements, and the Blackfeet, like other tribes, used the circle inclusive of intersecting roads as a symbol for life's activities. Life itself is seen as movement along a "trail" and the good life is spoken of as straight movement along the trail.[11] The movements that made up the activities of a good life were valid because, and only because, they reflected the archetypal cosmic pattern for life. Within this system of thought, order is good because it is natural. Anything that goes against the basic pattern is likely to result in sickness or even death. Along that archetypal trail of life, members of the tribe had to traverse specific distances before they could attain physical and spiritual necessities. This aspect of the symbol has a firm basis in reality. The Blackfeet were a nomadic people who had to travel to find the buffalo; so movement across the distance from one camp to another was literally the means to all power. The image of distance is a natural one in that vast country, and the Blackfeet have expanded its connotations over the centuries. Welch uses the image effectively and adds some connotations of his own. By tracing references to the distance theme in his poetry and in his novel, we can see how Welch relates the traditional meaning of distance to the life of his modern protagonist.

Once we understand the cultural overtones that give a particular sonority to the theme of distance, we can see that the omens are not all bad for the protagonist at the conclusion of the novel. In the course of the novel, Welch has effected a transformation from a negative distance that prevents the protagonist from attaining self-knowledge and separates him from nature and society to a positive distance that can allow him to relate to nature and society. The transformation is now possible because he understands the cultural meanings of distance among the Blackfeet. Welch's use of a cultural symbol enables him to show that, while the world remains cockeyed and stupidity continues to flourish, there are still possibilities of growth within the tradition. And one must understand that the possibilities exist within a particular tradition. They exist because of the culture's own history and geographical location and because of the conflicts that the people have endured over the years. The artist who works within a developing tradition speaks out of an experience of sharing in the known and the hidden sources of strength that belong to it. By examining the imaginative possibilities present in one mode of adaptation and transformation of a traditional thematic structure,

Welch shows how it is possible to move in the direction defined by tradition without falling back on the past as the solution to present-day problems.

Because Momaday and Welch are Indians who have lived among the people they write about, they understand how certain cultural images function as ways of perceiving.[12] The images enable people to think about phenomena in terms of unique constitutive qualities instead of such extrinsic considerations as quantity and monetary value. Momaday and Welch use these basic images as skillfully as the best of the oral literary artists. They do it, not to make the written form as much like the oral as possible, as in the intermediate works, but to tap some of the same creative energies that the oral artist uses. What is more, Welch and Momaday show these same cultural forces at work in the complex environment of a pluralistic society. The good novelist, if he or she wishes, can use the genre not only to show how the traditional structures can absorb and organically transform new content (a function of all the oral literary genres) but also to show how the tradition can function within new structures. Critics must be aware of the structural potential that the many oral genres have for written forms of literature.

Conclusion

The history of scholarship in the field of American Indian oral literary forms is not at all impressive. All too often scholars have treated these forms as simple, even simplistic, renderings of obvious truths. Therefore, anyone who lacks direct personal experience with oral forms may think that a wide gulf lies between the sophisticated contemporary novels of writers like Momaday, Welch, or Silko and the folktale or the legend. It may be easier to see how poets use a mythic context of language as a foundation for their art, but even that insight is all too often ignored when the mythic context is not directly reflected in the work. If the study of oral literary forms is to have any real value to the critic of American Indian literature, the critic must start with the premise that oral forms reflect particular ways of knowing, that they are epistemological realities. They exist both as artifact and as process. Comparison of the oral artifact with the written artifact might be sterile, but comparison of the processes related to the various oral forms and those related to the written genres can give the critic a sense of the genuine artistry of both modes of composition and of communication among individuals as well as among cultures.

Notes

1   Cook-Lynn. *Then Badger Said This*, p. 1.
2   Ben-Amos, "Analytical Categories and Ethnic Genres," p. 231.

3   Maranda's comments on the way myths manifest a culture's deep structure constitute a concise statement of the views of structuralist scholars. "Myths display the structured, predominantly culture-specific and shared semantic systems which enable the members of a culture area to understand each other and to cope with the unknown. More strictly, myths are stylistically definable discourses that express the strong components of semantic systems" (*Mythology*, p. 10).

See also Hymes's approach to genre classification and interpretation. "One assumes that persons growing up in the community in question acquire a grasp of the structures and functions of the genre, such that they are able to judge instances as appropriate or inappropriate not only in terms of overt formal features ('surface structures') but also in terms of underlying relations ('deep structure')" ("The 'Wife' Who 'Goes Out' like a Man").

4   *Wellspring*, p. 96.

5   *Hungarian Folklore*, p. 214.

6   "The Man Made of Words," in Henry, *Indian Voices*, p. 59.

7   An interesting attempt is Storm's *Seven Arrows*. A debate over the relative merits of *Seven Arrows* appeared in *Wassaja*, the newspaper published by the American Indian Historical Association, April-May 1974 and August 1974. V. Deloria wrote a positive review of the book in *Natural History*.

8   The most complete and authoritative essay on Momaday's novel published to date is Evers, "Words and Place."

9   See Matthews, *The Night Chant*.

10   Reichard, *Navaho Religion*, p. 517

11   McClintock, *The Old North Trail*, pp. 33, 179. Many of the prayers and ceremonies that McClintock records refer to traveling "the straight path" and proceeding along the "trail of life."

12   See Momaday's autobiography *The Names*: "In general my narrative is an autobiographical account. Specifically it is an act of the imagination. When I turn my mind to my early life, it is the imaginative part of it that comes first and irresistibly into reach, and of that part I take hold. This is one way to tell a story. In this instance, it is my way, and it is the way of my people."

In "The Only Good Indian," Welch has written, "There are exceptions . . . but for the most part only an Indian knows who he is—an individual who just happens to be an Indian—and if he has grown up on a reservation he will naturally write about what he knows. And hopefully he will have the toughness and fairness to present his material in a way that is not manufactured by conventional stance. . . . What I mean is whites have to adopt a stance; Indians already have one" (in *The American Indian II*, ed. Milton, p. 54).

Introductory Courses in American Indian Literature

American Indian literature is a continuum of imaginative uses of language. The continuum ranges in form from traditional oral narratives and songs to transitional forms such as oratory and autobiography, to written genres such as the essay, poem, short story, and novel. This continuum of form does not necessarily imply a chronology. Each form, each genre, has historical depth. The conventional rigid division of American Indian literature into past oral and present written literature is misleading. American Indians were writing imaginatively well before Momaday won a Pulitzer Prize, and American Indian oral traditions continue today.

Methodology and Description

The major organizing concept of all three introductory courses is genre. Included in each course are oral literature (narrative, song, ceremony); transitional literature, which combines oral and written expression (treaty oration, as-told-to autobiography, and personal narrative); and written literature (essay, poem, short story, novel).

All three courses impose a second organizing feature—region. Intensive treatment of American Indian literature is preferable to an extensive but superficial survey. Given the enormous number of different types of oral literature created by hundreds of tribes and given the variety of intermediate forms and the increasing amount of written material published by American Indian authors, no course can cover every narrative and song, every oration and autobiography, every essay, poem, short story, and novel. Instructors must make choices. One sensible way to inform those choices is to use a regional focus.

This approach offers several advantages in introductory courses: (1) Limiting the number of American Indian cultures to be covered in the course should enable instructors to devote time to the development of adequate contexts for the literature. This is very important in an introduction to Indian literature since the material is usually unfamiliar to the students. (2) A regional focus should allow instructors to develop clearly defined continuities between the written work of individual American Indian authors and the oral traditions that constitute part of their tribal heritages. (3) Much, if not all, American Indian literature is firmly tied to particular physical landscapes, hence it is logical to focus on a particular area. (4) Focusing an introductory course on the geographic area in which the course is taught offers students the opportunity to deal with literature shaped by a landscape with which the students are familiar.

Two of the introductory courses outlined below focus on the Southwest. This region has been a fertile landscape for excellent oral and written Indian literature: the Navajo, Pueblo, and Kiowa narratives and ceremonies include some of the most complex and beautiful examples of Indian oral literature, and many of the well-known contemporary authors—including N. Scott Momaday, Simon Ortiz, and Leslie Silko—come from the Southwest. The focus on the Southwest also helps to offset the stereotype of the nineteenth-century Plains Indian as the universal Indian.

The other introductory course focuses on the Northern Plains, the area that inspired the Plains stereotype. After studying the literature of this area, students will be encouraged to go beyond the stereotype—to become aware of the complexities of the Plains cultures' varying degrees of emphasis on individual glory, visions, courage, resistance, and adaptability to non-Indian settlers and miners and to the railroad. Although there aren't yet as many well-known contemporary authors in the area, one major American Indian poet and novelist, James Welch, is from the area; his views of modern Montana reservation and town life are among the most powerful examples of written Indian literature. Two of the best-known autobiographies, *Black Elk Speaks* and *Lame Deer*, recount different types of Sioux experiences, and the area is famous for its oratory, ghost dance and sun dance ceremonies, and oral narratives, especially those that recount the vision quest. A number of poets from the Northern Plains are also publishing work that movingly depicts contemporary Plains life and culture.

The regional bias we propose prompts us to call the three courses "introductory" courses rather than "survey" courses. A survey suggests a sampling of Indian literatures from all areas in North and possibly South America. The introductory courses outlined here attempt to provide instructors and students with a set of strategies for approaching examples from literature produced in one region rather than a superficial acquaintance with all Indian literatures. We assume, however, that this set of strategies can be used to approach the literatures of other regions. In other words, we hope that these introductory courses will acquaint instructors and students with a process rather than an established canon of works. This attitude is reflected by the organization of the courses and by the inclusion of non-southwestern and non-Plains reading assignments to supplement the regional readings in each course.

Thematic and Stylistic Continuities

The introductory courses contain several unifying principles besides the emphasis on genre and region. The oral, transitional, and written literatures examined also suggest thematic and stylistic links. One major theme in the American Indian literature of the Southwest is the emergence-regeneration theme. Many origin narratives, especially in the Southwest, tell of the emergence of the people through various lower worlds into the present world. This tribal journey usually advances in a series of movements from states of imbalance and disharmony to states of balance and harmony. The emergence narratives constitute a kind of tribal history from which the people can learn who and what they are. This collective emergence journey is often repeated in ritual dramas and in hero narratives by individual participants or protagonists. These individual journeys, which can be seen as a kind of retracing of the people's collective journey, appear not only in the oral traditions but also in the autobiographical sections of works such as Momaday's *Way to Rainy Mountain,* in novels such as *House Made of Dawn* and Silko's *Ceremony,* and in collections of poetry such as Simon Ortiz' *Going for the Rain* and *A Good Journey.* Just as the people moved from disharmony to harmony, so too do individual participants in ceremonies, autobiographers, and fictional protagonists or poetic personae.

A principal theme in the Northern Plains literature is the individual's quest for self-understanding, a search that often takes the form of a vision quest or a personal test. In the early oral traditions this theme appeared in hero tales, war songs, chants, and visions. The autobiographies *Black Elk Speaks* and *Lame Deer, Seeker of Visions* both follow this pattern. Even James Welch's description of his narrator's attempts to understand his tribal, family, and personal past reflects the quest for self-understanding.

In spite of the importance of the emergence theme and the vision quest in the introductory courses, these two themes should not become strait-jackets. Like the focus on genre and region, the thematic emphasis should be used to encourage students to look for links between written and oral traditions. They will discover other thematic and stylistic connections such as repetition and parallelism, recurring characters such as the Trickster, and the importance of the land.

Alternative Introductory Course

Although all three of the introductory courses emphasize genre, region, and theme, the alternative Southwestern course suggests a variety of options.

In this course the instructor emphasizes contemporary writings and begins the course with modern literature, whereas most introductory American Indian literature courses begin with oral literatures. There are several reasons for this approach: (1) Most students can easily understand the work of contemporary writers, whereas many (especially non-Indian) students have difficulty with the oral literature. Thus, beginning with contemporary works is a good way to ease students into a very complex body of literature, the understanding of which depends on familiarity with traditions that most university students know nothing about. (2) Most contemporary Indian authors use European-American literary forms to express Indian views. Hence their works—especially *The Way to Rainy Mountain* and *Ceremony*—often combine several different written and oral forms. Such works offer a provocative introduction to the variety of genres students will examine during the semester. (3) The emphasis on contemporary written literature should help to offset the stereotype of the "vanishing American" and the Indian as a museum relic.

Beginning with and emphasizing contemporary literature in an introductory course involves risks. Students will inevitably miss a lot when they plunge into the modern works. But the risks should be worth the gamble. What the students can't grasp should encourage them to seek information in the other forms—to rediscover, in effect, the meaning of the contemporary works later as they read the autobiographies, orations, narratives and ceremonies. This alternative introduction to Indian literature should thus be more than the conventional journey from one genre to the next. It should be a process of discovery that enables students to gain deeper insights into the origins and contexts of all the genres.

This is why this course opens and closes with *The Way to Rainy Mountain*. By the end of the course, students should be able to view this masterly synthesis of autobiography, written forms, and oral forms from perspectives they knew nothing about when they began the course. In other words, the students' ability to experience American Indian literature should be "regenerated" by the end of the course.

Course Design #1

An Introductory Course in American Indian Literature: Southwestern Literature

This course is designed for a three-hour, one-semester course at the sophomore or junior level and has no prerequisites other than freshman writing and an introductory course in literature. Because of limitations in time and expertise, the course does not include all tribes or all the literature reflecting a given tribe's culture.

The structure of the course allows examination of the myths and stories, central elements of which appear in written material, and an integration of the past and present, the cultural themes of the past being woven into the present experience. For example, the emergence story is echoed in Momaday's *House Made of Dawn*. The Trickster (Coyote) and some of his adventures, part of the oral tradition, appear in Simon Ortiz' poem "The Creation According to Coyote," and in Leslie Silko's poem "Toe'osh: A Laguna Coyote Story."

A study of the Night Chant should clarify the significance of ceremonial aspects in *House Made of Dawn*. The creation stories, accounts of the gifts of food, and an understanding of the sacred nature of those gifts provide insight into Abel's response to the evil that threatens the community and its life-sustaining food in *House Made of Dawn*. Thus each part of the course should complement the other.

To underline the continuing nature of the oral tradition, the instructor should try to arrange presentations by American Indian guests. Participation in local powwows or singings should be a part of the course, if possible, after the instructor has explained the Indian views of courtesy expected at such events. Some films and videotapes such as the *Words and Place* series are also useful in demonstrating the continuing presence of the oral tradition.

The term paper can be adapted to the individual student's interests or major. If the student's paper focuses on the literature, however, as it must at least as a springboard, the literature should be that of the American Indian, with other literature mentioned only for the purpose of contrast, comparison, or analysis.

Materials

Readings in oral literature should include Paula Allen, "The Sacred Hoop," and N. Scott Momaday, "The Man Made of Words," as introductory readings; creation stories told by Hastin Tlo'tsihee, "The Beginning," and Albert Yava, "Way Back in the Distant Past," from Evers, *The South Corner of Time*; Coyote stories and Yellow Woman stories from Boas, *Keresan Texts*, and Silko, *Storyteller*; the Navajo Night Chant from Bierhorst, *Four Masterworks*; and a selection of Hopi, Navajo, Papago, and Yaqui songs from *The South Corner of Time*. These readings in oral literature should be supplemented by oral presentations by American Indian singers or tellers where that is possible. Canyon Records (4143 N. Sixteenth St., Phoenix, AZ 85016) has made an enormous number of sound recordings of American Indian singers available on phonograph records. Videotapes of Navajo, Hopi, Apache, Keresan, and Yaqui singers and storytellers are available in the *Words and Place* series distributed by Clearwater Publishing Company (1995 Broadway,

New York, NY 10023). They are in native languages with English subtitles and come with study guides.

Appropriate readings in what we are calling transitional literature might include Mitchell, *Navajo Blessingway Singer,* Chona, *Papago Woman,* and Tom Ration's "A Navajo Life Story" and Nancy Woodman's "The Story of an Orphan" from *The South Corner of Time.*

Poetry and short fiction should include selections from Hobson, *The Remembered Earth,* and Evers, *The South Corner of Time.* Students should read two novels: Momaday, *House Made of Dawn,* and Silko, *Ceremony.*

Supplementary readings could include: McNickle and Fey, *Indians and Other Americans,* for historical contexts; Ortiz, *The Southwest,* gives concise ethnological perspectives on each of the Pueblos. Volume 10 of the *Handbook of North American Indians* will cover the non-Pueblo native peoples of the Southwest.

Finnegan, *Oral Poetry,* provides discussion of the processes that maintain oral traditions. Witherspoon, *Language and Art in the Navajo Universe;* K. Kroeber, *Traditional Literatures;* Hymes, *In Vain,* and Swann, *Smoothing the Ground,* provide critical perspectives on American Indian story and song. Bierhorst, *The Red Swan,* is a good collection of oral narratives. A. Grove Day, *The Sky Clears,* is an excellent collection of song texts, as is Swann's *Song of the Sky.*

Brumble, *American Indian and Eskimo Autobiographies,* provides information on many other autobiographies. Arnold Krupat, "The Indian Autobiography," gives very helpful perspectives on the transitional literature.

Other good sources for written literature are Niatum (Klallam), *Carriers of the Dream Wheel;* Rosen, *The Man to Send Rain Clouds;* and Fisher, *The Third Woman.* Lincoln, *Native American Renaissance,* provides critical perspectives. Fiedler, *The Return of the Vanishing American,* is helpful in providing a more general literary context.

Course Design #2

Northern Plains Indians

The principal themes of the oral literature of the Northern Plains are the search for individualism and self-understanding, the performance of heroic deeds, the relation of person to environment, and the relation of personal experience to group heritage and continuity. These themes can be traced through the oral literature, several important autobiographies, and contemporary fiction.

The Northern Plains region is rich in narrative materials that recount individual heroic achievement. Belief in the necessity for heroic action did

not disappear with the Indians' confinement on reservations, but opportunities for personal achievement were severely restricted.

The concern for history that we find in oral narratives and winter counts
extends to the nonfiction of today as typified by the works of Vine Deloria,
Jr., D'Arcy McNickle, and Robert Burnett. Reflected in the literature is a
strong element of the mystical and visionary, as seen in ghost dance materials
and earlier autobiographies. Viewing the literature exclusively from this
perspective is perhaps inadequate, but it is one way to relate the literature to
the Northern Plains landscape.

One can show the transition from oral to written literature by tracing the
tradition of personal narratives, biographies, and autobiographies and by
examining the oral and pictorial winter counts. One can extend the geographical limits of this study to include a comparison of Fred McTaggart's
Wolf That I Am with the poetry of Ray Young Bear.

Another important theme in all but the oldest oral literature concerns
Indian-white relations and the difficulties of cross-cultural understanding.
Several different treatments of this theme appear in oral narrative materials,
autobiographies, winter counts, and modern prose.

Materials

For background, students may begin by reading McNickle (Salish) and
Fey, *Indians and Other Americans*. For the oral traditions (legends, hero tales,
and narratives), students may read selections from Clark, *Indian Legends*; E.
Deloria (Sioux), *Dakota Texts*; Mooney, *Ghost Dance Religion*; Radin, *The
Trickster*; and Theisz, *Buckskin Tokens*. A selection from the following transi-
tional autobiographies can be made: Black Elk (Sioux), *Black Elk Speaks*;
Campbell (Métis), *Halfbreed*; Eastman (Sioux), *Indian Boyhood*; Fire (Sioux),
Lame Deer; and Stands in Timber (Cheyenne), *Cheyenne Memories*. For
fiction, students should read Welch (Blackfeet-Gros Ventre), *Death of Jim
Loney* and *Winter in the Blood*. For nonfiction, students should read V.
Deloria (Sioux), *Custer Died for Your Sins*.

Course Design #3

*Introduction to American Indian Literature with an Emphasis on the
Navajo, Pueblo, and Kiowa (Alternative Introduction to
Southwestern Literature)*

This is a three-hour, one-semester course for sophomores and juniors.
Prerequisites are freshman composition and one literature course.

Methodology and Description

The first course session should include an explanation of the nature of the course and the assignments, information about the instructor's background and interests, and an in-class writing assignment in which students state their reasons for taking the course and their attitudes toward American Indians. To introduce students to the historical background, the instructor should in one class session offer a general survey of major historical trends relating to Indians in the United States. The following material, to supplement the lecture, should be placed on reserve in the library: McNickle (Salish) and Fey, *Indians and Other Americans*; the brief historical essay in *American Indian Today* (ed. Levine and Lurie); and Chapman, Introduction, *Literature of the American Indians*. Students who want to begin to gather historical and cultural material about the Southwest might read Kluckhohn and Leighton, *The Navaho*; A. Ortiz (San Juan), *Tewa World*; and Waters and Fredericks (Hopi), *Book of the Hopi*. Required reading for historical background is Deloria (Sioux), *Custer Died for Your Sins*. This book will serve to expand the students' general historical background. Most students either really like or really dislike the book, and the strong opinions result in good discussion.

Students should then read works that combine oral and written forms: Silko (Laguna), *Storyteller*; and Momaday (Kiowa), *The Way to Rainy Mountain*. These books—which combine oral narrative, autobiography, essay, poetry, and fiction—provide a provocative introduction to the continuum of American Indian literature and acquaint students with traditional Indian themes. These books may be supplemented by Momaday, "The Man Made of Words" and *The Names*; Silko, "Language and Literature from a Pueblo Indian Perspective"; and Roemer, "Survey Courses."

Required reading in fiction are Momaday, *House Made of Dawn*; and Silko (Laguna), *Ceremony* and *Storyteller*. The emergence-migration theme is quite important in the two novels. Most of the stories in *Storyteller* draw on Keresan tales and illustrate the vitality of the oral tradition, as do Silko's use of Pueblo and Navajo legends throughout *Ceremony* and Momaday's use of the Navajo Night Way in *House Made of Dawn*. These readings may be supplemented by the filmed version of *House Made of Dawn*, directed by Larry Littlebird and distributed by New Line Cinema (852 Broadway, New York, NY 10003), and by "Running on the Edge of the Rainbow," a film about Silko in the *Words and Place* series.

The first course examination should follow these readings and discussions.

Required readings for poetry include Hobson, *The Remembered Earth*; and S. Ortiz (Acoma), *Going for the Rain*. The emergence-migration theme is central in Ortiz' collection. The diversity of the poetry in *The Remembered*

Earth offers numerous opportunities to stress stylistic links between oral and written poetry. These texts may be supplemented by Roemer's "Bear and Elk" (in this collection) and by the series of videotapes *Words and Place.*

The first course paper should be due following the poetry unit. The paper can compare two poems or two stories, or it can explore the links between oral and written traditions.

The next major unit of the course involves transitional literature. Required readings should be selected from Chona (Papago), *Autobiography;* F. Mitchell, *Navajo Blessingway Singer;* E. Mitchell (Navajo), *Miracle Hill;* and Talayesva (Hopi), *Sun Chief.* Evers, *The South Corner of Time,* contains shorter Hopi, Navajo, Papago, and Yaqui life stories. These books offer opportunities to consider the links between traditional and modern literary materials.

This unit should be followed by the second course examination.

The balance of the course deals with oral literatures: narratives and songs and ceremonials. Required reading for narratives is Marriott and Rachlin, *American Indian Mythology,* and *The South Corner of Time.* Some of the Kiowa, Pueblo, and Navajo narratives can be linked with the traditional themes in the fiction and poetry. A useful exercise for this section is to have students tell stories that elaborate on the narratives. Again the *Words and Place* video series can supplement the required readings. It contains programs with Navajo, Hopi, Laguna, Yaqui, and Apache singers and storytellers.

The required reading for songs and ceremonials is the Navajo Night Way (in Bierhorst, *Four Masterworks*). Since American Indian ceremonialism is a complex topic, any study of the subject should be intensive. Day's *The Sky Clears* can provide a useful overview, but the instructor will have to allow ample time to prepare for the Night Way (see the bibliography in Bierhorst). The result will be worth the effort, though. The Night Way is beautiful, and examining the links between it and *House Made of Dawn* and *Ceremony* will help to unify the course. Supplementary reading is Bevis, "American Indian Verse Translations" (in Chapman, *Literature of the American Indians*).

The second paper of the course should now be due. Students may compare origin narratives, compare different translations of the same selection, or trace a traditional theme or symbol in a contemporary poem, novel, or short story.

The course concludes with the students rereading *Way to Rainy Mountain* and *Storyteller* with their new awareness of the continuum of American Indian literature.

A review of the course work should precede the final examination.

Survey Courses

Course Design #1

The Contemporary American Indian Experience

This three-hour course will study the movement between urban and reservation/rural life in the contemporary American Indian experience by examining American Indian literature and sociological studies.

Methodology and Description

To study the movement between urban and reservation/rural life, the course will be structured around Simon Ortiz' book of poems, *Going for the Rain*. Ortiz' work provides insight into contemporary American Indian experience. For example, contemplating life's journey, Ortiz writes in the prologue: "The Man returns to the strength that his selfhood is, his home, people, his language, the knowledge of who he is. The cycle has been travelled; life has beauty and meaning, and it will continue because life has no end."

Using Ortiz' book as a base, we can view as cyclical concepts the four sections: "Preparation," "Leaving," "Returning," and "Going for the Rain" (rebirth). In turn, we can trace these ideas through poems, short stories, and novels by other contemporary American Indians. At the same time, we can learn about urban and reservation/rural settings by looking at data from sociological studies. Thus, the various facets of a kaleidoscopic movement of ideas, people, and places come into focus as we gain a deeper understanding of the American Indian experience.

Suggested methods of helping students reach this understanding include interweaving Ortiz' poems with the assigned short stories, novels, and sociological studies. For example, when students are reading about Abel moving to the city in Momaday's *House Made of Dawn*, they can read Ortiz' poem "Relocation" in class.

Additional poems by contemporary American Indians can supplement the assigned readings. For example, Ray A. Young Bear's "Coming Back

Home" (in Niatum, *Carriers of the Dream Wheel*) reflects the cyclical concepts in the novels. Students can read poems such as Wendy Rose's "Vanishing Point: Urban Indian" (in her *Long Division*) along with the interviews of Indians in *Native American Families in the City*. The class can compare Dolly Bird's poem "Return to the Home We Made" (in Lowenfels, *From the Belly of the Shark*) with the government programs and statistics presented in *Indian Giving*.

The interweaving of selected poems can add depth and dimension to the study of the movement between urban and reservation/rural life. "A Long Way" by Elizabeth Cook-Lynn charts this tension. When the uncle returns home to his people, they ask, "You're back . . . ?" But he responds, "No . . . I'm a long way from back. . . . "

Materials

Required readings are Levitan and Johnston, *Indian Giving*; Momaday (Kiowa), *House Made of Dawn*; Native American Research Group, *Native American Families in the City*; S. Ortiz (Acoma), *Going for the Rain*; Rosen, *The Man to Send Rain Clouds*; and Welch (Blackfeet-Gros Ventre), *Death of Jim Loney* and *Winter in the Blood*. Supplementary readings include Hobson (Cherokee), *The Remembered Earth*; Milton, *The American Indian Speaks*; Niatum (Klallam), *Carriers of the Dream Wheel*; Waddell and Watson, *The American Indian in Urban Society*; and Washburn, *The Indian in America*. Supplementary reading can include Lincoln, *Native American Renaissance*.

Course Design #2

Survey of American Indian Literature, 1772–1959

This course presents the major works of American Indian literature written in English from 1772 to 1959. It is designed for juniors, seniors, and graduate students who have taken three or more courses in American Indian studies or in literature.

The goals of the course are (1) to trace the evolution of American Indian literature written in English; (2) to understand the variety of genres in which American Indian authors work and the themes around which they write; (3) to compare the themes, genres, and techniques used by American Indian authors with those present in tribal oral literatures and in the written literatures of America and Europe; and (4) to examine the connection between the works of Indian authors and the history of Indian-white relations during the period in which the works were written.

This course is arranged chronologically to reflect the evolution of Indian writers, which corresponds to the pattern of white migration westward and the education of Indian youth in white schools. Genre designations should facilitate organization by literary form, if the instructor so desires. Much of the Indian literature of the late eighteenth and nineteenth centuries consists of works in which several genres are combined, such as mythology, history, and autobiography. Such combinations permitted authors to convey to their readers their tribes' mythic origins, culture, and history since contact, as well as their own personal experiences.

Instructors should discuss the relationship of Indian literature to the popular American taste for stories about conversion, tales of the "vanishing noble savage," and life stories of whites held captive by Indians. Also relevant to an understanding of the literary context of the works are such popular genres as the "dime western," the outlaw novel, regional literature, dialect satire, realistic works, and the social novels of the 1930s. Larson, *American Indian Fiction,* is a helpful study of American Indian novels from 1899 to the late 1970s.

Important to understanding the historical context of the works are the major events of Indian-white relations. A good guide to these is Hagan, *American Indians*, which is strongest in its coverage of Indian-white relations before 1900. Helpful sources on this subject after 1900 are McNickle (Salish) and Fey, *Indians and Other Americans*, and McNickle, *Native American Tribalism*. A brief but excellent survey of federal policies toward Indians is Dorris, "The Grass Still Grows, the Rivers Still Flow."

Materials

Readings before the passage of the Indian Removal bill (1830) should include Occom (Mohegan), *A Sermon Preached at the Execution of Moses Paul* (1772); and Apes (Pequot), selections from *A Son of the Forest* (1829). The period of removal, reservations, and allotment (from the late 1830s to World War I) can be covered by selections among nine authors: Copway (Ojibwe), selections from *Life, Letters and Speeches* (1847; autobiography) or from *Indian Life and Indian History* (1850; history, autobiography); Ridge (Cherokee), *Life and Adventures of Joaquín Murieta* (1854; fiction) and *Poems* (1868; autobiographical letter and such poems as "Mount Shasta" and "Humboldt River"); Pokagon (Potawatomi), *Queen of the Woods* (1899; fiction); La Flesche (Omaha), *The Middle Five* (1900; autobiography); Eastman (Sioux), *Indian Boyhood* (1902) or *From the Deep Woods* (1916; both autobiography; for background, see E. Deloria, *Speaking of Indians*, an excellent ethnographic account of how the Sioux adapted to reservation living while retaining traditional world views and customs); Zitkala-Sa

(Sioux), *American Indian Stories* (1921; mythology, tales, autobiography); Posey (Creek), *Poems* (1910) and selections from "Fus Fixico Letters" (political satire); Johnson (Mohawk), selections from *Legends of Vancouver* (1911; interpretations of myths and tales) and "A Red Girl's Reasoning" and "My Mother" (in Van Steen, *Pauline Johnson*; fiction).

The literature since World War I should be covered by selections from five authors: Rogers (Cherokee), selections from his political satire; Mourning Dove (Okanogan), *Co-ge-we-a* (1927; fiction); Mathews (Osage), *Wah'Kon-Tah* (1932; fiction) or *Sundown* (1934; fiction) and *Talking to the Moon* (1945; mythology, history, and autobiography); Oskison (Cherokee), *Brothers Three* (1935; fiction); and McNickle (Salish), *The Surrounded* (1936; fiction), which may be compared with *Wind from an Enemy Sky* (1978; fiction).

Course Design #3

Twentieth-Century American Indian Literature

This course is a survey of the contribution of twentieth-century American Indian writers to prose, fiction, and poetry in American literature. It is open to juniors, seniors, and graduate students who have had three courses in literature or in American Indian studies.

The course has two main goals: (1) to develop an appreciation of and respect for the variety of genres in which twentieth-century American Indian writers have written and are writing and the number of different themes they have developed in their works, and (2) to develop an understanding of the influences of both Indian and non-Indian world views, themes, genres, and techniques on the work of American Indian writers.

Methodology and Description

The course begins with an introduction to the histories and cultures of American Indians and then studies autobiographies and memoirs, other prose, fiction, and poetry. The introduction to histories and cultures provides a good approach to understanding Indian world views. Required texts are Dorris (Modoc), "The Grass Still Grows, the Rivers Still Flow"; Lurie, "Historical Background" (in Levine and Lurie, *The American Indian Today*, pp. 49–81); and V. Deloria (Sioux), *God Is Red* (esp. Ch. 3, "Indians of America"; Ch. 6, "The Problem of Creation"; and Ch. 7, "The Concept of History"). These can be supplemented by two films from Encyclopaedia Britannica Films, *Indians of Early America* and *Indian Families of Long Ago* (Sioux).

Autobiography and memoir, early forms of personal narrative by Indians, provide a valuable introduction to the cultures, literatures, and experiences of the tribes represented and of the narrators or authors themselves. Four of the suggested titles deal with the Sioux and cover the period from just before their settlement on reservations through the recent past. Focusing on the life stories of members of a single tribal group provides the student with a sense of the continuity of the American Indian experience. In addition, each work represents a different type of autobiography. Inviting Indian guest speakers to share their experiences with the class in exchange for an appropriate fee will enhance the learning experience. Required reading: Eastman (Sioux), *From the Deep Woods* or *Indian Boyhood*; Standing Bear (Sioux), selections from *My People, the Sioux* or *Land of the Spotted Eagle,* especially the chapters on his experience at Carlisle Indian School; Fire (Sioux), selections from *Lame Deer,* especially Chapter 1, "Alone on the Hilltop," and Chapter 7, "Talking to Owls and Butterflies"; Zitkala-Sa (Sioux), *American Indian Stories*; Momaday (Kiowa), *The Names,* especially Chapter 2, on his visit to his Kiowa grandmother, and Chapter 3, on growing up during the 1940s; and Vizenor (Chippewa), "I Know What You Mean, Erdupps MacChurbbs," one of the few works on Indian life in the city.

Within the category of prose, traditional narratives usually are presented in written form either as they were gathered from tribal storytellers or as they have been recreated by Indian writers. Written versions of traditional narratives told by storytellers can be found in Vizenor (Ojibwe), *Summer in the Spring,* tales originally published in an Ojibwe newspaper at the turn of the century; and *Stories of Traditional Navajo Life and Culture* (ed. Johnson). Works that include recreations by Indian authors of traditional stories include Mathews (Osage), *Talking to the Moon,* a Thoreauvian account of Mathews' return to the Oklahoma blackjacks region, interwoven with Osage traditions and history; and Momaday, *The Way to Rainy Mountain,* an account of a personal quest to find family and tribal roots in the recent, historic, and mythic past.

The satiric writing of Indian authors provides a good example of Indian humor. The earliest political satire appears in the work of Posey (Creek), whose "Fus Fixico Letters" were widely read but are now out of print. Readings for this unit are Rogers (Cherokee), selections from *Letters of a Self-Made Diplomat* or *Autobiography*; and V. Deloria, *Custer Died for Your Sins,* especially the chapter "Indian Humor."

The instructor can select fiction that focuses on the search for identity. Among the novels of the twenties and thirties that deal with the mixed-blood's search for Indian identity are Mourning Dove (Okanogan), *Co-ge-we-a,* the first novel by an Indian woman; Mathews, *Sundown*; and McNickle (Salish), *The Surrounded.* A selection of novels of the sixties and seventies can focus on the protagonist's search for Indian identity. Among the novels suggested, Momaday's *House Made of Dawn* might be taught with Silko's *Ceremony* because both deal with the adjustment problems of World War II veterans. Suggested readings: Welch (Blackfeet-Gros Ventre), *Winter in the Blood* or *Death of Jim Loney*; Momaday, *House Made of Dawn*; Silko (Laguna), *Ceremony* or *Storyteller*; McNickle, *Wind from an Enemy Sky*; and Markoosie (Eskimo), *Harpoon of the Hunter*.

Most available poetry is contemporary. Among the poets most frequently anthologized are Paula Gunn Allen, Caroll Arnett, Liz Sohappy Bahe, Peter Blue Cloud [Aroniawenrate], James Barnes, Joseph Bruchac, Barney Bush, Janet Campbell Hale, Joy Harjo, Lance Hensen, Roberta Hill, Maurice Kenny, N. Scott Momaday, Duane McGinnis Niatum, Simon Ortiz, Carter Revard, Wendy Rose, Norman Russell, Leslie Marmon Silko, Gerald Vizenor, Marnie Walsh, James Welch, and Ray Young Bear. Three important anthologies of contemporary poetry will be helpful: Hobson, *The Remembered Earth*; Niatum, *Carriers of the Dream Wheel*; and Rosen, *Voices of the Rainbow*. Selections from these anthologies may be supplemented by collections of poetry by individual authors, such as Niatum, *Songs for the Harvester of Dreams*; S. Ortiz, *Going for the Rain*; Welch, *Riding the Earthboy 40*; and Young Bear, *Winter of the Salamander*.

The modern drama written by American Indians can be presented through the work of [Rolla] Lynn Riggs (Cherokee) and Hanay Geiogamah (Kiowa), both from Oklahoma. The most prolific Indian dramatist, Riggs had many of his plays produced on Broadway. Unfortunately his tragedy *Cherokee Night* (1936), which is most appropriate for the course, is out of print. Its theme is the problem of Indian identity among Oklahoma mixed-bloods. His best play, available in several anthologies, is *Green Grow the Lilacs* (1931), the basis of the hit musical *Oklahoma!* Riggs's plays reveal a flair for capturing Oklahoma dialect and folk culture. His optimistic, rousing comedies make an excellent contrast with the dramas of Hanay Geiogamah, three of which are available in *New Native American Drama: Three Plays*. Jeffrey Huntsman's introduction provides a valuable commentary. *Body Indian*, one of Geiogamah's best plays, deals realistically with Indian alcoholism and with Indians' interrelationships with each other. *49* uses the theme of the "49" songs sung after powwows as a vehicle for presenting the theme of death and rebirth in Indian cultures.

The Indian in American Literature

Discovering America: Mary Austin and Imagism

James Ruppert

During the 1910s and 1920s, America experienced an explosion of literary talent concurrent with the rise of movements that revitalized Western dance, music, and painting. American writers at home and expatriates writing from abroad were not only assuming importance in the eyes of the world but were for the first time actually changing the direction of Western literature. During these fascinating years, American poetry was reborn and endowed with an astounding variety of new forms, techniques, and theories. For convenience, many literary historians date the beginning of this "poetry renaissance" from the publication of the first issue of *Poetry: A Magazine of Verse* in October 1912.

Interestingly, the surging force of American nationalism and the antinationalism of the exiles together produced reanimating experimentation in the forms of poetry as well as in the subject matter. Proponents of Imagism, vorticism, oral poetry, and vers libre attempted to liberate poetry from the superfluities of the past. The subject matter of the new poems ranged from psychological probings of the American character to the impact of technology on human beings. The study and translation of world literature was seen as a means of finding the true and eternal power of poetry. Writers wanted to create a new art that would reflect the unique quality of modern life and that was conscious of its effect and of the power it could produce. Most poets felt that in the distant past poetry was more powerful, more affective, and that the modern spiritual and artistic wasteland invalidated most Victorian attitudes. The time was ripe for a strong intellectual and scholastic struggle over what constituted the origins of poetry and how writers could use this knowledge to fortify poetry.

American Indian literature had always been like a silent figure, standing half-hidden in the forest ready to feed those American writers who could handle its assumptions. From Freneau to Longfellow, from Thoreau to Twain and Garland, American Indians and their literatures served as subject, symbol, natural object, and source of innovation in form. It is only logical that American Indian poetry should be bound up with this intellectual probing into the origins of poetry. The tremendous increase in the number of translations of all literatures during the early part of this century facilitated exploration of literatures of the past and of primitive peoples. Through this bright awakening to the world of today and yesterday, writers hoped to understand the origins of poetry and so its power.

Earthier literatures such as Chinese, Old English, and Greek were popular because their simplicity, imagistic unity, and hard precise language suited the modern temperament. Amy Lowell reveals the modern approach in a letter to Mary Austin concerning Pueblo poetry: "The extremes of sophistication and the aboriginal are not so far apart; man returns to simplicity when he has gone along the road of sophistication far enough."[1] Many writers, however, turned to American Indian literature following their impulse to learn from literatures and languages that were closer to the basic emotions of humanity. Simplicity, power, imagistic unity, and precise language forged out of the essentials of life were exactly what American Indian poetry offered to the poet/student of the 1910s and 1920s. Alice Corbin Henderson, assistant editor of *Poetry*, offered this:

> It is possible that Indian poetry may be more closely allied to Chinese poetry than to that of any other race; it has the same realism, the same concrete simplicity, and acceptance of the commonplace experience, as well as the exceptional, as the material of poetry.[2]

Or as Mary Hunter Austin puts it with brevity uncommon to her, "there is no question that in making poetry the mind of the Amerind moves in a fashion not dissimilar from the early Chinese."[3] The large number of translations from both literatures that appeared at this time would seem to confirm the validity of this comparison, as did the more specific explorations of both literatures and cultures by respected poets such as Amy Lowell and Witter Bynner.

Parallel to the writers' interest in the essence of poetry and its origins was the scholastic investigation into early literatures. The study of Old English literature, Greek poetry, and primitive literatures increased significantly. One of the most popular theories of poetic origin was the "ballad" theory, which held that poetry began as short narrative events portrayed in song and lyrically held together with communal song and then immediately presented in dance. The ballad/dance was the most primitive literary form. Richard G. Moulton is quoted as saying, "Literature, when it first appears spontaneously, takes this form: a theme or story is at once versified, accompanied by music and suggested in action."[4] This theory emphasized the origin of poetry in communal action.[5]

Many scholars, however, believed that much was to be learned from a study of a still-flourishing ancient literature, that of the American Indians. Typical of this branch of scholastic thought is an article by Louise Pound, in a 1917 issue of *PMLA*, entitled "The Beginnings of Poetry," in which she explores the tension between communal and private songs, concluding that private songs are much more basic and that ballads are a later development. In her attack on the ballad theory, she looks closely at Densmore's 1910 *Chippewa Music* and other ethnographic examples and decides that the origin of the "primitive lyric is not the ballad but the song or songlet" (p. 230). Interestingly, her concept of the songlet is similar to Ezra Pound's definition of the image as "that which presents an intellectual and emotional complex in an instant of time."[6] Consequently, Louise Pound's study unconsciously defends and explains contemporaneous trends in American poetry. These studies were complemented by some serious scholastic studies of the stylistics of American Indian literature and the literatures of various tribes, and American Indian literature began to become a legitimate area of research.[7]

Much of this literary and scholastic interest resulted from the increasing number of studies of primitive literature, particularly that of the American Indian, produced by prominent anthropologists. The original impetus may have been Brinton's pioneering work in the 1890s, but the field lay relatively fallow until 1907, when Curtis brought out *The Indians' Book*. In the 1910s and 1920s, studies appeared by Burton, Curtis, Densmore, Fletcher, Goddard, Sapir, and Spinden, perhaps culminating in Boas' classic "Stylistic Aspects of Primitive Literature." Curiously, many of these stylistic studies spoke of Indian poetry in concepts and terminology common to discussions of the poetry of the day. These anthropologists were undoubtedly aware of the continuing interest of poets and the general public in Indian song-poetry. The *Dial*, the *Nation*, the *New Republic*, *Scribner's*, the *Bookman*, and the *Atlantic* all did their part in the 1910s and 1920s to publish commentary on the style and content of Indian poetry.[8] *Poetry: A Magazine of Verse*, the most respected poetry magazine in America at that time, was deeply involved with the general interest in publishing Indian poetry, and it featured numerous notes and reviews on the subject. Its format, however, could not accommodate major articles.

Poetry began its illustrious career in October 1912. With its first issue, Ezra Pound joined the staff as foreign editor, and almost immediately the magazine was publishing Imagist statements and the first Imagist poems in America. In the March 1913 issue, F. S. Flint listed three principles of Imagism: "(1) Direct treatment of the 'thing,' whether subjective or objective, (2) To use absolutely no word that does not contribute to the presentation, and (3) As regarding rhythm: to compose in sequence of the musical phrase, not in sequence of the metronome" (p. 199). In 1914 the anthology *Des Imagistes* was published, solidifying Imagism as a school.

Poetry championed the new movement, but the magazine was not tied solely to Imagism. It was passionately committed to publishing new and truly American forms and writers, and it was uniquely successful in this effort. *Poetry* published work by every major poet writing at that time in America as well as many from England and the Continent, and consequently all those poets read the magazine. Besides Pound, Eliot, Sandburg, Frost, Moore, Aiken, Lindsay, Williams, Yeats, Stevens, Lowell, Lawrence, and Jeffers, *Poetry* published the works of numerous writers who were on their way to a limited popularity, although they have dropped from sight as poets today: Witter Bynner, J. G. Neihardt, Hartley Burr Alexander, Edward Sapir, Yvor Winters, Lew Sarett, Frank Gordon, and John Gould Fletcher. No magazine in America could come close to *Poetry* for quality or reputation.

Poems about Indians, or with Indian themes, appeared in the magazine from the beginning, but direct translations or so-called interpretive renderings started around 1914. In fact, Chief Joseph was the first Indian published in the magazine, when in a note in the November 1914 issue, the end of his surrender speech appeared as a fine example of war poetry. The entire February 1917 issue was an "aboriginal number," which included a wide variety of literary translations, interpretations, and retellings. From that point on, the number, frequency, and variety of poems, reviews, and notes dealing with Indian poetry and its use in contemporary poetry increased.

The popular interest continued and grew to a point where George W. Cronyn had no problem convincing Boni and Liveright to publish an anthology of Indian poetry. Cronyn collected the poems from the *Poetry* number and added to them BAE material and other translations published in popular magazines. *The Path on the Rainbow: An Anthology of Songs and Chants from the Indians of North America* came out in 1918, the first anthology of translations of Indian song-poetry. It contained a frontispiece translation by Carl Sandburg and an introduction by Mary Austin. Its publication provoked an almost unending discussion by critics and writers of the value of American Indian literature and its translations.

After the publication of this anthology, popular magazines seemed more receptive than ever to Indian poems. Other magazines joined in an awakened concept of an all-inclusive America. Many poets who had received professional encouragement from publishing in *Poetry* now found other editors interested in them. The "aboriginal" songs and Indian poems of Frank Gordon, Constance Skinner, Alice C. Henderson, J. G. Neihardt, Lew Sarett, Witter Bynner, Hartley Burr Alexander (one critic for the *Outlook* in 1925 called these last three "truly American"), and sometimes desert Imagist John Gould Fletcher found homes in magazines with good circulation. Amy Lowell's "Pueblo Songs" appeared in the *Dial* in 1919, along with Ezra

Pound's "Hugh Selwyn Mauberley," and were later collected in *Ballads for Sale*. She also reworked (wrote) a Central American Indian myth and a eulogy to a dying chief in *Legends*. These efforts were characteristic of this current of publications. With all this activity, a literary observer would doubtless have been tempted to agree with belles lettres celebrity Mabel Luhan, when she remarked in a 1922 letter to Mary Austin, "The country almost has seemed to *go indian* [sic]."[9]

These writers saw American Indian poetry as a great untapped source, truly American and full of lessons on poetry's origins, spiritual power, and natural forms. Their desire was to make a new, powerful poetry based on a knowledge of ancient literatures. This new poetry would be effective, both communally and psychically; it would reach into the unconscious. American Indian poetry was exceptionally suited to these requirements, revealing a unified response to the American experience and being more easily accessible than dead literatures and distant cultures. By studying American Indian poetry to discover the origins of verse, one could bypass years of dreary book peeling or the physical hardships of extended anthropological field work while still remaining in a truly American environment. Alice Henderson contributed this to the cross-cultural traveler:

> It is not impossible to know what preceded Homer, it is not impossible to learn first hand that symbolism has always preceded legend or narrative; and to make this discovery one need not project oneself imaginatively backward through time or immure oneself in a library: one need merely project oneself physically on a two or three days' journey from any of the principal cities of the United States, and witness a dance-drama of the southwestern Indians, in order to discover first hand what primitive poetry is like.[10]

Henderson's Imagistic conviction that the symbol or image functions as the essential and original unit of poetry is reinforced by the holistic nature of Indian song-poetry. The Imagists' desire to know the origin and essence of poetry and to blend into their own artistic ideas some elements of a vital primitive literature perfectly attuned to its environment and the culture that created it brought many writers, such as Williams and Lawrence, to the Southwest and to American Indian literature. Still, only a few writers found their information through in-depth firsthand explorations. Many of the poets who worked with American Indian material obtained their information from the Bureau of American Ethnology and folklore journals. To culture-locked writers like Amy Lowell, such publications provided access to the literatures of primitive American cultures. The poets who engaged in this study saw in the journals a rich and unmined vein of poetic material with which to revitalize their overly sophisticated responses with a wealth of fresh images, strong emotions, and new forms, all of which seemed to confirm and expand the directions that modern poetry was taking.

In an article for *Poetry*, Henderson colors Indian poetry with a Poundian brush:

> In the beginning therefore primitive poetry is brief, staccato, ejaculatory, like a cry or a wish or an aspiration; sometimes a mere mood of longing, or an observation whose deeper significance is felt by the singer and hearer. It is usually a single image, simple or complex, and the variations are in the nature of amplifications of this image, through restatement with slight changes or through reiteration. As the song progresses in the dance, action accompanies this image, which seems to grow, and expand with a life of its own, to be, in short, a symbol capable of creatively projecting that which it symbolizes.[11]

This appraisal explicitly conforms to the Imagistic principles of direct treatment of the thing with no unnecessary words, while it expands on the concept of the image. Implicit in this passage is the understanding that the poem is a song and therefore should be composed, in accordance with the third Imagist principle of composition, in the sequence of the musical phrase.

Many early modern poets attempted to bring the oral quality of primitive poetry back into modern poetry. Some sought to isolate speech rhythms unique to regions of the United States; some Imagists tried to bring back Greek rhythms through vers libre. Song-poems and chants abounded. Gordon, Skinner, and other published aboriginal "songs" in their efforts to capture the oral quality of Indian poetry. Nicholas Vachel Lindsay reports that Yeats asked him, "What are we going to do to restore the primitive singing of poetry?" Lindsay offered his "Fireman's Ball" as an example of a modern attempt to capture the spirit of primitive singing.[12] The concerns motivating modern poets coincided with and provided a justification for the literary study of Indian poetry.

Other writers envied the Indian's close spiritual relationship with nature and sought to use that unity to inform their art. They realized that the West, especially the Southwest, contained the only untamed nature left in America, and there they found the Indian still living in true harmony with a grand and elevating nature. Through their descriptions of this unity, these writers expressed an undying Romanticism.

Perhaps one of *Poetry*'s deepest commitments was to publish this particular kind of nature writing in which a spiritual nature instructed man. American Indians and their art became an ideal example of this unity. Harriet Monroe, the magazine's founder and editor, once referred to nature as "the Ultimate Modernist." Her magazine continually published poetry that explored the American landscape and the effects of nature on American writers. Her commitment to publishing western and midwestern writers reflected not only her belief that the eastern establishment had ignored these writers but also her belief that their calling up of the spirits of place and of the unique power of nature in the West, especially the Southwest, was a revitalizing force for the decaying values and communities of the East. Southwestern aboriginals, she believed, were destined through their art and its unity with the environment to reanimate the art of the Western world. In her article "The Great Renewal" she predicts a new art:

> Our painters are going there [the Southwest] more and more, and more and more not only our painters but our sculptors and architects as well, will inevitably feel the primitive art of this region and its more developed masterpieces among the kindred Aztecs and Incas to the south as a newly revealed ancient style of imperishable power and beauty—a style as authentic as the Greek or Chinese, as fit in its human expression of a region and a race. In nature of such incomparable forms and colors and in primitive art so right, so expressive, our artists should slough off their sophistication and find the Great Renewal which may energize the art of the world. (pp. 323–24)

Though this glowing prediction does not mention writers specifically, a look at Monroe's magazine confirms the extension of this attitude. The study of American Indian art and literature held out great rewards for artists and their cultures. Writers, editors, and scholars found insight into and justification for the new trends of vers libre and Imagism that were under attack by the literary conservatives. Artists also found new formal models. Indian poetry represented to some a spiritual/natural unity that could reinvigorate the oversophisticated literature that had lost its sense of community and was becoming increasingly divorced from the land. Many regional writers sought to reestablish this unity. In Indian literatures they saw a singularly American poetry of landscape, a poetry in which the unity of people and environment was at the core. Consequently, many could agree with Monroe and foresee a revolutionary effect on America through the study of American Indian literature and life.

Clearly writers and editors were aware of this general interest and recognized its force, with *Poetry* acting as its literary center. They could not be oblivious to it even if they did not agree with the reasons behind the study or the conclusions reached by some authors. The interaction between modern American poetry and American Indian literature was an accepted fact and not dissimilar to the current proportions of the ethnopoetics movement. Many writers saw that the desires of Imagists, regionalists, and other moderns coincided with the study of Indian poetry and concluded that the two were moving together. Alice Corbin Henderson brings this assumption to the forefront in her review of Cronyn's anthology for a 1919 issue of *Poetry*:

> The way this book has eventually crystalized, so to speak, is in itself indicative of a growing perception on our part of the literary and artistic value of Indian motives.
>
>   Certain it is that these Indian poems are very similar in spirit and method to the poetry of our most modern poets. Stephen Crane would have qualified as an

Indian poet, and in the *Mid-American Chants* of Sherwood Anderson one finds almost precisely the mood of the songs accompanying the green corn dances of the Pueblo Indians.[13]

On this similarity, Carl Sandburg, in a sincerely appreciative note on Frances Densmore, makes this tongue-in-cheek remark: "Suspicion arises definitely that the Red Man and his children committed direct plagiarism on the modern Imagists and vorticists."[14]

Mary Hunter Austin would have been in total agreement with the spirit of that statement. During her forty-some years as a poet and writer, she was continually involved with the American Indian cultures and literatures of the Southwest, and she knew what insights she could garner from cross-cultural experiences. In the 1910s and 1920s she was asked to write numerous introductions to books because of her many articles on American Indians and her popular translations of Indian works. She was greatly complimented when asked to write the chapter on aboriginal literature for the *Cambridge History of American Literature.* In short, she was commonly regarded as an expert on all things Indian.

As a major spokesperson for the study of Indian poetry and its importance to modern poetry, Austin is an interesting person on whom to focus after surveying the wider general interest in American Indian studies. Perhaps she carried this study to an extreme, but she is an excellent example of how one popular writer incorporated this study into her own work. She is clearer and more articulate than many of the other advocates. As she accurately reads the desires and directions of modern poetry, she funnels them ingeniously into the study of American Indian literatures. Mary Austin, then, may be a pivotal figure in understanding the relation between American Indian literature and modern American literature.

Mary Austin wrote prolifically during the sixty-six years of her life: over thirty books, well over a hundred articles, hundreds of poems and short stories, and numerous forewords and introductions. Her work appeared in many magazines, including *Everybody's Magazine, Harper's, Poetry, Nation, Saturday Review of Literature, Dial, Atlantic Monthly, Century, New Republic, North American Review,* and *English Journal.* Of course, not all of her publications were concerned with American Indian poetry, but a third to half either talk directly of American Indian literature and life or derive from insights and stories of the Indian experience.

Through her many translations, reexpressed Indian stories, articles on American Indian literature and life, fiction based on Indian ideas, and Indian plays, Austin established herself as an expert. In the late twenties and early thirties, she was in contact with many government agencies concerned with Indian reform and protection. Of her role as a protector of Indian arts from commercialization, she says, "It begins to look as though, having spent the last twenty-five years largely explaining the Indian to the American public, I am going to have to spend another twenty-five in defending him from the too great enthusiasm which the public has conceived for him."[15] She testified before a number of Senate and agency hearings, but more important than the government's recognition of her authority was the acknowledgment of her position by writers and editors. Despite her popularity in her own time, however, Mary Austin's work is now generally ignored by literary critics. Those who mention her do so rather grudgingly, assigning her a place as a regional or nature writer. Little if any critical effort is spent on her translations and theories about Indian poetry. Perhaps this neglect merely reflects the general perplexity that appears on the faces of students of modern American poetry when one mentions the intertwining of American Indian literature and modern American poetry, or perhaps it results from the critical style that sees only Pound, Eliot, and Williams writing in the early twentieth century.

Central to the understanding of Austin and her work is the realization that it is infused with mystical ideas, nearly all of which are connected directly or indirectly with American Indian experience. From the time of her direct experience, at the age of six, of the unity of all things in a living entity, God, she sought to experience God through nature: "I have always felt that I was part of everything around me, that it was moving somewhere with me. From the time I was thirteen, there has been nothing new in my life."[16] Later, in her late twenties and early thirties, she received a direct introduction into American Indian religious thought at the hands of Tinnemaha, a medicine man of the Paiutes. He revealed to her that the great reality of life was that the Friend-of-the-Soul-of-Man really did exist and that it could be touched directly to strengthen one's personal power or the power of the tribe.

She began to see American Indian poetry as the medium through which one could communicate with the Friend-of-the-Soul-of-Man. Songs welded the members of a group together so that they as a group could become one with the Friend. The Indian poet, then, creates a suggestive, provocative poetry with a form organically shaped by its intended function, that of uniting the community with a spiritual nature, a poetry more dependent on the experience of the poet and listener than on expression. Austin saw these as extremely modern qualities.

She regarded modern society as a spiritual wasteland, out of touch with itself and the environment. Modern poets perceived this, too, and were striving toward awakening the sleeping spirit of America, as they worked toward a suggestive, unified, organic poetry of experience. But Mary Austin saw that this alienated society grossly misunderstood and perversely disrespected the work of the artist: "There is no use wasting words on the fact that the great artist, whose genius is in advance of his age, has a bad time of it in the United States. He has always had a bad time of it and probably always will."[17] The poet, Austin believed, could bind people together, help produce a unified, progressive society that would strive to nurture the physical and the spiritual. Mary Austin was convinced that Indian poetry was perfectly attuned to the environment (thus ideal in its ability to provoke mystical communion among men, nature, and the Friend-of-the-Soul-of-Man, as experienced in the past); it was a goal toward which a groping and struggling new American poetry could strive.

With this conviction, she promoted the study of American Indian poetry. Austin affirms to America that all great cultures of the past have possessed a native treasure of aboriginal literature owing no influence but that of the native environment. She believed that, if American poets were truly to capture the American experience and create an art that is truly American, an art that reaches into the collective unconscious of a people of any particular area and spiritually unites them to one another and to the land, they must study the Indian's art, for in it they find a clear, evocative expression of the American environment.

All of this, of course, hinges on an assumption that I must call geographic determinism. Austin felt that anyone sensitive to life, as a good poet should be, would find native rhythms—rhythms determined by the environment and the life work necessary to survive in that environment, rhythms that would rise up from the subconscious fusion of the writer and the landscape. A writer could make contact with the Friend and feel oneness with all things. The more a writer is able to make this mystical fusion and let those natural rhythms rise up, the better that writer's work will become and the more useful he or she will become to American society.

After talking with writers and poets and reading their works, she accurately pinpointed their desire to try something new. The striving of Frost, Sandburg, Lindsay, Masters, and many American novelists to capture not only the image of American life but its natural rhythms as well gave her hope that the goals of this new American poetry and those of the aboriginal poets might meet.[18] After discussing the influence of rhythm on an audience in her book *The American Rhythm*, she links these two together:

> It is here, in the verbal realization, that we come upon the common root of aboriginal and modern Americanness. We have seen how native rhythms develop along the track of rhythmic stimuli arising spontaneously in the environment and are coordinated by the life-sustaining gestures imposed upon us by that environment. Although we have not yet achieved the communality into which the Amerind has entered by easy evolution, there is evident straining toward it in the work of such men as Masters, Frost and Sandburg; all our recent poetic literature touched [sic] with a profound nostalgia for those happy states of reconciliation with the Allness through group communion, which it is the business of poetry to promote. (p. 54)

Poets strive for communality, but the landscape, the environment, and the life work in that environment determine the rhythm and the form of the poet's "reconciliation with the Allness" and any effective striving toward communality. This determined form is what she refers to as "the landscape line." She claimed that by reading any author's lines, she could discover his or her landscape. An often-repeated anecdote tells of Mary Austin, before a general audience in Fort Worth, Texas, elaborating on a definition of the landscape line by rocking back and forth, swinging an imaginary axe while reciting Lincoln's Gettysburg Address to illustrate the midwestern rhythms of a prairie rail-splitter. As far as I know, no one ever put her to an objective test. In *The American Rhythm*, she defines the landscape line in such a way as to bring out its affinities with vers libre:

> It is this leap of the running stream of poetic inspiration from level to level, whose course cannot be determined by anything except the nature of the ground traversed, which I have called the landscape line. The lengths of leaps, and the sequence of pattern recurrence will be conditioned by the subjectively coordinated motor rhythms associated with a particular emotional flow.
>
> This landscape line may of course involve several verse lines as they appear on the printed page and is described by the term cadenced verse. In the placing of this line and the additional items by which it is connoted and decorated, the aboriginal process approaches closest to what is known as Imagism, unless you will accept my term and call it glyphic. (pp. 55–56)

Austin affirms that the landscape line in American Indian poetry coheres to the third principle of Imagism: it is composed in the sequence of the musical phrase as opposed to stiffly defined metrics, and it produces an art that modern America would recognize as Imagism and vers libre. Modern American poetry, then, gives us a way to understand the Indian compositional process. Austin hoped that modern poetry would explore this similar form and learn from its wholeness, rhythmic intricacies, and unique visual qualities. In using the term "glyphic," Austin is trying to particularize this compositional process because clearly she recognizes the distinct differences between "Amerind" poetry and Imagist poetry. The glyph indicates the unified, single impression of "Amerind" poetry in much the same way that the ideogram becomes a meaningful exemplar to other poets. Here more clearly is what she means when she speaks of the glyph:

> a translator's first care, then, would be to state the experience itself, usually by stating its most important reaction on himself. To this he would add no more than he found absolutely necessary by way of descriptive and associative phrases, to define the path of the experience through his own consciousness.
>
> Now this is precisely the way the primitive, when he first arrives at writing, begins to evolve what is called a glyph. (p. 51)

Austin sees the glyph and the ideogram as very similar, but the glyph adheres to the first two principles of Imagist doctrine. This is an important and accurate insight because much traditional American Indian poetry was

composed in a manner that would appeal to those who upheld these principles. The most obvious examples are Chippewa songs and ghost dance
songs, but others abound. In *The American Rhythm*, Austin gives us two
rather convincing examples of this kind of glyph—one by a modern poet and
the other by a Washoe boy.

> Washoe Charlie's girl had gone away to Indian Boarding School and Charlie
> had given her a grass-green ribbon for remembrance. A few days later, while his
> loss was sorest, he had a glimpse of another girl wearing an identical green
> ribbon. Any lover will understand what happened to Charlie, though as he
> expressed it in the song recording the experience, whole, as it occurred to him,
> there were only half as many words as I have put into it: "The Green Ribbon,
> when I saw a girl wearing it, my girl existed inside me." One touch more Charlie
> added by calling his song the magic ribbon. The rest any Washoe was supposed
> to understand by the likeness of all Washoe lovers one to another.
>   Stephen Crane has left us no note of what happened to him in the neigh-
> borhood of Yellow Sky to explain how he happened to write, "If I should cast off
> this tattered coat," and
>
>   I looked here
>   I looked there
>   Nowhere could I see my love,
>   And—this time—
>   She was in my heart.
>   Truly then, I have no complaint,
>   For though she be fair and fairer,
>   She is not so fair as she
>   In my heart.
>
> . . . It is this similarity of primary processes which has led me to adopt the term
> "glyph" for a type of Amerind song which is lyric in its emotional quality and
> yet cannot be completely expressed by the simple lyric cry. (pp. 52–53)

In this effort to tie American Indian poetry to modern American poetry,
Austin is trying not only to point out two similar compositional processes but
also to establish a precedent for the new developments in American poetry.
She, of course, was not alone in this effort, for many writers sought such
precedents in Chinese, Japanese, and early European literatures. In her view,
the glyph represented one such precedent. The Imagist poem, like the glyph,
was concerned with the importance of the unsaid. The glyph becomes a
symbol of. or a key to, the inner song, to the meaning not expressed. Imagists
hoped to provoke a similar resonance by quickly capturing that intellectual-
emotional complex that exists in time.
    In her 1919 reply to Untermeyer's negative review of *The Path on the
Rainbow*, she blatantly proclaims that precedent:

> But I feel the failure to get anything out of this edition as it stands is wholly Mr.
> Untermeyer's. It would be a great deal, for instance, to have fully established, as

this volume does, that vers libre and Imagism are in truth primitive forms, and both of them generically American forms, forms instinctively selected by people living in America and freed from outside influence.[19]

In her "Non-English Writings: Aboriginal" in the *Cambridge History of American Literature*, Austin articulates her belief in the common impetus of the American Indian and the non-Indian poetry of her day and her certainty about the immense advantages available to writers who study American Indian poetry in their search for a forerunner of modern poetry. She quotes liberally from the work of Densmore, Boas, and Fletcher, presenting translations that are strikingly imagistic, while explaining that American Indian principles of composition include an effort to avoid unnecessary words and to compose the line along the flow of the emotions and the words. In considering the Mide'-wiwin songs of the Chippewa, she concludes:

> "The form of these songs closely resembles the modern poetic mode which goes by the name of Imagism." The one convention of Indian verse which must not be broken is also the convention of Imagism, that the description must not merely describe, but must give witness to something that has occurred in the soul of the singer. (pp. 626, 628)

In keeping with these principles and the theme of the article, in which she postulates that the roots of modern tendencies lie in primitive verse, Austin points to the Walum Olum of the Leni-Lenape. As if to emphasize the imagistic quality that Indian languages place on their presentation, she produces two examples of ideographic writings that she feels will be of interest to modern Americans. Both ideographs concern the "advent of the first Tammany chief (Tamenend) and the coming of the Discoverers" (p. 620):

Weninitis Tamenend
sakimanep nekohatami

All being friendly,
the Affable was chief
the first of that name.

Wonwihil wapekunchi
wapsipsyat

At this time Whites
came on the
eastern sea.

In a similar vein, she believed that the principles of Indian storytelling had a unique parallel in modern American fiction. In her review of

Thompson's *Tales of the North American Indians*, she lists three principles essential to Indian storytelling: (1) sparing use of names (of characters for example), (2) detachment of the narrator, and (3) immediate establishment of the mood.[20] She saw these principles at work in the best writing of Lewis, Anderson, and Garland, and she judged these writers truly American, for they were attuned to the American environment and caught the forms inherent in the landscape.

Austin believed that the story was older than the storyteller. The emotions in and the structural basis for all plots that were truly "folk," of the people, were embedded in the land. Through archetypes, through the racial unconscious, people built up the possible stories created by the landscape and by the work necessary to survive in it. The good writer caught these and used them effectively. Since Indian storytelling had been developing for such a long time, it was intricately bound up with the goals of the modern American writer who tried to create a real and true American art that rose from the peoples of all regions and went back to them, alive and vital.

In this understanding of the nature of storytelling Austin felt she made her most lasting contribution. She was so thoroughly convinced of the validity of this theory that she presented the incredible claim that she could tell stories to sheep dogs, because of her understanding of the stories inherent in the life of the land. She challenged people seriously to bring her a trained sheep dog to which she could not tell a story and from which she could not then elicit an enthusiastic response.

It should be clear by now that Mary Austin considered writing fiction and translating poetry not so much the result of an excruciating study of social structure and laborious ethnological and linguistic research as a mystical communion of the writer and the land, a touching of the Friend-of-the-Soul-of-Man that resided in the land and through which the writer received power. This spiritual, humanistic communion was what many American writers were rather myopically seeking. Even as a literary translator, she was concerned with making poetry. Her attitude toward translation was similar to Pound's; she wanted to "make it new":

> My method has been by preference to saturate myself in the poem, in the life that produced it and the environment that cradled it, so that when the point of crystallization is reached, I myself give forth a poem which bears, I hope, a generic resemblance to the Amerind song that was my point of contact. (*American Rhythm*, p. 38)

Though this may sound somewhat romantic, it closely resembles recent statements that Gary Snyder and Kenneth Rexroth have made about poetic translation,[21] and it echoes in works like Lowell's *Imitations* and the writings of many poets associated with the ethnopoetics movement.[22] Because of this parallel, we may consider Austin a forerunner of some of our contemporary poets and translators, and we may find that a study of her work will illumi-nate theirs.

Mary Hunter Austin explored both modern American and American Indian poetry and found in Indian poetry forms that American poets were beginning to use. The modern poets' desire to develop a truly American art seemed to her to call for a close study of the work of the first Americans, whose poetry reached a spiritual and effective ideal that modern American poets searched for in vain. By studying American Indian poetry, modern writers could find the true origins of poetry and use this knowledge to re-vitalize their art. Even writers of fiction could learn from the true folk art of the American Indians, and it seemed to her that the best writers and poets had already done so, not necessarily by studying, but by achieving a close-ness to the source of poetry—the land and the Friend-of-the-Soul-of-Man that charged the land with power.

In looking back, we must remember that the writer's world in the 1910s and the 1920s was much more circumscribed than it is now. Contemporary fragmentation forces us to be skeptical of the desire and ability of writers to keep up with the mountains of published work. Writers in earlier times could seriously survey the work of most writers of their generation in a way we cannot.

We might regard Mary Austin's work and the enthusiasm of writers in the twenties as a high point in one of the recurring cycles of interest in the arts of the American Indian or as a high point in the continuing dialogue between scholars of American Indian and non-Indian literatures. One thing is certain, however: Mary Austin would have us know that any complete discussion of American literature or of its future must include a consideration of the contributions of American Indians and of the American landscape itself.

Notes

1   Amy Lowell, Letter to Mary Austin, 24 April 1923, Mary Austin Papers, Huntington Library, San Marino, Calif.

2   Henderson, "Poetry of the North American Indians," p. 42.

3   Austin, "Indian Songs," p. 704.

4   Moulton, *The Modern Study of Literature* (Chicago, 1915) as quoted by Louise Pound, "The Beginnings of Poetry," p. 217.

5   Compare Gummere, *The Beginnings of Poetry*; Gummere, *The Popular Ballad*; and Krapp, *The Rise of English Literary Prose*.

6   Pound, "A Few Don'ts by an Imagiste," p. 202.

7   For example: Barnes, *American Indian Verse*; Walton and Waterman, "American Indian Poetry"; Montgomery, "A Method of Studying Primitive Verse Applied to the Songs of the Teton-Sioux"; Walton, "Navajo Song Patterning"; and Reichard, "Literary Types and Dissemi-nation of Myths."

8   Examples are Alexander, "The Poetry of the American Indian"; Austin, "The Road to Spring"; Bryson, "Amerindian Poet"; Daugherty, "The Techniques of Indian Composition";

Lehmer, "The Music and Poetry of the American Indians"; and Walton, "Navajo Verse Rhythms"; books include Alexander, *The Mystery of Life*, and Eastman, "Music, Dancing, Dramatic Art," in *The Indian To-day*.

9 Luhan, "Letter to Mary Austin, December, 1922?" Austin, *Literary America 1903–1934*, p. 172.

10 Henderson, "A Note on Primitive Poetry," p. 330.

11 Henderson, "A Note on Primitive Poetry," p. 331.

12 Lindsay, "Notes," p. 161.

13 Henderson, "Poetry of the North American Indians," p. 41.

14 Sandburg, "Aboriginal Poetry," p. 255.

15 Doyle, *Mary Austin*, p. 273.

16 Pearce, *The Beloved House*, p. 17.

17 Austin, "Artist Life in the United States," pp. 151–52.

18 For a rather unsympathetic and careless exploration of this parallel see Ford, *"The American Rhythm."*

19 Austin, "Imagism," p. 163.

20 Austin, "Aboriginal Fiction," p. 597.

21 See Hymes, "Some North Pacific Coast Poems."

22 This influence may often be undesirable. See Hobson, "The Rise of the White Shaman."

"The White Man Will Never Be Alone": The Indian Theme in Standard American Literature Courses

Joseph M. Backus

I

In conventional programs, one can most readily teach Indian-related literature by following the Indian theme through established courses in American literature, an approach that can lead to development and establishment of any of the more specialized courses outlined in this publication. In the meantime, juxtaposing the two literatures offers a forceful introduction to Indian literature because European and traditional Indian cultures and world views contrast so markedly. Conversely, consideration of American Indian literature in an American literature course provides an illuminating cultural background against which to read the works of immigrant Europeans. For the conventionally educated instructor, this approach also has the advantage of not initially demanding a great deal of training beyond that required for the teaching of standard courses. Certainly the more an instructor can learn about Indian life and literature, the more effectively he or she can teach Indian literature, but starting "unprepared" can offer the best stimulus and guide for continuous self-teaching in this wide and relatively "new" field. In any case, interested teachers of American literature can begin immediately to teach Indian or Indian-related literature in existing courses, at the same time strengthening rather than distorting or diluting the students' knowledge of both Indian and European-American literature.

Because many classic American authors make reference to Indians, a fair number of Indian-related texts are already on book lists for standard American literature courses. The instructor can supplement these works about Indians with works *by* Indians without making the reading list too long. Even the briefest Indian poem set in the same time and place as a European-American novel, for example, can serve to balance a key incident or scene in that novel or even to clarify the novel's theme or tone. Moreover, consideration of a few traditional Indian works at the beginning of a chronologically ordered course can effectively set the scene for all that follows. Then, at the end of the course, literary works by contemporary Indian authors can legitimately represent the literature of our own time, thus completing the course in a satisfyingly cyclical way that is fittingly Indian. But even without free choice of texts, and with materials selected without regard for the Indian theme (as are most anthologies of American literature), an instructor can make this approach work by pointing out the Indian theme where it does appear and by adding a few short Indian-related pieces.

During the past half-dozen years, I have found that the most effective way to begin a survey course in American literature is to assign a few works from tribes such as the Algonquin and Iroquois, with whom English settlers first made contact. For this purpose, the instructor can present the Algonquin through Wabanaki songs, tales, and reminiscences gathered by Curtis (see the bibliography at the end of this volume), the lyric and imagistic works of the Chippewa (Astrov), and the ceremonial literature and pre-European tribal history of the Delaware (or Lenape) (Astrov and Cronyn), effectively concluding with the often reprinted few lines culminating in the ominous first sighting of foreign ships: "They are peaceful; they have great things; who are they?" From Iroquois literature one can choose, for example, the night-long "Ritual of Fire and Darkness" (as compressed to six pages in Cronyn) as well as shorter Iroquois (or Senecan) poems (Bierhorst, *In the Trail of the Wind*; Rothenberg, *Shaking the Pumpkin*). If, instead of duplicating selections from various sources, the instructor can assign a full Indian text, two recent serviceable ones covering the whole 360 years of the course are Sanders and Peek, *Literature of the American Indian,* and Velie, *American Indian Literature.*

From even a small selection, students can sense something of the diversity, sensitivity, grace, and wisdom of American Indian literature while also getting some indication of what pre-European America itself must have been like. For example, the atmosphere pervading the entire northern woodlands seems to emanate from this very brief Chippewa song:

> A loon I thought it was
> But it was
> My love's
> Splashing oar.

If the quiet ripple of deep human feeling here, so aptly reinforced by restrained artistry and so closely attuned to natural harmony and calm, is followed by the turgid anti-Indian excesses of so early an intruder as Cotton Mather, whose words echo still across the wide span of continent and years, a basic contrast between the two cultures becomes strikingly evident at the outset: "forlorn and wretched *Heathen*," he calls the natives of New England, "the veriest *Ruines of Mankind,* which are to be found any where upon the Face of the Earth." Indeed,

> we may guess that probably the Devil decoy'd those miserable Salvages hither, in hopes that the Gospel of the Lord Jesus Christ would never come here to destroy or disturb his *Absolute Empire* over them. . . . These abject Creatures, live in a Country full of *Mines*; we have already made entrance upon our *Iron*; and in the very Surface of the Ground among us, 'tis thought there lies *Copper* enough to supply all this World; besides other Mines hereafter to be exposed; but our shiftless *Indians* were never Owners of so much as a *Knife*, till we come among them; their Name for an *English-man* was a *Knife-man*. . . . Their way of living, is infinitely Barbarous. . . . No *Arts* are understood among them, unless just so far as to maintain their Brutish Conversation, which is little more than is to be found among the very *Bevers* upon our Streams. ("The Life of John Eliot")

If students can glimpse the truth about American Indians through what remains of their early literature (and through the eyes of tolerant Englishmen such as William Byrd), they will find that Matheresque misconceptions and animus quickly show themselves for what they are. With better understanding of American Indians comes better understanding of Europeans, especially when one pays attention to their many varied responses to the Indians, responses that continued to manifest themselves even after the Indian spirit seemed to be completely broken. A sense of the American Indian's presence that lurks in the land, or at the back of the European-American mind, is perhaps most consciously articulated in "The Indian Burying Ground" by Philip Freneau, whose largely sympathetic perception of the spiritual world of the American Indian neatly marks a turning point between an age of reason and one of romance:

> And long shall timorous fancy see
> The painted chief, and pointed spear,
> And Reason's self shall bow the knee
> To shadows and delusions here.

From time to time during all periods of European-American literature, the dead or dying Indian is summoned back to fulfill a number of different purposes as literary or philosophical fashions come and go. Sometimes the Indian is made to inform a character or idea—sometimes fleetingly as a touch of local color but often more lingeringly as a figure of fear or of unspoiled nobility or as a symbol of countless changing concepts, feelings, and dilemmas projected on the Indian by an uneasy successor. "There may be a devilish Indian behind every tree," frets the tormented Puritan, young Goodman Brown, as he makes his way through the dark Massachusetts woods. Here Hawthorne is looking back two hundred years to give specificity to fears that derive from the growing darkness within his protagonist and to anticipate and help identify the satanic figure soon to emerge in a shape suggestive of Goodman Brown's father—whose sins, significantly, include the burning of an Indian village. "And when the last Red Man shall have perished, and the memory of my tribe shall have become a myth among the White Men," warns one of Hawthorne's contemporaries, the far-seeing Chief Seattle,

> these shores will swarm with the invisible dead of my tribe, and when your children's children think themselves alone in the field, the store, the shop, upon the highway, or in the silence of the pathless woods, they will not be alone. . . . The White Man will never be alone. ("The Indians' Night Promises to Be Dark," in Vanderwerth, *Indian Oratory*)

While the American Indian today is far from extinct, the central truth of Chief Seattle's prediction is borne out by so many white writers that the very absence of Indians in the work of an American author can be worth noting. Most non-Indian authors look sympathetically on Indians, often sharing to some degree the traditional Indian's fundamental holistic understanding of things and admiring the balanced perspective and poetic harmony that often characterize American Indian verbal expression. But in the late nineteenth-century response to Romanticism by certain authors who considered themselves realists, the reader encounters some extraordinary—and dismaying—exceptions.

II. Mark Twain's Literary Offenses

The author most dismayingly exposed by this approach to American literature is Mark Twain, probably the most revered of all American writers for his down-to-earth clarity of vision, for the humanity and wisdom of his works, and for the squarely American character of his writing. Most scholars agree that these qualities characterize most of Twain's work, including the widely read "lecture" in which he ridicules the professional ineptitude of the unrealistic James Fenimore Cooper and in the process turns the American Indian into a ridiculous figure of fun. Cooper "was almost always in error about his Indians," says Twain. "There was seldom a sane one among them."[1] These are summary statements calculated for humorous effect rather than as a defense of Indians against Cooper.

Twain himself has been taken to task for both his seemingly deliberate misrepresentation of Cooper and his consistently savage attack on the Indian.[2] But "Fenimore Cooper's Literary Offenses" is still reprinted without apology or qualification to mislead the unsuspecting student (and teacher), and here and elsewhere readers take Twain's word on both Cooper and Indians as final. The instructor can provide balance for Twain's views, however, by presenting traditional Indian literature and one of Cooper's Indian novels before introducing Mark Twain. Students can then see for themselves something of the truth about Indians and about Cooper as a writer. Then, if the instructor assigns *The Last of the Mohicans*, followed by *The Adventures of Tom Sawyer*—published exactly a half-century later and only six months after Custer made his last stand—an awareness of Twain's offenses will come to the reader with full impact. Because *Tom Sawyer* responds to a moral problem more complex than the one dealt with in the more often studied *Adventures of Huckleberry Finn*,[3] its inclusion in a standard American literature course may be well justified.

Most of Mark Twain's criticism of Cooper's Indians is based on Twain's belief that Indians are not the noble children of the forest that Cooper makes them out to be; they are mean, vengeful, deceitful, dirty, stupid, and in all ways depraved. Twain has met them face to face on the western frontier and therefore, unlike Cooper, knows what he's talking about. But in fact he saw American Indians only briefly and from a distance: Indians of quite another time and place, dispossessed and demoralized. What irks Twain most about Cooper, says Leslie Fiedler, is the "woodland romance" between whites and Indians that runs through Cooper's Indian tales, for "Twain is, by instinct and conviction, an absolute Indian hater, consumed by the desire to destroy not merely real Indians, but any image of Indian life which stands between White Americans and a total commitment to genocide."[4] In Twain there would seem to be an inherited puritanical blindness that causes him to see all Indians as agents of Satan. And the persistent popularity of Cooper's Indian books in Mark Twain's time must have rankled. Still, Twain seems to have had a personal axe to grind, perhaps as a result of a frustrating inability to rid his own writing of the influence of Cooper. Scholars have shown that, when Twain set about writing an Indian book of his own ("Huck Finn and Tom Sawyer among the Indians"), he could do little more than parody Cooper,[5] and for this reason, perhaps, he left the book unfinished. Others have pointed out, too, that the villainous Injun Joe, Twain's only fully developed Indian character, is related to Cooper's Indians. "That murderin' half-breed," as Huck calls him, has retained only the savagery of the noble savage and none of the nobility.[6] But of course not all of Cooper's savages are noble, and certain aspects of Injun Joe bear a striking resemblance to one of Cooper's most ignoble.

In his memoirs, Twain identifies Injun Joe as a drunken Indian of his boyhood,[7] and much of what Injun Joe does in *Tom Sawyer* must represent an enlargement of fearful boyhood imaginings. But for motivation and for many specific details in the fictive representation of this lone dark non-

European townsman, Twain seems to have depended heavily on Cooper's portrayal of the villainous Magua.

One similarity between these two fictitious Indians is their strong feeling of aggrievement and lust for revenge, which each means to satisfy by victimizing a person close to the man who has wronged him rather than the man himself. A second similarity is that both are impelled by the memory of humiliation. Magua intends to take the dark-eyed Cora Munro for his wife because, at the command of her military father, as punishment for a single instance of drunkenness, Magua "was tied up before all the pale-faced warriors, and whipped like a dog."[8] Similarly, Injun Joe intends to murder a young doctor because the doctor's father had him jailed for vagrancy when he came to beg for food.[9] Both aggrieved Indians make their motives clear to their intended victims by direct declamation, and both conclude their speeches by emphasizing their undying memory. "The spirit of a Huron is never drunk; it remembers for ever!" asserts Magua. And "Did you think I'd forget?" asks Injun Joe. "The Injun blood ain't in me for nothing." But Twain goes Cooper one better by giving Injun Joe two scores to settle, the second involving the defenseless Widow Douglas because her husband, fulfilling his provincial duty as a justice of the peace much like Colonel Munro in his treatment of Magua, "had me *horsewhipped!*—horsewhipped in front of the jail, like a nigger!" (p. 267; Ch. 29). Here the word "nigger" can be seen as a significant intensification of the word "dog," used similarly by Magua, for Twain thus seems to be adding to the sins of Injun Joe (already well established as the lowest of the low, "the veriest ruin of mankind") a wholly unfounded and thus especially reprehensible sense of racial superiority. In this way Twain paints him more villainous still, at the same time providing the reader with some fairly solid grounds for Jungian speculation: Is the ultimate source for Injun Joe neither Cooper nor boyhood memory but Mark Twain's own unconfronted shadow?

Other details suggesting Cooper's influence on Twain's presentation of Injun Joe range from small matters of diction—the quaint word "miscreant," which Cooper is fond of applying to his bad Indians, also describes Injun Joe (p. 122; Ch. 11)—to the use of dramatic devices. The "Leatherstocking Series," says Twain in his essay on Cooper, "ought to have been called the Broken Twig Series" because "Every time a Cooper person is in peril, and absolute silence is worth four dollars a minute, he is sure to step on a dry twig" (p. 64). But so too in *Tom Sawyer.* When Huck and Tom think they have come upon Injun Joe asleep in the darkened tannery, "Tom stepped on a stick, and it broke with a sharp snap" (p. 115; Ch. 10); and as Huck tries to slip silently away from Injun Joe after overhearing him plotting against the Widow Douglas, "a twig snapped under his foot." (p. 268; Ch. 29). Similarly, while trying to escape the sleeping Injun Joe at the haunted house, where there are no sticks or twigs to step on, "the first step [Tom] made wrung such a hideous creak from the crazy floor that he sank down almost dead with fright" (p. 243; Ch. 26).

There are still other, more significant similarities between the two novels. In *The Last of the Mohicans* Hawkeye repeatedly insists that he is a "man without a cross"; that is, in spite of his proficiency in woodsmanship and his friendship with the noble savage, he is a true full-blooded Englishman; and in *Tom Sawyer* this emphasis on purity of blood is inverted to become an emphasis on mixed blood, certain anathema in the eyes of the polite white reader of both Cooper and Twain. While the name "Injun Joe" may suggest mixed ancestry, far more pointed and more damaging is the much-used epithet "half-breed." But, paradoxically enough, while Twain frequently reminds the reader of this most undesirable quality in Injun Joe, he makes the qualities that he identifies as being purely Indian the chief source of Injun Joe's villainy. In so doing, Twain adapts for his own purpose Cooper's repeatedly mentioned concept of "gifts"—seemingly immutable traits of character and capabilities that are racial in origin. White men "don't take that sort of revenge," says one of Twain's most trustworthy white characters in reference to Injun Joe's sadistic plans for the widow. "But an Injun! That's a different matter altogether" (p. 275; Ch. 30). And neither will an Injun stop at murder. Injun Joe and Magua attack their victims in almost the same bloodthirsty way: Injun Joe "drove the knife to the hilt in the young man's breast," thus killing the doctor (p. 105; Ch. 9), and Magua "buried his weapon in the back of the prostrate Delaware," killing the young Uncas (p. 427; Ch. 32). Finally, having been made to suffer much in life, both Magua and Injun Joe die hideous deaths.

"I think that in *Tom Sawyer* I starved Injun Joe to death in the cave," recalled Twain long after he wrote the novel. "But that may have been to meet the exigencies of romantic literature."[10] Most of the trappings of romance that both Twain and Cooper use—the unlikely coincidence and improbable disguise, the exemplary heroics and subscription to a chivalric code—may be justified in telling the tale of a young romantic like Tom Sawyer (or Sam Clemens). But it is difficult to justify the unremitting evil of Injun Joe, who is made to bear a heavy cross indeed, combining as he does in his character the darkness of Gothic romance and the anti-Romantic's dark view of reality. Even Magua, a noble tribal chief until his public whipping for having succumbed to the white man's drink, is not altogether an unsympathetic character; nor does his punishment, as Cooper puts it, fail to prompt moral questioning. As a vagrant and one of the last of his race (like Uncas, whose idealized portrayal he may be meant to invalidate), Injun Joe, like Magua, may be seen as the victim of white oppression, but that is not part of the story that Twain is telling. And Mark Twain seems to have added even Injun Joe's reputed addiction to drink as but one more indication of an evil inherent and pure. In this way, Twain makes his Indian less real than his prototype in Cooper, and the reader may sympathize with Injun Joe largely because Twain is so set against him.

And yet, in attacking Cooper, Twain claims strict adherence to reality in his depiction of Indians here and elsewhere, thus creating an effect more pernicious than the one of which he accuses Cooper. The image of the duplicitous, vengeful, murdering half-breed, with few or no redeeming qualities and with no noble counterpart among his race to offset his own ignobility, has been implanted for more than a century now in the impressionable minds of innumerable young readers as the typical American Indian: worse than untamable, wholly abject, and yet perversely clinging to life. And making this impression more indelible still is Twain's intimidating attack not only on Injun Joe but also on anyone daring to side with him or (by easy extension) with any Indian so importunate as to survive into modern times. Tom himself, like much of America when the last warring Indian bit the dust, is "touched" by Injun Joe's death, as may be only natural in a boy who lives a life of romance. But, as mature realist, Twain continues with mounting outrage:

> a committee of sappy women [had] been appointed to go in deep mourning and wail around the governor, and implore him to be a merciful ass and trample his duty under foot. Injun Joe was believed to have killed five citizens of the village, but what of that? If he had been Satan himself there would have been plenty of weaklings ready to scribble their names to a pardon-petition, and drip a tear on it from their permanently impaired and leaky waterworks. (pp. 303–04; Ch. 33)

A "belief" that Injun Joe killed as many as five citizens in one otherwise quiet small town might have been realistically voiced by frightened townspeople when he roamed at large after the disclosure of his one known murder, but there is no mention of other murders then. Such mention occurs only in Twain's impassioned vilification of Injun Joe and his sympathizers near the end of the story, at best echoing the thoughts held then by like-minded villagers. At worst, as for Mather before him and for young Goodman Brown, the murderous half-breed may have really been for Twain something like Satan: a manifestation of some killing, unkillable psychological force given a menacing outward form, which, when thus externalized, is made more real than real can be. A similar but conscious and positive projection of inner reality by the Missouri Osage, possible kin to Injun Joe, would have been regarded as rank superstition. According to an Osage ceremonial song, a pipe smoked before battle for tribal unity and as an offering to the supernatural powers becomes a man, for

> Within it I have placed my being.
> Place within it your own being, also,
> Then free shall you be from all that brings death.[11]

III. The Indian Theme in Introductory Major-Authors Courses

Emphasis on the Indian theme can broaden and deepen a student's understanding of American literature and life on any level of instruction and in courses of any kind: survey, period, genre, major-authors, and so forth. But perhaps I can best indicate here the ways in which the theme might be developed through a full semester by referring to my own experience in teaching an introductory major-authors course. For this one-semester course, I could select texts freely, as long as they represented several important literary periods, genres, and authors; and I could organize the course in any way. With ground rules as liberal as these, I could vary texts and course theme from semester to semester in the interest of meeting changing needs, and I could include the Indian theme every time. In fact, to judge from results of my three-semester "experiment," course materials can be combined in a great many satisfactory ways. For this reason, the following report is meant only to suggest a sampling of the kinds of material that one can use with, it seems, a fairly high degree of success.

Basic reading materials for the first of the three semesters included *The House of the Seven Gables* (Romantic period); poems by Whitman and Dickinson and a collection of stories by Henry James (realism and naturalism); poems by Cummings and *Go Down, Moses* (modern period); and *House Made of Dawn* (contemporary)—a list that on the surface promises little study of American Indian literature. But if the instructor offers a small selection of traditional Indian pieces (as suggested at the beginning of this essay) as a preface to such works, he or she can establish a workable Indian frame of reference for the rest of the course. The general theme for the course during this particular semester was natural simplicity and man-made complexity as alternative ways of American life, to which the Indian theme added considerable dimension.

Of course, many European-American authors, even those who are critical of the increasing complexity of their own culture, do not consciously endorse the contrasting way of the Indian. Hawthorne, the first author on our list, is one of these. Yet the Indian, while not participating as a character in *The House of the Seven Gables,* is nonetheless fundamental to the story of the Pyncheon family, because most of the dark complexities with which the family is concerned derive from a belief among its succeeding generations that somewhere there still exists a long-lost Indian deed to a portion of Maine "more extensive than many a dukedom, or even a reigning prince's territory, on European soil" (Ch. 1). Here the instructor can remind the students of the traditional Indian concept of free but responsible communal use of ownerless land, a concept that contrasts sharply and instructively with the fatal materialistic greed and self-aggrandizement of the coldly calculating villain of this piece, who cares not a whit for his fellows or for any of the qualities that both the humanitarian European-American author and the traditional Indian value. And if students have been able to gain a sense of the Indian feeling of oneness with nature and with all life, they are well on the way to understanding the basic principles of the Romantic movement, as well as its frequent and still recurring theme of "head" versus "heart."

Whitman, who can follow Hawthorne as a transcendental bridge between the Romantic and realistic periods, juxtaposes scattered references to Indians with references to other peoples to show the constant ebb and flow of life in its many varied forms—a transcendental concept that might itself be called Indian. And thus Whitman's response to the death of Custer is "a glad triumphal sonnet," for once again is "The loftiest of life upheld by death, / The ancient banner perfectly maintain'd" ("From Far Dakota's Canons," 1876). Students can also discuss the possibility that Whitman's unconventional rhythms and other characteristic techniques, such as anaphora and lack of rhyme, are the result of Indian influence. And when they observe that Whitman's verse is usually more complex than the "translations" of Indian expression that might have contributed to it, while being essentially no more profound, they may wonder at the premium we tend to put on complexity as a mark of cultural advance: by making our lives so intricately involved have we also made them unnecessarily difficult—and essentially empty rather than full? Perhaps Whitman most closely echoes Indian poetry in Section 6 of "The Sleepers," whose seventeen lines constitute one of the shortest and most simply rendered appearances of the Indian in all European-American literature, yet one of the strongest and most haunting:

> My mother look'd in delight and amazement at the stranger,
> She look'd at the freshness of her tall-borne face and full and pliant limbs,
> The more she look'd upon her she loved her,
> . . . .
> She remember'd her many a winter and many a summer,
> But the red squaw never came nor was heard of there again.

When a long-expatriated American dowager seeks to dampen the enthusiasm of her nephew for Daisy Miller by declaring her too "common," the effete young man is moved to strongest rebuttal: "But, my dear aunt, she's not, after all, a Comanche savage" (*Daisy Miller*, Ch. 2). That is the only reference to anything Indian that I could find among eight representative stories by James about well-to-do Americans who have fled their crude and commercially despoiled homeland for the cultural refinements of the mother continent. Written shortly after the Battle of Little Big Horn (like Whitman's "Dakota's Canons" and Twain's *Tom Sawyer*), this single, brief, offhanded remark gives the reader pause to wonder: how can so extraordinary a lack of interest in native peoples be accounted for in a writer so gifted, productive, and time-honored as James? Was he, in spite of all his sophistication and probing psychology no less ethnocentric and contemptuous of the American Indian than the vociferously anti-Indian Mark Twain? And what further significance can we see in the responses to the Indian of these two major American literary figures of the time, America's two leading realists and the spokesmen (we may assume) for this country's late nineteenth-century ruling class?

Answers to such questions help to sharpen the edge of the protest in much of the poetry by Cummings, most pertinently in his often anthologized "Buffalo Bill's Defunct," first collected in 1923, six years after the death of the celebrated exploiter of native peoples and at the beginning of a new wave of sympathy for them. And some understanding of American Indian concepts can help students understand both Cummings and Dickinson, two latter-day New Englanders who share something of the old Indian reverence for nature and natural cycles.

Some knowledge of Indian concepts also helps clarify the meaning of *Go Down, Moses*, where Faulkner's adaptation of Indian feeling for the land—"the earth was no man's but all men's, as light and air and weather were" ("Was," Part I)—is basic to Ike McCaslin's climactic decision to free himself from ownership of the family plantation and its accumulating evils, a decision that follows years of quiet tutelage by Sam Fathers, his half-Indian mentor. The main course of action in this novel can be seen as just the reverse of that in Hawthorne's, where the self-destructing Judge Pyncheon is guided by his own egoistic ideal of increasing ownership. As a further means of drawing materials for this semester together, I would point out that the first and last titles on the reading list sum up the basic differences between Europeans and American Indians: the dark, static, and oppressively complex angularity implicit in the title *The House of the Seven Gables* and the natural image in the title of the Momaday novel, *House Made of Dawn*, with its bright fragile promise of renewal.

In the second semester that I taught the course in this way, I changed its general theme to Looking Backward to See Ahead, a reference to the Indian consciousness of repeating cycles. The reading list this time included duplicated selections from the Indian literature of the eastern woodlands in addition to works by four non-Indian authors: Hawthorne, Crane, Faulkner, and Kesey. I replaced *The House of the Seven Gables* with *The Scarlet Letter*. In this "romance," too, the Indian theme is more significant than it may at first appear, for the presence of Indians on the streets keeps reminding the reader that the Boston of the story's setting is still a remote English outpost in the midst of "wilderness," a narrow, ingrown little community that offers fit setting for the story's unhappy events. Moreover, the English doctor of physic learned native medicines during his captivity by Indians. His use of such medicines to destroy the lover of his young wife might seem to the uninstructed reader the darkest of Indian witchery. But with some knowledge of

Indian healing, the reader may come to suspect the vengeful Chillingworth of misapplying natural remedies, an interpretation consistent with the perversion of natural human impulses into which his coldhearted intellectualizing has led him. Again, as in "Young Goodman Brown," evil comes not from without but from the gathering darkness within.

While Crane's Indian tales were not available for this course, one non-Indian tale, "His New Mittens," incidentally includes a boys' game called Indians and Militia, in which the self-serving whimsy of bullying players takes on considerable potency as a possible parallel of duplicity in government dealings with actual Indians during Crane's time. By the time they read *One Flew over the Cuckoo's Nest*, the last selection of the semester, students had an awareness of the Indian world view that enabled them to empathize with Chief Bromden's mute withdrawal from the sterile unnatural world that European America has become and thus to heed the book's central message.

During the third semester, readings for this course included Quasha and Rothenberg's *America a Prophecy* (1974), an inspired collection of American Indian and European-American poetry ranging from pre-Columbian times to the present and thus usable all semester. Because of the clearly "new age" consciousness that integrates its more than three hundred offerings, this anthology can also serve as an example of a contemporary text. Prose works this time included much of the fiction previously mentioned, by Hawthorne, James, and Faulkner. And the course theme this time, Magic in Literature (magic that can apply to creative process, content, and effect on the reader), constantly brought into illuminating contrast Indian and non-Indian views of reality.

"In America, the Indians did not share the same world view as the European Americans," wrote an undeclared arts-and-sciences major during this semester, in a midterm paper called "A Dichotomous Discrimination":

> They did not see the world [as being] composed of contradictions but as a world flowing with harmony. Their world was not divided into societies and wilderness, for all was nature. And nature was not separated from God or the other spirits. There was a one-ness toward all things. No doubt this kind of perception reflected or emanated from the inner harmony and integration of their cognitive patterns. They did not separate the mind from emotion, or logic from intuition. Thus, in all of their writings there seems to be no object, but to simply describe it in its state of being, thereby capturing its fullness immediately and not through the tedious procession of logic. Compare the "Song of the Butterfly" [a Chippewa poem translated by Frances Densmore] (p. 414) to "Reflex Action and Theism" [a short paragraph from William James] (p. 481) in *America, a Prophecy*, for an appreciative awareness of existence, and this [distinction] becomes clear. The titles themselves are suggestive. . . .
>
> Almost all of our suffering is caused by our inability to resolve the apparent dichotomy of reality and understand its harmony. Almost everyone takes it for

granted as a concrete fact that the world operates dichotomously. What a grand illusion.

By the time he made these observations, the student was able to draw together information from many class discussions as background for his own further explorations. While his statement needs elaboration and qualification, it does at least indicate that introduction of the Indian theme in standard American literature courses can do much to expand perspectives for the inquiring student. At the same time, it gives a vital new dimension to the study of this country's literature.

IV. In Conclusion: A Beginning

Today, in seeking a more satisfying view of the world than the one most commonly taught and in trying to right some old wrongs, non-Indian Americans are quick to attribute to the traditional Indian what seems an ideal kind of existence. Before renascent Europe swept the world, so the story goes, the American Indian was truly noble and far from savage, living according to a cosmic plan that other Americans are only now beginning to understand. By drawing on their store of ancient wisdom, moreover, the peoples native to this hemisphere were able to nurture and preserve in its nearly natural state a greatly varied but thoroughly integrated ecological system for countless thousands of years; and, as a conscious participant in this system, the individual Indian was centered, balanced, at peace with self and universe, almost perfectly realized. Because much of the current popularity of this ideal is clearly due to disenchantment with narrow rationalism and the ravaging materialism to which that realism gives license, this present-day view of the traditional Indian is sometimes dismissed, especially by rationalists, as nothing more than a backward swing of the European-American pendulum to something like Rousseauistic notions of Utopia—as little more than yet another form of racial misunderstanding and exploitation.

And maybe so, although many American Indians seem to share the vision. Maybe we all see only what we seek, not distorting the truth but, as an ancient principle would have it, creating reality as we go along, looking backward to see ahead and to form new coherent patterns. Indications of the validity of current interpretations of the old Indian way, at least in very general terms, are to be found these days wherever one looks: in scientific explorations of mind and universe that go beyond the confines of established psychological and physical realities; in sociological and anthropological studies of premodern or nonmaterialistic cultures on every continent; in the attentive reading of literary works by and about the North American Indian. But even if we imperfectly understand the old ways, as seems inevitable in a time and place so radically different as ours, this study of the Indian can take us away from contemporary imbalances and fragmentation toward a stabilizing harmony and wholeness, at the same time allowing us to gain for American Indians a solid and long overdue respect. Even if pursuit of the Indian theme through a course in American literature is frankly exploratory, with teacher and student tentatively guiding each other along an uncertain path, much can be learned that will benefit individuals and thus, as a result of their awakening understanding of the Indians' holistic scheme of things, humanity as a whole.

Notes

1   "Fenimore Cooper's Literary Offenses," p. 68.
2   Krause, "Cooper's Literary Offences"; and Harris, "Mark Twain's Response to the Native American."
3   Tracy, "Myth and Reality in *The Adventures of Tom Sawyer.*"
4   *The Return of the Vanishing American*, pp. 122–23.
5   Blair, ed., *Mark Twain's Hannibal, Huck & Tom,* pp. 81–140.
6   Tracy, p. 535.
7   Neider, ed., *The Autobiography of Mark Twain*, pp. 68–69.
8   *The Last of the Mohicans*, Vol. 2 of *Cooper's Novels* (New York: Appleton, 1892), p. 129; Ch. 11. All quotations from Cooper are from this edition.
9   *The Adventures of Tom Sawyer*, Vol. 12 of Author's National Edition of *The Writings of Mark Twain* (New York: Harper, 1903), p. 105; Ch. 11. All quotations from *Tom Sawyer* are from this edition.
10   *Autobiography of Mark Twain*, p. 68.
11   Bierhorst, ed., *In the Trail of the Wind*, p. 70.

Teaching the Indian in American Literature

Course Design #1
The Indian in American Literature

This course is designed for inclusion in academic programs concerned with American studies and especially with American literature, but instructors can alter its general pattern and title or expand the course to accommodate other concerns and programs as well. Titles of related courses might be, for example, Literature by and about Native Peoples of the Western Hemisphere, The American Indian in World Literature, or Views of American Indian Life in Literature. Instructors can follow this general pattern in reduced form to include works by and/or about Indians in standard literature courses, tracing the Indian theme to provide students with deeper insights and wider perspectives.

The course proposed here is limited to literature about the native peoples of what is now the United States, written by both Indians and non-Indians. To indicate the earlier Indians' way of life, character, and outlook, the course begins with translations of the literature of those Indians with whom Europeans first came in contact. It then continues by examining European-American literary works related to the Indian, in various genres, chiefly poetry and imaginative prose, which can be juxtaposed with Indian works of corresponding times and regions. The course concludes with a consideration of contemporary works in English by American Indian authors who are currently enriching and enlarging the scope of American literature. The course is designed for undergraduates and can serve as a basis for more specialized study at upper-division and graduate levels.

Rationale

Reasons for offering such a course as The Indian in American Literature are several:

1. To gain familiarity with an integral and necessary part of American literature that, as a frequently recurring theme and influence, has often been
   overlooked.
2. To add to the corpus of American literature the rich and highly poetic
   Indian oral tradition, which is echoed later by Indian authors writing in
   English and, indeed, in much of the literary output of non-Indian American authors.
3. To identify a constantly recurring major theme that helps to bring into
   focus and to reflect American Indians as they were and are, as opposed to
   the changing non-Indian views of Indians occurring from early colonial
   time to the present.
4. To promote an understanding of the continuing intercultural conflict,
   which, often as metaphor for intrapersonal conflict, is a repeated theme in
   literature by and about post-Columbian American Indians.
5. To help the student of American Indian ancestry increase his or her knowledge of American Indian values as they are conflictingly portrayed in both
   American Indian and European-American literatures.
6. To promote insight into the Indians' holistic, cyclical understanding of
   humanity's relationship with the universe, which informs most Indian-
   related literature and which helps to balance the more linear and fragmented approaches to life and learning that characterize present-day
   Western civilization.

Methodology and Description

Since the organizing principles of the course are thematic and
chronological, students can easily trace certain illuminating subthemes.
Most prominent of these is the oppression of American Indians by Europeans,
especially as reflected in portrayals of defeated and demoralized natives
who live as outcasts in their own land. Students can consider the way in
which this theme progresses from one work to another, and they can examine the ways in which both Indian and non-Indian authors respond to this
situation. A variation on this theme is the attitude toward the American
Indian reflected in the works of non-Indian authors—the Puritans' hellhound
and heathen, Cooper's noble savage, Thoreau's fellow human being, and so
forth—especially when compared with the image of the Indian projected by,
say, Black Elk, with his great sensitivity, perception, and wisdom. Closely
related to images of Indians is the theme of ecological or environmental
awareness, with its concomitant sense of the oneness of all things, the way of
the circle. Another subtheme is the Indian's opinion of the non-Indian and of
the non-Indian scale of values, with its reliance on empirical investigation as
the way to knowledge and on the accumulation of material wealth as the key
to well-being.

From the beginnings of European-American literary history, the American Indian has been drawn into discussions of what is "American," for from the beginning American Indians and their literature have affected American literature no less substantially than they have affected American life. We see their influence in the puritanical tirades of Cotton Mather, for example, and in the Romanticism of Longfellow and in Mark Twain's denigratory "realistic" portraits of Indians in *Roughing It* and *Tom Sawyer*. In the twentieth century, we find the attempted assimilation of the Indian world view in Faulkner's *Go Down, Moses* and the sympathetic concern for the liberation of Chief Bromden from the dehumanizing mechanization of contemporary life in Kesey's *One Flew over the Cuckoo's Nest*. The Adam myth, the Columbus archetype, the concept of manifest destiny, and the regenerative result of violence are all approaches that American scholars have used to establish the Indian's place, or lack of place, in non-Indian America and in American literature. These attempts indicate the importance of understanding the Indian in order to determine the essence of what non-Indians have come to call the "American experience." Here non-Indian students are forced to consider a culture alien to their own: a view of the world that is holistic rather than pluralistic and one to which writers and thinkers have continually turned for inspiration. A unique advantage in the study of this "alien" view is that it exists within this country and has been in a struggle with European-American culture for hundreds of years. We need not look as far as Asia for alternate philosophies or realities.

By considering the ways in which non-Indian authors have drawn on Indian tradition, we can see how oral literature and oral history are incorporated into written tradition. Our own literary models of this may be the tall tale, the story, and the sketch—all forms of European-American literature—and the fiction and verse of contemporary Indian authors. In addition to the "matter of the red man" in American literature, there is the influence of the Indian on the American language, on poetic imagry (as in nineteenth- and twentieth-century verse), and on form (as in the unrhymed verse of Whitman). And once we become aware of the Indian influence on American literature, we should realize that this influence is increasing and that only with some knowledge of American Indian literature can our understanding of the literature of this country begin to be complete.

Materials

Students can sample pre-European Indian literatures in selections from Astrov, *American Indian Prose and Poetry*; Bierhorst, *Four Masterworks* and *In the Trail of the Wind*; Cronyn, *American Indian Poetry*; Curtis, *The Indians' Book*; Day, *The Sky Clears*; Underhill, *Singing for Power*; and Zuni People, *The Zunis*.

The following non-Indian works of the colonial and federal periods contain portraits or discussions of Indians: Brackenridge, *Modern Chivalry*; Bradford, *A History of Plymouth Plantation*; Brown, *Edgar Huntly*; Byrd, *History of the Dividing Line*; Freneau, *Poems* (esp. "The Prophecy of King Tammany," "The Dying Indian," "The Indian Burying Ground," "The Indian Student," and "The Indian Convert"); Jefferson, *Notes on the State of Virginia*; C. Mather, "The Life of John Eliot"; Morton, *Ouâbi, or, The Virtues of Nature* (poem); Rowlandson, *The Soveraignity and Goodness of God*; and Smith, *General Historie of Virginia, New England Trials*, and *A True Relation*.

In the Romantic period, a selection may be made among Bird, *Nick of the Woods*; Bryant, *Poems* (esp. "The Indian Girl's Lament," "An Indian Story," "An Indian at the Burial Place of His Fathers," and "The Prairies"); Cooper, the Leatherstocking Tales; Eastburn and Sands, *Yamoyden* (poem); Irving, *Adventures of Captain Bonneville, Astoria,* and *A Tour on the Prairies*; Longfellow, *Song of Hiawatha*; Melville, *The Confidence Man* (Ch. 26); Parkman, *The Oregon Trail*; Paulding, *Konigsmarke*; Simms, *The Wigwam and the Cabin* (tales) and *Yemasee*; Stone, *Metamora*; Street, *Frontenac*; Thoreau, *The Maine Woods*; and Whitman, *Leaves of Grass* (esp. "Starting from Paumanok," "From Far Dakota's Canons," "Yonnondio," and "Osceola").

Among the nineteenth-century realists and naturalists, a selection may be made from Clemens, "Fenimore Cooper's Literary Offenses," *Roughing It* (esp. passages on "Goshoot" Indians), and *Tom Sawyer* (esp. passages about Injun Joe); Crane, Indian tales (in *Complete Short Stories*); Garland, *Book of the American Indian* and *Captain of the Gray-Horse Troop*; Harte, "The Princess Bob and Her Friends" (tale); Jackson, *Ramona*; Miller, *Unwritten History*; Stephens, *Malakeska*; Wheeler, Deadwood Dick novels; and Wister, *The Virginian*.

From literature of the modern period, one may select among Austin, *Isidro*; Black Elk, *Black Elk Speaks*; Cather, *Death Comes for the Archbishop*; Corle, *Fig Tree John*; Faulkner, *Go Down, Moses*; Ferber, *Cimarron*; Grey, *Vanishing American*; La Farge, *Laughing Boy*; A. Lowell, *Ballads for Sale* and *Legends*; McNickle, *The Surrounded*; Roberts, *Northwest Passage*; and Waters, *The Man Who Killed the Deer*.

In the contemporary period, one may select from Berger, *Little Big Man*; Craven, *I Heard the Owl Call My Name*; De Angulo, *Indian Tales*; Dodge and McCullough, *Voices from Wah'Kon-Tah* (poems); Hobson, *The Remembered Earth*; Kesey, *One Flew over the Cuckoo's Nest*; Kopit, *Indians*; T. Kroeber, *Ishi in Two Worlds* (biography); Momaday, *House Made of Dawn*; Niatum, *Carriers of the Dream Wheel* (poems); S. Ortiz, *Going for the Rain*; Quasha and Rothenberg, *America* (poems); Richter, *Light in the Forest*; Rosen, *The Man to Send Rain Clouds* (short stories) and *Voices of the Rainbow* (poems); Sanchez, *Rabbit Boss*; Sandoz, *The Horsecatcher*; Silko, *Cere-*

mony; Snyder, *Earth House Hold* (essays); and Welch, *Death of Jim Loney* and *Winter in the Blood.*

Useful secondary materials include the bibliographies by Dockstader, Stensland, and Ullom and the following historical and critical works: Barnett, *The Ignoble Savage*; Chapman, *Literature of the American Indians*; Fiedler, *The Return of the Vanishing American*; Keiser, *The Indian in American Literature*; McNickle, *Indian Tribes of the United States*; Pearce, *Savagism and Civilization*; and Zolla, *The Writer and the Shaman*.

Course Design #2

Teaching Indian Materials in Established American Literature Courses

The most readily available means of teaching materials related to the American Indian may be simply to point out and discuss occurrences of the Indian theme in works that are already included in general courses on American literature on all levels of instruction. The instructor can greatly enhance this approach by beginning the course with a few duplicated materials (or, better still, with an anthology of early Indian literature) to indicate what the Indian and the Indian's land were like before the arrival of the first colonists from Europe. Especially telling in contrast to the European or Jacobean mentality are literary expressions from the traditions of the American Indian peoples in the Northeast—those with whom Europeans first came into contact. Even a small selection of liberal translations demonstrates the diversity, sensitivity, and beauty of American Indian expression.

With this background, students will have a base from which to compare the descriptions of Indians in such early European-American writers as Cotton Mather, William Byrd, and Philip Freneau.

Throughout any course in American literature, the instructor can usually find references to American Indians or Indian themes that can be illuminated by reading works by and about American Indians. (Many specific examples as well as a course description and suggested methodology are included in Joseph Backus, " 'The White Man Will Never Be Alone,' " in this volume.)

Resources

American Indian Literatures: A Guide to Anthologies, Texts, and Research

A. LaVonne Brown Ruoff

Aboriginal people have inhabited this continent for between 20,000 and 28,000 years. When Columbus mistook the Bahamas for India, Native America north of Mexico contained more than three hundred cultural groups, each with different customs, social structures, and world views. These cultural groups spoke 250 separate languages, plus many dialects, derived from seven basic language families. By 1940, at least 149 of these languages were still in use, many broken up into local dialects. Such diversity precluded the existence of a single American Indian culture or literature—a fact essential to understanding the complexity of American Indian oral literatures. Because each literature is interwoven with the religious beliefs, customs, and social structures of an individual Indian group, each body of tribal literature must be studied within the cultural context of the group that produced it. Also interwoven with the literature of each tribe are elements taken from the literatures of other tribes and of non-Indian groups. The continuing strength of Indian oral traditions has been their ability to survive through the power of tribal memory and to renew themselves by incorporating new elements. After Indians were educated in the white man's literature, they began to express their creative imagination in written as well as oral forms.[1]

Because few teachers are familiar with the vast and rich American Indian oral and written literatures, this essay will focus on the resources the nonspecialist needs to teach these literatures. This survey of literary scholarship is selective rather than comprehensive. It does not discuss essays appearing in this volume. It does include selected sources on ethnohistorical backgrounds because of their importance to understanding the diversity and complexity of Indian literatures.

Teaching Aids, Bibliographies, and Handbooks

In "Native American Literature in an Ethnohistorical Context," Michael Dorris (Modoc) gives a brief but enlightening overview of the field. Writing from the perspective of an anthropologist, Dorris emphasizes that teachers must avoid generalizing about "Indian literature," which is pluralistic in nature. Jarold W. Ramsey expands Dorris' general bibliography in "A Supplement to Michael Dorris's 'Native American Literature.'" The teaching of oral literature has received too little scholarly attention. Dorris discusses the subject, but Larry Evers treats it in great detail in "Native American Oral Literatures in the College English Classroom." Evers demonstrates how to use an Omaha Culture-Hero myth to teach basic elements of oral narratives. Although Evers includes in this article a short bibliography, he provides a more detailed one in his edition of *The South Corner of Time*, pp. 235–40. This volume originally appeared as volume six of *Sun Tracks* (1980). Karl Kroeber and A. LaVonne Brown Ruoff have prepared a substantial annotated bibliography designed for the teacher new to the field: *American Indian Literatures*.

In the last decade, several book-length bibliographies in the field have been published. Jack Marken's unannotated *The American Indian: Language and Literature* is more helpful as a guide to oral than to written literature. The most comprehensive guide to written literature is *A Biobibliography of Native American Writings, 1772–1924*, compiled by Daniel F. Littlefield, Jr., and James W. Parins, which has sections on Native American writers (including those known only by pen names) and biographical notes. It includes not only writers of belles lettres but also of political documents, tribal addresses, and letters. Useful in locating Indian authors and transmitters of oral literatures is Arlene Hirschfelder's *American Indian and Eskimo Authors*. Hirschfelder, however, does not list all Indian authors and occasionally gives the dates of later or reprint editions rather than of first editions. Anna Lee Stensland's *Literature by and about the American Indian* is very helpful for selecting books for high school courses and for establishing curriculum libraries. Containing descriptions of elementary-level books prepared by Aune M. Fadum, this bibliography stresses books printed after 1973, when Stensland published the first edition, and includes brief biographies of fifty-four nineteenth- and twentieth-century authors. Also valuable for establishing curriculum libraries is *American Indian Authors for Young Readers*, compiled by Mary G. Byler (Cherokee). More specialized is *Annotated Bibliography of American Indian and Eskimo Autobiographies*, compiled by H. David Brumble III. Brumble describes individual life histories, comments on the degree of editorial intrusion, gives biographical information about the subject of the autobiography, and provides indexes to tribes. A general bibliography that contains a section on literary works is *Index to Literature on the American Indian*, edited by Jeannette Henry et al. Individual indexes cover 1970–73.

In addition, bibliographies on specific topics and on individual tribes contain relevant material. *Native American Women*, compiled by Rayna

Green (Cherokee), includes material on Indian women writers. An expanded version of this bibliography is forthcoming through Garland Press. Bibliographies exist for many tribal groups. Among the most recent is W. David Laird's *Hopi Bibliography*, which is a sound guide to the literature. *Bibliography of the Sioux*, compiled by Jack W. Marken and Herbert T. Hoover, contains a special section on literature. The volume is part of the Native American Bibliography series, edited by Marken, which, when complete, will include comprehensive bibliographies on the major tribes and on various aspects of Indian cultures.

An excellent reference work in the field of Indian languages is *Native Languages of the Americas*, edited by Thomas A. Sebeok, issued in two volumes. Of special interest is Harry Hoijer's "History of American Indian Linguistics," which surveys the evolution of the field and analyzes the contributions made by important scholars. Two classic works by pioneers in the classification of Indian languages are *Indian Linguistic Families of America North of Mexico* by John Wesley Powell and *Handbook of American Indian Languages*, edited by Franz Boas.

Valuable for its review essays on basic reference works and for its bibliographies is the series edited by Francis Jennings, sponsored by the American Indian History Center of Newberry Library, and published by Indiana University Press. Each annotated bibliography contains approximately two hundred items. Prepared by scholars for use in high schools and community colleges, these bibliographies are more helpful for anthropological and historical background than for literature, which receives less than its due in the series. An informative one-volume work on nonliterary background is Francis P. Prucha's *A Bibliographical Guide to the History of Indian-White Relations in the United States*. Especially relevant are the sections on concepts and images of the Indian in America, on Indian writers, and on Indian tribes. For information on cultural background a fine source is George P. Murdock's *Ethnographic Bibliography of North America* (4th ed., 5 vols., rev. Timothy J. O'Leary). Volume one, *General North America*, provides a bibliography of the major culture areas.

Among the numerous general reference works containing useful background material is Harold E. Driver's *Indians of North America* (2nd ed.), which provides a good topical survey and excellent maps. The standard guide to the study of the American Indian is Frederick W. Hodge's *Handbook of the American Indians North of Mexico* (2 vols.). Updated volumes are being published under the general editorship of William C. Sturtevant. Now available are new volumes on California, the Southwest, and the Northeast (including the Great Lakes), each of which constitutes an authoritative guide to the tribes in these areas.

At present there is no bibliography of Indian biography, and few Indian authors are included in the *Dictionary of American Biography*. *Great North*

American Indians, compiled by Frederick J. Dockstader (Oneida), contains short biographies of three hundred Indians, presented in varying degrees of accuracy. Dockstader's bibliography lists many biographical sources. Several Indian authors are included in this volume and in *American Indian Intellectuals*, edited by Margot Liberty. Biographies of past and present Indian leaders have been compiled by R. David Edmunds (Cherokee) in *American Indian Leaders*.

General Anthologies

At present there is no general anthology of oral and written American Indian literatures comparable to the standard survey anthologies of English and American literature. Such an anthology is very much needed. The *Portable North American Indian Reader*, edited by Frederick W. Turner III, reprints a varied selection of myths and tales, as-told-to autobiographies, and works by a few contemporary authors. The texts of the oral selections, however, are not always accurate. The informative introduction focuses on the characteristics of Indian literatures. *American Indian Prose and Poetry*, formerly entitled *The Winged Serpent*, edited by Margot Astrov, contains a diverse collection of North and South American narratives and songs, plus a few orations. All selections are divided according to culture area and subdivided according to tribe. Astrov's introduction gives a helpful, if generalized, analysis of the cultural and stylistic characteristics of the literature, as well as a commentary on the problems of translation. In his "Some North Pacific Coast Poems," Dell Hymes examines the weaknesses of Astrov's dependence on available translations for her analysis of the original stylistic features. Hymes emphasizes that such analysis should be based on the original texts and on the linguistic aids necessary for their interpretation.

Literature of the American Indian, edited by Thomas E. Sanders (Cherokee) and Walter W. Peek (Narragansett-Wampanoag), demonstrates the weaknesses in many such anthologies. Although the section on oral literature is stronger than that on written literature, it nevertheless does not contain the ethnographic notes and introductions necessary for students to understand oral literature. It includes a miscellany of origin, hero, and Trickster tales and of songs from a variety of tribes. The section on written literature emphasizes contemporary work. A similar emphasis marks *American Indian Literature*, edited by Alan R. Velie, which includes lengthy oral selections to enable the teacher to focus on the complexity of specific works, such as a complete Acoma Pueblo origin myth or a substantial portion of Paul Radin's edition of the Winnebago Trickster cycle. Unfortunately, Velie, like Sanders, omits the valuable ethnographic notes that accompanied the original texts. The written selections are primarily by Oklahoma males.

Regional approaches have also been used in preparing anthologies. *The South Corner of Time: Hopi, Navajo, Papago, and Yaqui Tribal Literature*, edited by Larry Evers, includes traditional and contemporary oral literature (some with bilingual texts) as well as short stories, essays, songs, and poems. Maps, orthographies, and tribal ethnohistories are provided. A volume on Indian literature of Oklahoma is forthcoming. Jarold W. Ramsey has gathered a fine collection of narratives, songs, and speeches from Oregon tribes in his *Coyote Was Going There*, which contains a sound introduction and ethnographic notes from the original texts.

One of the few books that include criticism of both oral and written genres is *Literature of the American Indians*, edited by Abraham Chapman. While the volume contains some examples of oral narrative and of autobiography, it is primarily an anthology of critical essays done both by earlier and by more recent critics on such topics as thematic content, style, and translation. In addition to selections from well-known non-Indian critics of the nineteenth and twentieth centuries, the book also includes the work of such contemporary writers as N. Scott Momaday (Kiowa), Paula Gunn Allen (Laguna-Sioux), Vine Deloria, Jr. (Sioux), and Hyemeyohsts Storm (Cheyenne).

Oral Literatures

The chief library resources for oral literatures are the Bulletins and Annual Reports of the Bureau of American Ethnology, Anthropological Papers and Memoirs of the American Museum of Natural History, Publications of the American Ethnological Society, and the Journal and Memoirs of the American Folklore Society. Additional resources can be found in the anthropological series published by several universities, notably Columbia and California-Berkeley.

An excellent introduction to the strengths and weaknessses of the various approaches used in the collection and analysis of oral materials is Melville Jacobs' "A Look Ahead in Oral Literature Research." According to Jacobs, undisputed acceptance of the scientific virtue in "unselective datagathering, comparativism, and historicism" has characterized folklore research from the 1890s to the present. Franz Boas and his followers focused their scholarly attention on the study of minimal or micro-units called tribal "culture traits," which they listed and charted by geographic distribution. They did not, however, apply these micro-units to the study of oral literature, choosing instead to categorize this literature according to such macro-units as the "motifs" popular among historicogeographical folklorists. Jacobs particularly criticizes folklorists' adherence to motifs and archetypal themes because they impose an external structure onto the oral literature that may not accurately reflect its expressive content. Instead, Jacobs proposes close analysis of texts based on a knowledge of the dynamics of the contents' origin, maintenance, and style. He expresses similar views in his earlier "Oral Literature" (in *Pattern in Cultural Anthropology*), which contains suggestions for further reading. Although these articles deal primarily with narratives, their emphasis on the importance of the expressive content of oral literature is equally applicable to other genres and provides the beginner with a critical basis on which to evaluate the approaches used by scholars to analyze these genres.

A good example of Franz Boas' historicogeographical approach to American Indian oral literature is his "Stylistic Aspects of Primitive Literature" (rpt. in Boas, *Race, Language, and Culture,* which contains many of Boas' folklore essays discussed later). Here Boas states that the literary style of a people is not uniform and may vary according to the occasion. In his discussion of both narrative and song, Boas stresses that the literature of primitive societies, like that of civilized societies, undergoes development.

For ease of discussion, we divide oral literatures into the following categories: (1) chants, ceremonies, and rituals; (2) narratives; (3) songs; (4) ritual oratory. Chants, ceremonies, and rituals form a separate category because such sacred rites can combine several genres, such as narrative, song, and oratory. Because categories used by individual tribes vary considerably, the teacher must approach each literature through categories assigned by the tribe rather than through those assigned broadly to American Indian Literature. The problem of categorization is further complicated when scholars treat the mythological sections of sacred rites as narratives and portions of full chants as songs. Texts and criticism devoted primarily to specific genres are discussed in the sections devoted to these genres.

Chants, Ceremonies, Rituals

Among the few anthologies containing full rituals is *Four Masterworks of American Indian Literature,* edited and partially translated by John Bierhorst. This anthology, which includes the Iroquois Ritual of Condolence and the Navajo Night Chant, offers the opportunity to study individual works in depth. Bierhorst has wisely retained the notes from the original texts. The Navajo ceremonials have been reprinted more than those of any other tribe. Authoritative texts have been prepared by such scholars as Charlotte Johnson Frisbie, Berard Haile, Karl W. Luckert, Washington Matthews, Leland C. Wyman, and Mary Wheelwright. Both the Museum of Northern Arizona, Flagstaff, and the Museum of Navaho Ceremonial Art, Santa Fe, publish texts (those from the former are now being reprinted, under the direction of Karl W. Luckert, by the Univ. of Nebraska Press).

Washington Matthews edited two of the best-known Navajo rituals: *The Night Chant, a Navajo Ceremony* and *The Mountain Chant: A Navajo*

Ceremony. A frequently cited example by an early scholar is Alice C. Fletcher's edition of *The Hako: A Pawnee Ceremony*. She and Francis La Flesche (Omaha) collaborated on the publication of Osage ceremonies in *The Osage Tribe* (Pt. 1: *Rite of the Chiefs;* Pt. 2: *Rite of Vigil;* Pt. 3: *Two Versions of the Child-Naming Rite*). All the texts prepared by these scholars contain full commentaries and interpretative notes.

In general, some of the most helpful criticism of the rituals is contained in the scholarly editions of individual texts, which contain discussions of the ethnohistorical and linguistic aspects of the rites. A body of critical scholarship distinct from textual editions is emerging as well. Among the most interesting studies of Navajo ceremonies, from a cultural point of view, is Katharine Spencer's *Mythology and Values,* which analyzes the Holyway, Evilway, and Lifeway chants from the perspective of Navajo culture. (See also the discussion of her work in the section on narratives.) Andrew O. Wiget takes a more literary approach in "Sayatasha's Night Chant." Wiget uses Ruth Bunzel's translation of this midwinter Shalako ritual as the basis for his analysis. (Aspects of ritual are also discussed in the sections of this essay on narrative, song, oratory, and philosophy and religion.)

Narratives: Anthologies and Texts

Narratives have received more scholarly attention than any other genre in American Indian oral literatures. *Traditional Literatures of the American Indian,* edited and compiled by Karl Kroeber, exemplifies the kind of text especially appropriate for literary study. Kroeber provides an illuminating introduction to the art of oral narrative and to the fine essays by Dell Hymes, Jarold Ramsey, Dennis Tedlock, and Barre Toelken (with Tacheeni Scott); he also reprints the narratives discussed. While this book emphasizes depth study of a limited number of works, *Tales of the North American Indians,* edited by Stith Thompson, emphasizes breadth. Organized primarily according to myth motifs developed by Thompson, this anthology is an excellent guide to some of the major motifs in Indian mythology classified by standard categories. Thompson includes detailed notes on the background of the stories and on the relationship of an individual story to similar stories from other tribes. As the title indicates, John Bierhorst's anthology *The Red Swan: Myths and Tales of the American Indians* distinguishes between myths (generally sacred) and tales (generally secular). This collection of narratives from both North and South America contains translations by standard authorities as well as some of Bierhorst's own reworkings of these. Bierhorst's introduction outlines psychoanalytical and structural approaches to interpretations of the annotated texts.

The most extensive scholarly work has been done in preparing editions of narratives. In his landmark studies of the Tsimshian and Kwakiutl tribes, Franz Boas established the principle of studying oral literatures as a means of understanding American Indian cultures. Among his best-known works are *Tsimshian Mythology,* coauthored with Henry W. Tate, *Kwakiutl Tales,* and *Kwakiutl Culture as Reflected in Mythology.* Boas' *Keresan Texts* is important to understanding the work of the contemporary writers Leslie Marmon Silko (Laguna) and Simon Ortiz (Acoma). Melville Jacobs provides an excellent analysis of Boas' critical methodology in his article "Folklore." An examination of Boas' contributions to anthropology, linguistics, and folklore and a bibliography of his work can be found in *Franz Boas, 1858–1942,* by Alfred L. Kroeber et al.

The influence of Boas is evident in the work of such scholars as Ruth Benedict, Leonard Bloomfield, Ruth Bunzel, George A. Dorsey, Pliny E. Goddard, Melville Jacobs, A. L. Kroeber, Robert H. Lowie, Elsie Parsons, Paul Radin, Edward Sapir, and Clark Wissler, all of whom made important contributions to the collection and analysis of Indian literatures. The texts edited by these scholars, as well as by such pioneers as James Mooney, provide literal translations, careful analyses of the cultural backgrounds of the tribes, and full notes. Representative examples of the work of the Boasian scholars are the following: Benedict, *Zuni Mythology* and *Tales of the Cochiti Indians;* Bloomfield, *Menominee Texts;* Bunzel, *Zuni Texts;* Dorsey, *The Pawnee Mythology;* Goddard, *Myths and Tales from the San Carlos Apache;* Jacobs, *Clackamas Chinook Texts* and *The Content and Style of an Oral Literature: Clackamas Myths and Tales;* Kroeber, *Yurok Myths;* Lowie, *Myths and Traditions of the Crow Indians;* Radin, *The Trickster;* Sapir, *Wishram Texts, Together with Wasco Tales and Myths,* collected by Jeremiah Curtin; Wissler and D. C. Duvall, *Mythology of the Blackfoot Indians;* Mooney, *Myths of the Cherokees.*

Anthropological and linguistic scholars have recently published additional authoritative texts, many of which are available in paperback. Excellent examples of scholarly bilingual editions suitable for the classroom are *O'otham Hoho'ok A'agitha: Legends and Lore of the Papago and Pima Indians,* edited by Dean Saxton and Lucille Saxton and *Hopitutuwutsi,* edited by Ekkehart Malotki. Such bilingual texts are preferable for class use because they enable the students to compare the English translations with the native-language versions. Another excellent text for class use is Melville Jacobs' *The People Are Coming Soon: Analyses of Clackamas Chinook Myths and Tales,* which offers the opportunity for depth discussion of a limited body of narratives from one tribe. A regional collection of narratives, presented only in translation, is *Wisconsin Chippewa Myths and Tales and Their Relation to Chippewa Life,* edited by Victor Barnouw. Barnouw examines the tales from psychological and sociological perspectives. The most innovative edition of narratives presented in translation is Dennis Tedlock's *Finding the Center: Narrative Poetry of the Zuni Indians.* Tedlock uses special typography to enable one to read aloud the narratives in a manner approximating the original performances. His perceptive discussion of the performance context provides a fine background for the stories.

When considering the variety of texts available, one should not forget the importance of the work done by such skilled storytellers as George Bird Grinnell, whose interpretations and commentaries are significant early contributions to American Indian literatures. Among the best of Grinnell's works are *Blackfoot Lodge Tales, By Cheyenne Campfires,* and *Pawnee Hero Stories and Folk Tales.* Howard A. Norman achieves an imaginative rendering of oral narratives in *The Wishing Bone Cycle,* which contains a complete Trickster cycle. Norman's translations capture the conversational tone and wit of Cree storytelling.

Indians themselves, both as individuals and as tribes, have increasingly published accounts of their oral traditions. Boasian-trained scholars Ella Deloria (Sioux), William Jones (Fox), and Archie Phinney (Nez Perce) and other scholars, such as John N. B. Hewitt (Tuscarora), Francis La Flesche (Omaha), William Morgan (Navajo), and Arthur C. Parker (Seneca), collected and translated the oral literatures of Native America, thereby adding an important Indian perspective that was missing from earlier scholarship. Examples of their work include Deloria, *Dakota Texts;* Hewitt, *Iroquoian Cosmology;* Jones, *Fox Texts,* ed. Franz Boas; La Flesche, see discussion of chants, ceremonies, and rituals; Morgan, Robert W. Young, and Hildegard Thompson, *Coyote Tales;* Parker, *Seneca Myths and Folktales;* Phinney, *Nez Perce Texts.* Alfonso Ortiz (San Juan) uses Tewa legends as the basis of his explanation of tribal world views in *The Tewa World.* Jack F. Kilpatrick and Anna G. Kilpatrick (Cherokee) have published several volumes of Cherokee oral literature, including *Friends of Thunder.*

Less scholarly but valuable nonetheless are the collections prepared by Mourning Dove [Humishuma] (Okanogan) in *Tales of the Okanogans,* edited by Donald M. Hines (see also an earlier version of these tales in *Coyote Stories,* ed. Heister D. Guie), and by Edmund Nequatewa (Hopi) in *Truth of a Hopi.* Collections of narratives published under the aegis of individual tribes include *Anadu Iwacha, The Way It Was: Yakima Legend Book,* project directed by Virginia Beavert (Yakima), and *Nu Mee Poom Tit Wah Tit (Nez Perce Stories),* compiled by Allen P. Slickpoo (Nez Perce) et al. An example of a tribally sponsored history based on oral tradition is *Navaho History,* edited by Ethelou Yazzie (Navajo). Bill Vaudrin (Ojibwe) gathered anecdotal narratives of the Tanaina Indians in *Tanaina Tales from Alaska.*

Narratives: Criticism

For a historical perspective on the development of critical approaches to American Indian oral literatures, the work of Franz Boas is an excellent starting point. The introductions and commentaries to his *Tsimshian Mythol-*

ogy and *Kwakiutl Culture as Reflected in Mythology* exemplify his belief that oral literatures mirror the cultures of Indian tribes. His best statement on the method of gathering and publishing oral literatures is contained in "Mythology and Folk-Tales of the North American Indians." Here Boas deals with the types and distribution of narratives, delineating such types as creation and origin, Trickster-Transformer, and animal. Boas discusses the diffusion of narratives in "The Dissemination of Tales among the Natives of North America" and "The Growth of Indian Mythologies." Boas expands his diffusion theory in "The Development of Folk-Tales and Myths" by illustrating from the mythology of the North Pacific Coast how incidents with wide distribution develop characteristic peculiarities in restricted parts of the territory in which they occur.

Boas' influence on the criticism of American Indian oral narratives can be seen clearly in the works by his disciples that trace the dissemination of narratives and categorize myth motifs, themes, and elements. In his *Literary Aspects of North American Mythology,* Paul Radin emphasizes the need for an examination of the literary aspects of American Indian mythology. Radin convincingly demonstrates the fallacy of the theory that there can be only one correct version of a myth by analyzing four examples to illustrate their complexity of plot, dramatis personae, motifs, and other elements.

Margaret W. Fisher's "Mythology of the Northern and Northeastern Algonkins in Reference to Algonkian Mythology as a Whole" is a good introduction to the broad characteristics and distribution of Algonkin oral literature. Fisher tabulates the appearance in many tribal literatures of various episodes from different types of narratives. More specific in focus is Robert H. Lowie's "Test Theme in North American Mythology." In "The Explanatory Element in the Folk-Tales of the North-American Indians," T. T. Waterman demonstrates that this element is secondary rather than primary in the plots of these narratives.

Most of the criticism of oral narratives has been devoted to the examination of themes, elements, or motifs. The analysis of oral literature through the use of motifs is advocated by Stith Thompson in *Narrative Motif-Analysis as a Folklore Method;* the results of Thompson's research are contained in his *Motif-Index of Folk-Literature.* A good starting point for the study of motifs in American Indian Literatures is Gladys A. Reichard's "Literary Types and Dissemination of Myths." After a general discussion of the issues involved in establishing myth types, Reichard applies her criteria to the analysis of the Earth-Diver, Star-Husband, Lodge-Boy, and Thrown-Away myths.

Creation myths are widespread among North American Indians, as Jeremiah Curtin demonstrates in his early *Creation Myths of Primitive America.* Anna Birgitta Rooth has done a careful analysis of over three hundred such myths in her "Creation Myths of the North American Indians." She distinguishes eight basic types, of which she finds the Earth-Diver the most prevalent. In "The Emergence Myth in Native North America," Ermine Wheeler-Voegelin and Remedios W. Moore trace the distribution of emergence myths and their relation to migration tales. Both these articles are good places to begin the study of these myths. Aileen O'Bryan analyzes Navajo myths in *The Diné,* and Katharine Spencer examines the relationship of these narratives to Navajo life in *Reflections of Social Life in the Navaho Origin Myth.* In "From Performance to Print," Paul G. Zolbrod illustrates the complexities of translating Navajo origin legends and analyzes the weaknesses in Washington Matthews' renditions. Dennis Tedlock treats a Zuni origin myth in "The Spoken Word and the Work of Interpretation in American Indian Religion."

The most thought-provoking discussion of the Earth-Diver myth is that by Alan Dundes in "Earth Diver." Dundes' interpretation of the myth as a male anal-creation story, however, is offensive to many Indian people. Earl W. Count examines the connections between the myths of North America and those of Eurasia in "The Earth-Diver and the Rival Twins." In "The Earth-Diver," Elii Kaija Köngäs expands on Count's study, concluding that though distributed worldwide, the myth always has four traits: the earth covered with water, the creator, the diver, and the making of the earth.

Two frequently discussed myths are the Orpheus and Star-Husband. In "Orpheus and Star Husband," Guy E. Swanton analyzes these two myths in terms of their revelation of tribal corporate structure. He also provides a useful summary of the numerous approaches taken by earlier scholars. A. H. Gayton's "Orpheus Myth in North America" is an informative guide to the distribution of the many versions of that narrative among Indian tribes. Åke Hultkrantz utilizes Gayton's research as well as his own in his definitive study of the myth's religious implications, *The North American Indian Orpheus Tradition.* Taking a Nez Perce version used by neither Gayton nor Hultkrantz, Jarold Ramsey gives a perceptive analysis of the meaning and structure of the myth among that tribe in his "From 'Mythic' to 'Fictive' in a Nez Perce Orpheus Myth."

Stith Thompson's construction of a hypothetical archetype and of various subarchetypes in "The Star Husband Tale" has stimulated considerable discussion of this narrative. Claude Lévi-Strauss uses a structuralist approach in his analysis of Plains Star-Husband tales in *The Origin of Table Manners.* Alan Dundes takes a morphological approach in *The Morphology of North American Folktales.* George W. Rich, in "Rethinking the 'Star Husbands,' " finds Dundes' approach to the tale's structure superior to that of Thompson in dealing with variations. In his articles on the narrative, "A Fifth Analysis of the Star Husband Tale" and "Folktales and Social Structure," Frank W. Young provides good summaries and informed criticism of the major theoretical studies, arguing that greater research is needed to determine links between social organizations and folktales.

Another important category of myths centers on the Culture Hero and the Trickster-Transformer. Daniel G. Brinton surveys the variety of myths in which the Culture Hero appears in his *American Hero-Myths*. Far more provocative, however, is Franz Boas' classic analysis in his introduction to *Traditions of the Thompson River Indians of British Columbia*, compiled by James Teit. Examining these figures as they appear in selected tribal literatures in North America, Boas distinguishes three types: the egocentric (who accidentally may benefit mankind); a combination of egocentric and altruistic; and two separate characters as Culture Hero (altruistic) and Trickster-Transformer (egocentric). Paul Radin provides the fullest discussion of the Trickster-Transformer in his analysis of the Winnebago cycle in *The Trickster*. Though critics increasingly question the extent to which the evolutionary structure of the cycle in Radin's edition accurately reflects the organizational pattern of the original oral narrative, the text itself and especially Radin's ethnographic and comparative notes and his discussion of the character are important contributions to our understanding of this figure so universal in American Indian mythology. Radin's analyses of the cycle's structure and of the character of the Trickster should be compared to those done by Barbara Babcock-Abrahams in her fine " 'A Tolerated Margin of Mess.' " Babcock-Abrahams focuses on the Trickster as an expression of the ambiguous and paradoxical power derived from the figure's ability to live interstitially, to confuse, and to escape the structures of society and of cultural order. After discussing the concepts of "marginality," cultural negation, and powers available to "outsiders," she carefully analyzes the Winnebago cycle to show that there is structuring beyond the level of the episode, as suggested by other critics. She also rejects as reductionist Jung's view, shared by Radin, that the myth reflects an earlier, rudimentary stage of consciousness. Mac-Linscott Ricketts also rejects Radin's Jungian perspective in his "The North American Indian Trickster." Using Radin's view of the Trickster as representing man's coming to consciousness, Ricketts delineates the specific aspects of this state through an examination of various Trickster myths. He concludes that the Trickster/Transformer/Culture Hero is a complex but essentially unified figure. The article provides a good commentary on the validity of criticism of the figure by Brinton, Boas, and Radin.

Frequently included in the Culture Hero or Trickster-Transformer cycles are the Bumbling-Host tales, the basic elements of which Boas outlines admirably in *Tsimshian Mythology* (pp. 694–702). Polly Pope analyzes the activities that occur in the tale and outlines its structure in "Toward a Structural Analysis of North American Trickster Tales."

The impact of modern psychology is evident in the work of many twentieth-century scholars. Benedict includes a discussion of dreams in her influential introduction to *Zuni Mythology*. Astrov's interest in psychology is reflected both in her introduction to *American Indian Prose and Poetry* and her "The Concept of Motion as the Psychological Leitmotif of Navaho Life and Literature." Dundes' discussion of the Earth-Diver myth reflects this impact, as do Radin's commentary in *The Trickster* and Barnouw's in *Wisconsin Chippewa Myths and Tales*. In "Psychological Inferences from a Chinook Myth," Jacobs uses "The Basket Ogress Snatched the Baby" to test the Freudian concepts of oral and genital stages of psychic development. He finds evidence of the Clackamas concept of the connection between excessive oral interest and failure to develop normal genital activity within both the myth and Clackamas culture. A. Irving Hallowell emphasizes the importance of tribal concepts of psychology, as opposed to Western European concepts. His collected writings in *Culture and Experience* provide an illuminating introduction to the interrelation between tribal culture and world view.

Clyde Kluckhohn in "Recurrent Themes in Myths and Mythmaking," however, rejects the overemphasis on the culture of a specific tribe in the analysis of a myth or motif common throughout the world. Kluckhohn and others have examined the structure of narratives to determine their universal elements. The most controversial of these scholars is Lévi-Strauss, who seeks the true meaning of myths by analyzing their Hegelian dialectal structure and developing universal models for this structure. An excellent overview of his structuralist theories is given by Edmund Leach in *Claude Lévi-Strauss*. The following works provide a good introduction to his theories: "The Structural Study of Myth," "The Story of Asdiwal," and "Overture" to *The Raw and the Cooked*. See also "Four Winnebago Myths." Lévi-Strauss' structuralism, too well known to require elaboration here, is opposed by many scholars as reductionist because it denies the significance of cultural, literary, and performance contexts.

A different kind of approach to examining the structure of narrative is offered by Alan Dundes, who advocates breaking motifs into motifieme sequences. Dundes' approach is an attempt to deal with micro- rather than macrounits within mythology. His *Morphology of North American Folktales* contains the fullest statement of his motifieme theory. The book is also an excellent guide to the strength and weaknesses of earlier critical approaches to American Indian oral narratives. Dundes includes discussion of many of the myth types described earlier in this essay.

In "Texture, Text, and Context," Dundes proposes the use of "internal criteria" of interacting narrative levels (texture, text, and context) to determine the meaning of folklore items. Karl Kroeber shows how the application of "internal criteria" can reveal the artistry of Indian oral narratives in "An Introduction to the Art of Traditional American Indian Narration." Kroeber's essay provides a clear and effective guide to understanding the complexity of these narratives.

Scholars have also focused on stylistic aspects of oral narrative. "Catchwords" are examined early in this century by Alfred L. Kroeber in

"Catch-words in American Mythology" and by Robert H. Lowie in "Catch-Words for Mythological Motifs" and "Additional Catch-Words." More recently Melville Jacobs examines the significance of the titles given Clackamas Chinook stories by native narrators in "Titles in an Oral Literature." Gladys Reichard discusses the relation between individual narrative style and story content in "Individualism and Mythological Style." She uses internal evidence of myth to determine the individual character of the narrator and how his or her control of the ritualistic medium affects the treatment of literature. Reichard uses four versions of Navajo creation myth as her examples.

The research of Melville Jacobs ushered in an era of scholarly focus on the expressive content of narrative. A helpful introduction to Jacobs' theories of pattern in culture is his *Pattern in Cultural Anthropology;* of particular interest to literature scholars are the essays on "Oral Literature," "Humor and Tragedy," "Religion," and "World View." Especially important for an understanding of Jacobs' concepts about the expressive content of narrative is *The Content and Style of an Oral Literature.* Here Jacobs emphasizes the need to examine oral literature as a total literary event within a native setting. In his discussion of the content of selected myths and tales, Jacobs delineates the stories' use of emphases, social relationships, personality traits, humor, world views, and perception of the good. In his discussion of style, Jacobs suggests that the performance of oral stories is a form of drama. To elucidate his thesis, he examines the variability in the structures of the stories as well as the stylized devices and motifs present. Jacobs treats humor as a significant unit in oral literature in "Humor and Social Structure in an Oral Literature"; after outlining sixteen types of humor in Clackamas Chinook stories, he concludes that analysis of a people's humor can point to some values in their social system the attainment of which is marked by uncertainties. In "A Few Observations on the World View of the Clackamas Chinook Indians" Jacobs analyzes a myth entitled "Coyote Made Everything Good," which expresses two kinds of symbiotic relationships: intimate interconnections of food, kindred, spirit powers, and people and the interconnection between the fatherlike authoritarian who heads the village and his people. Maureen E. Connors has compiled a limited bibliography of Jacobs' work.

Dell Hymes, using his corrected versions of texts collected by earlier scholars, has greatly elaborated on the principles outlined by Jacobs. Hymes provides a clear discussion of his concept of the role of folkloristic study of language and literature in "Folklore's Nature and the Sun's Myth." Hymes advocates a general conception of folklore based on genre, performance, tradition, situation, and creativity, and applies this conception to the analysis of a Kathlamet Chinook text. In "Discovering Oral Performance and Measured Verse in American Indian Narrative," Hymes, who considers himself a structuralist, emphasizes that traditional Chinookan narratives possess linguistically marked presentational segments. Hymes divides the narratives, which he calls "measured verse," into acts, scenes, verses, and lines. Discussing how to discover oral performance in printed texts, Hymes convincingly demonstrates how Jacobs' misreading of linguistic markings led him to an incorrect interpretation of "Seal and Her Younger Brother Lived There." Hymes also argues against limiting the study of oral narrative to texts transcribed from tape-recorded performances, pointing out that such a restriction would eliminate from scholarly study most of what has been recorded of Native American oral tradition. Hymes outlines the achievements of Melville Jacobs and discusses the differences between their approaches in "The Methods and Tasks of Anthropological Philology." Hymes has gathered together many of his most important essays on the linguistic methodology of interpreting Indian oral literatures in his recent *In Vain I Tried to Tell You,* a valuable guide to the study of these literatures.

Basing his own work on that of Hymes, Jarold W. Ramsey has done a perceptive article on the structure of the Oregon transformation narratives, "The Wife Who Goes Out like a Man, Comes Back as a Hero."

Dennis Tedlock's important work on oral performance differs from that of Jacobs and Hymes in its emphasis on performed as opposed to dictated or transcribed texts. In "On the Translation of Style in Oral Narrative" and in "Pueblo Literature: Style and Verisimilitude," Tedlock argues convincingly that the translation problems in Pueblo literature stem from the insistence of the Boasian school on literal translation and from the predilection of other translators for literary embellishment and stilted diction. In both articles Tedlock uses examples from Zuni literature to illustrate the importance of voice quality, pause, loudness, and other qualities of oral performance as guides to the structure of the narrative. Tedlock urges in "Toward an Oral Poetics" that greater attention be paid to spoken performances because they contain patterns of repetition on various scales—patterns that he believes are more typical of written poetry and song than of prose. Tedlock emphasizes the primary significance of verbal performance, although he acknowledges the secondary importance of studying texts taken down by early ethnographers and linguists. In "The Spoken Word and the Work of Interpretation in American Indian Religion," Tedlock stresses the difference between his approach and that of Hymes, who he says distinguishes between *telling* about the story and *doing* the story. Tedlock uses a Zuni origin story to illustrate his belief that for the tribal storyteller-interpreter, the relation between text and interpretation is dialectical: the teller both respects and revises the text.

Barre Toelken analyzes the nature of both oral performance and audience response to Navajo coyote myths in his "The 'Pretty Language(s)' of Yellowman." Toelken finds that part of the significance of Navajo coyote narratives resides in their texture, which he defines as any coloration given a traditional item or statement as it is being made. Too often scholars ignore texture in their search for structure. Toelken further elaborates on the nature of audience response in "Poetic Retranslation and the 'Pretty Languages' of Yellowman," written with Tacheeni Scott (Navajo). Through a reanalysis and retranslation of the Navajo story discussed in the previous article, Toelken illustrates that structure and meaning unite in the story to provide an excitement of meaning already present in the shared world views and customs of people living in a traditional society.

The kind of analysis of style, performance, and audience participation now being conducted by scholars such as Hymes, Tedlock, and Toelken has yielded important insights into the form and content of American Indian oral narratives. Karl Kroeber uses another method of analysis in "Deconstructionist Criticism and American Indian Literature" to show how the principles of deconstructionism outlined by J. Hillis Miller provide a means of understanding Trickster-Transformer narratives.

Songs: Anthologies and Texts

Although songs, often categorized as poetry, have received far less scholarly attention than have narratives, they are an important area of oral literature. The best anthology is *The Indians' Book,* edited by Natalie Curtis [Burlin], second edition. Published two years after Curtis' death, this fine anthology contains careful ethnographic introductions and notes, bilingual texts, and musical transcriptions as well as relevant myths and tales. Many of the songs, arranged by culture area and tribe, were collected by Curtis herself; others are taken from authoritative sources. It is selective rather than comprehensive in its coverage of tribes. Less reliable is *American Indian Poetry,* edited by George W. Cronyn, an enlarged edition of *The Path on the Rainbow.* This anthology contains an introduction by Mary Austin and songs from many tribes, arranged by culture areas. It includes some fraudulent Eskimo songs as well as a section of interpretations by modern writers, including E. Pauline Johnson (Mohawk). Both this book and A. Grove Day's edition of *The Sky Clears* reprint translations done by scholars, omitting the original texts and most of the notes. Day, however, provides a lengthy introduction, short commentaries on the cultural contexts of the songs, and a bibliography. Far less satisfactory are the anthologies of free interpretations of standard translations prepared by William Brandon in *The Magic World* and Jerome Rothenberg in *Shaking the Pumpkin.*

Regrettably, there is no good book-length study of the broad subject of American Indian songs as literature. The best discussions exist in the commentaries and notes to texts prepared by such scholars as Natalie Curtis, Alice C. Fletcher, Frances Densmore, Herbert J. Spinden, and Ruth M. Underhill. The work of Fletcher, who pioneered in the field, is exemplified by her often cited *Study of Omaha Indian Music.* She examines the relation between narrative and song in her anthology *Indian Story and Song from North America.* The most prolific pioneer in the field of Indian music was Densmore, who collected, transcribed, and translated songs from many tribes. Excellent examples of her work are *Chippewa Music* and *Teton Sioux Music.*

Herbert Joseph Spinden has prepared a useful volume in *Songs of the Tewa.* His translations of the songs are preceded by an essay on American Indian poetry in general and on Tewa poetry in particular. Ethnographic notes are also provided. Especially valuable as a text for class use is Ruth M. Underhill's *Singing for Power: The Song Magic of the Papago Indians of Southern Arizona.* Underhill translates the songs and describes the contexts of the rituals of which they are a part. David P. McAllester analyzes the musical and cultural dimensions of a Navajo ceremonial in *Enemy Way Music.* He and Susan W. McAllester have prepared an interesting volume on house poems from Navajo rituals in *Hogans: Navajo Houses and House Songs,* for which he translated and interpreted the songs and she provided the accompanying photographs. A good example of the techniques of modern methodologies in collecting Indian music is Alan P. Merriam's *Ethnomusicology of the Flathead Indians.* The secular songs of the Lakota are presented in a bilingual edition entitled *Songs and Dances of the Lakota,* compiled by Ben Black Bear, Sr. (Sioux), and R. D. Theisz. It includes historical and explanatory notes and suggestions for further reading.

Songs: Criticism

Nellie Barnes examines the shaping forces and characteristics of style of American Indian song in *American Indian Verse.* Barnes overgeneralizes, however, and ignores cultural contexts. In contrast, Eda Lou Walton and T. T. Waterman concentrate on specific tribal patterns in versification in their "American Indian Poetry." As Walton and Waterman demonstrate in their analyses of songs from Southwestern tribes, these patterns can differ greatly. Gladys A. Reichard's *Prayer* contains incisive commentary on the songs that constitute or are included within prayers. Excellent commentaries are contained in the texts cited above.

Helen Addison Howard's *American Indian Poetry* is an informative survey of the theories and practices of some of the major collectors, translators, and interpreters of songs in the twentieth century. Although it purports to survey the field of Indian poetry, in reality the book is a series of critical biographies.

An influential discussion of style and translation is "Some North Pacific Coast Poems" by Dell Hymes. Here Hymes summarizes the theories of translation used by collectors and anthologists, particularly the work of Margot Astrov in *American Indian Prose and Poetry,* and closely analyzes six songs. Hymes's research has stimulated other scholars to address these issues. William Bevis, in his examination of the strengths and weaknesses of anthologies of songs, is especially critical of the free interpretations done by Brandon and Rothenberg. Bevis effectively illustrates the distortions present in their versions by comparing these with scholarly texts in his "American Indian Verse Translations." Gretchen Bataille addresses the translation problem in her "American Indian Literature: Traditions and Translations." The kind of ethnographic and literary analysis Hymes urges is provided by Kathleen M. Sands and Emory Sekaquaptewa (Hopi) in "Four Hopi Lullabies." Using tape recordings made by Emory's mother Helen, Sekaquaptewa and Sands give detailed commentary on the meaning and form of the songs.

Although the ethnomusicology of American Indian song is beyond the scope of this essay, a few references are included to help the beginner. David P. McAllester's *Readings in Ethnomusicology* contains Bruno Nettle's "What Is Ethnomusicology," articles by George Herzog, McAllester, and Willard Rhodes on Indian music, and a selected annotated bibliography. A general study of Indian music is Nettl's *North American Indian Musical Styles*, which surveys the scholarship in the field and delineates the characteristics of the music of various culture areas. An excellent regional guide is Charlotte Johnson Frisbie's *Music and Dance Research of Southwestern United States*. This work surveys the history of the collection and analysis of Southeastern Indian music and provides a substantial bibliography.

Ritual Oratory

Relatively little has been published on ritual oratory. (Speeches by individual Indians are discussed later in this essay.) Among the few such studies is *Rainhouse and Ocean: Speeches for the Papago Year* by Ruth M. Underhill, Donald M. Bahr, Baptisto Lopez, Jose Pancho, and David Lopez. Bahr has prepared a bilingual text in *Pima and Papago Ritual Oratory*. Both works contain valuable introductions and notes.

Philosophies and Religions

Familiarity with the world views of North American Indians is important in understanding both oral and written literatures. Indeed, because sacred oral literature is so closely interwoven into the fabric of traditional Indian religious life, it is difficult to distinguish between literature and religion. Sam D. Gill provides an informative overview of the scholarship in tribal philosophies and religions in his "Native American Religions." The most comprehensive analysis of American Indian religions is Åke Hultkrantz's *The Religions of the American Indian*. One of the foremost scholars of American Indian religions, Hultkrantz has done numerous comparative studies of Indian world views and has argued persuasively that a knowledge of these views is important to an understanding of world religion. The bibliography to the book is a good guide to the field. Ruth M. Underhill provides a sound general survey in *Red Man's Religion*. Two volumes that are useful introductions to traditional and current religious movements and world views are *Teachings from the American Earth*, edited by Dennis Tedlock and Barbara Tedlock, and *Seeing with a Native Eye*, edited by Walter Holden Capps.

A number of books on American Indian philosophies have been written by Indians themselves. Ella Deloria (Sioux) gives a clear and perceptive account of Sioux kinship systems, values, modes of education, and adaptation to reservation living in her *Speaking of Indians*. This very readable book is excellent as a resource for helping students understand Indian world views. Vine Deloria, Jr. (Sioux), has written two books on American Indian philosophies: *God Is Red* contrasts American Indian and Judeo-Christian world views, which he outlines in broad strokes and presents with satiric wit; more scholarly in tone is *Metaphysics of Modern Existence*, in which he urges that we turn to American Indian world views in order to understand today's realities. His provocative study is stronger in its interpretation of tribal views than in its interpretation of modern non-Indian religious and philosophical thought. Alfonso Ortiz combines anthropological perspectives and Tewa oral traditions to elucidate the dualism present in the beliefs of his tribe in *The Tewa World*. The book is among the best on Indian religion. The collections of oral literature and the autobiographies of American Indians contain valuable insights into tribal world views.

Numerous studies of the religions of specific tribes are available as well. Two fine studies of the Sioux are Joseph Epes Brown's *The Sacred Pipe*, which describes the seven rites of this pipe as outlined by Black Elk, and William K. Powers' *Oglala Religion*, which surveys in detail Oglala rituals and beliefs. Essential to understanding Navajo religious practices and beliefs is Gladys A. Reichard's *Navaho Religion* and Sam D. Gill's *Sacred Words*. Though criticized by Pueblo people, Elsie C. Parsons' *Pueblo Indian Religion* is an important guide to their world views. Hamilton Tyler has prepared a series of careful studies of Pueblo mythology: *Pueblo Birds and Myths, Pueblo Animals and Myths*, and *Pueblo Gods and Myths*. Karl W. Luckert, who has written many excellent books on Navajo religious beliefs and ceremonies, is editing a series, American Tribal Religions, published by the University of Nebraska Press.

Personal Narratives: Oral and Written

The genre of personal narrative spans both oral and written literatures, incorporating elements of oral storytelling and of written autobiography.

During the nineteenth and early twentieth centuries, the personal narrative achieved a popularity second only to that of the narrative. Much of this popularity was the result of the great interest in the lives of the "vanishing Americans" as well as in the slave narratives and formal autobiographies of the period. Most of the personal narratives were of the as-told-to variety. Because they were narrated to a translator or collaborator, these life histories should be classified as oral rather than written literature. However as Indians became educated in the white man's language and literature, they began to write autobiographies that frequently combined oral history, myths and tales, and personal experience.

The only bibliographic guide to this genre is *Annotated Bibliography of American Indian and Eskimo Autobiographies,* compiled by H. David Brumble III (see Bibliography section). In "American Indian Autobiographies," William F. Smith, Jr., suggests that most of these works contain a mixture of narrative and cultural essay, illustrating his thesis with examples from nine autobiographies. Arnold Krupat, in "The Indian Autobiography," argues that Indian life histories exemplify bicultural authorship. To demonstrate his point, he analyzes the relationship between J. B. Patterson's *Life of Black Hawk* and non-Indian personal narratives typifying Western autobiography. Lynn Woods O'Brien presents a regional view of the genre in *Plains Indian Autobiographies.*

Editors of as-told-to autobiographies have used a variety of approaches in shaping the texts. Excellent examples of two Winnebago personal narratives structured as anthropological documents are Sam Blowsnake [Big Winnebago and Crashing Thunder], *The Autobiography of a Winnebago,* ed. Paul Radin, and Mountain Wolf Woman, *Mountain Wolf Woman, Sister of Crashing Thunder,* ed. Nancy O. Lurie. Other examples of good editions of oral autobiographies from a variety of tribes are the following: Maria Chona, *Autobiography of a Papago Woman,* ed. Ruth M. Underhill; John Stands in Timber, *Cheyenne Memories,* ed. Margot Liberty assisted by Robert M. Utley; James Sewid (Kwakiutl), *Guests Never Leave Hungry,* ed. James P. Spradley; and Left Handed (Navajo), *Left Handed, Son of Old Man Hat,* ed. Walter Dyk. Some subjects told their life stories to friends who recorded them: Helen Sekaquaptewa's *Me and Mine* typifies this form.

Two of the most widely read as-told-to personal narratives deal with Sioux life. Far more literary than most such works is John G. Neihardt's edition of *Black Elk Speaks,* which vividly portrays Sioux world views and customs both before and after the tribe was forced onto reservations. *Black Elk Speaks* has received greater critical attention than any other life history. Sally McClusky examines both the book's literary reception and Neihardt's role as transmitter in *"Black Elk Speaks: And So Does John Neihardt."* Neihardt's role is also discussed by Robert Sayre in "Vision and Experience in *Black Elk Speaks,"* the best discussion of the book's themes and structure.

Holly Carol thoughtfully analyzes the relationship of this personal narrative to autobiography as a literary genre in *"Black Elk Speaks* and the Making of Indian Autobiography." Much of the discussion of Neihardt's role must be reexamined in the light of the research done by Michael A. Castro in his unpublished dissertation "Interpreting the Indian." Castro demonstrates that a comparison of Neihardt's notes with his final manuscript reveals that Neihardt made some significant changes in material Black Elk gave him. Though less polished stylistically, *Lame Deer, Seeker of Visions* by John Fire [Lame Deer] (Sioux) and Richard Erdoes gives a humorous and often forceful account of the life and times of Lame Deer. Part holy man and part scamp, Lame Deer represents the generation born after settlement on reservations.

In addition to these life histories of individuals collections from specific tribes are available. Especially well done is *Navajo Stories of the Long Walk Period,* edited by Broderick H. Johnson, made from tape-recorded accounts of experiences during the time of the forced march to the Bosque Redondo in 1864. Another example is *The Zunis: Self Portrayals,* translated by Alvina Quam.

Falling somewhere between narrated and written personal narratives are those set down in manuscript by the subjects and later edited by scholars. Among the most interesting of this genre is *The Warrior Who Killed Custer,* edited and translated by James H. Howard. In 1931 Chief White Bull (Sioux) wrote the life history in the Dakota language; both his original text and his illustrations are reproduced in the volume. Others wrote their stories in English. The long manuscript written by Don Talayesva (Hopi) was revised and restructured extensively by Leo W. Simmons prior to publication as *Sun Chief.* Refugio Savala's manuscript, published as *Autobiography of a Yaqui Poet,* received much less editorial interference by Kathleen M. Sands. Both in this edition and in "A Man of Words" Sands provides detailed commentary on the background and literary qualities of the manuscript.

Though Indians began writing their autobiographies early in the nineteenth century, most of those published in that century have not yet been reprinted. Further, little has been written on these works. In "Sarah Winnemucca," Catharine S. Fowler gives an excellent account of the life of this author and of her long out-of-print *Life among the Piutes.* (For a discussion of William Apes, see below.) Autobiographies written since the late nineteenth century have been reprinted, however, often in paperback. One of the earliest of these is Francis La Flesche's descriptive portrayal of his life as a schoolboy during the mid-1860s in *The Middle Five.* Margot Liberty briefly chronicles La Flesche's life in "Francis La Flesche." Further information on La Flesche and his family is contained in *Iron Eye's Family* by Norma Kidd Green.

The most widely read autobiographies continue to be those written by Charles Alexander Eastman (Sioux) and his wife Elaine Goodale Eastman:

Indian Boyhood, which covers Eastman's life to age fifteen, and *From the Deep Woods to Civilization,* which covers his subsequent life. Both books provide memorable descriptions of Sioux family life, customs, and legends as well as of Eastman's experiences in the white world. Informative accounts of Eastman's life and writings and of the collaborative role played by Elaine Eastman are given by David R. Miller in "Charles Alexander Eastman, the 'Winner'" and by Raymond Wilson in "The Writings of Ohiyesa— Alexander Eastman, M.D." The first analysis of Eastman's literary and historical achievements is Anna L. Stensland's "Charles Alexander Eastman," in which she emphasizes that Eastman was more a creative storyteller than an ethnohistorian steeped in scholarship. She stresses the importance of his historical portraits of Indian leaders.

Autobiographies were written by other Sioux as well. Luther Standing Bear's *My People, the Sioux,* edited by E. A. Brininstool, contains interesting vignettes of Sioux life and a powerful description of Standing Bear's life as a member of the first class at Carlisle Indian School. Among the very few autobiographies by Indian women during this period is that by Zitkala Sa [Gertrude Bonnin], *American Indian Stories.* In essays originally published 1900–02, Zitkala Sa recounts her girlhood and school experiences and retells traditional stories. Dexter Fisher traces Zitkala Sa's life and work in her unpublished dissertation "The Transformation of Tradition" and in her fine article "Zitkala Sa: The Evolution of a Writer."

Later Indian authors have written autobiographies reflecting a high degree of literary sophistication. Among the most beautifully crafted is that of John Joseph Mathews (Osage), *Talking to the Moon;* a Thoreauvian portrait of Mathews' return to the Oklahoma blackjacks region, the book is a beautiful blend of myth, history, and personal experience. N. Scott Momaday (Kiowa) achieves a similar blend in *The Way to Rainy Mountain,* a chronicle both of the Kiowas' origin and ultimate migration to Oklahoma and of Momaday's quest for his tribal roots. Momaday's *The Names* is a more conventional life history. Gerald Vizenor (Chippewa) has written an imaginative short autobiography in which he describes growing up as a mixed-blood in Minneapolis, "I Know What You Mean, Erdupps MacChurbbs," one of the few creative works about urban Indian life. Less literary but delightful nevertheless is *The Reservation* by Ted Williams (Tuscarora).

Speeches: Oral and Written

The speeches of Indian people constitute another genre that spans both oral and written literature. (Ritual orations are discussed earlier in this essay.) The authenticity of the orations attributed to Indian leaders before the twentieth century, however, is increasingly questioned by scholars because our records usually are based on translations or reports that cannot be checked against the original orations. To use these speeches as examples of Indian oratorical style is problematic because the structure and language of the speech may be closer to those of the translator or transmitter than to those of the speaker. In *Indian Oratory* W. C. Vanderwerth has collected speeches dating from 1758 to 1910 and provided short biographical sketches of the orators. In *I Have Spoken* Virginia Armstrong has collected statements and speeches dating from 1609 to 1971. Unfortunately, most of these are brief excerpts, some consisting of one or two lines. The selections are arranged chronologically, with notes indicating the sources. Both Armstrong and Vanderwerth provide bibliographies. Additional statements and speeches can be found in Peter Nabokov's *Native American Testimony*, which focuses on Indian-white relations.

Written Literature: Prose, Fiction, Poetry, and Drama

The literary achievements of American Indian writers before 1968 have been largely unexplored. Bernd C. Peyer calls attention to the works of the late eighteenth- and nineteenth-century writers and provides a somewhat inaccurate bibliography in his "A Bibliography of Native American Prose Prior to the 20th Century." In "The Nineteenth-Century Native American Poets," Linda Hogan (Chickasaw) discusses briefly the non-Indian literary influences on the work of Alexander Posey (Creek), John Rollin Ridge (Cherokee), and E. Pauline Johnson (Mohawk).

Little scholarly attention has been paid to sermons and hymns written by American Indians. "A Sermon . . . at the Execution of Moses Paul, an Indian" (1772), by Samson Occom (Mohegan), the first Indian best-seller, has been reprinted by the Association for Study of American Indian Literatures. A careful study of Occom's life and career is Harold Blodgett's *Samson Occom*, which contains generous excerpts from Occom's letters, journals, and hymns. Occom's relation to the history of New England Indians is traced by W. Deloss Love in his detailed *Samson Occom and the Christian Indians of New England*. Love quotes extensively from Occom's works.

An example of early nineteenth-century Indian protest literature in an edition suitable for class use is *Indian Nullification of the Unconstitutional Laws of Massachusetts Relative to the Marshpee Tribe: . . . ,* by William Apes (Pequot) (1835). For a 1979 reprint edition, Jack Campisi provides a foreword that gives the political backgrounds of the treatise. Kim McQuaid's "William Apes, Pequot: An Indian Reformer in the Jackson Era" is a careful examination of Apes's life and career which contains much useful information about Indian-white relations of the period.

James E. Murphy and Sharon M. Murphy have recently examined Indian journalism. In *Let My People Know* the Murphys provide a brief history of American Indian presses, a discussion of contemporary Indian journalism, and a directory of Indian print and broadcast media. Ralph Henry Gabriel chronicles the life of one of the earliest Indian journalists in *Elias Boudinot, Cherokee, and His America.* Carolyn Thomas Foreman traces the careers of two Indian editors in "Edward W. Bushyhead and John Rollin Ridge."

Two figures dominate the field of journalistic satire: Alexander Posey (Creek) and Will Rogers (Cherokee). Though he was a poet, Posey is remembered primarily for his satiric "Fus Fixico Letters," written in Creek-style English. Unfortunately, these have not yet been reprinted. Posey's journals, which provide illuminating insights into his reading and composition methods, have been edited by Edward Everett Dale. Most of the extant scholarship on Posey is biographical. William Elsey Connelly provides a detailed account of the writer's life and death in *The Poems of Alexander Lawrence Posey*, collected and arranged by Mrs. Minnie H. Posey. Doris Challacombe gives a brief survey in "Alexander Lawrence Posey," and Leona G. Barnett gives a fuller survey, especially of his journalistic career, in *"Este Cate Emunkv."*

Far more scholarship has been done on Will Rogers than on Posey. Reprint editions of Rogers' voluminous works are now being published jointly by the Will Rogers Memorial Commission and Oklahoma State University Press. *Will Rogers: A Centennial Tribute,* edited by Arrell M. Gibson, contains numerous essays on the humorist's life and work as well as an excellent bibliographical essay by Blue Clark (Creek) entitled "The Literary Will Rogers." Two good biographies are by Richard M. Ketchum and Donald Day, neither of which is annotated. Betty Rogers has written a warm memoir of her husband, *Will Rogers: His Wife's Story.* An overview of Rogers' life and work is given by E. Paul Alworth in *Will Rogers.* Several collections of Rogers' comments and writings have been edited to serve as autobiographies: Donald Day, ed., *Autobiography of Will Rogers*; Paula McSpadden Love (Rogers' niece), ed., *The Will Rogers Book*; and Margaret S. Axtell, ed., *Will Rogers Rode the Range.* Bruce Southard examines Rogers' use of language in "Will Rogers and the Language of the Southwest"; Rogers' influence on the American public is the subject of William R. Brown's *The Imagemaker.*

Until recently, the only book-length study of Indian novelists was Charles R. Larson's *American Indian Fiction.* Larson covers only novels written since 1899, omitting John Rollin Ridge's novel and the short fiction of writers like E. Pauline Johnson. Although Larson provides good plot summaries of the novels and incisive commentary on their relation to mainstream American fiction, his interpretations and categorizations pay insufficient attention to the novels' cultural contexts. Priscilla Oaks surveys the development of Indian fiction during the single decade in "The First Generation of Native American Novelists," which focuses on the work of John Joseph Mathews (Osage), D' Arcy McNickle (Salish), and John Oskison (Cherokee).

In a recent book, *Four American Indian Masterworks*, Alan R. Velie examines the novels of Momaday, Silko, Welch, and Vizenor.

The earliest novel by an American Indian is John Rollin Ridge's *The Life and Adventures of Joaquín Murieta, the Celebrated California Bandit* (1854). In addition to the account of Ridge's life and journalistic career written by Caroline Thomas Foreman, a good account appears in Angie Debo's "John Rollin Ridge." Ridge's place in the San Francisco literary milieu and his treatment of the Murieta legend are discussed in detail by Joseph Henry Jackson in his introduction to the novel and by Franklin Walker in *San Francisco Literary Frontier*. Remi Nadeau traces the historical and mythic bases for the Murieta legend in *The Real Joaquín Murieta*.

O-gî-mäw-kwĕ Mit-i-gwä-kî, Queen of the Woods by Simon Pokagon (Potawatomi) has received scant critical attention. The only biographical study of Chief Leopold and his son Simon is Cecilia Buechner's *The Pokagons*. In "Chief Simon Pokagon: The Indian Longfellow," David H. Dickason discusses the relation between Pokagon's work and that of Henry Wadsworth Longfellow. He also analyzes the literary reception, content, and style of *Queen of the Woods*.

The work of E. Pauline Johnson (Mohawk), author of fiction, essays, and poetry at the turn of the century, has been the subject of several studies. A good introduction to her writing is Marcus Van Steen's *Pauline Johnson*, which contains a biography and selections from her prose and poetry. Her former manager Walter McCraye warmly portrays her life in *Pauline Johnson and Her Friends* and in *Town Hall Tonight*. A less authoritative life is Mrs. Garland Foster's *The Mohawk Princess*.

The work of Mourning Dove [Humishuma] (Okanogan) is surveyed by Dexter Fisher in a fine introduction to the reprint edition of *Co-ge-we-a*, coauthored with Lucullus McWhorter. Particularly helpful are Fisher's examination of the nature of the collaboration and her discussion of the ethnographic and historical backgrounds to the novel.

John Joseph Mathews' novel *Sundown* is available in reprint. Unfortunately Priscilla Oaks's introduction is too brief to provide necessary background. The best guides to this novel are Mathews' own books: *Wa'Kon-Tah: The Osage and the White Man's Road,* an account of the tribe's acculturation; and *The Osages,* a comprehensive history based on both oral and written accounts. Garrick Bailey describes the author's career in "John Joseph Mathews." Further biographical information can be found in Guy Longsdon's "John Joseph Mathews—A Conversation." *The Surrounded,* the superb first novel of D'Arcy McNickle (Salish), Mathews' fellow writer in the 1930s, has also been reprinted. William Towner, in his introduction, provides a warm biographical tribute to his friend and colleague.

Although much of the literature written before 1968 remains out of print, numerous anthologies of contemporary literature exist. Kenneth Rosen has collected the work of contemporary writers in *The Man to Send Rain Clouds,* an anthology greatly enriched by several stories by Leslie Marmon Silko (Laguna) and by two stories by Simon Ortiz (Acoma). Witty and trenchant discussions by Vine Deloria, Jr. (Sioux), of the cycles of popularity experienced by American Indian authors and of the problems presented by anthologies appear in "A Conversation with Vine Deloria, Jr." and in "Anthologies: Main Course or Left-Overs?" The latter is a review of *The Remembered Earth,* edited by Geary Hobson (Cherokee), an anthology that contains substantial samples from the prose and poetry of the best recent Indian writers. James Welch (Blackfeet-Gros Ventre), Gerald Vizenor (Ojibwe), and Roberta Hill (Oneida), however, are not included. Two useful collections of contemporary Indian poetry are *Carriers of the Dream Wheel,* edited by Duane Niatum (Klallam), which also includes Hawaiian selections, and *Voices of the Rainbow,* edited by Kenneth Rosen. Among the first collections of contemporary Indian writing and art to be published were John Milton's editions of *The American Indian Speaks* (1969) and *American Indian II* (1971). Both originally appeared as special issues of *South Dakota Review.* Milton also published *Four Indian Poets* in 1974. Other anthologies of contemporary poetry as *Voices from Wa'Kon-Tah,* edited by Robert K. Dodge and Joseph B. McCullough; *Come to Power,* edited by Dick Lourie; and *From the Belly of the Shark,* edited by Walter Lowenfels. The work of contemporary Canadian Indian poets has been collected by David Day and Marilyn Bowering in *Many Voices.*

Most critics have limited their inquiries into written American Indian literature to the work of contemporary authors. Galen Buller, in "New Interpretations of Native American Literature," sets forth a theory of literary criticism for American Indian literature, arguing that the characteristics unique to this literature include a reverence for words, a sense of place, a feeling for and participation in ritual, and an affirmation of Indian assumptions about the nature of the universe. Although Buller examines the appearance of these characteristics in the works of contemporary authors, he does not demonstrate how these traits are uniquely Indian, as opposed to tribal. Jarold W. Ramsey offers a perceptive analysis of why teachers should avoid the extremes of seeing all contemporary works either as ethnographic mirrors of specific tribes or as reflections of pan-Indianism. In "The Teacher of Modern American Indian Writings as Ethnographer and Critic," Ramsey points out the need for relevant ethnographic information but emphasizes that works of art exist beyond cultural contexts. He suggests that the best approach to contemporary works incorporating oral traditions is through the study of the oral literatures from the tribes about which the authors write.

Out of her own experience, Paula Gunn Allen (Laguna-Sioux) writes a moving study of contemporary writers' treatment of the theme of alienation and the mixed-blood in "A Stranger in My Own Life," a good guide to the work of contemporary poets. James Ruppert, in "The Uses of Oral Tradition in Six Contemporary Native American Poets," uses the poetry of Maurice Kenny, Peter Blue Cloud, Wendy Rose, Liz Sohappy Bahe, Ray Young Bear, and Elizabeth Cook-Lynn to demonstrate that the use of oral tradition distinguishes American Indian poetry from other contemporary poetry. The essay is a sound introduction to these writers. Another helpful introduction to contemporary poetry is *The Magic of Names: Three Native American Poets. Interviews with Norman H. Russell, Lance Henson, Jim Weaver Barnes* (ed. Patrick Hundley).

Much critical discussion has been devoted to the work of N. Scott Momaday, James Welch, and Leslie Marmon Silko. Among the articles discussing all three is Peter G. Beidler's "Animals and Human Development in the Contemporary American Indian Novel," in which he traces the authors' use of animals as fictional characters. Any study of Momaday's works should begin with his own essays on the power of oral tradition and the importance of place: "Man Made of Words," "An American Land Ethic," and "The Morality of Indian Hating." In "A Conversation with N. Scott Momaday," edited by Larry Evers, Momaday elaborates on these ideas and also explains why he feels that the ending of *House Made of Dawn* is optimistic. Momaday discusses the film of *House Made of Dawn* in "Interview with N. Scott Momaday," edited by Gretchen Bataille. Larry Evers' "Words and Place" is an authoritative and careful analysis of this difficult book. Also well done is Floyd Watkins' "Culture versus Anonymity in *House Made of Dawn*" (in his *In Time and Place*). Both articles illuminate Momaday's use of Jemez Pueblo and Navajo oral traditions. In "Incarnate Grace and the Paths of Salvation in *House Made of Dawn*," Harold S. McAllister carefully outlines the relation between the novel's Catholicism and its theme of regeneration or redemption, though he may overemphasize the role of Catholicism. Nora Baker Barry gives a good analysis of Momaday's and Hal Borland's use of a folktale in "The Bear's Son Folk Tale in *When the Legends Die* and *House Made of Dawn*." Roger Dickinson-Brown examines the significance of Momaday's work as a whole in "The Art and Importance of N. Scott Momaday." Martha Scott Trimble gives a similar survey and a brief biography in *N. Scott Momaday*.

James Welch's *Winter in the Blood* is the subject of a special issue of *American Indian Quarterly*, edited by Peter Beidler. Of special interest are the following essays from that issue: Kathleen M. Sands, "Alienation and Broken Narrative"; Nora Baker Barry, "*Winter in the Blood* as Elegy"; and A. LaVonne Brown Ruoff, "Alienation and the Female Principle." Also included are an essay and a bibliography by Ruoff on the historical background of the novel. William Thackeray thoroughly examines Welch's use of Gros Ventre oral traditions in the novel; his essay "Crying for Pity in *Winter in the Blood*" illustrates how the book's structure follows the stages of that ceremony. Both *Winter in the Blood* and Welch's poetry are discussed in provocative essays by Elaine Jahner, "Quick Paces and a Space of Mind," and by Kenneth Lincoln, "Back-Tracking James Welch." Jahner examines Welch's concept of "distance," and Lincoln suggests that Welch's sense of reality is the key to his art. "James Welch's Poetry," by Alan Velie, is the most informative analysis of Welch's poetry. Velie reveals the influence of South American surrealism on some of Welch's poems. *The Death of Jim Loney*, Welch's second novel, is discussed in a special issue of *Studies in American Indian Literatures* containing three essays: William Thackeray, "*The Death of Jim Loney* as a Half-Breed's Tragedy"; Robert Lewis, "*The Death of Jim Loney*"; and Kathleen M. Sands, "*The Death of Jim Loney*: Indian or Not."

Important to understanding the work of Leslie Marmon Silko are her own essays and interviews. In "An Old-Time Indian Attack Conducted in Two Parts," Silko criticizes white poets who use Indian themes. Silko expresses her views on literature in "Language and Literature from a Pueblo Indian Perspective." Two interviews with Silko give valuable insights into her works: "A Conversation with Leslie Marmon Silko," edited by Larry Evers and Dennis Carr, and "Stories and Their Tellers: A Conversation with Leslie Silko," edited by Dexter Fisher. Additional information appears in Silko's letter to Abraham Chapman, published in his *Literature of the American Indians*. The best general introduction to Silko's work is Per Seyersted's *Leslie Marmon Silko*. A. LaVonne Brown Ruoff examines Silko's short stories in "Ritual and Renewal." The *American Indian Quarterly* has devoted a special issue, edited by Kathleen M. Sands, to Silko's *Ceremony*. Especially helpful is Elaine Jahner's analysis of the novel's organization in "An Act of Attention." In the same issue Robert Bell illustrates Silko's use of the Navajo Red Antway Chant in "Circular Design in *Ceremony*," and Larry Evers emphasizes Silko's role as a storyteller and cautions against reducing our examination of what is American Indian in texts to mere ethnographic analysis in his "A Response: Going along with the Story."

Increasingly, critics are giving attention to the works of other contemporary American Indian writers as well as to Momaday, Welch, and Silko. Hyemeyohsts Storm (Cheyenne) has aroused controversy with his novel *Seven Arrows*. Rupert Costo (Cahuilla) attacks Storm's misrepresentation of Cheyenne rituals, an issue voiced first by members of the Northern Cheyenne tribe, in "*Seven Arrows* Desecrates Cheyenne." In "A Conversation with Vine Deloria, Jr.," edited by Larry Evers, Deloria defends the right of Storm or any writer to deal with Indian subject matter creatively. Bernd Peyer discusses the novel at length in his *Hyemeyohsts Storm's Seven Arrows*.

Among the most prolific contemporary writers is Gerald Vizenor (Ojibwe), who discusses his treatment of fictitious Indians and the evolution of his work in "An Interview with Gerald Vizenor," edited by Neal Bowers and Charles L. P. Sllet. A. LaVonne Brown Ruoff examines Vizenor's use of the Trickster/Transformer—Culture Hero cycle in her review of *Darkness in Saint Louis Bearheart*.

Two essays by Simon Ortiz (Acoma) are good introductions to his work: "Song/Poetry and Language" and "Toward a National Indian Literature." Willard Gingerich, in "The Old Voices of Acoma," discusses the extent to which Ortiz incorporates into his work the oral traditions of his pueblo.

The poetry of Ray A. Young Bear (Mesquakie) is the subject of two recent studies. Robert L. Gish, Young Bear's former teacher, comments on three poems about old songs in "Mesquakie Singer." In "On Stereotypes," the poet Duane Niatum (Klallam) uses Young Bear's poetry to illustrate his thesis that American Indian writers are influenced by Indian as well as by Western European literary traditions.

The satire of Vine Deloria, Jr. (Sioux), is best exemplified in his *Custer Died for Your Sins* and *We Talk, You Listen: New Tribes, New Turf*. Deloria gives a good introduction to the tradition of American Indian humor in "Indian Humor." Deloria's satire continues the long tradition of Indian humor first expressed in written form by Alexander Posey and Will Rogers. Like Momaday, Deloria is a voice of the Indian literary renaissance.

Another such voice is Hanay Geiogamah (Kiowa), one of the very few Indian dramatists. His *New Native American Drama* includes three plays: *Body Indian, Foghorn,* and *49*. Jeffrey Huntsman provides a careful and informative introduction to the volume.

Contemporary American Indian literature has received a disproportionate amount of study by literary scholars. The evolution of American Indian written literature, however, and its relation to oral literatures need much more study. Research is also needed into the literary aspects of oral literatures, which scholars have neglected as an area of inquiry. As a result, the major scholarship in Indian oral literatures has been done by anthropologists, linguists, and folklorists who, for the most part, have not dealt with the literary dimensions of the material. Another area needing study is the place of American Indian literary works in mainstream American literature. While scholars have pored over the literature by immigrant Americans and their descendants, they have ignored the literatures created by American Indians. This imbalance can be addressed only through the inclusion of selections from this vast body of literature in courses on American literature and culture.

Note

1   In an earlier version, part one of this article appeared in the bibliography issue of *American Studies International*, 33, No. 3 (1981), 327–38.

Selected Periodicals

The following periodicals publish oral and written American Indian literary works or articles about Indian literatures.

A: A Journal of Contemporary Literature. 4905 Stratford Rd. East, Eagle Rock Station, CA 90041. Creative writing and essays emphasizing but not limited to American Indian literatures.

Akwesasne Notes. Mohawk Nation, via Rooseveltown, NY 13683. Issued periodically. Comprehensive newspaper that publishes its own news stories as well as reprints from both the Indian and the non-Indian press. Also publishes poetry.

American Indian Culture and Research Journal. American Indian Studies Center, 3220 Campbell Hall, Univ. of California, Los Angeles, CA 90024. Quarterly. Interdisciplinary journal.

American Indian Quarterly. Native American Studies, Univ. of California, Berkeley, CA 94720. Journal of anthropology, history, and literature.

Blue Cloud Quarterly. Marvin, SD 57251. Formerly a creative writing journal; now issues chapbooks quarterly.

Conditions. P.O. Box 56, Van Brunt Sta., Brooklyn, NY 11215. Women's literary magazine that frequently publishes poetry, fiction, essays, and art by American Indian women.

Contact II. PO Box 451, Bowling Green Sta., New York, NY 10004. Publishes creative writing and articles on creative work and small presses. Frequently publishes works by American Indian authors.

Greenfield Review. RD 1, Box 80, Greenfield Center, NY 12833. Publishes creative writing. Frequently publishes American Indian authors.

Indian Historian. American Indian Historical Soc., 1451 Masonic Ave., San Francisco, CA 94117. Quarterly indisciplinary journal. Merged with *Wassaja*, below. Included stories and poems.

Journal of American Folklore. 1703 New Hampshire Ave., NW, Washington, DC 20009. Publication of American Folklore Soc. Contains many articles on American Indian oral literatures.

Journal of Cherokee Studies. Cherokee Museum, PO Box 770-A, Cherokee, NC 28719. Interdisciplinary journal; often publishes bilingual texts of Cherokee stories.

Journal of Ethnic Studies. Western Washington Univ., Bellingham, WA 98225. Interdisciplinary journal publishing articles on multiethnic cultures.

Latin American Indian Literatures. Dept. of Hispanic Languages and Literatures, Univ. of Pittsburgh, Pittsburgh, PA 15260. Semiannual. Scholarly articles on Indian cultures in Latin America and United States (Southwest and California).

MELUS (Multi-Ethnic Literature of the United States). Dept. of English, Univ. of Cincinnati, Cincinnati, OH 45221. Scholarly articles and reviews, including many on American Indian literatures.

Minority Voices. Paul Robeson Cultural Center, 101 Walnut Bldg., Pennsylvania State Univ., University Park, PA 16802. Interdisciplinary journal of the arts.

El Nahuatzen. Room 310, Calvin Hall, Univ. of Iowa, Iowa City, IA 52242. Poetry magazine with emphasis on Chicano and American Indian writers.

NAIES. Ethnic Studies Dept., California State Polytechnic Univ., Pomona, CA 91768. Newsletter of the National Assn. of Interdisciplinary Ethnic Studies.

New Mexico Magazine. Santa Fe, NM 87501. Often publishes work of American Indian writers in its poetry section.

Puerto del Sol. Box 3E, New Mexico State Univ., Las Cruces, NM 88003. Southwestern literary magazine that frequently publishes work by American Indian authors.

SCREE. Duck Down Press, PO Box 1047, Fallon, NV 89406. Publishes work by American Indian writers.

Shantih. Box 125, Bay Ridge Sta., Brooklyn, NY 11220.

Sinister Wisdom. P.O. Box 186, Montague, MA 01351. Devoted to women's writing. Frequently publishes poetry, fiction, and biography by American Indian women. Special American Indian woman's issue, ed. Beth Brant (Mohawk), forthcoming.

South Dakota Review. Univ. of South Dakota, Vermillion, SD 57069. Quarterly. Interdisciplinary, with emphasis on Western America and Great Plains. Publishes scholarly articles as well as creative works, many about or by American Indians.

Studies in American Indian Literature. Dept. of English and Comparative Literature, Columbia Univ., New York, NY 10027. Quarterly newsletter of the Assn. for Studies in American Indian Literatures. Publishes short articles, reviews, and bibliographies as well as special issues.

Sun Tracks: An American Indian Literary Annual. Dept. of English, Univ. of Arizona, Tucson, AZ 85721. Formerly a quarterly. Best source for contemporary Indian writing. Has also published interviews with Indian writers and collections of regional Indian literature.

Wassaja. 1451 Masonic Ave., San Francisco, CA 94117. Originally a newspaper. Merged with *Indian Historian* to become an Indian journal. Ceased publication.

Western American Literature. Dept. of English, Colorado State Univ., Ft. Collins, CO 80521. Quarterly. Publishes articles on literature of the American West, including several on American Indian literatures.

Yardbird Reader. Yardbird Publishing, Inc., Box 2370, Sta. A, Berkeley, CA 94702. Literary magazine of minority poetry.

Special Issues of Periodicals

A: A Journal of Contemporary Literature. 4905 Stratford Rd. East, Eagle Rock Station, CA 90041.

Education Issue: Contemporary Native American Literature, 4, No. 2 (Fall 1979). Criticism of Indian writers, essays, poetry.

Native Women of New Mexico, 3, No. 2 (Fall 1978). Selections by American Indian women writers.

Special Native People's Issue, 2, No. 2 (Fall 1977).

American Indian Culture and Research Journal. American Indian Studies Center, 3220 Campbell Hall, Univ. of California, Los Angeles, CA 90024.

American Indian Translation, 4, Nos. 1 and 2 (1980). Ed. Kenneth Lincoln. Includes introduction, critical analyses, and translations of Indian texts as well as poetry by William Oandasan.

American Indian Quarterly. Native American Studies, Univ. of California, Berkeley, CA 94720. For back issues of vols. 1–5, write PO Box 443, Hurst, TX 76053.

Symposium Issue on Leslie Marmon Silko's *Ceremony*, 5, No. 1 (1979). Ed. Kathleen M. Sands. Critical essays, discussions, and response. For authors and titles see page 308.

Symposium Issue on James Welch's *Winter in the Blood*, 4, No. 2 (1978). Ed. Peter G. Beidler. Critical essays, history, discussion, and responses. For authors and titles see pages 307–08.

Book Forum. Hudson River Press, Box 126, Rhinecliff, NY 12574.

American Indians Today: Their Thought, Their Literature, Their Art, 5, No. 3 (1981). Ed. Elaine Jahner.

Chronicles of Oklahoma. Oklahoma Historical Soc., Historical Bldg., Oklahoma City, OK 73105.

Will Rogers: A Centennial Tribute, 57, No. 3 (1979). Ed. Arnell M. Gibson. Biographical, bibliographic, and critical essays on Rogers.

Dakotah Territory. Black Hills Genealogy Club, Box 372, Rapid City, SD 57701.

Native American Issue, 6 (1973–74). Genealogical magazine.

Denver Quarterly. Univ. of Denver, Denver, CO 80208.

Native American Literature, 14, No. 4 (Winter 1980). Ed. Leland Chambers. Critical essays, fiction, and poetry.

Greenfield Review. RD 1, Box 80, Greenfield Center, NY 12833.
  American Indian Writing Issue, 9, Nos. 3–4 (Winter 1981–82). Ed. Joseph
  Bruchac. Prose and fiction, poetry and translations.
Indian Historian. 1451 Masonic Ave., San Francisco, CA 94117.
  Dreams and Drumbeats, 9, No. 2 (Spring 1976). Poems, stories.
New America: A Review. Dept. of American Studies, Univ. of New Mexico,
  Albuquerque, NM 87131.
  Native American Issue, 2, No. 3 (Summer-Fall 1975). Ed. Geary Hobson.
  Essays, poems, stories.
New Literary History. Johns Hopkins Univ., Baltimore, MD 21218.
  Oral Cultures and Oral Performances, 8, No. 3 (Spring 1977). Essays on
  oral traditions, including two on Indian literature by Dennis Tedlock and
  Dell Hymes.
Nimrod. Univ. of Tulsa, Tulsa, OK 74104.
  Native American Issue, 16, No. 2 (Spring-Summer 1972). Ed. William
  Brandon. Essays on Indian arts and history and creative writing by In-
  dian authors.
SCREE. Duck Down Press, Box 1047, Fallon, NV 89406.
  Native American Issue, Nos. 11–12 (1979). Ed. Kirk Robertson. Poetry and
  fiction.
Shantih. PO Box 125, Bay Ridge Sta., Brooklyn NY 11220.
  Native American Issue, 4, No. 2 (Summer-Fall 1979). Ed. Roberta Hill
  (Oneida) and Brian Swann. Essays, creative writing, and art.
Sinister Wisdom. PO Box 186, Montague, MA 01351. Forthcoming special
  American Indian woman's issue, ed. Beth Brant (Mohawk).
South Dakota Review. Dakota Press, Univ. of South Dakota, Vermillion, SD
  57069.
  American Indian II, 9, No. 2 (Summer 1971). Ed. John Milton. Rpt. Ver-
  million: Dakota Press, 1971. Essays, creative writing, art.
  The American Indian Speaks, 7, No. 2 (Summer 1969). Ed. John Milton.
  Rpt. Vermillion: Dakota Press, 1969. Essays, creative writing, art.
Spawning the Medicine River. U.S. Dept. of the Interior, Bureau of Indian
  Affairs, Inst. of American Indian Arts, College of Santa Fe Campus, St.
  Michael Dr., Santa Fe, NM 87501.
  Special issue. Nos. 2–3 (Winter-Spring 1980). Guest author Ray A. Young
  Bear. Includes Native American High School Creative Writing Awards.
  Works by students in Inst. of American Indian Arts.
Studies in American Indian Literature. Dept. of English and Comparative
  Literature, Columbia Univ., New York, NY 10027.
  American Indians in Film and Literature, 4, No. 1 (Winter 1980). Ed.
  Gretchen Bataille. Articles, interview with N. Scott Momaday, anno-
  tated bibliography, "Indians in the Movies."

Hanta Yo Issue, 3, No. 4 (Winter 1979). Collection of reviews on the novel by Ruth Beebe Hill.

James Welch, *The Death of Jim Loney*, 5, Nos. 3–4 (Fall 1981). Critical essays on Welch's second novel.

Forthcoming: special issues on Ray A. Young Bear's *Winter of the Salamander* and Duane Niatum's *Harvester of Dreams*.

Selected Presses

Small Presses

The following presses publish works by American Indian authors or books about American Indians:

A Press
4905 Stratford Rd. East
Eagle Rock Station, CA 90041

Ahsahta Press
University Bookstore
Boise State Univ.
Boise, ID 83725

Akwesasne Notes.
Mohawk Nation
Via Rooseveltown, NY 13683

American Indian Studies Center
3220 Campbell Hall
Univ. of California
Los Angeles, CA 90024

Apple-wood Press
Box 2870
Cambridge, MA 02139

Archangel Books
2922 C Otis St.
Berkeley, CA 94703

Association for Study of American Indian Literatures
Dept. of English and Comparative Literature
Columbia Univ.
New York, NY 10027

Bear Claw Press
215 Bucholz Ct.
Ann Arbor, MI 48104

Blackberry Press
Box 186
Brunswick, ME 04011

Blue Cloud Quarterly (poetry chapbooks)
Marvin, SD 57251

Blue Moon Press
Dept. of English
Univ. of Arizona
Tucson, AZ 85721

Bookslinger Press
2163 Ford Parkway
St. Paul, MN 55116
(formerly associated with Truck Distribution)

Chalatien Press
5859 Woodleigh Dr.
Carmichael, CA 95608

Clearwater Publishing Company
1995 Broadway
New York, NY 10023

Earl M. Coleman Enterprises
PO Box 143
Pine Plains, NY 12567

The Consortium of Johnson-O'Malley
  Committee of Region Four
State of Washington
PO Box 341
Toppenish, WA 98948
(Yakima materials)

Crossing Press
17 West Main St.
Trumansburg, NY 14886

Duck Down Press
Box 1047
Fallon, NV 89406

Energy Earth Communications
PO Box 8431
Houston, TX 77004
(distributor of Third World publishers)

Greenfield Review Press
RD 1, Box 80
Greenfield Center, NY 12833

Gusto Press
2960 Philip Ave.
Bronx, NY 10465

Hardscrabble Books
Rt. 2, Box 285
Berrien Springs, MI 49103
(local or regional Michigan books)

Heidelberg Graphics
PO Box 3606
Chico, CA 95927

Indian Historian
1451 Masonic Ave.
San Francisco, CA 94117

Jawbone Press
17023 Fifth Ave., NE
Seattle, WA 98155

Kennikat Press
90 South Bayles Ave.
Port Washington, NY 11050

Kitchen Table: Women of Color Press
PO Box 592, Van Brant Sta.
Brooklyn, NY 11215

NAIES Publications (National Assn. of
  Interdisciplinary Ethnic Studies)
Ethnic Studies Dept.
California State Polytechnic Univ.
Pomona, CA 91768

Naturegraph Publishers, Inc.
PO Box 1075
Happy Camp, CA 96039

Navajo Community College Press
Many Farms, AZ 86538

Nez Perce Tribe
Box 305
Lapwai, ID 83540

Nodin Press
c/o The Bookmen, Inc.
519 N. Third St.
Minneapolis, MN 55401

North Country Community College
  Press
Saranac Lake, NY 12983

Northland Press
PO Box N
Flagstaff, AZ 86002

Point Riders Press
Box 2731
Norman, OK 73070

Reed & Cannon
Room 311
2140 Shattuck Ave.
Berkeley, CA 94704
(Third World authors)

Samisdat
Box 129
Richford, VT 05476

Serendipity
1790 Shattuck Ave.
Berkeley, CA 94709

Seven Buffaloes Press
Box 214
Big Timber, MT 59011

Sinte Gleska College Bookstore
Rosebud, SD 57570
(Sioux materials)

Strawberry Press
PO Box 456
Bowling Green Sta.
New York, NY 10004

Sun Stone
PO Box 2321
Sante Fe, NM 87501

Sun Tracks Press
Dept. of English
Univ. of Arizona
Tucson, AZ 85721

Taurean Horn
601 Leavenworth St., #45
San Francisco, CA 94109

Territorial Press
PO Box 775
Moorhead College
Moorhead, NM 56560

Unicorn Press
PO Box 3307
Greensboro, NC 27402

Walking Bull, Gilbert and Montana
11750 Mistletoe Rd.
Monmouth, OR 97361
(publish and distribute
own books)

White Pine Press
109 Duerstein St.
Buffalo, NY 14210

Working Man's Press
1790 Shattuck Ave.
Berkeley, CA 94709

Ye Galleon Press
PO Box 25
Fairfield, WA 99012

Canadian Presses

J. J. Douglas
1875 Welch St.
North Vancouver, B.C. V7P 1B7

McClelland & Stewart
25 Hollinger Rd.
Toronto, Ont. M4B 3G2

Press Gang Publishers
602 Powell St.
Vancouver, B.C.

Reprint Presses

The following reprint presses publish American Indian materials. Because some reprint presses advertise large selections of materials that may not be in print or even scheduled, ask if the material is actually available before ordering:

AMS Press, 56 E. 13th St., New York, NY 10003
   Special catalog: *The Indians of North America in Reprint Editions.* Not all listed are
   actually available.

Johnson Reprint Corporation, 111 Fifth Ave., New York, NY 10003

No special catalog; see general catalog under "American Indian Languages," "Anthropology," and "Archaeology."

Kraus Reprint Co., Route 100, Millwood, NY 10546

Special catalog: *Indians of North America: Books and Monographs Immediately Available.*

Rio Grande Press, PO Box 33, Glorieta, NM 87535

Specializes in reprinting basic source documents of American history, many with new introductions, maps, indexes. Reprints many classics of history and anthropology. Uses strong bindings, not always the case with other reprint houses.

Scholarly Press, 19722 E. Nine Mile Rd., Saint Clair Shores, MI 48080

Selected reprints; publishes *Encyclopedia of Indians of the Americas.*

Works Cited

The list that follows is composed primarily of works cited in shortened form in the essays in this volume. A few other works, of interest to those studying American Indian literatures, are also included.

American Indian authors are identified by their tribal affiliations, within parentheses; alternative given names are included within brackets. The names of publishers have been shortened, usually to the first word of a multiple-word firm (e.g., Harcourt Brace Jovanovich is cited as Harcourt). The following abbreviations are used for frequently cited journals and series:

AICRJ	American Indian Culture and Research Journal
AIQ	American Indian Quarterly
APAMNH	Anthropological Papers of the American Museum of Natural History
ARBAE	Annual Report of the Bureau of American Ethnology
BBAE	Bulletin of the Bureau of American Ethnology
CE	College English
CO	Chronicles of Oklahoma
CUCA	Columbia University Contributions to Anthropology
JAF	Journal of American Folklore
JES	Journal of Ethnic Studies
MAAA	Memoirs of the American Anthropological Association
MAFS	Memoirs of the American Folklore Society
PAES	Publications of the American Ethnological Society
PBHS	Publications of the Buffalo [N.Y.] Historical Society
SAIL	Studies in American Indian Literature
WAL	Western American Literature

Abeita, Louise [Eyehshire] (Isleta). *I Am a Pueblo Indian Girl.* New York: Morrow, 1939.

Alexander, Hartley Burr. "Indian Songs and English Verse." *American Speech,* 1 (1926), 571–75.

———. *The Mystery of Life: A Poetization of the "Hako," a Pawnee Ceremony.* Chicago: Open Court, 1930.

———. "The Poetry of the American Indian." *Nation,* 13 Dec. 1919, pp. 757–59.

———. *The World's Rim: Great Mysteries of the North American Indians.* 1953; rpt. Lincoln: Univ. of Nebraska Press, 1967.

Allen, Paula Gunn (Laguna-Sioux). "Answering the Deer: Genocide and Continuance in American Indian Women's Poetry," *AICRJ*, 6, No. 1 (1982).

———. *The Blind Lion*. Berkeley: Thorp Springs, 1975.

———. *A Cannon between My Knees*. New York: Strawberry, 1981.

———. *Coyote's Daylight Trip*. Albuquerque: La Confluencia, 1978.

———. "The Feminine Landscape of Leslie Marmon Silko's *Ceremony*." *AIQ*, 5, No. 1 (1979), 7–12.

———. "The Grace That Remains." In Jahner, *Book Forum*, 5, No. 3 (1981). Rpt. as *American Indians Today*. New York: Horizon, 1982.

———. "The Sacred Hoop: A Contemporary Indian Perspective on American Indian Literature." In Chapman, *Literature of the American Indians*, pp. 111–36.

———. *Shadow Country*. Native American Series. Los Angeles: Univ. of California, 1982.

———. "Sipapu: A Cultural Perspective." Diss. Univ. of New Mexico, 1975.

———. *Star Child*. Marvin, S. Dak.: Blue Cloud Quarterly, 1981.

———. "A Stranger in My Own Life: Alienation in American Indian Prose and Poetry." *MELUS*, 7, No. 2 (1980), 3–19.

———. *The Woman Who Owned the Shadows*. Boston: Persephone, 1983.

———. *Woman's Way*. New York: Kitchen Table: Women of Color Press. Forthcoming.

———, and Patricia Clark Smith. "Chee Dostoyevsky Rides the Reservation: American Indian Literature since Momaday." In Taylor, *Literary History*.

Allen, T. D. See Mitchell, Emerson Blackhorse.

Allen, Terry, ed. *Arrows Four: Prose and Poetry by Young American Indians*. New York: Pocket, 1974.

———, and Mae Durham, eds. *The Whispering Wind: Poetry by Young American Indians*. Garden City: Doubleday, 1972.

Alworth, E. Paul. *Will Rogers*. United States Authors, 236. Boston: Twayne, 1974.

Anauta (Eskimo). *Land of Good Shadows: The Life Story of Anauta, an Eskimo Woman*. Ed. Heluiz Chandler Washburne. New York: Day, 1940.

Anderson, Chester G., ed. *Growing Up in Minnesota*. Minneapolis: Univ. of Minnesota Press, 1976.

Anderson, Lynn. *Medicine Woman*. New York: Harper, 1981.

Apes, William (Pequot). *Eulogy on King Philip, as Pronounced at the Odeon, in Federal Street, Boston, by the Rev. William Apes, an Indian*. Boston: Author, 1836.

———. *The Experience of Five Christian Indians of the Pequod Tribe; or, The Indian's Looking-Glass for the White Man*. Boston: J. B. Dow, 1833.

———. *Indian Nullification of the Unconstitutional Laws of Massachusetts, Relative to the Marshpee Tribe; or, The Pretended Riot Explained*. 1835; rpt. with Foreword by Jack Campisi, Pine Plains, N.Y.: Coleman, 1980.

———. *A Son of the Forest: The Experience of William Apes, a Native of the Forest, Comprising a Notice of the Pequod Tribe of Indians, Written by Himself*. New York: Author, 1829; New York: G. E. Bunce, 1831.

Armstrong, Robert Plant. *Wellspring*. Berkeley: Univ. of California Press, 1975.

Armstrong, Virginia, ed. *I Have Spoken: American History through the Voices of the Indians*. Chicago: Swallow, 1971.

Arnett, Carroll (Cherokee). *Tsalagi*. New Rochelle, N.Y.: Elizabeth, 1976.

Astrov, Margot. "The Concept of Motion as the Psychological Leitmotif of Navaho Life and Literature." *JAF*, 63 (1950), 45–56.

——, ed. *The Winged Serpent: An Anthology of American Indian Poetry*. 1946; rpt. as *American Indian Prose and Poetry*. New York: Capricorn, 1962.

Austin, Mary. "Aboriginal Fiction." *Saturday Review of Literature*, 28 Dec. 1929, pp. 597–99.

——. *The American Rhythm: Studies and Reexpression of Amer-Indian Songs*. 1923; rpt. Boston: Houghton, 1930; Totowa, N.J.: Cooper Square, 1971.

——. "Artist Life in the United States." *Nation*, 11 Feb. 1925, pp. 151–52.

——. "Imagism: Original and Aboriginal." *Dial*, 23 Aug. 1919, pp. 162–63.

——. "Indian Songs." Rev. of *Dawn Boy* by Eda Lou Walton. *Saturday Review of Literature*, 10 April 1924, p. 704.

——. *Isidro*. 1904; rpt. New York: Irvington, 1979.

——. *Literary America: The Mary Austin Letters*. Ed. T. M. Pearce. Westport, Conn.: Greenwood, 1979.

——. "Non-English Writings: Aboriginal." In *Cambridge History of American Literature*. Cambridge: Cambridge Univ. Press, 1933, III, 626–28.

——. "The Path on the Rainbow." *Dial*, 31 May 1919, pp. 569–70.

——. "The Road to Spring." *Nation*, 13 Oct. 1926, pp. 77–80.

Babcock-Abrahams, Barbara. "'A Tolerated Margin of Mess': The Trickster and His Tales Reconsidered." *Journal of the Folklore Institute*, 11, No. 3 (1975), 147–86.

Bahr, Donald M. *Pima and Papago Ritual Oratory: A Study of Three Texts*. San Francisco: Indian Historian, 1975.

——. *Rainhouse and Ocean: Speeches for the Papago Year*. Flagstaff: Museum of Northern Arizona Press, 1979.

——. *Staying Sickness*. Tucson: Univ. of Arizona Press, 1971.

——, et al. *Piman Shamanism and Staying Sickness: Ká:cim Múmkidag*. Tucson: Univ. of Arizona Press, 1974.

——. See also Underhill, Ruth M.

Bahti, Tom. *Southwestern Indian Arts and Crafts*. Las Vegas: K. C. Publications, 1966.

Bailey, Garrick. "John Joseph Mathews." In Liberty, *American Indian Intellectuals*, pp. 205–14.

Bannan, Helen M. "Spider Woman's Web: Mothers and Daughters in Southwestern Native American Literature." In Broner and Davidson, *Embraced and Embattled*, pp. 268–79.

Barnes, Nellie. *American Indian Verse: Characteristics of Style*. Bulletin of the University of Kansas Humanistic Studies, 2, No. 4. Lawrence: Univ. of Kansas.

Barnett, Leona G. "*Este Cate Emunkv:* Red Man Always." *CO*, 46 (1968), 20–40.

Barnett, Louise K. *The Ignoble Savage: American Literary Racism, 1790–1890*. Westport, Conn.: Greenwood, 1975.

Barnouw, Victor. "A Psychological Interpretation of a Chippewa Origin Legend." *JAF*, 68 (1955), 73–85, 211–23, 341–55.

——, ed. *Wisconsin Chippewa Myths and Tales and Their Relation to Chippewa Life*. Madison: Univ. of Wisconsin Press, 1977.

Barry, Nora Baker. "The Bear's Son Folk Tale in *When the Legends Die* and *House Made of Dawn*." *WAL*, 12 (1978), 275–87.

——. "*Winter in the Blood* as Elegy." *AIQ*, 4 (1978), 149–57.

Bataille, Gretchen M. "American Indian Literature: Traditions and Translations." *MELUS*, 6, No. 4 (1979), 17–26.

———, ed. "Interview with N. Scott Momaday." *SAIL*, 4, No. 2 (1980), 1–3.

———, David Gradwohl, and Charles L. Silet, eds. *The Worlds between Two Rivers: Perspectives on American Indians in Iowa.* Ames: Iowa State Univ. Press, 1978.

———, and Kathleen Mullen Sands. *Native American Women in a Changing World: Their Lives as They Told Them.* Lincoln: Univ. of Nebraska Press, forthcoming.

———, and Charles L. Silet, eds. *The Pretend Indians: Images of Native Americans in the Movies.* Ames: Iowa State Univ. Press, 1980.

Bauman, Richard. "Differential Identity and the Social Base of Folklore." In Paredes and Bauman, *Towards New Perspectives in Folklore.*

———. *Verbal Art as Performance.* Rowley, Mass.: Newberry, 1978.

———, and Joel Sherzer, eds. *Explorations in the Ethnography of Speaking.* New York: Cambridge Univ. Press, 1974.

Beavert, Virginia (Yakima), et al., eds. *Anadu Iwacha; The Way It Was: Yakima Indian Legend Book.* Yakima, Wash.: Franklin, 1974.

Beckwith, Martha Warren. "Mythology of the Oglala Dakota." *JAF*, 43 (1930), 339–442.

Beckwourth, James P. *The Life and Adventures of James P. Beckwourth, Mountaineer, Scout and Pioneer, and Chief of the Crow Nation of Indians.* Ed. Thomas D. Bonner. 1856; rpt. Lincoln: Univ. of Nebraska Press, 1972.

Begay, Harrison. *Sacred Mountains of the Navajo in Four Paintings.* Introd. Leland Clifton Wyman. Flagstaff: Museum of Northern Arizona, 1967.

Beidler, Peter G. "Animals and Human Development in the Contemporary American Indian Novel." *WAL*, 14 (1979), 133–48.

Bell, Robert. "Circular Design in *Ceremony.*" *AIQ*, 5 (1979), 47–62.

Ben-Amos, Dan. "Analytical Categories and Ethnic Genres." In Ben-Amos, *Folklore Genres.*

———, ed. *Folklore Genres.* Austin: Univ. of Texas Press, 1976.

Benedict, Ruth F. *Concept of the Guardian Spirit in North America.* 1923; rpt. Millwood, N.Y.: Kraus, n.d.

———, ed. *Tales of the Cochiti Indians.* 1931; rpt. New York: Gordon and Breach, 1976; Saint Clair Shores, Mich.: Scholarly, n.d.; Albuquerque: Univ. of New Mexico Press, 1981.

———. "The Vision in Plains Culture." *American Anthropologist*, 24 (1922), 1–23.

———. *Zuni Mythology.* CUCA, 21. 1935; rpt. 2 vols. New York: AMS, 1969.

Bennett, Kay (Navajo). *Kaibah: Recollections of a Navajo Girlhood.* Los Angeles: Western Lore, 1964.

Bennett, Noël. *The Weaver's Pathway: A Clarification of the Spirit Trail in Navajo Weaving.* Flagstaff: Northland, 1974.

Berger, Thomas. *Little Big Man.* 1964; rpt. New York: Fawcett, 1978; New York: Delacorte, 1979.

Berkhofer, Robert F., Jr. *The White Man's Indian: Images of the American Indian from Columbus to the Present.* New York: Knopf, 1978.

Berry, Brewton. *Almost White.* New York: Macmillan, 1969.

Betzinez, Jason (Apache). *I Fought with Geronimo.* With Wilbur Sturtevant Nye. Harrisburg, Pa.: Stackpole, 1959.

Bevis, William. "American Indian Verse Translations." *CE*, 35 (1974), 693–703. Rpt. in Chapman, *Literature of the American Indians*, pp. 306–23.

Bierhorst, John. "American Verbal Art and the Role of Literary Critics." *JAF*, 88 (1975), 401–08.

——, ed. *Four Masterworks of American Indian Literature*. New York: Farrar, 1974.

——. *In the Trail of the Wind: American Indian Poems and Ritual Orations*. New York: Farrar, 1971.

——, trans. *The Red Swan: Myths and Tales of the American Indians*. New York: Farrar, 1976.

Big Winnebago. See Blowsnake, Sam.

Bird, Robert Montgomery. *Nick of the Woods*. 1837. Ed. Curtis Dahl. New Haven: College and University Press, 1967.

Black Bear, Ben, Sr. (Sioux), and R. D. Theisz, eds. *Songs and Dances of the Lakota*. Rosebud, S. Dak.: Sinte Gleska College, 1976.

Blackbird, Andrew J. [Mackawdebenessy] (Ottawa). *History of the Ottawa and Chippewa Indians of Michigan; a Grammar of Theirr [sic] Language, and Personal and Family History of the Author*. 1887. Republished as *Complete Both Early and Late History of the Ottawa and Chippewa Indians. . . .* 1897; rpt. Petosky, Mich.: Little Traverse Regional History Soc., 1977.

Black Elk (Sioux). *Black Elk Speaks: Being the Life Story of a Holy Man of the Oglala Sioux*. Ed. John G. Neihardt. 1932; rpt. Lincoln: Univ. of Nebraska Press, 1961; New York: Pocket, 1961.

——. *The Sacred Pipe: Black Elk's Account of the Seven Rites of the Oglala Sioux*. Ed. Joseph Epes Brown. 1953; rpt. Baltimore: Penguin, 1971; Norman: Univ. of Oklahoma Press, 1975.

Black Hawk (Sioux). *Black Hawk: An Autobiography*. Ed. Donald Jackson. Gloucester, Mass.: Peter Smith, 1955; Urbana: Univ. of Illinois Press, 1964.

Blish, Helen H. *A Pictographic History of the Oglala Sioux*. Lincoln: Univ. of Nebraska Press, 1967.

Blodgett, Harold. *Samson Occom*. Dartmouth College Manuscript Series, 3. Hanover, N.H.: Dartmouth Coll. Press, 1935.

Bloomfield, Leonard. *Menominee Texts*. PAES, 12. 1928; rpt. New York, AMS, n.d.

Blowsnake, Sam [Big Winnebago; Crashing Thunder] (Winnebago). *The Autobiography of a Winnebago*. Ed. Paul Radin. 1920; rpt. New York: Dover, 1963.

Boas, Franz. "The Development of Folk-Tales and Myths." *Scientific Monthly*, 3 (1916), 335–43. Rpt. in Boas, *Race, Language, and Culture*, pp. 397–406.

——. "Dissemination of Tales among the Natives of North America." *JAF*, 4 (1891), 13–20. Rpt. in Boas, *Race, Language, and Culture*, pp. 437–45.

——. "The Growth of Indian Mythologies." *JAF*, 9 (1896), 1–11. Rpt. in Boas, *Race, Language, and Culture*, pp. 425–36.

——. *Handbook of American Indian Languages*. BBAE, 40, Pts. 1–2. 1911–22; rpt. New York: Humanities, 1969.

——. *Keresan Texts*. 2 vols. PAES, 8. 1928; rpt. New York: AMS, 1974.

——. *Kwakiutl Culture as Reflected in Mythology*. MAFS, 28. 1935; rpt. Millwood, N.Y.: Kraus, 1970.

——. *Kwakiutl Tales*. CUCA, 2. 1910; rpt. New York: AMS, 1969.

————. "Mythology and Folk-Tales of the North American Indians." *JAF*, 27 (1914), 374–410. Rpt. in Boas, *Race, Language, and Culture*, pp. 451–90.

————. *Race, Language, and Culture*. 1940; rpt. New York: Free Press, 1966.

————. "Stylistic Aspects of Primitive Literature." *JAF*, 38 (1925), 329–39. Rpt. in Boas, *Race, Language, and Culture*, pp. 491–502; Chapman, *Literature of the American Indians*, pp. 240–52.

————, and Henry W. Tate, eds. *Tsimshian Mythology*. BBAE, 31. 1916; rpt. New York: Johnson, 1970.

————. See also Teit, James.

Bonnin, Gertrude. See Zitkala Sa.

"Bonnin, Gertrude Simmons." *Notable American Women, 1607–1950: A Biographical Dictionary*. Cambridge: Harvard Univ. Press, 1971.

Bowering, Marilyn, and David Day, eds. *Many Voices: An Anthology of Contemporary Canadian Indian Poetry*. Vancouver: Douglas, 1977.

Boudinot, Elias [Galagina] (Cherokee). *Poor Sarah; or, Religion Exemplified in the Life and Death of an Indian Woman*. 1823. Rpt. as *Poor Sarah; or, The Indian Woman*. 1833; rpt. New Echota, Okla.: Mission, 1843.

Brackenridge, Hugh Henry. *Modern Chivalry*. 1792–97. Ed. Lewis Leary. New Haven: Coll. and Univ. Press, 1965.

Bradford, William. *A History of Plymouth Plantation*. 1646. Ed. Charles F. Adams et al. 2 vols. 1912; rpt. New York: Russell, 1968.

Brand, Johanna. *The Life and Death of Anna Mae Aquash*. Toronto: J. Lorimer, 1978.

Brandon, William. *The Last Americans: The Indian in American Culture*. New York: McGraw-Hill, 1974.

————, ed. *The Magic World: American Indian Songs and Poems*. New York: Morrow, 1970.

Brant, Charles S. See Whitewolf, Jim.

Braudy, Susan. "'We Will Remember' Survival School: The Women and Children of the American Indian Movement." *Ms. Magazine*, July 1976, pp. 77–80, 94, 120.

Brininstool, E. A. See Standing Bear, Luther.

Brinton, Daniel G. *Aboriginal American Authors and Their Productions, Especially Those in the Native Language: A Chapter in the History of Literature*. 1883; rpt. New York: Gordon, n.d.

————. *American Hero-Myths: A Study in the Native Religions of the Western Continent*. 1882; rpt. New York: Johnson, 1970.

Bromwich, David. "New Poetry Made a Little Less Private." *New York Times Book Review*, 16 June 1974, p. 7.

Broner, E. M., and Cathy N. Davidson, eds. *Embraced and Embattled: A History of Mothers and Daughters*. New York: Ungar, 1979.

Bronson, Ruth Muskrat (Cherokee). *Indians Are People Too*. New York: Friendship, 1944.

Brown, Charles Brockden. *Edgar Huntly; or, Memoirs of a Sleepwalker*. 1799. Ed. David Stineback. New Haven: Coll. and Univ. Press, 1973.

Brown, Dee. *Bury My Heart at Wounded Knee: An Indian History of the American West*. New York: Holt, 1970; rpt. New York: Bantam, 1972; New York: Washington Square, 1981.

Brown, Joseph Epes. See Black Elk.

Brown, Judith K. "Economic Organization and the Power of Women among the Iroquois." *Ethnohistory*, 17 (1970), 151–67.

Brown, Roger Dickinson. "The Art and Importance of N. Scott Momaday." *Southern Review*, 14, No. 1 (1978), 30–45.

Brown, William R. *The Imagemaker: Will Rogers and the American Dream*. Columbia: Univ. of Missouri Press, 1970.

Bruchac, Joseph (Abenaki-Métis). *The Dreams of Jesse Brown*. Austin: Cold Mountain, 1978.

———. *Entering Onondaga*. Austin: Cold Mountain, 1976.

———. *Translator's Son*. Merrick, N.Y.: Cross-Cultural Communications, 1980.

Brumble, H. David, III, ed. *An Annotated Bibliography of American Indian and Eskimo Autobiographies*. Lincoln: Univ. of Nebraska Press, 1981.

Bruns, Gerald L. *Modern Poetry and the Idea of Language: A Critical and Historical Study*. New Haven: Yale Univ. Press, 1974.

Bryant, William Cullen. *Poems*. 1821, 1875. Ed. H. C. Sturges and R. H. Stoddard. 1903; rpt. New York: AMS, 1969.

Bryde, John. *Modern Indian Psychology*. Vermillion: Dakota, 1971.

Bryson, Lyman. "Amerindian Poet." *New Republic*, 4 Jan. 1928, p. 200.

Buechner, Cecelia Bain. *The Pokagons*. 1933; rpt. Berrien Springs, Mich.: Hardscrabble, 1976.

Buller, Galen. "New Interpretations of Native American Literature: A Survival Technique." *AICRJ*, 4 (1980), 165–77.

Bunzel, Ruth, ed. *Zuni Origin Myths*. ARBAE, 47, pp. 545–609. Washington: GPO, 1932.

———. *Zuni Ritual Poetry*. ARBAE, 47. Washington, D.C.: GPO, 1930.

———. *Zuni Texts*. PAES, 15. 1933; rpt. New York, AMS, n.d.

Burlin, Natalie Curtis. See Curtis, Natalie.

Burns, Thomas. "Folkloristics: A Conception of Theory." *Western Folklore*, 36 (April 1977), 109–34.

Burnshaw, Stanley. *The Seamless Web*. New York: Braziller, 1970.

Byler, Mary G. (Cherokee), ed. *American Indian Authors for Young Readers: A Selected Bibliography*. New York: Assn. on American Indian Affairs, 1973.

Byrd, William. *History of the Dividing Line*. 1737. Ed. William K. Boyd. Raleigh, N.C.: North Carolina Historical Commission, 1929.

Cameron, Anne. *Daughters of Copper Woman*. Vancouver: Press Gang, 1981.

Campbell, Maria (Métis). *Halfbreed*. Toronto: McClelland and Stewart, 1973.

Capps, Walter Holden, ed. *Seeing with a Native Eye: Essays on Native American Religion*. New York: Harper, 1976.

Carius, Helen Slwooko (Eskimo). *Sevukakmet: Ways of Life on St. Lawrence Island*. Anchorage: Alaska Pacific Univ. Press, 1979.

Carol, Holly. "*Black Elk Speaks* and the Making of Indian Autobiography." *Genre*, 12 (1979), 117–36.

Carpenter, Edmund. "Eskimo Poetry." *Explorations*, 4 (1955), 101–11.

Castañeda, Carlos. *Journey to Ixtlan: The Lessons of Don Juan*. New York: Simon, 1972.

———. *A Separate Reality: Further Conversations with Don Juan.* New York: Simon, 1971.

———. *Tales of Power.* New York: Simon, 1974.

———. *The Teachings of Don Juan: A Yaqui Way of Knowledge.* Berkeley: Univ. of California Press, 1968; New York: Simon, 1973.

Castro, Michael A. "Interpreting the Indian: Twentieth-Century Poets and the Native Americans." Diss. Washington Univ. 1981.

Cather, Willa. *Death Comes for the Archbishop.* 1926; rpt. New York: Random, 1971.

Challacombe, Doris. "Alexander Lawrence Posey." *CO,* 11 (1933), 1011–18.

Chapman, Abraham, ed. *Literature of the American Indians: Views and Interpretations.* New York: Meridian-NAL, 1975.

Chester, Laura, and Sharon Barba, eds. *Rising Tides: Twentieth Century American Women Poets.* New York: Washington Square Pocket, 1973.

Chief Eagle, Dallas (Sioux). *Winter Count.* Denver: Golden Bell, 1968.

Chona, Maria (Papago). *The Autobiography of a Papago Woman.* Ed. Ruth M. Underhill. MAAA, 46. 1936; rpt. Millwood, N.Y.: Kraus, 1974; New York: Holt, 1979.

Christensen, Rosemary A. "Indian Women: An Historical and Personal Perspective." *Pupil Personnel Services,* 4 (July 1975), 12–22.

Clark, Blue (Creek). "The Literary Will Rogers." *CO,* 57 (1979), 385–94; and in Gibson, *Will Rogers,* pp. 133–42.

Clark, Ella E. *Indian Legends from the Northern Rockies.* 1966; rpt. Norman: Univ. of Oklahoma Press, 1977.

Clark, Julius Taylor. *The Ojibway Conquest.* New York: Putnam, 1850.

Clark, La Verne H. *They Sang for Horses: The Impact of the Horse on Navajo and Apache Folklore.* Tucson: Univ. of Arizona Press, 1966.

Clarke, Peter Dooyentate (Wyandott). *Origin and Traditional History of the Wyandotts, and Sketches of Other Indian Tribes of North America: True Traditional Stories of Tecumseh and His League, in the Years 1811 and 1812.* Toronto: Hunter, Ross, 1870.

Clemens, Samuel L. *The Adventures of Tom Sawyer.* 1876. Ed. John C. Gerber et al. Berkeley: Univ. of California Press, 1980.

———. *The Autobiography of Mark Twain.* Ed. Charles Neider. New York: Harper, 1959.

———. "Fenimore Cooper's Literary Offenses." In *Literary Essays,* Vol. 10 of Author's National Edition of *The Writings of Mark Twain.* New York: Harper, 1918.

———. *Mark Twain's Hannibal, Huck & Tom.* Ed. Walter Blair. Berkeley: Univ. of California Press, 1969.

———. *Roughing It.* 1872. Ed. Franklin R. Rogers and Paul Baender. Berkeley: Univ. of California Press, 1972.

Cochise, Ciye N. (Apache). *The First Hundred Years of Nino Cochise.* New York: Pyramid, 1972.

Collaer, Paul, et al. *Music of the Americas: An Illustrated Music Ethnology of Eskimo and American Indian Peoples.* London: Curzon, 1970.

Collier, John, Sr. *Patterns and Ceremonials of the Indians of the Southwest.* New York: Dutton, 1949.

Colson, Elizabeth, ed. *Autobiographies of Three Pomo Women.* Berkeley: Dept. of Anthropology, Univ. of California, 1974.

Concha, Joseph L. (Taos). *Lonely Deer.* Taos, N. Mex.: Red Willow Soc., 1969.

Connors, Maureen E. "A Selected Bibliography of Melville Jacobs through Early 1966." *International Journal of American Linguistics*, 32 (1968), 288–89.

Cook[-Lynn], Elizabeth (Sioux). "American Indian Literature in Servitude." *Indian Historian*, 10 (Winter 1977), 3–6.

———. *Then Badger Said This.* New York: Vantage, 1977.

Copway, George (Ojibwe). *The Life, History, and Travels of Kah-ge-ga-gah-bowh (George Copway), a Young Indian Chief of the Ojebwa Nation, with a Sketch of the Present State of the Ojebwa Nation, in Regard to Christianity and Their Future Prospects.* . . . Albany, N.Y.: Weed and Parsons, 1847; Philadelphia: James Harmstead, 1847. Republished as *The Life, Letters and Speeches of Kah-ge-ga-gah-bowh, or G. Copway.* . . . New York: Benedict, 1850; and as *Recollections of a Forest Life; or, The Life and Travels of Kah-ge-ga-gah-bowh, or George Copway.* London: Gilpin, 1851.

———. *Running Sketches of Men and Places, in England, France, Germany, Belgium, and Scotland.* New York: Riker, 1851.

———. *The Traditional History and Characteristic Sketches of the Ojibway Nation.* London: Gilpin, 1851. Republished as *Indian Life and Indian History, by an Indian Author, Embracing the Traditions of the North American Indians Regarding Themselves, Particularly of That Most Important of All the Tribes, the Ojibways.* 1858; rpt. New York: AMS, 1977.

———, ed. *Copway's American Indian.* 10 July 1851. New York.

Corle, Edwin. *Fig Tree John.* 1935; rpt. New York: Liveright, 1971; New York: Pocket, 1972.

Costo, Rupert (Cahuilla). "*Seven Arrows* Desecrates Cheyenne." In Chapman, *Literature of the American Indians*, pp. 149–51.

Count, Earl W. "The Earth-Diver and the Rival Twins: A Clue to Time Correlation in North-Eurasiatic and North American Mythology." In Tax, *The Civilizations of Ancient America*, pp. 55–62.

Crane, Stephen. *Complete Short Stories and Sketches.* Ed. Thomas A. Gullason. Garden City: Doubleday, 1963.

Crashing Thunder. See Blowsnake, Sam.

Craven, Margaret. *I Heard the Owl Call My Name.* Garden City: Doubleday, 1973.

Cronyn, George W., ed. *The Path on the Rainbow: An Anthology of Songs and Chants from the Indians of North America.* Introd. Mary Austin. New York: Liveright, 1918. Republished, enlarged, as *American Indian Poetry: An Anthology of Songs and Chants.* New York: Liveright, 1934, 1970. Originally published as a special issue of *Poetry*, 1917.

Cruikshank, Julie. "Native Women in the North: An Expanding Role." *North/Nord*, 18 (Nov.-Dec. 1971), 1–7.

Crying Wind (Kickapoo). *Crying Wind.* Chicago: Moody, 1977.

Cuero, Delfina (Dieguero). *The Autobiography of Delfina Cuero, a Dieguero Indian.* Ed. Florence Shipek. Los Angeles: Dawson's Book Shop, 1968.

Cuffe, Paul (Pequot). *Narrative of the Life and Adventures of Paul Cuffe, a Pequot*

Indian, during Thirty Years Spent at Sea, and in Traveling in Foreign Lands. Vernon, [N.Y.?]: H. N. Bill, 1839.

Curtin, Jeremiah. *Creation Myths of Primitive America.* 1898; rpt. New York: Bloom, 1969.

———. See also Sapir, Edward.

Curtis, Natalie [Natalie Curtis Burlin] ed. *The Indians' Book: Songs and Legends of the American Indians.* 1907. 2nd ed. 1923; rpt. New York: Dover, 1968.

Cushing, Frank H. *Zuni Folk Tales.* 1901; rpt. New York: AMS, 1976.

Cusick, David (Tuscarora). *Sketches of Ancient History of the Six Nations.* . . . Lewiston, N.Y.: Author, 1827. 2nd ed. Lockport, N.Y.: Colley Lathrop, 1828.

Dale, Edward Everett. See Posey, Alexander Lawrence.

Darnell, Regna. "Correlates of Cree Narrative Performance." In Bauman and Sherzer, *Explorations in the Ethnography of Speaking.*

Daugherty, George. "The Techniques of Indian Composition." *The Open Court,* 41 (March 1927), 150–66.

Day, A. Grove, ed. *The Sky Clears: Poetry of the American Indians.* 1951; rpt. Lincoln: Univ. of Nebraska Press, 1964.

Day, Donald. *Will Rogers: A Biography.* New York: McKay, 1962.

De Angulo, Jaime. *Indian Tales.* 1953; rpt. New York: Hill and Wang, 1962; New York: Ballantine, 1976.

Debo, Angie. "John Rollin Ridge." *Southwest Review,* 17 (1932), 59–71.

Deloria, Ella (Sioux). *Dakota Texts.* PAES, 14. 1932; rpt. New York: AMS, 1974.

———. *Speaking of Indians.* Ed. Agnes Picotte and Paul Pavich. 1944; rpt. Vermillion: Dakota, 1979.

Deloria, Vine, Jr. (Sioux). "Anthologies: Main Course or Left-Overs?" *Journal of Ethnic Studies,* 8, No. 1 (1980), 111–15.

———. "A Conversation with Vine Deloria, Jr." *Sun Tracks,* 4 (1978), 80–88.

———. *Custer Died for Your Sins: An Indian Manifesto.* New York: Macmillan, 1969; New York: Avon, 1970.

———. *God Is Red.* New York: Grosset, 1973; New York: Macmillan, 1975; New York: Dell, 1975.

———. "Indian Humor." In his *Custer Died for Your Sins,* pp. 146–67. Rpt. in Chapman, *Literature of the American Indians,* pp. 152–69.

———. *Metaphysics of Modern Existence.* New York: Harper, 1979.

———. *We Talk, You Listen: New Tribes, New Turf.* New York: Macmillan, 1970.

DeMallie, Raymond. *Lakota Society.* Lincoln: Univ. of Nebraska, 1982.

Demetracopolou, D. "The Loon Woman Myth." *JAF,* 46 (1933), 101–28.

Densmore, Frances. *The American Indians and Their Music.* 1926; rpt. New York: Johnson, n.d.

———. *The Belief of the Indian in a Connection between Song and the Supernatural.* BBAE, 151. Washington, D.C.: GPO, 1953.

———. "The Use of Meaningless Syllables in Indian Songs." *American Anthropologist,* 45 (1943), 160–62.

———. "The Words of Indian Songs as Unwritten Literature." *JAF,* 63 (1950), 450–58.

———, ed. *Chippewa Music.* BBAE, 45 and 53. 1910 and 1913; rpt. Millwood, N.Y.: Kraus, n.d.

————. *Teton Sioux Music.* BBAE, 61. 1918; rpt. New York: Da Capo, 1972; Saint Clair Shores, Mich.: Scholarly, 1977.

Diamond, Stanley, ed. *Culture in History: Essays in Honor of Paul Radin.* New York: Columbia Univ. Press, 1961.

Dickason, David H. "Chief Simon Pokagon: The Indian Longfellow." *Indiana Magazine of History,* 52 (1961), 127–40.

Dickson, Lovat. *Half-Breed: The Story of Grey Owl (Wa-Sha-Quon-Asin).* London: Davies, 1939, 1946, 1947.

Dobie, J. Frank. *The Voice of the Coyote.* 1949; rpt. Lincoln: Univ. of Nebraska Press, 1961.

Dockstader, Frederick J. (Oneida). *The American Indian in Graduate Study: A Bibliography of Theses and Dissertations.* New York: Museum of the American Indian, 1957.

————, ed. *Great North American Indians: Profiles in Life and Leadership.* New York: Van Nostrand, 1977.

Dodge, Robert K., and Joseph B. McCullough, eds. *Voices from Wah'Kon-Tah: Contemporary Poetry of Native Americans.* New York: International, 1974.

Dominguez, Chona (Cahuilla). "Bygone Days." In Seiler, *Cahuilla Texts,* pp. 148–52.

Dorris, Michael A. (Modoc). "The Grass Still Grows, the Rivers Still Flow: Contemporary Native Americans." *Daedalus,* 110, No. 2 (1981), 43–69.

————. "Native American Literature in an Ethnohistorical Context." *CE,* 41 (1979), 147–62.

Dorsey, George A. *The Pawnee Mythology.* 1906; rpt. New York: AMS, 1974.

Dorsey, James O. *A Study of Siouan Cults.* ARBAE, 11. 1894; rpt. Seattle: Shorey, n.d.

Doyle, Helen MacKnight. *Mary Austin: Woman of Genius.* New York: Gotham, 1939.

Dozier, Edward P. *The Pueblo Indians of North America.* New York: Holt, 1970.

Drinnon, Richard. *Facing West: The Metaphysics of Indian-Hating and Empire Building.* Minneapolis: Univ. of Minnesota Press, 1980; New York: NAL, 1980.

Driver, Harold E. *Indians of North America.* 2nd ed. Chicago: Univ. of Chicago Press, 1969.

Dundes, Alan. *Analytic Essays in Folklore.* Studies in Folklore, 2. The Hague: Mouton, 1976.

————. "Earth Diver: Creation of the Mythopoeic Male." *American Anthropologist,* 64 (1962), 1032–51.

————. *Interpreting Folklore.* Bloomington: Indiana Univ. Press, 1980.

————. *The Morphology of North American Folktales.* Folklore Fellows Communications, 195. Helsinki: Suomalainen Tiedeakatemia, 1964.

————. "Texture, Text, and Context." *Southern Folklore Quarterly,* 28 (1964), 251–65.

————, ed. *The Study of Folklore.* Englewood Cliffs, N.J.: Prentice-Hall, 1965.

Durham, Mae. See Allen, Terry.

Dyk, Walter. See Left Handed and Old Mexican.

Eastburn, James W., and Robert C. Sands. *Yamoyden: A Tale of the Wars of King Philip, in Six Cantos.* New York: Author, 1820.

Eastman, Charles Alexander (Sioux). *From the Deep Woods to Civilization: Chapters in the Autobiography of an Indian.* 1916; rpt. Lincoln: Univ. of Nebraska Press, 1977.

———. *Indian Boyhood.* 1902; rpt. New York: Dover, 1971; with Introd. Frederick W. Turner III, Greenwich, Conn.: Fawcett, 1972.

———. *Indian Child Life.* Boston: Little, 1913.

———. *Indian Heroes and Great Chieftains.* Boston: Little, 1918.

———. *The Indian To-day: The Past and Future of the First Americans.* 1915; rpt. New York: AMS, 1975.

———. *Old Indian Days.* 1907; rpt. Rapid City, S. Dak.: Fenwyn, 1970.

———. *Red Hunters and the Animal People.* 1904; rpt. New York: AMS, 1976.

———. *The Soul of the Indian: An Interpretation.* 1911; rpt. New York: Johnson, 1970; Rapid City, S. Dak.: Fenwyn, 1970; Lincoln: Univ. of Nebraska Press, 1980.

———, and Elaine Goodale Eastman. *Wigwam Evenings: Sioux Folktales Retold.* Boston: Little, 1909. Republished as *Smoky Day's Wigwam Evenings: Indian Stories Retold.* Boston: Little, 1910.

Edmunds, R. David (Cherokee). *American Indian Leaders: Studies in Diversity.* Lincoln: Univ. of Nebraska Press, 1980.

Eggan, Fred. *Social Organization of the Western Pueblos.* Chicago: Univ. of Chicago Press, 1950.

Ehanni Ohunkakan. Curriculum Material Resource Unit. Pine Ridge, S. Dak.: Red Cloud Indian School, n.d.

Eliade, Mircea. *Myth and Reality.* Trans. Willard R. Trask. New York: Harper, 1963.

———. *The Quest: History and Meaning in Religion.* Chicago: Univ. of Chicago Press, 1969.

———. *The Sacred and the Profane: The Nature of Religion.* Trans. Willard R. Trask. 1959; rpt. New York: Harper, 1973.

Encyclopedia of World Mythology. New York: Galahad, 1975.

Erdoes, Richard. See Fire, John.

Estrada, Álvaro. *María Sabina: Her Life and Chants.* Trans. Henry Mann. Preface Jerome Rothenberg. New Wilderness Poetics Series. Santa Barbara: Ross-Erikson, 1981.

Evers, Larry. "Further Survivals of Coyote." *WAL,* 10 (1975), 233–36.

———. "Native American Oral Literatures in the College English Classroom: An Omaha Example." *CE,* 36 (1975), 649–62.

———. "A Response: Going Along with the Story." *AIQ,* 5 (1979), 71–75.

———. Rev. of *American Indian Literature,* ed. Alan R. Velie. *SAIL,* 5 (Fall 1981), 15–17.

———. Rev. of *Literature of the American Indian,* ed. Thomas E. Sanders and Walter W. Peek. *College Composition and Communication,* 26 (Feb. 1975), 86–89.

———. "Words and Place: A Reading of *House Made of Dawn.*" *WAL,* 11 (1977), 297–320.

———, ed. "A Conversation with N. Scott Momaday." *Sun Tracks,* 2, No. 2 (1976), 18–21.

———. "A Conversation with Vine Deloria, Jr." *Sun Tracks,* 4 (1978), 80–88.

———. *The South Corner of Time: Hopi, Navajo, Papago, and Yaqui Tribal Literature.* Tucson: Univ. of Arizona Press, 1980.

———, prod. *Words and Place: Native Literature from the American Southwest.*

Tucson: KUAT-TV, 1978. Series of eight color videotapes of American Indian singers, storytellers, and authors. Dist. by Clearwater, 1995 Broadway, New York, NY 10023.

———, and Dennis Carr, eds. "A Conversation with Leslie Marmon Silko." *Sun Tracks*, 3 (Fall 1976), 28–33.

———, and Paul Pavich. "Native Oral Literatures." In Taylor, *The Literary History of the American West*, forthcoming.

Ewers, John C. "Deadlier Than the Male." *American Heritage*, 16 (1965), 10–13.

———. "Mothers of the Mixed-Bloods: The Marginal Woman in the History of the Upper Missouri." In Toole, *Probing the American West*, pp. 62–70.

Farb, Peter. *Man's Rise to Civilization: The Cultural Ascent of the Indians of North America*. 2nd ed. New York: Dutton, 1978; New York: Bantam, 1978.

Faulkner, William. *Go Down, Moses*. New York: Modern Library-Random, 1942.

Fenton, William. "This Island, the World on Turtle's Back." *JAF*, 75 (1962), 283–300.

Ferber, Edna. *Cimarron*. 1929. Garden City: Doubleday, 1951; New York: Fawcett, 1979.

Fewkes, J. Walter. "Sky God Personations in Hopi Worship." *JAF*, 15 (1902), 14–32.

Fiedler, Leslie. *The Return of the Vanishing American*. New York: Stein and Day, 1968.

———, and Houston A. Baker, Jr., eds. *Opening Up the Canon: Selected Papers from the English Institute*. Baltimore: Johns Hopkins Univ. Press, 1981.

Finnegan, Ruth. *Oral Poetry: Its Nature, Significance, and Social Context*. Cambridge: Cambridge Univ. Press, 1977.

Finster, David. *The Hardin Winter Count*. Spec. iss. of *Museum News*, 26, Nos. 3–4 (March–April 1968).

Fire, John [Lame Deer] (Sioux), and Richard Erdoes. *Lame Deer, Seeker of Visions*. New York: Simon, 1972.

Fisher, Dexter [Alice Poindexter Fisher]. "The Transformation of Tradition: A Study of Zitkala-Sa and Mourning Dove, Two Transitional Indian Writers." Diss. City Univ. of New York 1979.

———. "Zitkala Sa: The Evolution of a Writer." *AIQ*, 5 (1979), 229–38.

———, ed. *The Third Woman: Minority Women Writers of the United States*. Boston: Houghton, 1980.

Fisher, Margaret W. "The Mythology of the Northern and Northeastern Algonkins in Reference to Algonkian Mythology as a Whole." In Johnson, *Man in Northeastern North America*, pp. 226–62.

Fletcher, Alice C. *A Study of Omaha Indian Music*. Archaeological and Ethnological Papers of the Peabody Museum, Harvard Univ., 1, No. 5. 1893; rpt. Millwood, N.Y.: Kraus, n.d.

———, ed. *The Hako: A Pawnee Ceremony*. ARBAE, 22, Pt. 2. Washington: GPO, 1901.

———. *Indian Story and Song from North America*. 1900; rpt. New York: Johnson, n.d.

———. See also La Flesche, Francis.

Flint, F. S. "Imagism." *Poetry*, 1, No. 6 (March 1913), 198–200.

Forbes, Jack D., ed. *Nevada Indians Speak*. Reno: Univ. of Nevada Press, 1954.

Forche, Carolyn. *Gathering the Tribes.* New Haven: Yale Univ. Press, 1976.

Ford, Thomas. "*The American Rhythm:* Mary Austin's Poetic Principle." *WAL,* 5 (1970), 3–14.

Foreman, Carolyn Thomas. "Edward W. Bushyhead and John Rollin Ridge, Cherokee Editors in California." *CO,* 14 (1936), 295–311.

———. *Indian Women Chiefs.* 1954; rpt. Washington, D.C.: Zenger, 1976.

Foreman, Grant. *Indian Removal: The Emigration of the Five Civilized Tribes of Indians.* Norman: Univ. of Oklahoma Press, 1976.

Forrest, Linn A. See Garfield, Viola.

Foster, Annie [Mrs. W. Garland]. *The Mohawk Princess: Being Some Account of the Life of Tekahion-Wake* [E. Pauline Johnson]. Vancouver: Lions' Gate, 1931.

Fowler, Catharine S. "Sarah Winnemucca." In Liberty, *American Indian Intellectuals,* pp. 33–42.

Fredericks, Oswald White Bear. See Waters, Frank.

Freneau, Philip. *Poems of Freneau.* Ed. Harry Hayden Clark. New York: Harcourt, 1929.

Freud, Sigmund. *Totem and Taboo: Some Points of Agreement between the Mental Lives of Savages and Neurotics.* Trans. James Strachey. New York: Norton, 1952.

Freund, Philip. *Myths of Creation.* Levittown, N.Y.: Transatlantic Arts, 1975.

Friday, Nancy. *My Mother, My Self: The Daughter's Search for Identity.* New York: Delacorte, 1977; New York: Dell, 1978.

Frisbie, Charlotte Johnson. *Music and Dance Research of Southwestern United States: Past Trends, Present Activities, and Suggestions for Future Research.* Detroit Studies in Music Bibliography, 36. Detroit: Information Coordinators, 1977.

———. *Southwestern Indian Ritual Drama.* Albuquerque: Univ. of New Mexico Press, 1980.

Gabriel, Ralph Henry. *Elias Boudinot, Cherokee, and His America.* Norman: Univ. of Oklahoma Press, 1941.

Garfield, Viola, and Linn A. Forrest. *The Wolf and the Raven: Totem Poles of Southeastern Alaska.* 2nd ed. Seattle: Univ. of Washington Press, 1961.

Garland, Hamlin. *The Book of the American Indian.* 1923; rpt. Saint Clair Shores, Mich.: Somerset, n.d.

———. *The Captain of the Gray-Horse Troop.* 1902; rpt. Saint Clair Shores, Mich.: Somerset, n.d.; New York: Irvington, 1973.

Gayton, Anna H. "The Orpheus Myth in North America." *JAF,* 48 (1935), 263–93.

———. and Stanley S. Newman. *Yokuts and Western Mono Myths.* Univ. of California Anthropological Records, 5. Berkeley: Univ. of California, 1940.

Geiogamah, Hanay (Kiowa). *New Native American Drama: Three Plays.* Introd. Jeffrey Huntsman. Norman: Univ. of Oklahoma Press, 1980.

Geronimo (Apache). *Geronimo: His Own Story.* Ed. S. M. Barrett. Introd. Frederick Turner III. 1906; rpt. New York: Dutton, n.d.; New York: Ballantine, 1978.

Gibson, Arrell M., ed. *Will Rogers: A Centennial Tribute.* Oklahoma Series, 12. Oklahoma City: Oklahoma Historical Soc., 1979. Also published as *CO,* 57, No. 3 (1979).

Gill, Sam D. "Native American Religions: A Review Essay." *Religious Studies Review,* 5 (1979), 251–58.

———. "Prayer as Person." *History of Religions,* 17, No. 2 (1977).

————. *Sacred Words: A Study of Navajo Religion and Prayer*. Contributions in Intercultural and Comparative Studies, 4. Westport, Conn.: Greenwood, 1981.

————. "The Trees Stood Rooted." *Parabola*, 2, No. 2 (1977).

————, ed. *The Religious Character of Native American Humanities*. Tempe: Arizona State Univ., 1977.

Gingerich, Willard. "The Old Voices of Acoma: Simon Ortiz's Mythic Indigenism." *Southwest Review*, 64 (1979), 18–30.

Gish, Robert L. "Mesquakie Singer: Listening to Ray A. Young Bear." *A*, 4, No. 2 (1979), 24–28.

Goddard, Pliny E., ed. *Myths and Tales from the San Carlos Apache*. APAMNH, 24, Pt. 1. 1918; rpt. New York: AMS, n.d.

————. *White Mountain Apache Texts*. APAMNH, 24, Pt. 4. 1920; rpt. New York: AMS, 1977.

Goetz, Delia, and Sylvanus G. Morley. *Popol Vuh: The Sacred Book of the Ancient Quiche Maya*. From the trans. of Adrian Recinos. 1950; rpt. Norman: Univ. of Oklahoma Press, 1977.

Goldschmidt, Walter, ed. *The Anthropology of Franz Boas: Essays on the Centennial of His Birth*. MAAA, 89. Published as *American Anthropologist*, 61, No. 5, Pt. 2 (Oct. 1959).

Gossen, Gary. *Chamulas in the World of the Sun*. Cambridge: Harvard Univ. Press, 1974.

Green, Norma Kidd. *Iron Eye's Family: The Children of Joseph La Flesche*. Lincoln: Univ. of Nebraska Press, 1969.

Green, Rayna. "The Pocahontas Perplex: The Image of Indian Women in Popular Culture." *Massachusetts Review*, 16 (1975), 698–714.

————, ed. *Native American Women: A Bibliography*. Wichita Falls, Tex.: Ohoyo, 1981.

Grey, Zane. *The Vanishing American*. 1925; rpt. New York: Grosset, 1953.

Gridley, Marion E. *American Indian Women*. New York: Hawthorn, 1974.

————, comp. *Indians of Today*. 1936. 3rd ed. Chicago: Towerton, 1948.

Griffis, Joseph [Chief Tahan] (Osage). *Indian Circle Stories*. Burlington, Vt.: Free Press, 1928.

————. *Tahan: Out of Savagery into Civilization*. New York: Doran, 1915.

Grinnell, George Bird. *Blackfoot Lodge Tales: The Story of a Prairie People*. 1892; rpt. Lincoln: Univ. of Nebraska Press, 1962.

————. *By Cheyenne Campfires*. 1926; rpt. Lincoln: Univ. of Nebraska Press, 1971.

————. *Pawnee Hero Stories and Folk Tales*. 1889; rpt. Lincoln: Univ. of Nebraska Press, 1961.

Gummere, Francis B. *The Beginnings of Poetry*. 1901; rpt. New York: Arno, 1971; Philadelphia: Richard West, 1973.

————. *The Popular Ballad*. 1907; rpt. Magnolia, Mass.: Peter Smith, n.d.

Gunn, John M. *Schat-Chen: History, Traditions, and Narratives of the Queres Indians of Laguna and Acoma*. 1917; rpt. New York: AMS, 1977.

Hagan, William. *American Indians*. Rev. ed. Chicago: Univ. of Chicago Press, 1979.

Hail, Raven. *The Raven and the Redbird*. Dallas: n.p., 1965.

Haile, Berard, and Leland C. Wyman. *Beautyway: A Navajo Ceremonial*. New York: Pantheon, 1957.

Hale, Janet Campbell (Coeur d'Alene). "Desmet, Idaho, March 1969." In her *Custer Lives in Humboldt County.* Greenfield Center, N.Y.: Greenfield Review Press, 1978, p. 21.

———. *Owl Song.* Garden City: Doubleday, 1974.

Hallowell, A. Irving. *Culture and Experience.* 1955; rpt. New York: Schocken, 1971.

———. "Myth, Culture, and Personality." *American Anthropologist,* 49 (1947).

Hammond, Dorothy, and Alta Jablow. *Women: Their Economic Role in Traditional Societies.* Module in Anthropology, 35. Reading, Mass.: Addison-Wesley, 1973.

Hand, Wayland, ed. *American Folk Legend.* Berkeley: Univ. of California Press, 1971.

Harjo, Joy (Creek). *The Last Song.* Las Cruces, N. Mex.: Puerto del Sol, 1975.

———. *What Moon Drove Me to This.* Berkeley: Reed and Cannon, 1979.

———. "White Sands." In Kopp and Kopp, *Southwest,* p. 68.

Harris, Helen L. "Mark Twain's Response to the Native American." *American Literature,* 46 (1975), 495–505.

Harte, Bret. "The Princess Bob and Her Friends." In *The Writings of Bret Harte.* 20 vols. Boston: Houghton, 1896–1911, II, 51–66.

Haywood, Charles. *A Bibliography of North American Folklore and Folksong.* Vol. 2: *American Indians North of Mexico, including the Eskimos.* New York: Dover, 1961.

Heizer, Robert, and Albert B. Elsasser. *Original Accounts of the Lone Woman of San Nicholas Island.* Ramona, Calif.: Ballena, 1973.

Henderson, Alice Corbin. "A Note on Primitive Poetry." *Poetry,* 13 (Sept. 1919), 330–35.

———. "Poetry of the North American Indians." *Poetry,* 14, No. 6 (1919), 41–47.

Henry, Jeannette, ed. *The American Indian Reader: Literature.* San Francisco: Indian Historian, 1973.

———. *Indian Voices.* San Francisco: Indian Historian, 1970.

———, et al., eds. *Index to Literature on the American Indian.* 4 vols. San Francisco: Indian Historian, 1971–75.

Hewett, Edgar L., and Bertha P. Dutton. *The Pueblo Indian World: Studies on the Natural History of the Rio Grande Valley in Relation to Pueblo Indian Culture.* Albuquerque: Univ. of New Mexico Press, 1945.

Hewitt, John N. B. (Tuscarora), ed. *Iroquoian Cosmology, Part One.* ARBAE, 21. Washington: GPO, 1904.

———. *Iroquoian Cosmology: With Introduction and Notes, Part Two.* ARBAE, 43. 1928; rpt. New York: AMS, n.d.

Hirschfelder, Arlene, ed. *American Indian and Eskimo Authors: A Comprehensive Bibliography.* New York: Assn. on American Indian Affairs, 1973.

Hobson, Geary [Gearld] (Cherokee). "The Rise of the White Shaman as a New Version of Cultural Imperialism." *Yardbird,* 1, No. 1 (1977), 85–95. Rpt. in Hobson, *The Remembered Earth,* pp. 100–08.

———. "Round Dance: Native American Writing at the University of New Mexico." *New America,* 2 (1976), 4–16.

———, ed. *The Remembered Earth: An Anthology of Contemporary Native American Literature.* 1979; rpt. Albuquerque: Univ. of New Mexico Press, 1981.

Hodge, Frederick W. *Handbook of the American Indians North of Mexico.* 2 vols.

BBAE, 30. 1907; rpt. Totowa, N.J.: Rowman, 1970; Westport, Conn.: Greenwood, 1971; St. Clair Shores, Mich.: Scholarly, 1979.

Hogan, Linda (Chickasaw). "The Nineteenth-Century Native American Poets." *Wassaja*, 13, No. 4 (1980), 24–29.

————. *Calling Myself Home*. Greenfield Center, N.Y.: Greenfield, 1980.

————. *Daughters I Love You*. Denver: Loretto Heights Coll., 1981.

————. *Eclipse*. Los Angeles: UCLA-Native American Series, 1983.

Hoijer, Harry. "History of American Indian Linguistics." In Sebeok, *Native Languages of the Americas*, I, 3–22.

Hopkins, Sarah Winnemucca (Paiute). *Life among the Piutes: Their Wrongs and Claims*. Ed. Mrs. Horace Mann. New York: Putnam, 1883.

Howard, Helen Addison. *American Indian Poetry*. Boston: Twayne, 1979.

Howard, James H. *Dakota Winter Counts as a Source of Plains History*. BBAE, 173. Washington, D.C.: Smithsonian, 1960.

Howe, Oscar. "Theories and Beliefs." In Milton, *The American Indian Speaks*, pp. 69–79.

Hudson, Charles. *The Southeastern Indians*. Knoxville: Univ. of Tennessee Press, 1977.

Hultkrantz, Åke. *The North American Indian Orpheus Tradition*. Stockholm: Statens Ethnolografiska, 1957.

————. *The Religions of the American Indian*. 1967; trans. Monica Setterwall, Berkeley: Univ. of California Press, 1979.

Hundley, Patrick D., comp. *The Magic of Names: Three Native American Poets. Interviews with Norman H. Russell, Lance Henson, Jim Weaver Barnes*. Marvin, S. Dak.: Blue Cloud Quarterly, n.d.

Hungry Wolf, Beverly (Blackfeet). *The Ways of My Grandmothers*. New York: Morrow, 1980.

Hunt, Wolf Robe (Acoma). *The Dancing Horses of Acoma*. Cleveland: World, 1963.

Hunter, Lois Marie (Shinnecock). *The Shinnecock Indians*. Islip, N.Y.: Buys, 1950.

Hymes, Dell. "Discovering Oral Performance and Measured Verse in American Indian Narrative." *New Literary History*, 8 (1977), 431–57. Rpt. in *In Vain I Tried to Tell You*, pp. 309–41.

————. "Folklore's Nature and the Sun's Myth." *JAF*, 88 (1975), 345–69.

————. *In Vain I Tried to Tell You: Essays in Native American Ethnopoetics*. Studies in Native American Literature. Philadelphia: Univ. of Pennsylvania Press, 1981.

————. "Louis Simpson's 'The Deserted Boy.'" *Poetics*, 5 (1976), 119–55. Rpt. in *In Vain I Tried to Tell You*, pp. 142–83.

————. "The Methods and Tasks of Anthropological Mythology (Illustrated with Clackamas Chinook)." *Romance Philology*, 19 (1965), 325–40.

————. "Reading Clackamas Texts." In K. Kroeber, *Traditional Literatures of the American Indian*, pp. 117–59. Rpt. in *In Vain I Tried to Tell You*, pp. 342–48.

————. "Some North Pacific Coast Poems: A Problem in Anthropological Philology." *American Anthropologist*, 67 (1965), 316–41. Rpt. in *In Vain I Tried to Tell You*, pp. 35–62.

————. "The 'Wife' Who 'Goes Out' Like a Man: Reinterpretation of a Clackamas Chinook Myth." *Social Science Information*, 7, No. 3 (1967), 173–99. Rpt. in *In Vain I Tried to Tell You*, pp. 274–308.

Icolari, Dan, ed. *Encyclopedia of the American Indian.* 2nd ed. Rye, N.Y.: Todd, 1973.

Irvine, Judith. "Formality and Informality in Communicative Events." *American Anthropologist,* 81 (1979), 773–90.

Irving, Washington. *The Adventures of Captain Bonneville.* 3 vols. 1837. Ed. Robert A. Rees and Alan Sandy. Boston: Twayne, 1977.

———. *Astoria: or, Anecdotes of an Enterprize beyond the Rocky Mountains.* 1936. Ed. Richard D. Rust. Boston: Twayne, 1976.

———. *A Tour on the Prairies.* 1835. Ed. Dahlia Kirby Terrell. In *The Crayon Miscellany.* Boston: Twayne, pp. 5–122.

Jackson, Donald. See Black Hawk.

Jackson, Helen Hunt. *Ramona.* 1884. New York: Avon, 1970.

Jacobs, Melville. *The Content and Style of an Oral Literature: Clackamas Chinook Myths and Tales.* Chicago: Univ. of Chicago Press, 1959.

———. "A Few Observations on the World View of the Clackamas Chinook Indians." *JAF,* 68 (1955), 283–89.

———. "Folklore." In Goldschmidt, *The Anthropology of Franz Boas,* pp. 119–38.

———. "Humor and Social Structure in an Oral Literature." In Diamond, *Culture in History,* pp. 181–89.

———. "A Look Ahead in Oral Literature Research." *JAF,* 79 (1966), 413–27.

———. *Pattern in Cultural Anthropology.* Homewood, Ill.: Dorsey, 1964.

———. *The People Are Coming Soon: Analyses of Clackamas Chinook Myths and Tales.* Seattle: Univ. of Washington Press, 1960.

———. "Psychological Inferences from a Chinook Myth." *JAF,* 65 (1952), 121–37.

———. "Titles in an Oral Literature." *JAF,* 70 (1957), 157–72.

———, ed. *Clackamas Chinook Texts.* 2 vols. Indiana Univ. Research Center in Anthropology, Folklore, and Linguistics Publications, 8 and 11. Bloomington: Indiana Univ., 1958 and 1959.

Jacobs, Peter [Pahtahsega] (Ojibwe). *Journal of the Reverend Peter Jacobs, Indian Wesleyan Missionary, from Rice Lake to the Hudson's Bay Territory; and Returning. Commencing May 1852. . . .* Toronto: Anson Gree, 1853; Boston: Rand, 1853.

Jacobs, Sue-Ellen. *Women in Perspective: A Guide for Cross-Cultural Studies.* Urbana: Univ. of Illinois Press, 1974.

Jacobson, Angeline. *Contemporary Native American Literature: A Selected and Partially Annotated Bibliography.* Metuchen, N.J.: Scarecrow, 1977.

Jahner, Elaine. "An Act of Attention: Event Structure in *Ceremony.*" *AIQ,* 5 (1979), 37–46.

———. *American Indians Today: Thought, Literature, and Art.* New York: Horizon, 1982.

———. "Cognitive Domains and Oral Literary Style." *Language and Style,* Fall 1982.

———. "A Laddered Rain-Bearing Rug: The Poetry of Paula Gunn Allen." In Rosowski and Stauffer, *Women and Western American Literature.*

———. "Quick Paces and a Space of Mind." *Denver Quarterly,* 14, No. 4 (1980), 34–47.

———, ed. *Lakota Myth.* Lincoln: Univ. of Nebraska Press, 1983.

———. "Woman among the Wolves." In *Handbook of American Folklore.* Ed. Richard M. Dorsen. New York: McGraw-Hill, 1982.

————, ed., with Raymond J. DeMallie. *Lakota Belief and Ritual*. Lincoln: Univ. of Nebraska Press, 1983.

Jefferson, Thomas. *Notes on the State of Virginia*. 1784. Ed. William Peden. New York: Norton, 1972. Ed. Bernard Wishy and William E. Leuchtenburg. New York: Harper, 1977.

Johnson, Broderick H., ed. *Navajo Stories of the Long Walk Period*. Tsaile, Ariz.: Navajo Community Coll. Press, 1975.

————. *Stories of Traditional Navajo Life and Culture by Twenty-Two Navajo Men and Women*. Tsaile, Ariz.: Navajo Community Coll. Press, 1977.

Johnson, Elias (Tuscarora). *Legends, Traditions and Laws, of the Iroquois or Six Nations, and History of the Tuscarora Indians*. 1881; rpt. New York: AMS, 1977.

Johnson, Emily Pauline [Tehakionwake] (Mohawk). *Canadian Born*. Toronto: Morang, 1903.

————. *Flint and Feather*. Rev. ed. Introd. Theodore Watts-Dunton. 3rd ed. Toronto: Musson, 1914.

————. *Legends of Vancouver*. Vancouver: Saturday Sunset, 1911. New ed. Toronto: McClelland, 1911.

————. *The Moccasin Maker*. Introd. Sir Gilbert Parker. With an Appreciation by Charles Mair. Toronto: Ryerson, 1913.

————. *The Shagganappi*. Introd. Ernest Thompson Seton. Toronto: Briggs, 1913.

————. *The White Wampum*. London: Lane, 1895; Boston: Lamson, 1895.

Johnson, Frederick, ed. *Man in Northeastern North America*. Papers of the Robert S. Peabody Foundation for Archaeology, 3. Andover, Mass.: Phillips Acad., 1946.

Johnson, Pauline. See Johnson, Emily Pauline.

Johnston, Basil H. (Ojibwe). *Ojibwa Heritage*. Toronto: Stewart, 1976; New York: Columbia Univ. Press, 1976.

Johnston, Verna Patronella (Ojibwe). *I Am Nokomis, Too: The Biography of Verna Patronella Johnston*. Ed. Rosamund Vanderburgh. Don Mills, Ont.: General, 1977.

Jones, David. See Sanapia.

Jones, Louis Thomas. *Aboriginal American Oratory: The Tradition of Eloquence among the Indians of the United States*. Los Angeles: Southwest Museum, 1965.

Jones, Peter (Ojibwe). *History of the Ojebway Indians, with Especial Reference to Their Conversion to Christianity. . . .* 1861; rpt. New York: Arno, n.d.

————. *Life and Journals of Kah-ke-wa-quo-na-by (Rev. Peter Jones), Wesleyan Missionary*. 1860; rpt. New York: AMS, 1977.

Jones, William (Fox). *Fox Texts*. Ed. Franz Boas. PAES, 1. 1907; rpt. New York: AMS, 1978.

————. *Ojibwa Texts*. Ed. Truman Michelson. 2 vols. PAES, 8. 1917 and 1919; rpt. New York: AMS, 1973.

Jung, Carl G. *Four Archteypes*. Trans. R. F. Hull. Ed. G. Adler. Princeton: Princeton Univ. Press, 1973.

Karol, Joseph S. *Red Horse Owner's Winter Count: The Oglala Sioux, 1786–1968*. Martin, S. Dak.: Booster, 1969.

Katz, Jane B., ed. *I Am the Fire of Time: The Voices of Native American Women*. New York: Dutton, 1977.

————. *This Song Remembers: Self-Portraits of Native Americans in the Arts*. Boston: Houghton, 1980.

Kegg, Maude (Ojibwe). *Gii-Ikwezensiwiyaan / When I Was a Little Girl*. Ed. John Nichols. Onamia, Minn.: n.p., 1976.

Keiser, Albert. *The Indian in American Literature*. 1933; rpt. New York: Octagon, 1970.

Kelley, Jane Holden. *Yaqui Women: Contemporary Life Histories*. Lincoln: Univ. of Nebraska Press, 1978.

Kenny, Maurice (Mohawk). *Blackrobe*. Saranac Lake, N.Y.: North Country Community Coll. Press, 1982.

Keon, W., ed. *Sweetgrass: An Anthology of Indian Poetry*. Elliot Lake, Ont.: Algoma, 1971.

———. *Dancing Back Strong the Nation*. Marvin, S. Dak.: Blue Cloud Quarterly, 1978.

———. *Greyhounding This America*. Chico, Calif.: Heidelberg, 1983.

———. *Kneading the Blood*. New York, Strawberry.

———. *North: Poems of Home*. Marvin, S. Dak.: Blue Cloud Quarterly, 1977.

Kesey, Ken. *One Flew over the Cuckoo's Nest*. New York: Viking, 1962. Ed. John C. Pratt. New York: Penguin, 1977.

Ketchum, Richard M. *Will Rogers: His Life and His Times*. New York: Simon, 1973.

Keyes, Elisha Williams. "Julius Taylor Clark." *Proceedings* (Historical Soc. of Wisconsin), 56 (1909), 140–45.

Kidwell, Clara Sue. "Bright Eyes: The Story of Susette La Flesche, an Omaha Indian." *JES*, 2 (Winter 1975), 117–22.

———. "The Power of Women in Three American Indian Societies." *JES*, 6 (1979), 113–21.

Kilpatrick, Jack Frederick, and Anna Gritts Kilpatrick (Cherokee), eds. *Friends of Thunder: Folktales of the Oklahoma Cherokees*. Dallas: Southern Methodist Univ. Press, 1964.

———. *Run toward the Nightland: Magic of the Oklahoma Cherokees*. Dallas: Southern Methodist Univ. Press, 1967.

———. *Walk in Your Soul: Love Incantations of the Oklahoma Cherokees*. Dallas: Southern Methodist Univ. Press, 1965.

Klah, Hosteen (Navajo). *Navajo Creation Myth: The Story of the Emergence*. 1942; rpt. New York: AMS, 1977.

Klievan, Inge. "The Swan Maiden Myth among the Eskimos." *Acta Arctica*, 13 (1962).

Kluckhohn, Clyde. "Recurrent Themes in Myths and Mythmaking." *Daedalus*, 88 (1959), 268–79. Rpt. in Murray, *Myth and Mythmaking*, pp. 46–60.

———, and Dorothea Leighton. *The Navaho*. Rev. ed. Cambridge: Harvard Univ. Press, 1974.

Köngäs, Elii Kaija. "The Earth-Diver." *Ethnohistory*, 7, No. 2 (1960), 151–79.

Kopit, Arthur. *Indians: A Play*. New York: Hill and Wang, 1969.

Kopp, Karl, and Jane Kopp, eds. *Southwest: A Contemporary Anthology*. Albuquerque: Red Earth, 1977.

Krapp, George P. *The Rise of English Literary Prose*. New York: Oxford Univ. Press, 1915.

Krause, Sydney J. "Cooper's Literary Offences: Mark Twain in Wonderland." *New England Quarterly*, 38 (1965), 291–311.

Kroeber, Alfred L. "Catch-Words in American Mythology." *JAF*, 21 (1908), 222–27.

————. *Cultural and Natural Areas of Native North America.* 1939; rpt. Millwood, N.Y.: Kraus, n.d.

————. *The Nature of Culture.* Chicago: Univ. of Chicago Press, 1952.

————, ed. *Yurok Myths.* Berkeley: Univ. of California Press, 1976.

———— et al. *Franz Boas, 1858–1942.* MAAA, 61. 1943; rpt. New York: Kraus, 1969.

Kroeber, Karl. "Deconstructionist Criticism and American Indian Literature." *Boundary 2,* 7, No. 3 (1979), 73–89.

————. "An Introduction to the Art of Traditional American Indian Narration." In Kroeber, *Traditional Literatures,* pp. 1–24.

————, ed. *Traditional Literatures of the American Indian: Texts and Interpretations.* Lincoln: Univ. of Nebraska Press, 1981.

————, and A. LaVonne Brown Ruoff. *Native American Literatures: A Basic Bibliography for Teachers.* New York: Assn. for the Study of American Indian Literatures, 1981.

Kroeber, Theodora. *Ishi in Two Worlds: A Biography of the Last Wild Indian in North America.* Berkeley: Univ. of California Press, 1961.

————, and Robert F. Heizer. *Almost Ancestors: The First Californians.* Ed. F. David Hales. San Francisco: Sierra Club, 1968.

Krupat, Arnold. "The Indian Autobiography: Origins, Type, and Function." *American Literature,* 53 (1981), 22–42.

La Barre, Weston. *The Peyote Cult.* 1959. 4th ed. Hamden, Conn.: Shoe String, 1975.

La Farge, Oliver. *Laughing Boy.* 1929. New York: NAL, 1971.

La Flesche, Francis (Omaha). *The Middle Five: Indian School Boys of the Omaha Tribe.* 1900; rpt. Madison: Univ. of Wisconsin Press, 1963; Lincoln: Univ. of Nebraska Press, 1978.

————, and Alice C. Fletcher, eds. *The Omaha Tribe.* ARBAE, 27. 1911; rpt. in 2 vols. New York: Johnson, 1970; Lincoln: Univ. of Nebraska Press, 1972.

————. *The Osage Tribe.* ARBAE. *Rite of the Chiefs,* 36 (1921). *Rite of Vigil,* 39 (1925). *Two Versions of the Child-Naming Rite,* 43 (1928). *Rite of Wa-x'-be,* 45 (1930). Rpt. New York: Johnson, 1970.

Laird, W. David, ed. *Hopi Bibliography: Comprehensive and Annotated.* Tucson: Univ. of Arizona Press, 1977.

Lame Deer. See Fire, John.

Landes, Ruth. *The Ojibwa Woman.* 1938; rpt. New York: Norton, 1971.

LaRoque, Emma. *Defeathering the Indian.* Agincourt: Book Soc. of Canada, 1975.

Larson, Charles R. *American Indian Fiction.* Albuquerque: Univ. of New Mexico Press, 1978.

Latta, Frank F. *Handbook of the Yokut Indians.* 1949; rpt. Santa Cruz, Calif.: Bear State Books, 1979.

Leach, Edmund. *Claude Lévi-Strauss.* Modern Masters. New York: Viking, 1970.

————. "Genesis as Myth." 1962; rpt. in his *Genesis as Myth and Other Essays.* London: Cape, 1969, pp. 7–23.

————, ed. *The Structural Study of Myth and Totemism.* London: Tavistock, 1967.

Lee, Bobbi (Métis). *Bobbi Lee: Indian Rebel.* Ed. Don Barnett and Rick Sterling. Richmond, B. C.: LSM Information Center, 1975.

Left Handed (Navajo). *Left Handed, Son of Old Man Hat: A Navaho Autobiography.* Ed. Walter Dyk. 1938; rpt. Lincoln: Univ. of Nebraska Press, 1967.

Lehmer, Derrick. "The Music and Poetry of the American Indians." *Poetry Review*, 20 (1929), 333–440.

Levine, Stuart, and Nancy O. Lurie, eds. *The American Indian Today*. New York: Penguin, 1970. 2nd ed. DeLand, Fla.: Everett-Edwards, 1971.

Lévi-Strauss, Claude. "Four Winnebago Myths: A Structural Sketch." In Diamond, *Culture in History*, pp. 351–62.

———. *The Origin of Table Manners*. 1968. Trans. John Weightman and Doreen Weightman. New York: Harper, 1978.

———. *The Raw and the Cooked*. 1964. Trans. John Weightman and Doreen Weightman. New York: Harper, 1969.

———. "The Story of Asdiwal." In Leach, *The Structural Study of Myth and Totemism*, pp. 1–47.

———. *Structural Anthropology*. Trans. C. Jacobsen and B. G. Schoef. Garden City: Doubleday, 1967.

———. "The Structural Study of Myth." *JAF*, 68 (1955), 428–44. Rpt. in his *Structural Anthropology*, pp. 202–28.

Levitan, Sar A., and William B. Johnston. *Indian Giving: Federal Programs for Native Americans*. Baltimore: Johns Hopkins Univ. Press, 1975.

Lewis, Claudia. *Indian Families of the Northwest Coast: The Impact of Change*. Chicago: Univ. of Chicago Press, 1970.

Lewis, Robert. "The Death of Jim Loney." *SAIL*, 5, Nos. 3–4 (Fall 1981), 18–20.

Liberty, Margot. "Francis La Flesche: The Osage Odyssey." In Liberty, *American Indian Intellectuals*, pp. 45–59.

———, ed. *American Indian Intellectuals*. 1976 Proceedings of the American Ethnological Soc. St. Paul, Minn.: West, 1978.

———. See also Stands in Timber, John.

Lifshin, Lyn, ed. *Tangled Vines: A Collection of Mother and Daughter Poems*. Boston: Beacon, 1978.

Lincoln, Kenneth. "Back-Tracking James Welch." *MELUS*, 6, No. 1 (1979), 23–40.

———. *Native American Renaissance*. Los Angeles: Univ. of California Press, 1983.

———. "The Now Day Indi'n." *Four Winds*, Summer 1982.

Linderman, Frank B. See Pretty-Shield.

Lindsay, N. Vachel. "Notes." *Poetry*, 4, No. 4 (1914), 161.

Little Bear, Mary (Cheyenne). *Dance around the Sun: The Life of Mary Little Bear Inkanish, Cheyenne*. Ed. Alice Marriott and Carol K. Rachlin. New York: Crowell, 1977.

Littlefield, Daniel F., Jr., and James W. Parins, eds. *A Biobibliography of Native American Writings, 1772–1924*. Native American Bibliography. Metuchen, N.J.: Scarecrow, 1981.

Lone Dog, Louise (Mohawk-Delaware). *Strange Journey: The Vision Life of a Psychic Indian Woman*. Ed. Vinson Brown. Healdsburg, Calif.: Naturegraph, 1964.

Long, Charles. *Alpha: The Myths of Creation*. New York: Collier, 1963.

Long, James Larpenteur [First Boy] (Assiniboine). *The Assiniboines: From the Accounts of the Old Ones Told to First Boy*. Ed. Michael Stephen Kennedy. Norman: Univ. of Oklahoma Press, 1961.

Longfellow, Henry Wadsworth. *The Song of Hiawatha*. 1855. Facs. ed. New York: Crown, 1969.

Longsdon, Guy. "John Joseph Mathews—A Conversation." *Nimrod*, 16 (1972), 70–75.

Lopez, Barry Holstun, ed. *Giving Birth to Thunder, Sleeping with His Daughter: Coyote Builds North America.* Kansas City: Sheed, 1977.

Lord, Albert B. *The Singer of Tales.* 1960; rpt. New York: Atheneum, 1965.

Lourie, Dick, ed. *Come to Power: Eleven Contemporary Indian Poets.* Trumansburg, N.Y.: Crossing, 1973.

Love, W. Deloss. *Samson Occum and the Christian Indians of New England.* Boston: Pilgrim, 1899.

Lowell, Amy. *Ballads for Sale.* Boston: Houghton, 1927.

———. *Legends.* Boston: Houghton, 1921.

———. Letter to Mary Austin, 24 April 1923. Mary Austin Papers, Huntington Library, San Marino, Calif.

Lowenfels, Walter, ed. *From the Belly of the Shark: A New Anthology of Native Americans.* New York: Vintage-Random, 1973.

Lowenstein, Tom, trans. *Eskimo Poems from Canada and Greenland.* Pittsburgh: Univ. of Pittsburgh Press, 1973.

Lowie, Robert H. "Additional Catch-Words." *JAF*, 22 (1909), 332–33.

———. "Catch-Words for Mythological Motifs." *JAF*, 21 (1908), 24–27.

———. *Myths and Traditions of the Crow Indians.* APAMNH, 25, Pt. 1. 1918; rpt. New York: AMS, 1974.

———. "The Test Theme in North American Mythology." *JAF*, 21 (1908), 97–148.

Lowry, Annie (Paiute). *Karnee: A Paiute Narrative.* Ed. Lalla Scott. Reno: Univ. of Nevada Press, 1966; New York: Fawcett, 1973.

Luckert, Karl. *Coyoteway: A Navajo Healing Ceremony.* Tucson: Univ. of Arizona Press, 1979.

Lurie, Nancy Oestreich. "Indian Women: A Legacy of Freedom." In Robert Iacopi, ed. *Looking to the Mountaintop.* San Jose: Gousha, 1972, pp. 29–35.

———. See also Mountain Wolf Woman.

MacAdams, Lewis. *News from Niman Farm.* Bolinas, Calif.: Tombouctou, 1976.

Maclagan, David. *Creation Myths.* London: Thames and Hudson, 1977.

Madrano, Dan C. (Caddo). *Heap Big Laugh.* Tulsa, Okla.: Western, 1955.

The Magic of Names: Three Native American Poets. Interviews with Norman H. Russell, Lance Henson, Jim Weaver Barnes. Marvin, S. Dak.: Blue Cloud, 1980.

Mallery, Garrick. *Picture-Writing of the American Indians.* ARBAE, 11. 1893; rpt. 2 vols. New York: Dover, 1972.

Malotki, Ekkehart, ed. *Hopitutuwutsi: Hopi Tales. A Bilingual Collection of Hopi Indian Stories.* Flagstaff: Museum of Northern Arizona, 1978.

Maranda, Pierre. *Mythology.* Baltimore: Penguin, 1972.

Marken, Jack W., ed. *The American Indian: Language and Literature.* Goldentree Bibliographies. Arlington Heights, Ill.: AHM, 1978.

———. *The Indians and Eskimos of North America: A Bibliography of Books in Print through 1972.* Vermillion: Univ. of South Dakota Press, 1973.

———, and Herbert T. Hoover, eds. *Bibliography of the Sioux.* Native American Bibliography. Metuchen, N.J.: Scarecrow, 1980.

Markoosie (Eskimo). *Harpoon of the Hunter.* Montreal: McGill-Queen's Univ. Press, 1970.

Marquis, Thomas. See Wooden Leg.

Marriott, Alice. *Kiowa Years: A Study in Culture Impact.* New York: Macmillan, 1968.

———. *Maria, the Potter of San Ildefonso.* Rev. ed. 1948; rpt. Norman: Univ. of Oklahoma Press, 1976.

———, and Carol K. Rachlin. *American Indian Mythology.* New York: Crowell, 1968; New York: NAL, 1972.

———. *Peyote.* New York: Crowell, 1971; New York: NAL, 1972.

———. *Plains Indian Mythology.* New York: Crowell, 1975; New York: Mentor, 1975.

———. See also Little Bear, Mary.

Martinez, Maria (San Ildefonso). *The Story of an American Indian.* Ed. Mary C. Nelson. Minneapolis, Minn.: Dillon, 1974.

Mather, Cotton. "The Life of John Eliot." In his *Magnalia Christi Americana,* Bk. III. 1702; rpt. New York: Arno, 1971. Ed. Raymond J. Cunningham. New York: Ungar, 1971.

Mathes, Valerie Shirer. "American Indian Women and the Catholic Church." *North Dakota History,* 47 (Fall 1980), 20–25.

———. "A New Look at the Role of Women in Indian Society." *AIQ,* 2 (Summer 1975), 131–39.

Mathews, John Joseph (Osage), *Life and Death of an Oilman: The Career of E. W. Marland.* Norman: Univ. of Oklahoma Press, 1951, 1976.

———. *The Osages:Children of the Middle Waters.* 1961; rpt. Norman: Univ. of Oklahoma Press, 1973.

———. *Sundown.* 1934; rpt. with introd. Priscilla Oaks, Boston: Gregg, 1979.

———. *Talking to the Moon.* 1945; rpt. with introd. Elizabeth Mathews, Norman: Univ. of Oklahoma Press, 1980.

———. *Wah'Kon-Tah: The Osage and the White Man's Road.* Norman: Univ. of Oklahoma Press, 1932, 1968.

Mathur, Mary E. Fleming. "Who Cares That a Woman's Work Is Never Done . . . ?" *Indian Historian,* 4 (Summer 1971), 11–16.

Matthews, Washington, ed. *The Mountain Chant: A Navajo Ceremony.* ARBAE, 5. 1883–84; rpt. Glorietta, N. Mex.: Rio Grande, 1971.

———. *Navaho Legends.* MAFS, 5. 1897; rpt. Millwood, N.Y.: Kraus, 1969.

———. *The Night Chant, a Navajo Ceremony.* APAMNH, 6. 1902; rpt. New York: AMS, 1974.

McAllester, David. "A Different Drum: A Consideration of Music in Native American Humanities." In Gill, *The Religious Character of Native American Humanities,* pp. 155–83.

McAllester, David P. *Enemy Way Music: A Study of the Social and Esthetic Values as Seen in Navaho Music.* Archaeological and Ethnological Papers, 41, Pt. 3. Cambridge: Peabody Museum, Harvard Univ., 1954.

———, ed. *Readings in Ethnomusicology.* New York: Johnson, 1971.

———, and Susan W. McAllester. *Hogans: Navajo Houses and House Songs.* Middletown, Conn.: Wesleyan Univ. Press, 1980.

McAllister, Harold S. "Incarnate Grace and the Paths of Salvation in *House Made of Dawn.*" *South Dakota Review,* 12 (1974–75), 115–25.

————. "The Language of Shamans: Jerome Rothenberg's Contribution to American Indian Literature." *WAL*, 10 (1976), 293–309.

McClintock, Walter. *The Old North Trail: or, Life, Legends and Religion of the Blackfeet Indians.* 1910; rpt. Lincoln: Univ. of Nebraska Press, 1965.

McClusky, Sally. "*Black Elk Speaks:* And So Does John Neihardt." *WAL*, 6 (1972), 231–42.

McCraye, Walter. *Pauline Johnson and Her Friends.* Toronto: Ryerson, 1947.

————. *Town Hall Tonight.* Toronto: Ryerson, 1929.

McLaughlin, Marie L. *Myths and Legends of the Sioux.* Bismarck, N. Dak.: Bismarck Tribune, 1916.

McNickle, D'Arcy (Salish). *Indian Man: A Life of Oliver La Farge.* Bloomington: Indiana Univ. Press, 1971.

————. *The Indian Tribes of the United States: Ethnic and Cultural Survival.* New York: Oxford Univ. Press, 1962.

————. *Native American Tribalism: Indian Survivals and Renewals.* New York: Oxford Univ. Press, 1973.

————. *Runner in the Sun: A Story of Indian Maize.* New York: Holt, 1954.

————. *The Surrounded.* 1936; rpt. with Introd. William Towner, Albuquerque: Univ. of New Mexico Press, 1978.

————. *They Came Here First: The Epic of the American Indian.* 1949; rpt. New York: Octagon, 1975.

————. *Wind from an Enemy Sky.* New York: Harper, 1978.

————, and Harold E. Fey. *Indians and Other Americans: Two Ways of Life Meet.* New York: Harper, 1970.

McQuaid, Kim. "Williams Apes, Pequot: An Indian Reformer in the Jackson Era." *New England Quarterly*, 50 (1977), 605–25.

McTaggart, Fred. *Wolf That I Am: In Search of the Red Earth People.* Boston: Houghton, 1976.

Medicine, Bea (Sioux). "The Anthropologist as the Indian's Image Maker." *Indian Historian*, 4 (Fall 1971), 27–29.

————. "Role and Function of Indian Women." *Indian Education*, 7 (Jan. 1977), 4–5.

————. "The Role of Women in Native American Societies." *Indian Historian*, 8 (Summer 1975), 51–53.

Meinig, Donald W. *Southwest: Three Peoples in Geographical Change, 1600–1970.* New York: Oxford Univ. Press, 1971.

Melville, Herman. *The Confidence Man.* 1857. Ed. Hershel Parker. New York: Norton, 1971.

Merriam, Alan P., ed. *Ethnomusicology of the Flathead Indians.* Viking Fund Publ. in Anthropology, 44. New York: Werner-Gren Foundation, 1967.

Metoyer, Cheryl A. "The Native American Woman." In Eloise C. Snyder, ed. *The Study of Women: Enlarging Perspectives of Social Reality.* New York: Harper, 1979, pp. 329–35.

Michelson, Truman. *The Autobiography of a Fox Indian Woman.* ARBAE, 40, pp. 291–349. Washington: GPO, 1925.

————. "Narrative of an Arapaho Woman." *American Anthropologist*, 35 (1933), 595–610.

————. "Narrative of a Southern Cheyenne Woman." *Smithsonian Miscellaneous Collections*, 87 (1932), 1–13.

Miller, David R. "Charles Alexander Eastman, the 'Winner': From Deep Woods to Civilization." In Liberty, *American Indian Intellectuals*, pp. 61–73.

Miller, Dorothy I. "Native American Women: Leadership Images." *Integrateducation*, 16 (Jan.-Feb. 1978), 37–39.

Miller, Joaquin. *Unwritten History: Life among the Modocs*. 1873. Ed. A. H. Rosenus. Eugene, Ore.: Urion, 1972.

Milton, John R. *The Blue Belly of the World*. Vermillion, S. Dak.: Spirit Mound, 1974.

————, ed. *American Indian II*. Vermillion, Dakota, 1971.

————. *The American Indian Speaks in Poetry, Fiction, Art, Music, Commentary*. Vermillion: Dakota, 1969.

————. *Four Indian Poets*. Vermillion: Univ. of South Dakota Press, 1974.

Mitchell, Emerson Blackhorse (Navajo). *Miracle Hill: The Story of a Navaho Boy*. Ed. T. D. Allen. Norman: Univ. of Oklahoma Press, 1967, 1980.

Mitchell, Frank. *Navajo Blessingway Singer: The Autobiography of Frank Mitchell, 1881–1967*. Ed. Charlotte Johnson Frisbie and David P. McAllester. Tucson: Univ. of Arizona Press, 1979.

Mitchell, John G., with Constance L. Stallings. *Ecotactics: The Sierra Club Handbook for Environmental Activities*. New York: Pocket, 1970.

Moises, Rosalio (Yaqui). *The Tall Candle: The Personal Chronicle of a Yaqui Indian*. Ed. Jane Kelly Holden and William Curry Holden. Lincoln: Univ. of Nebraska Press, 1971. Reissued as *A Yaqui Life: The Personal Chronicle of a Yaqui Indian*. Lincoln: Univ. of Nebraska Press, 1977.

Momaday, N[atachee] Scott (Cherokee). *American Indian Authors*. Boston: Houghton, 1972.

Momaday, N[avarre] Scott (Kiowa). "An American Land Ethic." In Mitchell, *Ecotactics*, pp. 97–105.

————. *Angle of Geese and Other Poems*. Boston: Godine, 1974.

————. *The Gourd Dancer*. New York: Harper, 1976.

————. *House Made of Dawn*. New York: Harper, 1968; New York: Signet, 1969.

————. *House Made of Dawn* [movie]. Dir. Larry Littlebird. New York: New Line Cinema (distr.)

————. *The Journey of Tai-me*. Santa Barbara: privately printed, 1967.

————. "The Man Made of Words." In Henry, *Indian Voices*, pp. 49–84. Rpt. in Chapman, *Literature of the American Indians*, pp. 96–110; and Hobson, *The Remembered Earth*, pp. 162–73.

————. "The Morality of Indian Hating." *Ramparts*, 3 (1964), 30–34.

————. *The Names: A Memoir*. New York: Harper, 1976.

————. "Native American Attitudes to the Environment." In Capps, *Seeing with a Native Eye*, pp. 79–85.

————. *The Way to Rainy Mountain*. Albuquerque: Univ. of New Mexico Press, 1969; New York: Ballantine, 1972.

Monroe, Harriet. "The Great Renewal." *Poetry*, 12, No. 6 (1918), 323–24.

Montgomery, Guy. "A Method of Studying Primitive Verse Applied to the Songs of the Teton-Sioux." *University of California Publications in Modern Philology*, 11 (1922), 269–83.

Moon, Sheila. *A Magic Dwells: A Poetic and Psychological Study of the Navaho Emergence Myth.* Middletown, Conn.: Wesleyan Univ. Press, 1970.

Mooney, James. *Ghost Dance Religion.* ARBAE, 14. 1892–93; rpt. Seattle: Shorey, 1966; New York: Dover, 1973.

———, ed. *Myths of the Cherokees.* ARBAE, 19, Pt. 1. 1897–98; rpt. New York: Johnson, 1970; St. Clair Shores, Mich.: Scholarly, 1970.

Morgan, William (Navajo), Robert W. Young, and Hildegard Thompson, eds. *Coyote Tales.* Washington, D.C.: Bureau of Indian Affairs, 1968.

Morton, Sarah Wentworth. *Ouâbi: or, The Virtues of Nature: An Indian Tale in Four Cantos.* Boston: Thomas and Andrews, 1790.

Moulton, Richard G. *The Modern Study of Literature.* 1915; rpt. Folcroft, Pa.: Folcroft, 1973.

Mountain Wolf Woman (Winnebago). *Mountain Wolf Woman, Sister of Crashing Thunder: The Autobiography of a Winnebago Indian.* Ed. Nancy Oestreich Lurie. Ann Arbor: Univ. of Michigan Press, 1961.

Mourning Dove [Humishuma; Cristal McLeod Galler] (Okanogan). *Co-ge-we-a, the Half-Blood: A Depiction of the Great Montana Cattle Range, by Hum-ishu-ma, "Mourning Dove," . . . Given through Sho-pow-tan.* With Notes and Biographical Sketch by Lucullus Virgil McWhorter. 1927. Rpt. with Introd. Dexter Fisher, Lincoln: Univ. of Nebraska Press, 1981.

———. *Coyote Stories.* With Notes by Lucullus Virgil McWhorter [Old Wolf]. Foreword Chief Standing Bear. Ed. Heister Dean Guie. 1933; rpt. New York: AMS, 1977.

———. *The Tales of the Okanogans.* Ed. Donald M. Hines. Fairfield, Wash.: Ye Galleon, 1976.

Mullett, G. M. *Spider Woman Stories.* Tucson: Univ. of Arizona Press, 1979.

Munn, Henry. "The Mushrooms of Language." In Michael Harner, ed. *Hallucinogens and Shamanism.* New York: Oxford Univ. Press, 1973, pp. 86–122.

Murdock, George P. *Ethnographic Bibliography of North America.* 5 vols. 4th ed., rev. Timothy J. O'Leary. New Haven: Human Relations Area File Press, 1975.

Murphy, Edith V. A. See Young, Lucy.

Murphy, James E., and Sharon M. Murphy. *Let My People Know: American Indian Journalism, 1828–1978.* Norman: Univ. of Oklahoma Press, 1981.

Murray, Henry A., ed. *Myth and Mythmaking.* New York: Braziller, 1960.

Nabokov, Peter. *Indian Running.* Santa Barbara: Capra, 1981.

———, ed. *Native American Testimony: First Encounter to Dispossession.* New York: Harper, 1979.

———. See also Two Leggings.

Nadeau, Remi. *The Real Joaquín Murieta: Robin Hood Hero or Gold Rush Gangster?* Corona del Mar, Calif.: Trans-Anglo, 1974.

Native American Research Group. *Native American Families in the City.* San Francisco: Scientific Analysis, 1975.

Neihardt, John G. See Black Elk.

Nelson, Mary C. See Martinez, Maria.

Nequatewa, Edmund (Hopi). *Hopi Customs, Folklore and Ceremonies.* Flagstaff: Museum of Northern Arizona, 1954.

———. *The Truth of a Hopi and Other Clan Stories of Shungapovi.* 1936. Rpt. as

Truth of a Hopi: Stories Relating to the Origin, Myths, and Clan Histories of the Hopi. Flagstaff, Ariz.: Northland, 1967.

Nettl, Bruno. *North American Indian Musical Styles.* MAFS, 45. Philadelphia: American Folklore Soc., 1954.

—————. "What Is Ethnomusicology?" In McAllester, *Readings in Ethnomusicology*, pp. 3–14.

Neuman, Erich. *The Great Mother: An Analysis of the Archetype.* Trans. Ralph Manheim. Princeton: Princeton Univ. Press, 1972.

Nevada Indians Speak. See Forbes, Jack D.

Newcomb, Franc J. *Hosteen Klah: Navaho Medicine Man and Sand Painter.* Norman: Univ. of Oklahoma Press, 1971.

Niatum, Duane McGinnis (Klallam). *Ascending Red Cedar Moon.* New York: Harper, 1974.

—————. *Digging Out the Roots.* New York: Harper, 1977.

—————. "On Stereotypes." *Parnassus*, 7, No. 8 (1978), 160–66.

—————. *Songs for the Harvester of Dreams.* Seattle: Univ. of Washington Press. 1981.

—————, ed. *Carriers of the Dream Wheel: Contemporary Native American Poetry.* New York: Harper, 1975.

Nida, Eugene A. *Toward a Science of Translation.* Leiden: Brill, 1964.

Niethammer, Carolyn. *Daughters of the Earth: The Lives and Legends of American Indian Women.* New York: Collier, 1977.

Norman, Howard A., ed. and trans. *The Wishing Bone Cycle: Narrative Poems of the Swampy Cree.* New York: Stonehill, 1976.

northSun, nila (Shoshone: Chippewa). "the way and the way things are." In *Diet Pepsi and Nacho Cheese.* Fallon, Nev.: Duck Down, 1977.

Nowell, Charles James (Kwakiutl). *Smoke from Their Fires: The Life of a Kwakiutl Chief.* Ed. Chellan S. Ford. Hamden, Conn.: Archon, 1968.

Nuñez, Bonita [Wa Wa Calachaw] (Luiseno). *Spirit Woman.* Ed. Stan Steiner. New York: Harper, 1980.

Oaks, Priscilla. "The First Generation of Native American Novelists." *MELUS*, 5, No. 1 (1978), 57–65.

O'Brien, Lynne Woods. *Plains Indian Autobiographies.* Western Writers, 10. Boise: Boise State Coll. Press, 1973.

O'Bryan, Aileen. *The Diné: Origin Myths of the Navaho Indians.* BBAE, 163. 1956; rpt. Saint Clair Shores, Mich.: Scholarly, 1974.

Occom, Samson (Mohegan). *A Choice Collection of Hymns and Spiritual Songs Intented [sic] for the Edification of Sincere Christians of all Denominations.* London: Timothy Green, 1774.

—————. *A Sermon Preached at the Execution of Moses Paul, an Indian Who Was Executed at New-Haven, on the 2d of September 1772. . . .* 1772; rpt. New York: Assn. for Study of American Indian Literatures, 1982.

Old Mexican (Navajo). *Old Mexican, Navaho Indian: A Navaho Autobiography.* Ed. Walter Dyk. Viking Fund Publications in Anthropology, 8. 1947; rpt. New York: Johnson, n.d.

O'Meara, Walter. *Daughters of the Country: The Women of the Fur Traders and Mountain Men.* New York: Harcourt, 1968.

Oppler, Morris. "Three Types of Variation and Their Relations to Culture Change." In Spier, Hallowell, and Newman, *Essays in Memory of Edward Sapir.*

Ortiz, Alfonso (San Juan). *The Tewa World: Space, Time, Being, and Becoming in a Pueblo Society.* Chicago: Univ. of Chicago Press, 1969, 1972.

———, ed. *New Perspectives on the Pueblos.* Albuquerque: Univ. of New Mexico Press, 1972.

———. *The Southwest. Handbook of North American Indians,* vol. 9. Washington, D.C.: Smithsonian Institution, 1979.

Ortiz, Simon J. (Acoma). *Fight Back: For the Sake of the People, for the Sake of the Land.* Albuquerque: Univ. of New Mexico, 1980.

———. *From Sand Creek.* New York: Thunder's Mouth, 1981.

———. *Going for the Rain.* New York: Harper, 1976.

———. *A Good Journey.* Berkeley: Turtle Island, 1977.

———. "Men on the Moon." *Howbah Indians.* Tucson: Blue Moon, 1977, pp. 11–19.

———. "Song/Poetry and Language: Perception and Expression." *Sun Tracks,* 3 (Spring 1977), 9–12. Rpt. *A,* 4, No. 2 (1979), 2–9.

———. "Towards a National Indian Literature: Cultural Authenticity in Nationalism." *MELUS,* 8 (1981), 7–12.

Ortutay, Gyula. *Hungarian Folklore: Essays.* Trans. István Butykai. Budapest: Akadémiai Kiadó, 1972.

Oskison, John Milton (Cherokee). *Black Jack Davy.* New York: Appleton, 1926.

———. *Brothers Three.* New York: Macmillan, 1935.

———. *Tecumseh and His Times: The Story of a Great Indian.* New York: Putnam, 1938.

———. *A Texas Titan: The Story of Sam Houston.* Garden City: Doubleday, 1929.

———. *Wild Harvest: A Novel of Transition Days in Oklahoma.* New York: Appleton, 1925.

"Oskison, John" [obituary]. New York Times, 27 Feb. 1947, p. 27.

Otto, Walter F. *Dionysus: Myth and Cult.* Trans. Robert B. Palmer. Bloomington: Indiana Univ. Press, 1965.

Paredes, Americo, and Richard Bauman, eds. *Towards New Perspectives in Folklore.* Austin: Univ. of Texas Press, 1972.

Parker, Arthur C. (Seneca). *Seneca Myths and Folktales.* PBHS, 27. 1923; rpt. New York: AMS, n.d.

Parker, Chief Everett (Seneca), and Oledoska (Abnaki). *The Secret of No Face: An Ireokwa Epic.* Healdsburg, Calif.: Native American Publishing, 1972.

Parkman, Francis. *The Oregon Trail.* 1849. Ed. E. N. Feltskog. Madison: Univ. of Wisconsin Press, 1969.

Parsons, Elsie Clews. *American Indian Life.* 1922; rpt. Lincoln: Univ. of Nebraska Press, 1967.

———. *Hopi and Zuni Ceremonialism.* MAAA, 39. 1933; rpt. Millwood, N.Y.: Kraus, n.d.

———. *Notes on Ceremonialism at Laguna.* APAMNH, 19, Pt. 4. New York: American Museum of Natural History, 1920.

———. *Pueblo Indian Religion.* 1933; rpt. Chicago: Univ. of Chicago Press, 1974.

———. *Tewa Tales.* MAFS, 19. 1926; rpt. Millwood, N.Y.: Kraus, 1971.

Pascal, Roy. *Design and Truth in Autobiography*. Cambridge: Harvard Univ. Press, 1960.

Paulding, James H. *Konigsmarke, the Long Finne*. 2 vols. 1823, 1835; rpt. New York: AMS, 1972.

Paytiamo, James (Acoma). *Flaming Arrow's People, by an Acoma Indian*. New York: Duffield and Green, 1932.

Paz, Octavio. *Alternating Current*. Trans. Helen R. Lane. New York: Viking, 1973.

———. *The Bow and the Lyre*. Trans. Ruth L. Simms. Austin: Univ. of Texas Press, 1973; New York: McGraw, 1973.

Pearce, Roy Harvey. *Savagism and Civilization: A Study of the Indian and the American Mind*. Baltimore: Johns Hopkins Press, 1953, 1967.

Pearce, T. M. *The Beloved House*. Caldwell, Id.: Caxton, 1940.

Peyer, Bernd C. "A Bibliography of Native American Prose Prior to the 20th Century." *Wassaja*, 13, No. 3 (1980), 23–25.

———. *Hyemeyohsts Storm's* Seven Arrows: *Fiction and Anthropology in the Native American Novel*. Wiesbaden: Steinver, 1979.

Phinney, Archie (Nez Perce), ed. *Nez Perce Texts*. CUCA, 25. 1934; rpt. New York: AMS, 1969.

Pitseolak (Eskimo). *Pitseolak: Pictures out of My Life*. Ed. Dorothy Eber. Seattle: Univ. of Washington Press, 1972.

Plenty Coups (Crow). *American: The Life Story of a Great Indian*. Ed. Frank B. Linderman. 1930. Rpt. as *Plenty Coups, Chief of the Crows*. Lincoln: Univ. of Nebraska Press, 1962.

Pokagon, Simon (Potawatomi). *O-gî-mäw-kwĕ Mit-i-gwä-kî (Queen of the Woods). Also Brief Sketch of the Algaic Language by Chief Pokagon*. 1899; rpt. Berrien Springs, Mich.: Hardscrabble, 1972.

Pope, Polly. "Toward a Structural Analysis of North American Trickster Tales." *Southern Folklore Quarterly*, 31 (1967), 274–86.

Popovi Da. "Indian Values." *The Living Wilderness*, 34 (Spring 1970), 26.

Posey, Alexander Lawrence (Creek). "Journal of Alexander Lawrence Posey with Annotations, January 1–September 4, 1897." Ed. Edward Everett Dale. CO, 45 (1967–68), 393–432.

———. "Journal of the Creek Enrollment Field Party 1905." Ed. Edward Everett Dale. CO, 46 (1968), 2–19.

———. *The Poems of Alexander Lawrence Posey*. Collected and Arranged by Mrs. Minnie H. Posey, with a Memoir by William Elsey Connelly. Topeka: Crane, 1910.

Pound, Ezra. "A Few Don'ts by an Imagiste." *Poetry*, 1, No. 6 (1913), 200–06.

Pound, Louise. "The Beginnings of Poetry." *PMLA*, 32 (1917), 201–32.

Powell, John Wesley. *Indian Linguistic Families of America North of Mexico*. ARBAE, 7. Washington: GPO, 1891.

Powers, William K. *Oglala Religion*. 1975; rpt. Lincoln: Univ. of Nebraska Press, 1977.

Pretty-Shield (Crow). *Red Mother*. 1932. Ed. Frank B. Linderman, as *Pretty-Shield, Medicine Woman of the Crows*. Lincoln: Univ. of Nebraska Press, 1974.

Price, Anna [Her Eyes Grey] (Apache). "Personal Narrative of Anna Price." In Keith H. Basso, ed. *Western Apache Raiding and Warfare*. Tucson: Univ. of Arizona Press, 1971, pp. 29–39.

Prucha, Francis P., ed. *A Bibliographical Guide to the History of Indian-White Relations in the United States.* Chicago: Univ. of Chicago Press, 1977.

Purley, Anthony F. "Keres Pueblo Concepts of Deity." *AICRJ,* 1, No. 1 (1974), 29–32.

Qoyawayma, Polingaysi [Elizabeth O. White] (Hopi). *No Turning Back: A True Account of a Hopi Indian Girl's Struggle to Bridge the Gap between the World of Her People and the World of the White Man.* Ed. Vada F. Carlson. Albuquerque: Univ. of New Mexico Press, 1964.

Quam, Alvina. See Zuni People.

Quasha, George, and Jerome Rothenberg, eds. *America a Prophecy: A New Reading of American Poetry from Pre-Columbian Times to the Present.* New York: Random, 1973.

Radin, Paul. *Literary Aspects of North American Mythology.* Canada Dept. of Mines, Museum Bull. 16, Anthropological Series 6. Ottawa: Government Printing Bureau, 1915.

––––––. *The Trickster: A Study in American Indian Mythology.* 1948; rpt. New York: Philosophical Library, 1969; New York: Schocken, 1972.

––––––. See also Blowsnake, Sam.

Ramsey, Jarold W. "The Bible in Western Indian Mythology." *JAF,* 90 (1977), 442–54.

––––––. "Coyote Goes Upriver: A Cycle for Story Theater and Mime." *Georgia Review,* 35 (1981), 534–51.

––––––. *Coyote Was Going There: Indian Literature of the Oregon Country.* Seattle: Univ. of Washington Press, 1977.

––––––. "From 'Mythic' to 'Fictive' in a Nez Percé Orpheus Myth." *WAL,* 12 (1978), 119–31. Rpt. in Kroeber, *Traditional Literatures,* pp. 25–44.

––––––. "A Supplement to Michael Dorris's 'Native American Literature.'" *CE,* 41 (1980), 933–35.

––––––. "The Teacher of Modern American Indian Writings as Ethnographer and Critic." *CE,* 41 (1979), 163–69.

––––––. "The Wife Who Goes Out like a Man, Comes Back as a Hero: The Art of Two Oregon Indian Narratives." *PMLA,* 92 (1977), 9–18.

Randle, Martha Champion. "Iroquois Women Then and Now." In William N. Fenton, ed. *Symposium on Local Diversity in Iroquois Culture.* BBAE, 149. Washington, D.C.: GPO, 1951, pp. 169–80.

Rasmussen, Knud J. V. *Report of the Fifth Thule Expedition.* 2 vols. Copenhagen: Gyldendal, 1927.

Reichard, Gladys A. *Dezba, Woman of the Desert: Life among the Navajo Indians.* 1939; rpt. Glorieta, N. Mex.: Rio Grande, 1971.

––––––. "Individualism and Mythological Style." *JAF,* 57 (1944), 16–25.

––––––. "Literary Types and Dissemination of Myths." *JAF,* 34 (1921), 269–307.

––––––. *Navaho Religion: A Study of Symbolism.* 2nd ed. Princeton: Princeton Univ. Press, 1963.

––––––. *Prayer: The Compulsive Word.* American Ethnological Soc. Monographs, 7. New York: Augustin, 1944; Seattle: Univ. of Washington Press, 1944.

Revard, Carter (Osage). "Deer Talk, Coyote Talk, Meadowlark Territory: The Muses Dance to Our Drum Now." Paper presented at the Modern Language Association, New York, 28 Dec. 1978.

Rich, George W. "Rethinking the 'Star Husbands.'" *JAF*, 84 (1971), 436–41.

Richter, Conrad. *The Light in the Forest*. New York: Knopf, 1953.

Ricketts, MacLinscott. "The North American Indian Trickster." *History of Religions,* 5 (1966), 327–50.

Ridge, John Rollin (Cherokee). *The Life and Adventures of Joaquín Murieta, the Celebrated California Bandit, by Yellow Bird*. 1854; rpt. with Introd. Joseph Henry Jackson. Norman: Univ. of Oklahoma Press, 1977.

———. *Poems*. San Francisco: Hayot, 1868.

Riggs, Lynn (Cherokee). *Big Lake*. New York: French, 1927.

———. *The Cherokee Night*. New York: French, 1936.

———. *Green Grow the Lilacs*. New York: French, 1931.

Roberts, Helen H., and Diamond Jenness. *Songs of the Copper Eskimo*. Report of the Canadian Arctic Expedition, 14. Ottawa: Acland, 1925.

Roberts, Kenneth. *Northwest Passage*. 1937. Garden City: Doubleday, 1959; New York: Fawcett, 1977.

Roemer, Kenneth. "Bear and Elk: The Nature(s) of Contemporary Indian Poetry." *JES*, 5 (1977), 69–79.

———. "Native American Oral Narratives: Context and Continuity." In Swann, *Smoothing the Ground*, forthcoming.

———. Rev. of *Darkness in Saint Louis Bearheart*, by Gerald Vizenor. *AICRJ*, 4, Nos. 1-2 (1980), 187–91.

———. "Survey Courses, Indian Literature, and *The Way to Rainy Mountain*." *CE* 37 (1976), 619–24.

Roessel, Ruth, ed. *Navajo Studies*. Many Farms, Ariz.: Navajo Community Coll. Press, 1971.

Rogers, Betty. *Will Rogers: His Wife's Story*. 1943; rpt. Norman: Univ. of Oklahoma Press, 1979.

Rogers, Will (Cherokee). *The Autobiography of Will Rogers*. Ed. Donald Day. 1949; rpt. New York: AMS, 1979.

———. *Convention Articles of Will Rogers*. Ed. Joseph A. Stout, Jr. Stillwater: Oklahoma State Univ. Press, 1976.

———. *Ether and Me, or "Just Relax."* 1929. Ed. Joseph A. Stout, Jr. Stillwater: Oklahoma State Univ. Press, 1973.

———. *The Illiterate Digest*. 1924. Ed. Joseph A. Stout, Jr. Stillwater: Oklahoma State Univ. Press, 1974.

———. *Letters of a Self-Made Diplomat to His President*. 1926. Ed. Joseph A. Stout, Jr. Stillwater: Oklahoma State Univ. Press, 1977.

———. *Rogerisms: The Cowboy Philosopher on the Peace Conference*. 1919. Ed. Joseph A. Stout, Jr. Stillwater: Oklahoma State Univ. Press, 1975.

———. *Rogerisms: The Cowboy Philosopher on Prohibition*. 1919. Ed. Joseph A. Stout, Jr. Stillwater: Oklahoma State Univ. Press, 1975.

———. *There's Not a Bathing Suit in Russia and Other Bare Facts*. 1927. Ed. Joseph A. Stout, Jr. Stillwater: Oklahoma State Univ. Press, 1973.

———. *The Will Rogers Book*. Ed. Paula McSpadden Love. Indianapolis: Bobbs-Merrill, 1961.

———. *Will Rogers' Daily Telegrams*. Ed. James M. Smallwood. Stillwater: Oklahoma State Univ. Press, 1978.

———. *Will Rogers Rode the Range.* Ed. Margaret S. Axtell. Phoenix: Allied, 1972.

Rooth, Anna Birgitta. "The Creation Myths of the North American Indians." *Anthropos,* 52 (1957), 497–508.

Rose, Wendy (Hopi). *Academic Squaw: Reports to the World from the Ivory Tower.* Moorhead, Minn.: Blue Cloud, 1977.

———. *Hopi Roadrunner, Dancing.* Greenfield Center, N.Y.: Greenfield Review, 1973.

———. *Long Division: A Tribal History.* New York: Strawberry, 1977.

———. *Lost Copper.* Banning, Calif.: Malki Museum, 1980.

Rosen, Kenneth, ed. *The Man to Send Rain Clouds: Contemporary Stories by American Indians.* New York: Viking, 1974; New York: Random, 1975.

———. *Voices of the Rainbow: Contemporary Poetry by American Indians.* New York: Viking, 1975; New York: Grove, 1980.

Rosowski, Susan, and Helen Stauffer, eds. *Women in Western American Literature.* Troy, N.Y.: Whitston, 1982.

Rothenberg, Jerome. "Total Translation: An Experiment in the Presentation of American Indian Poetry." In Chapman, *Literature of the American Indians,* pp. 292–307.

———, ed. *Shaking the Pumpkin: Traditional Poetry of the Indian North Americas.* Garden City: Doubleday, 1972.

———. See also Quasha, George.

Rowlandson, Mary. *The Soveraignity and Goodness of God. . . .* 1682; rpt. Boston: S. Phillips, 1720.

Roy, Cal. *The Serpent and the Sun: Myths of the Mexican World.* New York: Farrar, 1972.

Ruoff, A. LaVonne Brown. "Alienation and the Female Principle." *AIQ,* 4 (1978), 107–22.

———. "History in *Winter in the Blood:* Backgrounds and Bibliography." *AIQ,* 4 (1978), 169–72.

———. "Ritual and Renewal: Keres Traditions in the Short Fiction of Leslie Silko." *MELUS,* 5 (1978), 2–17.

———. Rev. of *Darkness in Saint Louis Bearheart,* by Gerald Vizenor. *MELUS,* 8 (1981), 69–71.

Ruppert, James. "The Uses of Oral Tradition in Six Contemporary Native American Poets." *AICRJ,* 4, No. 4 (1980), 87–100.

Rushmore, Helen, and Wolf Robe Hunt (Acoma). *The Dancing Horses of Acoma and Other Acoma Indian Stories.* New York: World, 1963.

Sanapia (Comanche). *Sanapia, Comanche Medicine Woman.* Ed. David E. Jones. New York: Holt, 1972.

Sanchez, Carol Lee (Laguna-Sioux). *Conversations from the Nightmare.* San Francisco: La Galleria, 1975.

———. *Message Bringer Woman.* San Francisco: Tauran, 1976.

Sanchez, Thomas. *Rabbit Boss.* New York: Knopf, 1973; New York: Ballantine, 1973.

Sandburg, Carl. "Aboriginal Poetry." *Poetry,* 9 (Feb. 1917), 254–55.

Sanders, Thomas E. (Cherokee), and William E. Peek (Narragansett-Wampanoag), eds. *Literature of the American Indian.* New York: Glencoe, 1973.

Sando, Joe (Jemez). *The Pueblo Indian.* San Francisco: Indian Historian, 1976.

Sandoz, Mari. *The Horsecatcher*. Philadelphia: Westminster, 1957.

Sands, Kathleen Mullen. "Alienation and Broken Narrative." *AIQ*, 4 (1978), 97–105.

——. "*The Death of Jim Loney*: Indian or Not?" *SAIL*, 5, Nos. 3-4 (1981), 5–8.

——. "A Man of Words: The Life and Letters of a Yaqui Poet." *AICRJ*, 4 (1980), 143–59.

——. See also Savala, Refugio.

——, and Emory Sekaquaptewa (Hopi). "Four Hopi Lullabies: A Study in Method and Meaning." *AIQ*, 4 (1978), 195–210.

Sapir, Edward. "Song Recitative in Paiute Mythology." *JAF*, 23 (1910), 455–72.

——, ed. *Wishram Texts, Together with Wasco Tales and Myths*. Collected by Jeremiah Curtin. PAES, 2. 1907; rpt. New York: AMS, 1974.

Savala, Refugio (Yaqui). *The Autobiography of a Yaqui Poet*. Ed. Kathleen M. Sands. Tucson: Univ. of Arizona Press, 1980.

Saxton, Dean, and Lucille Saxton, eds. *O'otham Hoho'ok A'agitha: Legends and Lore of the Papago and Pima Indians*. Tucson: Univ. of Arizona Press, 1973.

Sayre, Robert F. "A Bibliography and an Anthology of American Indian Literature." *CE*, 35 (1974), 704–06.

——. "Vision and Experience in *Black Elk Speaks*." *CE*, 32 (1971), 509–35.

Scarberry, Susan J. "Memory as Medicine: The Power of Recollection in *Ceremony*." *AIQ*, 5, No. 1 (1979), 19–26.

——. "Sources of Healing in *House Made of Dawn*." Diss. Univ. of Colorado 1982.

Scott, Lalla. See Lowry, Annie.

Sebeok, Thomas A., ed. *Native Languages of the Americas*. 2 vols. New York: Plenum, 1976.

Seiler, Hans J. *Cahuilla Texts*. Language Science Monographs, 6. Bloomington: Indiana Univ., 1970.

Sekaquaptewa, Helen (Hopi). *Me and Mine: The Life Story of Helen Sekaquaptewa as Told to Louise Udall*. Ed. Louise Udall. Tucson: Univ. of Arizona Press, 1969.

Sewell, Elizabeth. *The Orphic Voice*. New York: Harper, 1971.

Sewid, James (Kwakiutl). *Guests Never Leave Hungry: The Autobiography of James Sewid, a Kwakiutl Indian*. Ed. James P. Spradley. New Haven: Yale Univ. Press, 1969.

Seyersted, Per. *Leslie Marmon Silko*. Western Writers, 45. Boise, Id.: Boise State Univ. Press, 1980.

Shaw, Anna Moore (Pima). *Pima Indian Legends*. Tucson: Univ. of Arizona Press, 1968.

——. *A Pima Past*. Tucson: Univ. of Arizona Press, 1974.

Silko, Leslie Marmon (Laguna). *Ceremony*. New York: Viking, 1977; New York: NAL, 1978.

——. *Laguna Woman*. Greenfield Center, N.Y.: Greenfield Review, 1974.

——. "Language and Literature from a Pueblo Indian Perspective." In Fiedler and Baker, *Opening Up the Canon*, pp. 54–72.

——. Letter to Abraham Chapman. In Chapman, *Literature of the American Indians*, pp. 5–6.

——. "An Old-Time Indian Attack Conducted in Two Parts." *Shantih*, 4, No. 2 (1979), 3–5. Rpt. in Hobson, *The Remembered Earth*, pp. 211–16.

———. "Stories and Their Tellers: A Conversation with Leslie Silko." In Fisher, *The Third Woman*, pp. 18–23.

———. "Storyteller." *Puerto del Sol*, Fall 1975, pp. 11–25.

———. *Storyteller*. New York: Seaver, 1981; New York: Grove, 1981.

———. "Toe'osh, a Laguna Coyote Story." In Niatum, *Carriers of the Dream Wheel*, pp. 223–25.

———. "Yellow Woman." In Rosen, *The Man to Send Rain Clouds*, pp. 33–45.

Simmons, Leo W. See Talayesva, Don C.

Simms, William Gilmore. *The Wigwam and the Cabin*. 1853. Rev. ed., 1885; rpt. New York: AMS, 1970.

———. *Yemasee: A Romance of Carolina*. 1835. Ed. Joseph V. Ridgely. New Haven: Coll. and Univ. Press, 1964.

Skinner, Alanson, and John V. Satterlee (Menominee). *Folklore of the Menomini Indians*. APAMNH, 8, Pt. 3. 1915; rpt. New York: AMS, 1977.

Slickpoo, Allen P. (Nez Perce), et al., eds. *Nu Mee Poom Tit Wah Tit* (*Nez Perce Stories*). Lapwai, Id.: Nez Perce Tribe, 1972.

Smith, Dana Margaret. *Hopi Girl*. Palo Alto: Stanford Univ. Press, 1931.

Smith, John. *General Historie of Virginia, New England, and the Southern Isles*. 1624; rpt. Murfreesboro, N.C.: Johnson, n.d.

———. *New England Trials*. 1620; rpt. Norwood, N.J.: Johnson, 1971.

———. *A True Relation*. . . . 1608. New York: Lovell, 1896.

Smith, Patricia. "Coyote Ortiz: *Canis latrans latrans* in the Poetry of Simon Ortiz." *Minority Voices*, 3, No. 2 (1979), 1–17.

———, and Paula Gunn Allen. "Chee Dostoyevsky Rides the Reservation: American Indian Literature since Momaday." In Taylor, *Literary History*.

Smith, William F., Jr. "American Indian Autobiographies." *AIQ*, 2 (1975), 237–45.

Smith, William James. Rev. of *House Made of Dawn*, by N. Scott Momaday. *Commonweal*, 20 Sept. 1968, p. 636.

Smithson, Carma Lee. *The Havasupai Woman*. Anthropological Papers, 38. 1959; rpt. New York: Johnson, 1972.

Snyder, Gary. *Earth House Hold*. New York: New Directions, 1969.

———. "The Incredible Survival of Coyote." *WAL*, 9 (1975), 255–72.

Sokolov, Yuriy M. *Russian Folklore*. Trans. Catharine R. Smith. 1950; rpt. Detroit: Folklore Assn., 1971.

Southard, Bruce. "Will Rogers and the Language of the Southwest: A Centennial Perspective." In Gibson, *Will Rogers*, pp. 365–75.

Spencer, Katharine. *Mythology and Values: An Analysis of Navaho Chantway Myths*. MAFS, 48. 1957; rpt. Austin: Univ. of Texas Press, 1976.

———. *Reflections of Social Life in the Navaho Origin Myth*. Univ. of New Mexico Publications in Anthropology, 3. 1947; rpt. New York: AMS, 1981.

Sperry, James. See Waheenee.

Spicer, Edward H. *Cycles of Conquest: The Impact of Spain, Mexico, and the United States on Indians of the Southwest, 1533–1960*. Tucson: Univ. of Arizona Press, 1962.

Spier, Leslie, A. Irving Hallowell, and Stanley S. Newman, eds. *Essays in Memory of Edward Sapir*. Menasha, Wis.: Sapir Memorial Publishing Fund, 1941.

Spinden, Herbert Joseph. "American Indian Poetry." *Natural History*, 19 (1919), 301–08.

———, ed. *Songs of the Tewa*. 1933; rpt. Santa Fe, N. Mex.: Sunstone, 1976.

Spindler, Louise S. "Menomini Women and Culture Change." *MAAA*, 91 (1962), 14–20.

Spradley, James P. See Sewid, James.

Sprague, Marshall. Rev. of *House Made of Dawn*, by N. Scott Momaday. *New York Times Book Review*, 9 June 1968, p. 5.

Standing Bear, Luther [Ota Kte] (Sioux). *Land of the Spotted Eagle*. 1933; rpt. with foreword by Richard N. Ellis, Lincoln: Univ. of Nebraska Press, 1978.

———. *My Indian Boyhood, by Chief Luther Standing Bear, Who Was the Boy Ota K'te (Plenty Kill)*. Boston: Houghton, 1931.

———. *My People, the Sioux*. Ed. E. A. Brininstool. Introd. William S. Hart. 1928; rpt. with introd. Richard N. Ellis, Lincoln: Univ. of Nebraska Press, 1975.

———. *Stories of the Sioux*. Boston: Houghton, 1934.

Stands in Timber, John (Cheyenne). *Cheyenne Memories, a Folk History*. Ed. Margot Liberty and Robert M. Utley. 1967; rpt. Lincoln: Univ. of Nebraska Press, 1972.

Stanley, Mrs. Andrew. "Personal Narrative of Mrs. Andrew Stanley." In Keith H. Basso, ed. *Western Apache Raiding and Warfare*. Tucson: Univ. of Arizona Press, 1971, pp. 205–19.

Steiner, Stan. *The New Indians*. New York: Harper, 1968; New York: Dell, 1969.

Stensland, Anna Lee. "Charles Alexander Eastman: Sioux Storyteller and Historian." *AIQ*, 3 (1977), 199–208.

———. *Literature by and about the American Indian: An Annotated Bibliography*. 2nd ed. Urbana: National Council of Teachers of English, 1979.

Stephen, Alexander McGregor. "Hopi Tales." *JAF*, 42 (1929), 1–72, 187–91.

Stephens, Anna Sophia. *Malakeska: The Indian Wife of the White Hunter*. 1860; rpt. New York: Arno, 1975.

Stern, Theodore. "Some Sources of Variability in Klamath Mythology." *JAF*, 69 (1956), 1–12, 135–45, 377–86.

Steward, Julian H. "Two Paiute Autobiographies." *University of California Publications in American Archaeology and Ethnology*, 33 (1934), 423–38.

Stewart, Irene (Navajo). *A Voice in Her Tribe*. Ed. Doris Ostrander Dawdy and Mary Shepardson. Anthropological Papers, 17. Socorro, N. Mex.: Ballena, 1980.

Stirling, Matthew W. *Origin Myth of Acoma and Other Records*. BBAE, 135. 1942; rpt. Saint Claire Shores, Mich.: Scholarly, n.d.

———, ed. "Pictograph Autobiographies of Sitting Bull." *Smithsonian Institution Collections*, 97, No. 5 (1938), 1–57.

Stone, John Augustus. *Metamora, or the Land of the Wampanoags*. 1829. Ed. Eugene R. Page. Princeton: Princeton Univ. Press, 1941.

Stories of Traditional Navajo Life. See Johnson, Broderick H.

Storm, Hyemeyohsts (Cheyenne). *Seven Arrows*. New York: Harper, 1972.

Street, Alfred B. *Frontenac, or the Atotarho of the Iroquois*. New York: Baker and Scribner, 1849.

Stump, Serain (Shoshone). *There Is My People Sleeping: The Ethnic Poem-Drawings of Serain Stump*. Sidney, B.C.: Gray's, 1970.

Swann, Brian, ed. *Smoothing the Ground: Essays on Native American Oral Literature.* Los Angeles: Univ. of California Press, 1982.

————. *Song of the Sky: Versions of American Indian Songs.* Foreword Paula Gunn Allen. New York: Four Zoas, 1982.

Swanton, Guy E. "Orpheus and Star Husband: Meaning and the Structure of Myths." *Ethnology,* 15, No. 2 (1976), 115–33.

Sweezy, Carl (Arapaho). *The Arapaho Way: A Memoir of an Indian Boyhood.* New York: Potter, 1966.

Tahan. See Griffis, Joseph.

Talayesva, Don C. (Hopi). *Sun Chief: The Autobiography of a Hopi Indian.* Ed. Leo W. Simmons. 1942; rpt. New Haven: Yale Univ. Press, 1974.

Tall Mountain, Mary (Athalascan). *Nine Poems.* San Francisco: Friars, 1977.

————. *There Is No Word for Goodbye.* Marvin, S. Dak: Blue Cloud Quarterly, 1981.

Tax, Sol, ed. *The Civilizations of Ancient America: Selected Papers of the Twenty-Ninth International Congress of Americanists.* Chicago: Univ. of Chicago Press, 1952.

Taylor, Golden, ed. *The Literary History of the American West.* Lincoln: Univ. of Nebraska Press, forthcoming.

Tedlock, Dennis. "On the Translation of Style in Oral Narrative." *JAF,* 84 (1971), 114–33.

————. "Pueblo Literature: Style and Verisimilitude." In A. Ortiz, *New Perspectives on the Pueblos,* pp. 219–42.

————. "The Spoken Word and the Work of Interpretation in American Indian Religion." In Kroeber, *Traditional Literatures,* pp. 45–64.

————. "Toward an Oral Poetics." *New Literary History,* 8 (1977), 507–19.

————, ed. *Finding the Center: Narrative Poetry of the Zuni Indians.* 1972; rpt. Lincoln: Univ. of Nebraska Press, 1978.

————, and Barbara Tedlock, eds. *Teachings from the American Earth: Indian Religion and Philosophy.* New York: Liveright, 1975.

Teit, James, ed. *Traditions of the Thompson River Indians of British Columbia.* Introd. Franz Boas. MAFS, 6. 1898; rpt. Millwood, N.Y.: Kraus, 1970.

Terrell, John Upton, and Donna M. Terrell. *Indian Women of the Western Morning: Their Life in Early America.* New York: Dial, 1974; Garden City: Doubleday, 1976.

Thackeray, William. "Crying for Pity in *Winter in the Blood.*" *MELUS,* 7, No. 1 (1980), 61–78.

————. "*The Death of Jim Loney* as a Half-Breed's Tragedy." *SAIL,* 5, Nos. 3–4 (1981), 16–18.

Theisz, R. D., and Ben Black Bear, Sr. (Sioux), eds. *Buckskin Tokens: Contemporary Oral Narratives of the Lakota.* Rosebud, S. Dak.: Sinte Gleska Coll., 1975.

Thompson, Stith. *The Folktale.* 1946; rpt. Berkeley: Univ. of California Press, 1977.

————. *Motif-Index of Folk-Literature.* Rev. and enl. 6 vols. Bloomington: Indiana Univ. Press, 1955–58.

————. *Narrative Motif-Analysis as a Folklore Method.* Folk Fellows Communications, 161. Helsinki: Suomalainen Tiedeakatemia, 1955.

————. "The Star Husband Tale." 1953; rpt. in Dundes, *The Study of Folklore,* pp. 414–74.

————, ed. *Tales of the North American Indians.* 1929; rpt. Bloomington: Indiana Univ. Press, 1966.

Thoreau, Henry David. *The Maine Woods.* 1864. Ed. Joseph J. Moldenhauer. Princeton: Princeton Univ. Press, 1972.

Toelken, Barre. *The Dynamics of Folklore.* Boston: Houghton, 1978.

————. "*Ma'i Joldloshi*: Legendary Styles and Navajo Myth." In Hand, *American Folk Legend*, pp. 203–11.

————. "The 'Pretty Language(s)' of Yellowman: Genre, Mode, and Texture in Navajo Coyote Narratives." *Genre*, 2 (1969), 211–35. Rpt. in Ben-Amos, *Folklore Genres*, pp. 145–70.

————. "Seeing with a Native Eye: How Many Sheep Will It Hold?" In Capps, *Seeing with a Native Eye*, pp. 9–24.

————, and Tacheeni Scott (Navajo). "Poetic Retranslation and the 'Pretty Languages' of Yellowman." In Kroeber, *Traditional Literatures*, pp. 65–116.

Toole, Kenneth Ross, ed. *Probing the American West.* Santa Fe: Museum of New Mexico, 1962.

Tracy, Robert. "Myth and Reality in *The Adventures of Tom Sawyer.*" *Southern Review*, 4 (1968), 530–41.

Trimble, Martha Scott. *N. Scott Momaday.* Western Writers. Boise, Id.: Boise State Coll., 1973.

Turner, Frederick W., III, ed. *The Portable North American Indian Reader.* New York: Viking, 1973.

Two Leggings (Crow). *Two Leggings: The Making of a Crow Warrior.* Ed. Peter Nabokov. New York: Crowell, 1967; New York: Apollo, 1970.

Tyler, Hamilton A. *Pueblo Animals and Myths.* Norman: Univ. of Oklahoma Press, 1975.

————. *Pueblo Birds and Myths.* Norman: Univ. of Oklahoma Press, 1979.

————. *Pueblo Gods and Myths.* Norman: Univ. of Oklahoma Press, 1964.

Udall, Louise. See Sekaquaptewa, Helen.

Ullom, Judith C. *Folklore of the North American Indian: An Annotated Bibliography.* Washington: Library of Congress, 1969.

Underhill, Ruth M. *First Penthouse Dwellers of America.* 2nd ed. Santa Fe, N. Mex.: Laboratory of Anthropology, 1946.

————. *Hawk over Whirlpools.* New York: Augustin, 1940.

————. *Papago Indian Religion.* CUCA, 33. 1946; rpt. New York: AMS, 1969.

————. *The Papago Indians of Arizona and Their Relatives the Pima.* 1940; rpt. New York: AMS, 1977.

————. *Red Man's Religion: Beliefs and Practices of the Indians North of Mexico.* Chicago: Univ. of Chicago Press, 1965, 1972.

————. *Singing for Power: The Song Magic of the Papago Indians of Southern Arizona.* 1938; rpt. Berkeley: Univ. of California Press, 1976.

————. See also Chona, Maria.

————, Donald M. Bahr, Baptisto Lopez, Jose Pancho, and David Lopez. *Rainhouse and Ocean: Speeches for the Papago Year.* American Tribal Religions, 4. 1979; rpt. Lincoln: Univ. of Nebraska Press, 1981.

United States Department of Labor. *Native American Women and Equal Opportunity: How to Get Ahead in the Federal Government.* Washington, D.C.: GPO, 1979.

Untermeyer, Louis. Rev. of *The Path on the Rainbow*, ed. George Cronyn. *Dial*, 8 March 1919, pp. 240–41.

Utley, Robert M. See Stands in Timber, John.

Vanderburgh, Rosamund M. See Johnston, Verna Patronella.

Vanderwerth, W. C., ed. *Indian Oratory: Famous Speeches by Noted Indian Chieftains*. 1971; rpt. New York: Ballantine, 1975; Norman: Univ. of Oklahoma Press, 1979.

Van Steen, Marcus, ed. *Pauline Johnson: Her Life and Work*. Toronto: Hodder and Stoughton, 1965.

Vaudrin, Bill (Chippewa), ed. *Tanaina Tales from Alaska*. Norman: Univ. of Oklahoma Press, 1969.

Velarde, Pablita (Santa Clara). *Old Father, the Story Teller*. Globe, Ariz.: King, 1960.

Velie, Alan R. "James Welch's Poetry." *AICRJ*, 3, No. 1 (1979), 19–38.

————, ed. *American Indian Literature: An Anthology*. Norman: Univ. of Oklahoma Press, 1979.

————. *Four American Indian Literary Masters*. Norman: Univ. of Oklahoma Press, 1982.

Veselovsky, A. N. *Three Chapters from Historical Poetics*. Vol. I of *Collected Works*. St. Petersburg, 1913.

Vistal, Stanley, ed. *Warpath: The True Story of a Fighting Sioux*. Boston: Houghton, 1934.

Vizenor, Gerald (Ojibwe). *Anishinabe Adisokan: Tales of the People*. 1970. Rpt. in his *Summer in the Spring*.

————. *Anishinabe Nagamon*. 1965. Rpt. in his *Summer in the Spring*.

————. *Darkness in Saint Louis Bearheart*. St. Paul: Truck, 1978.

————. "I Know What You Mean, Erdupps MacChurbbs: Autobiographical Myths and Metaphors." In Anderson, *Growing Up in Minnesota*, pp. 79–111.

————. "An Interview with Gerald Vizenor." Ed. Neal Bowers and Charles L. P. Silet. *MELUS*, 8, No. 1 (1981), 41–49.

————, ed. *Summer in the Spring: Ojibwe Lyric Poems and Tribal Stories*. Minneapolis: Nodine, 1981.

Von Franz, Marie-Louise. *Patterns of Creativity Mirrored in Creation Myths*. Zürich: Spring, 1972.

Waddell, Jack O., and O. Michael Watson, eds. *The American Indian in Urban Society*. Boston: Little, 1971.

Waheenee [Buffalo Bird Woman] (Hidatsa). *An Indian Girl's Story*. Ed. Gilbert L. Wilson. 1921; rpt. Lincoln: Univ. of Nebraska Press, 1981.

Walker, Franklin. *San Francisco's Literary Frontier*. 1939; rpt. Seattle: Univ. of Washington Press, 1969.

Walker, James R. *Lakota Belief and Ritual*. Ed. Raymond DeMallie and Elaine Jahner. Lincoln: Univ. of Nebraska Press, 1980.

————. *Lakota Myth*. Ed. Elaine Jahner. Lincoln: Univ. of Nebraska Press, forthcoming.

————. *The Sun Dance and Other Ceremonies of the Oglala Division of the Teton Dakota*. APAMNH, 16. 1917; rpt. New York: AMS, n.d.

Walking Bull, Gilbert (Sioux), and Montana Walking Bull (Cherokee).

————. *Mi Ta-ku-ye: About My People*. Dallas, Ore.: Itemizer-Observer, 1977.

————. *O-hu-kah-kan: Poetry, Songs, Legends, and Stories by American Indians*. Dallas, Ore.: Itemizer-Observer, 1975.

————. *Wo Ya-ka-pi: Telling Stories of the Past and the Present*. Dallas, Ore.: Itemizer-Observer, 1976.

Wallis, Leslie A. "Folktales from Shumopovi, Second Mesa." *JAF*, 49 (1936), 1–68.

Walsh, Marnie (Dakota). *A Taste of the Knife*. 2nd ed. Ed. A. Thomas Trusky. Boise, Id.: Ahsahta, 1976.

Walters, Anna Lee. *Indian Time*. 1977. (Unpublished manuscript.)

Walther, Tom. *A Spider Might*. New York: Scribners, 1978.

Walton, Eda Lou. "Navajo Song Patterning." *JAF*, 43 (1930), 105–18.

————. "Navajo Verse Rhythms." *Poetry*, 24 (April 1924), 40–44.

————, and T. T. Waterman. "American Indian Poetry." *American Anthropologist*, 27 (1925), 25–52.

Waltrip, Lela, and Rufus Waltrip. *Indian Women*. New York: McKay, 1964.

Warren, William Whipple (Ojibwe). *History of the Ojibways, Based on Traditions and Oral Statements*. Collections of the Minnesota Historical Soc., 5. 1885; rpt. Minneapolis: Ross and Haines, 1957.

Washburn, Wilcomb E. *The Indian in America*. New York: Harper, 1975.

Waterman, T. T. "The Explanatory Element in the Folk-Tales of the North-American Indians." *JAF*, 27 (1914), 1–54.

Waters, Frank. *The Man Who Killed the Deer*. Athens, Ohio: Swallow, 1942; New York: Pocket, n.d.

————. *Masked Gods*. New York: Ballantine, 1950.

————, and Oswald White Bear Fredericks (Hopi). *Book of the Hopi*. New York: Viking, 1963; New York: Ballantine, 1974; New York: Penguin, 1977.

Watkins, Floyd. *In Time and Place: Some Origins of American Fiction*. Athens: Univ. of Georgia Press, 1977.

Wauneka, Annie D. (Navajo). "The Dilemma for Indian Women." *Wassaja*, 4 (Sept. 1976).

Webb, George E. (Pima). *A Pima Remembers*. Tucson: Univ. of Arizona Press, 1959.

Welch, James (Blackfeet–Gros Ventre). *The Death of Jim Loney*. New York: Harper, 1979.

————. *Riding the Earthboy 40*. 1971. Rev. ed. New York: Harper, 1975.

————. *Winter in the Blood*. New York: Harper, 1974.

Wheeler-Voegelin, Ermine, and Remedios W. Moore. "The Emergence Myth in Native North America." In *Studies in Folklore*. Ed. W. Edson Richmond. 1957; rpt. Westport, Conn.: Greenwood, 1972, pp. 66–91.

White, Elizabeth. See Qoyawayma, Polingaysi.

White, Hayden. "Introduction: The Poetics of History." Ch. 1 of *Metahistory: The Historical Imagination in Nineteenth-Century Europe*. Baltimore: Johns Hopkins Univ. Press, 1973.

White, James L., ed. *The First Skin around Me: Contemporary American Tribal Poetry*. Moorhead, Minn.: Territorial, 1975.

White, Leslie A. *The Acoma Indians*. ARBAE, 47. 1929–30; rpt. Glorieta, N. Mex.: Rio Grande, 1972.

————. "An Autobiography of an Acoma Indian." *BBAE*, 136 (1943), 326–37.

White Bull, Joseph (Sioux). *The Warrior Who Killed Custer: The Personal Narrative of*

Chief Joseph White Bull. Trans. and ed. James H. Howard. Lincoln: Univ. of Nebraska Press, 1968.

Whitewolf, Jim (Kiowa-Apache). *Jim Whitewolf: The Life of a Kiowa Apache.* Ed. Charles S. Brant. New York: Dover, 1969.

Whitman, Walt. *Leaves of Grass.* Ed. Harold W. Blodgett and Bradley Sculley. New York: New York Univ. Press, 1965; New York: Norton, 1968.

Whitman, William. "Xube, a Ponca Autobiography." *JAF*, 52 (1939), 180–93.

Wiget, Andrew O. "Aztec Lyrics: Poetry in a World of Continually Perishing Flowers." *Latin American Indian Literatures,* 4 (1980), 1–11.

———. "The Oral Literature of Native North America: A Critical Anthology." Diss. Univ. of Utah 1977.

———. "Sayatasha's Night Chant: A Literary Textual Analysis of a Zuni Ritual Poem." *AICRJ*, 4 (1980), 99–140.

Williams, Ted (Tuscarora). *The Reservation.* Syracuse: Syracuse Univ. Press, 1976.

Willoya, William, and Vinson Brown. *Warriors of the Rainbow: Strange and Prophetic Dreams of the Indian Peoples.* Happy Camp, Calif.: Naturegraph, 1962.

Wilson, Raymond. "The Writings of Ohiyesa—Alexander Eastman, M.D., Santee Sioux." *South Dakota History*, 5 (1975), 55–73.

Winnemucca. See Hopkins, Sarah Winnemucca.

Winnie, Lucille [Jerry; Sah-gan-de-oh] (Seneca-Cayuga). *Sah-gan-de-oh, the Chief's Daughter.* New York: Vantage, 1968.

Winters, Yvor. *Forms of Discovery: Critical and Historical Essays on the Forms of the Short Poem in English.* Chicago: Swallow, 1967.

Wissler, Clark, and D. C. Duvall (Blackfeet). *Mythology of the Blackfoot Indians.* APAMNH, 2, Pt. 1. 1908; rpt. New York: AMS, 1975.

Wister, Owen. *The Virginian: A Horseman of the Plains.* 1902; rpt. New York: Pocket, 1977; New York: NAL, 1979.

Witherspoon, Gary. *Language and Art in the Navajo Universe.* Ann Arbor: Univ. of Michigan Press, 1978.

Witt, Shirley Hill. "The Brave-Hearted Women." *Akwesasne Notes*, 8 (Summer 1976), 16–17.

———. "Native Women Today: Sexism and the Indian Woman." *Civil Rights Digest*, 6 (Spring 1974), 29–35.

———, and Stan Steiner, eds. *The Way: An Anthology of American Indian Literature.* New York: Knopf, 1972.

Women of All Red Nations. Porcupine, S. Dak.: We Will Remember Group, 1978.

Wooden Leg (Cheyenne). *Wooden Leg, a Warrior Who Fought Custer.* Trans. Thomas Marquis. 1931; rpt. Lincoln: Univ. of Nebraska Press, 1962.

Wyman, Leland, and Clyde Kluckhohn. *Navajo Classification of Their Song Ceremonials.* 1938; rpt. Millwood, N.Y.: Kraus, n.d.

Yava, Albert (Tewa-Hopi). *Big Falling Snow.* Ed. Harold Coulander. New York: Crown, 1978.

Yazzie, Ethelou (Navajo), ed. *Navaho History.* Many Farms, Ariz.: Navaho Community Coll. Press, 1971.

Yoimut (Chunut). "Yoimut's Story, the Last Chunut." In Latta, *Handbook of the Yokut Indians*, pp. 223–76.

Young, Frank W. "A Fifth Analysis of the Star Husband Tale." *Ethnology*, 9 (1970), 389–413.

———. "Folktales and Social Structure: A Comparison of Three Analyses of the Star-Husband Tale." *JAF*, 91 (1978), 691–99.

Young, Lucy (Wailaki). "Out of the Past: A True Indian Story as Told by Lucy Young of Round Valley Indian Reservation to Edith V. A. Murphy." *California Historical Society Quarterly*, 20 (1941), 349–64.

Young Bear, Ray A. (Mesquakie). *Winter of the Salamander.* New York: Harper, 1981.

Zitkala-Sa [Gertrude Bonnin] (Sioux). *American Indian Stories.* 1921; rpt. Glorieta, N. Mex.: Rio Grande, 1976.

———. "Impressions of an Indian Childhood." *Atlantic Monthly,* Jan. 1900, pp. 37–47.

———. "An Indian Teacher among Indians." *Atlantic Monthly,* March 1900, pp. 381 86.

———. *Old Indian Legends, Retold by Zitkala-Sa.* Boston: Ginn, 1901.

———. "The Schooldays of an Indian Girl." *Atlantic Monthly,* Feb. 1900, pp. 185–94.

———. "Why I Am a Pagan." *Atlantic Monthly,* Dec. 1902, pp. 801–03.

Zoellner, Robert. *The Salt-Sea Mastodon: A Reading of* Moby-Dick. Berkeley: Univ. of California Press, 1973.

Zolbrod, Paul G. "From Performance to Print: Preface to a Native American Text." *Georgia Review*, 35 (1981), 465–533.

Zolla, Elemire. *The Writer and the Shaman.* Trans. Raymond Rosenthal. New York: Harcourt, 1973.

Zuni People. *The Zunis: Self-Portrayals.* Ed. and trans. Alvina Quam. Albuquerque: Univ. of New Mexico Press, 1972; New York: NAL, 1974.

Index

The index lists names of writers and Indian tribes, titles of literary works, subjects and topics, discussed in some detail in the text. Alternative names and/or tribal affiliation follow writers' names in parentheses when one or both can be determined from the text.